Pirates in the Middle Kingdom:

The Art of Trademark War

RECOMMENDED STOCKISTS

Australia
Thomson Legal and Regulatory Limited
Sydney, Canberra, Melbourne,
Brisbane, Adelaide

Canada / USA
Carswell
Ontario
Canada

Hong Kong
Bloomsbury Books Ltd

Hong Kong Book Centre Ltd

Swindon Book Co. Ltd

Japan
Yushodo Fantas
Tokyo

Kokusai Shobo Ltd
Tokyo

Maruzen Co. Ltd
Tokyo, Osaka

Tokyo Publications
Tokyo

Malaysia / Singapore
Sweet & Maxwell Asia®
Petaling Jaya

New Zealand
Brookers Ltd
Wellington, Auckland

Singapore
Sweet & Maxwell Asia®
Singapore

Thailand
Source One Ltd
Bangkok

UK & Europe
Sweet & Maxwell Ltd
London

USA
Professional Publications
Services
New Jersey

West Group
Minnesota

Rest of the World
Sweet & Maxwell Asia®
Hong Kong

Pirates in the Middle Kingdom:
The Art of Trademark War

Tan, Loke Khoon

HONG KONG • SINGAPORE • MALAYSIA
SWEET & MAXWELL ASIA®
2004

Published in 2004 by
Sweet & Maxwell Asia®
a division of
The Thomson Corporation Hong Kong Ltd
20/F, Sunning Plaza, 10 Hysan Avenue,
Causeway Bay, Hong Kong
www.sweetandmaxwellasia.com

Reprinted 2005

Affiliated Companies

AUSTRALIA
Thomson Legal and Regulatory Limited
100 Harris Street
Pyrmont NSW 2009
www.lawbookco.com.au

CANADA
Carswell
Corporate Plaza
2075 Kennedy Road
Scarborough, Ontario M1T 3V4
www.carswell.com

MALAYSIA
Sweet & Maxwell Asia®
No 17 Jalan PJS 7/19
Bandar Sunway
46150 Petaling Jaya
Selangor, Malaysia
www.sweetandmaxwellasia.com

NEW ZEALAND
Brookers
Level 1, Guardian Trust House
15 Willeston Street, Wellington
www.brookers.co.nz

SINGAPORE
Sweet & Maxwell Asia®
6 Battery Road
#29–03
Singapore 049919
www.sweetandmaxwellasia.com

UNITED KINGDOM / EUROPE
Sweet & Maxwell Ltd
100 Avenue Road, London NW3 3PF
www.sweetandmaxwell.co.uk

UNITED STATES OF AMERICA
West Group
PO Box 64526
St Paul, Minnesota 55164–0526
www.westgroup.com

Typeset by Sweet & Maxwell Asia®

Printed in Hong Kong

ISBN 962 661 233 9

© SWEET & MAXWELL ASIA® 2004

To my one and only, Shirley,
and
our three loves
Christopher, Alistair and Olivia

FOREWORD

The law of trademarks in the People's Republic of China has undergone a metamorphosis since China's decision to join the World Trade Organisation. While trademarks, and rights pertaining to them, are part of Chinese history and culture – Chinese artisans and mandarins applied distinctive seals to their work in the Han dynasty – it is only in recent years that the importance of trademarks as individual, rather than collective rights, have been recognised. With China's economy expanding at a pace unparalleled, and both foreign and domestic enterprises gaining in scope and scale, protecting one's right to identify the source of one's goods and services has become of paramount importance.

While the importance is unquestioned, it is a difficult task for judges and practitioners alike to keep up with the staggering array of changes in the law. Even I, in my position as Chief Justice of the Intellectual Property Division of the Supreme People's Court, have often found it a formidable task. For that reason, I am very grateful for the recent addition of this excellent book to the intellectual property law resources available to those of us in the field. Tan Loke Khoon of Baker & McKenzie has written a clear, informative and entertaining guide to trademark law in the People's Republic. Mr Tan's book takes us from the inception of trademark law in China to its current avatar as a complex and comprehensive body of laws that rivals those in the United States and Europe. Along the way, the book covers everything a practitioner in the field would need to know. For example, Chapter 2 enumerates the importance of choosing the correct Chinese-language trademark, and how to go about doing so. This is of special pertinence for non-Chinese clients who are eager to take advantage of the Chinese market. Mr Tan's book clearly sets out the various methods of choosing a mark, along with examples of the same, which illustrate his points. As an adjudicator of many trademark disputes, it is my belief that a correct foundation often obviates future problems, and choosing the correct mark at inception often assuages problems foreign trademark holders may face when doing business in an unfamiliar setting. The book also thoroughly details the administrative and enforcement frameworks in the PRC, listing the numerous judicial and administrative bodies responsible for the protection of trademark rights, and their respective duties. Registrations, oppositions, cancellations, licensing and assignment of trademarks are all covered in separate chapters. Also explored in great detail is the issue that probably occupies most right holders' minds – trademark infringement and counterfeiting. The rampant counterfeiting in the PRC has garnered much media coverage, and it is no secret that counterfeiting of goods, along with the sister evils of infringement and cybersquatting, are the problems feared and faced most by trademark holders, both foreign and domestic. I am thus grateful to Mr Tan for covering these issues in a thorough and comprehensive manner, without being preachy or alarmist.

On that note, I have to commend Mr Tan on the eminent readability of his book. Tan Loke Khoon has put to good use his extensive personal experience as partner in one of Asia's largest and pre-eminent intellectual property law practices. Written from a practitioner's point of view, the book covers the key points of China's trademark law and the fine art of practicing it, while maintaining a style that is easy to read. With so many books on the subject being written, it is still refreshing to find something that contains the fruits of the author's personal experience and knowledge of the law. I commend Mr Tan on his fine book, and hope you will enjoy reading it.

Jiang Zhipei
蔣志培

Commissioner of the Judicial
Committee of the Supreme
People's Court

Chief Justice of the Third
Civil Trial Chamber
(Intellectual Property Right
Trial Chamber) of the
Supreme People's Court

Doctor of Laws

PREFACE

As a former soldier with the Singapore army during my National Service days, the idea of the business world as a battleground seemed natural when I started my intellectual property legal practice in Singapore in 1987. My decision to move to Hong Kong and the People's Republic of China two years later was a stroke of good fortune and a blessed mix of happenstance, wanderlust and opportunity. These early notions of warfare took greater shape as I found myself running from one unfamiliar province to another and from one Chinese counterfeiter factory to the next, championing the invisible rights of multinational brand owners who had fallen prey to piracy in the mainland. The terrain was harsh, and the learning curve was steep. It was no longer a case of knowing what the law stated but what it meant in actual practice.

As I rollercoasted through the myriad of trademark victories and losses, it became apparent to me that I could not win all of the battles but I should certainly live to fight another day. Once I reached that point of awareness, there was less angst about the Chinese civil law system as I knew that there would always be a solution, in some form or another.

Drawing from the wealth of military knowledge that the Chinese philosopher Sun Tzu bestowed upon Chinese culture and teachings, I applied many of these valued strategems to the growing trademark piracy caseload. Wary foreign investors were treading carefully but were wisely not turning their backs on the endless opportunities that China was offering. What everyone needed was a strategy to keep the Chinese pirates at bay!

It has been fifteen years since my adventure with China intellectual property first started and the excitement is as fresh as ever. With each new case, I am faced with yet another new learning opportunity, an unexplored way to combat the piracy and to reap better results. This book is an attempt to share some of the insights that my colleagues and I have gathered through our collective experiences with the Chinese pirates, so that you will learn to survive as we did, to fight back and to conquer new ground.

This project started around the time when Hong Kong and the region was battling SARS and it persevered because of the wonderful teamwork in the firm. My fellow comrades-in-arms at Baker & McKenzie who have contributed selflessly to the research, feedback and preparation of this book include the following: Anu Singh, Scott Palmer, Isabella Liu, Elaine Lee, Wan Shiu Man, Adrian Cook, Paul Schmidt, Zhang Hui, Hank Chong, Wang Jin, Violet Cheng, and my partners in the IP Group: Jeannie Smith, Joseph Simone, Chris Smith, Li Chiang Ling, Loo Shih Yann, Anita Leung and Peggy Cheung. I also wish to acknowledge the support and encouragement of my partner (China Group) and mentor, Winston Zee, throughout my career. I am also indebted to my Editors Jojo Mo and Claudia Pimenta for their patience in seeing this project through to completion; and also to Judge Jiang Zhi-Pei who has given me invaluable insight into this area of law. To all of these friends and colleagues, I am deeply grateful.

Finally, to the unsung heroes in the battlefield, all of our clients and supporters who held faith in us and shared their resources so generously, I am sincerely thankful.

To you, the reader, it is time to approach the Middle Kingdom ("Zhong Guo") and Carpe Diem / seize the day!

Loke-Khoon Tan
Old Peak Road
Hong Kong SAR
June 2004

ABOUT THE AUTHOR

Loke-Khoon Tan is an international partner with the Hong Kong / China offices of Baker & McKenzie and his area of practice is PRC and Hong Kong intellectual property. He is active on various IP committees in global trademark and domain name dispute resolution organisations including INTA, Marques, PTMG, ACG, IPBA, WIPO, CIETAC and HKIAC. He is an advocate / solicitor with the local bars of Singapore, Hong Kong and England & Wales.

He is the co-author of "Trademark Law in the PRC" (Oxford University Press) and is a regular contributor to IP journals and publications. He is also a regular speaker at IP forums in Asia and abroad.

Loke-Khoon is resident in Hong Kong with his wife Shirley and their three children. He is an avid waterskier and loves watching movies. He is working on his first novel and script based on what he calls the splendour and eccentricities of Asia.

© Photography by Shirley Kwan, 2004

TABLE OF CONTENTS

Chapter 7
Trademark Cancellations

Chapter Eight
Trademark Licensing and Assignment

Chapter 13
Domain Names and the Internet

TABLE OF CASES

TABLE OF LEGISLATION

CHAPTER 1

INTRODUCTION

HISTORICAL OVERVIEW
1.1

This book provides an introduction to the legal framework governing trademarks and trademark rights in the People's Republic of China ("PRC" or "China"). The emergence of a relatively complete body of laws in China dealing with trademark and other intellectual property rights is only a relatively recent occurrence. China began re-drafting its intellectual property laws in the late 1970s as a response to new policies geared towards modernising science and technology, towards developing a market economy and attracting foreign investment, and in response to a need for enhancing the position of intellectuals in China after the Cultural Revolution.

In large part, the development of trademark law in post-Mao China is directly related to economic reform and Beijing's openness to a wider range of linkages with the international economy. Eager to attract foreign investment and advanced technologies to fuel its growing economy, Chinese authorities realised that the licensing, sale, and transfer of technologies and goods from foreign investors would be stimulated by enforceable laws and regulations providing a higher degree of trademark protection.

Since the early 1980s, China has taken active and continuous steps to develop a comprehensive intellectual property framework governing trademarks, copyright, and patents, and has acceded to most international intellectual property-related conventions. In general, most "hard law" treaty regimes seek to harmonise national laws at the global level, and accordingly, the development of China's intellectual property laws reflects its adoption of international minimum standards of intellectual property protection as embodied in the relevant treaties.[1] China's intellectual property regime now provides a broad

---

1   For an overview of the law of treaties, see Ian Brownlie, *Principles of Public International Law*, 6th edn (Oxford University Press, 2003).

1

range of protection, and includes, *inter alia*, the protection of computer software, audio and video products, domain names, internet and enterprise names.

Despite such advances, serious problems remain, most notably in the area of enforcement. China's efforts to exact compliance with its existing body of laws and regulations have attracted a great amount of international attention. Nonetheless, with each trade-related confrontation, particularly those involving the United States during the mid and late 1990s, China has made great efforts to develop a more transparent legal system. Specialised tribunals handling cases involving intellectual property rights have been established in the People's Courts in the Special Economic Zones and in Beijing, Fujian, Guangdong, and Shanghai, as well as in other provinces and municipalities, and a wider range of legal remedies for trademark violations are now available, including increased fines, statutory damages, injunctive orders and prison sentences of up to seven years for egregious counterfeiters. Although it may take some time to reverse China's reputation as a major violator of intellectual property rights, a strong signal is being sent by the international business community to Chinese companies and individuals that large-scale counterfeiting and infringement will no longer be tolerated.

A primary goal of China's most recent efforts to improve trademark protection is the management and supervision of enterprises as to how to use and register trademarks. Educating its population on the importance of trademark protection is a novel and daunting task. Yet perhaps the greatest obstacle to achieving a standard level of understanding for trademark use, and enforcing protection, is literally a matter of numbers. China has 20 per cent of the world's population. Implementing any policy goal is a challenge unto itself, not to mention consistently supervising, managing, and enforcing its terms.

1.2 WHAT ARE TRADEMARKS AND SERVICE MARKS?

Trademarks and service marks are, on the most basic level, distinctive signs, words or symbols that identify a source of goods or services, and distinguish them from the goods and services provided by others. Trademarks and service marks are therefore distinguished only by virtue of the subject matter identified. In Anglo-American jurisprudence, trademark protection arose from the common law, and initially functioned to prevent manufacturers from passing off their goods as those of another. The grant of exclusive rights in a trademark also reflected a perceived need to protect the so-called "goodwill" that consumers associate with a certain manufacturer and its products.

Trademark law evolved in the early and mid nineteenth century in tandem with the demands of industry and the new industrial economies of Europe and North America. The first generation trademark laws provided limited protection, and in the United States for example, marks were only afforded protection if they included the name of the manufacturer. Gradually, protection was extended to symbols, arbitrary names, and geographic names that had come to be associated with particular products in the minds of consumers, or had otherwise acquired secondary meaning. In the twentieth century, protection was further extended to the novel packaging of products, or 'trade dress'. In many jurisdictions, protection has been extended to a vast array of visual forms, including colours and colour combinations, and three-dimensional marks. In some jurisdictions, the ambit of protection has been extended to sounds and smells.

The entitlements entailed in ownership of a trademark or service mark has also evolved. Early trademark protection extended only to use of identical marks and later similar marks by direct competitors. The doctrine of trademark 'dilution' developed in the latter half of the twentieth century to protect trademark owners from use of identical or similar marks by non-competitors, or by proprietors who use their marks on dissimilar goods or services. Such protection, however, has been generally reserved for marks that are determined to be well known or widely recognised by relevant consumers.

A BRIEF HISTORY OF TRADEMARKS IN CHINA   1.3

The Chinese practice of using proprietary symbols and marks to distinguish goods in commerce and to identify the source of goods dates back to at least the Han dynasty (206 BC – AD 220). Archaeological excavations have unearthed ironware and pottery dating from the Han and Tang dynasties that are engraved with the name of a craftsman, or places of production, or the name of a workshop.

The use of distinguishing marks later developed to include both words and pictures. For example, the 'White Rabbit' (*bai tu er*) mark, was used by the Liu family to identify sewing needles produced at their shop in Jinan (Shandong province), during the Song dynasty. It is often cited as the earliest known example of a trademark in China. The mark not only depicts a drawing of a white rabbit, but also contains the Chinese characters meaning "the rabbit is a sign". Other sources indicate that producers of silk, tea, paper, and medicines, among other products, developed brand names and symbols, and marked their products accordingly. Many producers practiced nepotism to maintain the secrecy of their manufacturing processes, or otherwise limited key areas of the manufacturing process to family-run operations.

Despite modest and local attempts to protect proprietary trademarks, counterfeiting and imitating confidential manufacturing processes was common, particularly during and after the Song dynasty. In most cases, assistance was sought from local officials such as village and guild leaders to order the infringers to cease production. Such pleas, however, generally met with little success.

In imperial China, the state's authority was felt and exercised through villages, guilds and families, and otherwise through local networks of family and quasi-family relationships. Social and economic stability was therefore maintained not through public or 'positive' law, but primarily through informal channels and institutions of social control.

Prior to the twentieth century, essentially all efforts by the Chinese state to provide protection for intellectual property concerned the protection of imperial power. Symbols associated with the imperial family, such as the five-clawed dragon, were excluded by law from reproduction by common citizens. It was not until the 1900s that a trademark law dealing with the interests of persons and entities other than the State was enacted.

THE DEVELOPMENT OF TRADEMARK LEGISLATION IN CHINA

1.4 TRADEMARK LAW IN DYNASTIC CHINA?

There is no indication of any kind of centrally administered formal legal protection for proprietary symbols, ie trademarks or service marks in the legal codes of dynastic China prior to 1904. This conclusion, however, requires a bit of contextual elaboration.

Most historians who concern themselves with early Chinese legal history focus their attention on dynastic codes rather than informal mechanisms of social ordering. This scholarly focus on dynastic codes reflects a tendency, particularly in the Western world, to emphasise public or 'positive law', and to characterise positive law in terms of the dichotomy between civil law and criminal law. In dynastic China, as suggested above, positive law was not a primary or desirable tool for maintaining social order, nor was it viewed in terms of a dichotomy between civil and criminal law. The various modes for administrating the state and, indeed, maintaining social harmony, were arranged into a hierarchical order, with heavenly reason (*tianli*) in the top position, followed by 'the way' (*dao*), morality (*de*), ritual propriety (*li*), custom (*xixu*), community agreements (*xiang yue*), family rules (*jia cheng*), and with the formal written law of the state (*lu li* or *fa lu*) at the bottom, the last resort.[2]

---

2   William P Alford, *To Steal a Book is an Elegant Offence, Intellectual Property Law in Chinese Civilization* (Oxford, 1995), p 10.

In light of the predominance of informal mechanisms of social ordering in China, searching for formal expressions of Western legal ideas and practices (such as the protection of something akin to intellectual property) in China's imperial past is problematic, to say the least. This is not to say that comparative studies of imperial Chinese and Western legal culture and history are impossible or useless. It is just to say that such scholarly work requires a familiarity with the intellectual history and political culture of imperial China, and entails an investigation of both formal and informal mechanisms for administering social order. Such an investigation, of course, is far beyond the scope of this book.

THE 1904 TRADEMARK LAW   1.5

After the Boxer Uprising of 1900, the British, the Americans and the Japanese were eager to see the establishment of a stable and predictable environment for international business in China. The British obtained a promise of trademark protection from China in the 1902 Mackay Treaty, and the Americans and the Japanese obtained similar promises in treaties concluded with China the following year. To comply with its treaty obligations, China's Ministry of Foreign Affairs called upon the Imperial Maritime Customs Authority to prepare a draft trademark law, which, after later revisions by the Chinese authorities, became the first model for a comprehensive trademark regime in China.

The original draft trademark law contained a number of provisions that clearly favoured foreign interests in China. Two of the most obvious provisions relate to the choice of a trademark registration authority and the protection of foreign marks. Trademark registrations were to be administered by the British-run Imperial Maritime Customs Authority, and foreign marks that were used in China were to be granted trademark protection regardless of whether they had obtained registration domestically or abroad.

China's newly formed Ministry of Commerce did not take favourably to this first draft, and in consultation with Japanese advisors, prepared a substantially revised version. This new version proposed a single trademark authority based in Beijing, with registration offices in Shanghai and Tianjin. Article 1 of the revised draft declared that anyone, "whether Chinese or foreigner, who desires to have the exclusive use of a trademark must first register the same."[3] As a concession to foreign interests, however, applicants of trademarks registered abroad were to be provided a six-month application priority period, which would later be reduced to four.

---

3   Trademark Regulations, from *Foreign Relations of the United States*, 15 August 1904, item no 1681, Article 1; see also *ibid*, p 39, cited in Tan Loke Khoon and Clifford Borg-Marks, *Trade Mark Law in the People's Republic of China*, (Oxford, 1998).

The draft trademark law envisioned a centrally administered registration and enforcement regime. Accordingly, registration would be granted to the first to apply. Opposition petitions would be heard within six months of filing an application, otherwise the application would proceed to registration. A registration would be effective for 20 years, and could be renewed within 6 months of expiration. Any changes in the use or ownership of a mark were to be registered with the registration authorities before taking effect. Trademark infringers would be liable for damages, a fine, or a term in prison, and the infringing goods would be destroyed and any items used for the manufacture of the infringing goods confiscated.

Although the foreign trading community initially pressured China into enacting a trademark law, none of the treaty powers in China approved of the Chinese draft. Since the Chinese authorities in turn refused to adopt a version more conciliatory to the foreign powers in China, a deadlock ensued. This deadlock persisted until 1923, when the first modern trademark law in China was enacted.

1.6 THE 1923 AND 1930 TRADEMARK LAWS

The revolution of 1911 led to the overthrow of the Qing and the end of dynastic rule in China. Revolutionaries had staged anti-Manchu uprisings with relative frequency during the last decade of the nineteenth century, and in 1905 in Tokyo, Sun Yat-sen allied his revolutionary group with a number of other radical groups to form the *'Tongmen Hui'* or 'Revolutionary Alliance'. On 9 October 1909, an accidental bomb explosion in Wuhan served as the catalyst for regime change. The event would have been forgotten had it not been for the general disenchantment that had weakened Qing rule. The explosion led to a string of army mutinies that ended a few weeks later with the complete collapse of imperial rule and the abdication of Pu Yi, the 'last emperor'.[4] Sun Yat-sen was named the first president of the new republic, but was soon replaced by Yuan Shikai who was elected by the new National Council in Nanjing on 14 February 1912.

The Revolutionary Alliance was renamed the National People's Party, or Guomindang, which in 1912 was completely dominated by Yuan Shi-kai and his supporters. The new Republican government, however, soon proved too weak to deliver its reform agenda, and infighting in China's new parliament in spring 1913 led Yuan to order the dissolution of the party and the eviction of its members from Parliament and positions of military power. Yuan soon yielded to

---

4   Jonathan D Spence, *The Search for Modern China*, 2nd edn (W W Norton & Co, 2001) pp 262–268.

foreign, particularly Japanese, demands for special privileges, and lived as the self-proclaimed 'emperor' of a short-lived dynasty. Revolts in the southern provinces and Yuan's death in 1916 left the country without a strong central authority, a situation that led to the militarisation of politics and an era of warlordism in China.

Nevertheless, amidst the political instability of the day, on 3 May 1923, the de facto government in Beijing issued a trademark law. The 1923 Trademark Law was based on Japanese regulations in force at the time, which called for the establishment of a trademark office under the Ministry of Agriculture and Commerce in Beijing. Detailed regulations outlining the classification of goods were promulgated shortly thereafter.

At the end of 1928, Guomindang troops under the leadership of Chiang Kai-shek had taken Beijing from the warlord Zhang Zuolin, unifying the country under a central nationalist government that was to be established in Nanjing. The bloody 'Northern Expedition' to unify the country was declared at an end and the task of rebuilding the country and its economy was to begin anew.

Two years later, in May 1930, the Guomindang government promulgated another trademark law, which was based largely on the 1923 Trademark Law. The 1930 Trademark Law is no longer in effect on mainland China, but is still in force in Taiwan today after a series of amendments, in 1935, 1958, and 1983 respectively. Detailed Implementing Rules for the Trademark Law were promulgated in late December 1930, and took effect on 1 January 1931. These Implementing Rules are also still in effect in Taiwan, also in amended form.

Trademark law in China prior to the communist revolution was informed by the laws of other nation states and was greatly influenced by international, and particularly Japanese participation in both drafting and implementation. Indeed, the Implementing Rules for the Trademark Law contained a table for the classification of goods taken directly from Japanese legislation. The presence of foreign powers continued to be strongly felt in China, and trading powers such as the Japanese had strong and vested interests in the development of China's trademark laws during this period.

Disputes over trademark rights during this period reflected an environment that favored foreign interests to the detriment of domestic enterprises. One such example is a case involving a Shanghai company that produced a brand of soap branded with the 'Three Stars' mark, and at the time of the dispute had used the mark in commerce for over ten years. Despite the fact that the mark was registered in China in 1924, the Shanghai enterprise lost its right to use the mark when challenged by a Japanese company claiming to have used it first. The decision ran counter to provisions in the law that limited cancellation actions based on 'first use' to marks that had been registered for less than three years. In a similar case, a Chinese tobacco company contested the right of an English company to use the 'Elephant' brand trademark, which had been registered in 1924. In this case, the trademark authorities ruled that the English firm could retain its rights to use the trademark because the mark had been registered for over three years.

Another indicator of the influence of foreign powers in China during this period is the statistics from the Trademark Office of the government in Nanjing. From 1928 to 1934, almost 68 per cent of the 24,747 trademarks registered were owned by foreign parties, most of which were Japanese. In 1948, after eight years of open war with the Japanese, and in the midst of a civil war between the Guomindang and Communist forces, there were only 50,000 trademarks registered by Chinese parties in China.

1.7 THE 1949 TRADEMARK LAW

By 1948, Chiang's forces were defeated in Northern China, and his power base was quickly deteriorating due to mass troop defections, paralysing inflation, and the dwindling allegiance of the majority of China's intellectuals, professionals and urban workers. In 1949, the Nationalist army was in complete disarray, and by the end of the year Chiang retreated with his remaining troops and supporters to the island of Taiwan. The communists had "liberated" most of China by 1 October 1949, when Mao Zedong in Beijing declared the founding of the new People's Republic of China.

During the period of civil war, the local governments in several 'liberated' areas had issued provisional trademark legislation. Before the promulgation of the PRC's national trademark regulations, local legislation existed in the Jiangsu and Anhui areas, the Shanxi, Hebei, Shandong and Henan areas, the Shanxi, Gansu, and Ningxia areas, and the areas of North China. In addition, the local Office for Administration and Commerce in the Taihang area of Shanxi and western Hebei province had issued a number of rules controlling the registration of trademarks in the region.

1.8 THE 1950 TRADEMARK LAW

One year after the founding of the PRC, the new government passed the Provisional Regulations for Trademark Registration, the Detailed Implementing Rules for the Provisional Regulations, and the Procedures for Dealing with Trademarks Registered at the Trademark Office of the Former Guomindang Government. The new trademark regime featured a central trademark registration authority in Beijing, and guaranteed protection only to trademarks that were registered under the new regime. As a result, the Communist Party was able to force the re-registration of all marks that were registered during the Nationalist period, and to purge any trademark registrations with apparent links to imperialist countries, or otherwise deemed anathema to the moral and ideological sensibilities of the Communist Party. As a result, almost one-third of the trademarks registered under the old system were no longer recognised in the PRC.

In 1954, the Government promulgated the Provisional Measures for the Administration of Unregistered Trademarks, encouraging the small enterprises to register their marks with the local Department for Industry and Commerce prior to use. The 1950 Trademark Law was only to be implemented, however, in 1957, when measures were adopted to establish a comprehensive trademark registration procedure. The measures provided the same set of procedures for the registration of marks by enterprises and cooperative organisations. The new measures focused trademark registration concerns on product quality, and required submission of a product quality standards form, and approval from the local administrative authorities prior to public announcement and registration.

THE 1963 TRADEMARK LAW   1.9

Most of China's intellectual property laws were amended during the early 1960s to respond to the political climate of the times. On 10 April 1963, the State Council promulgated new Regulations for the Administration of Trademarks, which made no mention of trademark 'rights' per se, or to 'exclusive use'. The declared purpose for the new Regulations was to strengthen "the control of trademarks and make enterprises safeguard and improve the quality of their products."[5]

These new Regulations were based on the principles of compulsory registration, product quality supervision, and simplified review procedures. The General Administration of Industry and Commerce was to assume oversight responsibility for product quality standards, to receive complaints, and to cancel registrations when necessary. In April 1966, it was even suggested that the Administration of Industry and Commerce at the provincial and municipal levels should assume responsibility for the examination and approval of trademarks on products for sale in China. This measure was never implemented, however, on account of the onset of the Cultural Revolution later the same year, ushering in a decade-long period when China's legal institutions were rendered redundant, and the very idea of trademarks,

---

5   Tan & Borg-Marks, p 18 (above, n 3).

even as a way to assure the quality of goods, was seen as a loathsome concession to a quasi-capitalist commodity economy, inappropriate for the new China.[6]

During the Cultural Revolution, China's compulsory trademark registration system came to a standstill. Many of China's well-known marks during the period were replaced with propagandist marks and slogans such as 'Red Flag' (*hong qi*), 'Red Wind' (*hong feng*), 'Liberation' (*jie fang*), and 'The East is Red' (*dong fang hong*). Trademarks were effectively politicised, and common trademarks became the targets of political theatre. In one case, the manufacturer of shoes bearing the mark '*gong zi pa*', which was normally printed on the soles of the shoes, became the victim of revolutionary fervor. As the first character of the trademark, '*gong*', is the same as the Chinese word for worker, the trademark was interpreted to mean 'trample the working class underfoot'. Thousands of shoes bearing the mark were confiscated, and the proprietors were branded counter-revolutionaries and arrested accordingly. In another case, the proprietors of a black shoe polish bearing the mark 'Red Flag Brand' (*hong qi pai*) were arrested as counter-revolutionaries for deceiving the masses by selling black market goods while waving the red flag.

TRADEMARK LEGISLATION IN POST-MAO CHINA

1.10 PRIOR DEVELOPMENTS

The 1978 *Communiqué of the Third Plenary Session of the Eleventh Central Committee of the Chinese Communist Party* contemplated the development of the socialist legal system, not only as a goal in itself, but as the basis of the government's efforts at political and economic reform after the chaos of the Cultural Revolution. China's so-called 'open door policy' envisioned a complete and gradual reorientation of its economy, an opening of China's markets to foreign investment and technology, and the development of new laws to encourage and protect its economic development.

In 1978, the Central Office for Administration and Commerce (later renamed the State Administration for Industry and Commerce ("SAIC")) was established under the State Council, with one of its many functions being the administration of China's trademark regime.

---

6   Alford, p 64 (above, n 2).

At the outset, trademark registrations by foreign parties were dealt with on the basis of reciprocity. In late 1979, China's central registration system was again fully functioning under the auspices of the newly formed Trademark Office ("TMO"). By the end of 1982, over 50,000 trademarks were registered, about 8,000 of which were registered by foreign enterprises. This brought the total number of registered trademarks to 85,000, with 13,500 registered by foreign parties.

1982 TRADEMARK LAW   1.11

China's first post-Mao trademark legislation consisted of 8 chapters and 43 articles. It was adopted by the National People's Congress on 23 August 1982, and along with the Implementing Rules of the Trademark Law, became effective in March 1983. China's new trademark regime envisioned a central registration system based in Beijing, and administrative and enforcement organs at the state, provincial and local levels.

Article 1 of the new law clearly linked trademark use with quality control and consumer protection as before, but it otherwise differed greatly from earlier PRC trademark laws. For instance, Article 3 resurrected the idea of "exclusive rights," which now were to be protected by law; and instead of compulsory registration, registration of a mark under the new legal regime was voluntary.

China's new trademark law established a purely 'first-to-file' system, and prior use was essentially irrelevant for purposes of establishing exclusive rights to use a particular mark. The only exception to the first-to-file rule is the 'simultaneous applicant' scenario, when two applicants file for identical or similar marks on identical or similar goods on the same day. In such a case, Article 18 provided that the first applicant to use the mark was to be approved for registration and otherwise published for opposition.

The opposition procedure was quite simple. Trademark applications that were suitably distinctive, did not conflict with any prior applications or registrations filed by third-parties, and did not contain prohibited or state-sensitive elements, would be preliminarily approved for registration and published for opposition in the PRC *Trademark Gazette*. Once a mark was published, third parties would have three months to oppose the registration of a mark. If no opposition were filed, the mark would proceed to registration.

1993 AMENDMENTS   1.12

China's 1983 Trademark Law and Implementing Regulations were amended in 1993. These amendments were noteworthy in that they extended all provisions for the registration and protection of trademarks to service marks as well. In addition, the amended law provided for the recognition of collective and certification marks, and for the enforcement of trademarks by administrations for industry and commerce ("AIC"s) at the provincial and local levels. Provisions relating to the protection of the exclusive right to use a trademark were also expanded to cover the unauthorised manufacture or sale of forged trademark representations.

Supplemental Regulations Regarding the Punishment of the Crime of Passing Off a Registered Trademark ("Supplemental Regulations") were also passed in 1993. These Supplemental Regulations provided for stiff fines and penalties for passing off and counterfeiting activities, including imprisonment of up to seven years in serious cases. The Supplementary Regulations on the Punishment of Crimes of Counterfeiting of Registered Trademarks were also passed in 1993 and were later adapted into China's Criminal Law. For crimes related to trademark infringement, penalties included fines and imprisonment of three years, and seven years in particularly serious cases.

1.13   2001 TRADEMARK LAW

China's Trademark Law was amended again on 27 October 2001 by the Standing Committee of the Ninth National People's Congress. These later amendments were geared towards bringing China's trademark regime in line with international standards and to facilitate China's impending entry into the World Trade Organisation ("WTO"). The new amended Trademark Law came into force on 1 December 2001. Ten days later, on 11 December 2001, China formally became a member of the WTO. The Implementing Regulations were also considerably revised, and became effective on 15 September 2002.

The 2001 Trademark Law consists of 64 articles, and with the newly revised Implementing Regulations, serves as the foundation for what has evolved into an extremely sophisticated and ambitious trademark regime. New amendments to the Trademark Law and Implementing Regulations addressed a number of shortcomings in the earlier law, most notably in the addition of provisions on the determination and protection of well-known marks, and the introduction of preliminary injunctions in trademark infringement cases. The new Trademark Law also provided for statutory damages in infringement cases where a plaintiff's damages and infringer's liability are difficult to determine, as well as provisions for the compensation of an aggrieved party's legal and investigation costs for pursuing infringers. The new Trademark Law also enhanced the powers of administrative enforcement authorities, and made sellers of infringing goods liable despite lack of 'intent'.

CHINA's TRADEMARK LEGISLATION IN THE INTERNATIONAL CONTEXT

DEVELOPMENT OF CHINA'S TRADEMARK LAW 1.14

Since the early 1980s, trademark law in China has developed in stride with PRC accession to the most prominent multinational treaty regimes. These treaty regimes seek the alignment or 'harmonisation' of national trademark laws, and at the very least, provide minimum standards for national legislation. In addition to China's accession to multinational treaties, bilateral agreements, particularly with the United States, have also shaped the development of trademark law in China, particularly in the area of enforcement.

Article 17 of China's 2001 Trademark Law provides that foreign parties who wish to register marks in China "shall handle matters in accordance with the agreements entered into between their country and the People's Republic of China or international treaties to which both parties have acceded" or to otherwise handle relevant matters in accordance with the 'principle of reciprocity'. In addition to this direct reference to the applicability of treaties and relevant agreements in the 2001 Trademark Law, Article 142 of China's Civil Code states that the provisions of international treaties shall apply in circumstances where China's civil law conflicts with the provisions of a treaty, provided that China has not announced a reservation to the relevant provision(s). Despite these provisions, the manner in which domestic legislation and international treaties interrelate and are interpreted by administrative and judicial authorities is often unpredictable, particularly in the enforcement context.

China joined the World Intellectual Property Organization ("WIPO") in 1980. WIPO is the specialised agency of the United Nations that administers the two primary trademark related treaty regimes, the Paris Convention for the Protection of Industrial Property ("Paris Convention") and the so-called Madrid system, an international trademark registration vehicle governed by the Madrid Agreement and the Protocol Relating to the Madrid Agreement ("Madrid Protocol").

THE PARIS CONVENTION 1.15

The Paris Convention was first concluded in 1883, but its current version is the result of six revisions, most currently revised in Stockholm in 1967. The Paris Convention is based on the "national treatment" principal that requires a contracting state to apply equal treatment and provide the same rights to both its own citizens and to foreign nationals. It also enables trademark applicants from member states to claim the date of application for a trademark registration in one member state as the priority date when applying in another.

China acceded to the Paris Convention in March 1983, at about the same time its first post-Mao trademark law came into effect.

As a member of the Paris Convention, China was not only obligated to provide national treatment to foreign applicants, but was required to provide protection to service marks and marks that were not registered in China but were deemed "well known." Nevertheless, it was not until the 1993 Trademark Law when service marks became registrable in China, and not until well into the 1990s when the first regulations regarding the recognition of well-known marks was passed by the SAIC.

Article 6 of the Paris Convention governs the protection of well-known marks. It provides that member states are to refuse or cancel the registration, and to prohibit the use of a trademark that is used for identical or similar goods, and liable to create consumer confusion by constituting a reproduction, imitation or translation of a mark considered to be well known. Article 13 of the 2001 Trademark Law provides such protection for well-known marks, and closely tracks the language of Article 6 of the Paris Convention. Article 6 also provides that such protection applies when the "essential part" of the mark in question constitutes a reproduction or imitation of a well-known mark and is liable to create consumer confusion. Language to this effect is not included in Article 13 of the 2001 Trademark Law, but by virtue of China's accession to the Paris Convention, it is technically applicable in the PRC as well.

On 14 August 1996, the SAIC promulgated the Provisional Regulations for the Determination and Administration of Well-known Trademarks ("Provisional Measures"). The Provisional Measures were China's first attempt at standardizing the requirements and procedures for determining marks as well known, as well as the type of protection accorded such marks. The Provisional Measures were limited only to marks that were registered in China, and arguably fell short of the minimum standards for protection set out in Article 6 of the Paris Convention. This changed, however, when the 2001 Trademark Law and Implementing Regulations extended such protection to marks that were not registered in China. Also, on 1 June 2003, the Provisional Measures were repealed when new Regulations for the Recognition and Protection of Well-Known Trademarks came into effect. These new Regulations, as well as the new procedures for the recognition and protection of well-known marks are discussed in detail in Chapter 3.

In addition to the protection of well-known marks, the Paris Convention contains provisions that protect trade names, and provide for protection to foreign entities against passing off and other forms of unfair competition. These topics will be discussed in detail in Chapter 14 below.

THE MADRID SYSTEM   1.16

In addition to overseeing matters related to the Paris Convention, WIPO also administers the Madrid system of international registration of marks ("Madrid system"), maintains the International Register, and publishes the *WIPO Gazette of International Marks*. The Madrid system is governed by two treaties: the Madrid Agreement Concerning the International Registration of Marks ("Madrid Agreement" or "Agreement"), which dates to 1891, and the more recent Protocol Relating to the Madrid Agreement ("Madrid Protocol" or "Protocol"). Any state that is a party to the Paris Convention may become a party to the Madrid Agreement, the Protocol, or both. China became a party to the Madrid Agreement on 4 October 1989, and acceded to the Protocol on 1 September 1995.

The Madrid Agreement is the oldest international filing system, but it has been amended multiple times since its inception in 1891. The Agreement provides for international registration of marks based on the 'extension principle'. An applicant must first obtain a trademark registration in its country of origin, which must be a contracting state of the Agreement. After obtaining a home country registration, the applicant can complete an application for international registration, which must be submitted in French. The application will be accepted by the International Bureau of WIPO if it satisfies various procedural requirements, and is then sent to the National Offices nominated by the applicant.

The National Offices may reject the extension application within 12 months, but if accepted, the application is valid for 20 years and renewable for additional 20-year periods. Each national registration is dependent on the home registration, which makes possible what is referred to as 'central attack'. In other words, if within five years of the date of initial registration, the mark is declared invalid or otherwise cancelled in the country of origin, all dependent national registrations are also lost.

The Protocol was conceived to overcome a number of the perceived shortcomings of the Madrid Agreement, and it became operational on 1 April 1996. It differs from the Madrid Agreement in that international registration for a mark is based on a home country registration *or* application. In addition, applications can be submitted in English, Spanish or French, and National Offices are provided with up to 18 months to refuse an extension application.

Perhaps the most prominent difference between the Madrid Agreement and the Protocol is that the Protocol provides for the transformation of marks into national registrations in the case of central attack. Registrations under the Protocol are also valid for 10 years and renewable for further 10-year periods, which is more consistent with international practice than the 20-year rule under the Madrid Agreement.

On 17 April 2003, the SAIC promulgated the Implementing Procedures for the Registration of Marks under the Madrid System ("Madrid Implementing Procedures" or "Procedures"). The Procedures supersede 1996 regulations under the same name, and clarify the procedures for applying for international registration designating China as the home country. The Procedures also delineate the responsibilities of the Trademark Office when handling and processing requests for international registration, territorial extension to China, and the transfer of rights to an internationally registered trademark under the Madrid System. As for licensing, the procedures outlined in the 2001 Trademark Law also apply to internationally registered marks, and accordingly, the license must be filed with the Trademark Office.

1.17 THE NICE AGREEMENT

The Nice Agreement for the International Classification of Goods and Services (ICG) entered into force on 15 June 1957, and although the ICG system has been used in China since 1988, China formally became a member of the agreement on 9 August 1994. The ICG provides the international standard for the classification of goods and services for the purposes of trademark and service mark registration in the various member states. Under the ICG system, goods and services identified in trademark applications are organised into numbered classes that contain similar or related goods and services. Membership allows China an opportunity to provide input into the classification of goods and services, and the opportunity to lobby for the addition of new goods, such as Chinese herbal medicines, unique foodstuffs, musical instruments, etc, to the international classification scheme.

WIPO also administers the ICG system, and recently introduced the eighth edition of the Nice Classification of Goods and Services, which provides for the addition of three additional classes (ie classes 43–45). The eighth edition entered into force on 1 January 2002.

1.18 BILATERAL IPR / TRADEMARK AGREEMENTS: CHINA AND THE UNITED STATES

Since the mid 1980s, intellectual property issues have played a prominent role in Sino-American relations.[7] Twice the United States has threatened China with trade sanctions under the so-called "Special 301" provisions of the Trade Act of 1974. In 1992, and in early 1995, by classifying China as a 'priority foreign country', the United States was

---

7 For a detailed discussion, see Alford, pp 112–123 (above n 2).

able to gain leverage in ensuing negotiations over intellectual property concerns without actually initiating a Special 301 action.

The first threat of imposition of tariffs from the United States resulted in the landmark 1992 Memorandum of Understanding on the Protection of Intellectual Property ("1992 MOU"). The 1992 MOU was geared towards providing "effective procedures and remedies to prevent or stop, internally, and at their borders, infringements of intellectual property rights." It required China to make changes to its existing laws and otherwise bring them up to international standards, but did not delineate specific changes to be made. Shortly after concluding the 1992 MOU, China acceded to several international treaty regimes regarding copyright and patent protection, and promulgated a revised version of its 1982 Trademark Law as discussed above, which included, most notably, criminal penalties for trademark violations.

Despite the promulgation of new intellectual property laws and accession to various international conventions, the United States was soon to become dissatisfied with China's intellectual property enforcement efforts. As a result, in early 1995 the United States Trade Representative ("USTR") again listed China as a priority foreign country, and Special 301 investigations were resumed. China averted a trade war with the United States by agreeing to a new bilateral accord, the 1995 Enforcement Agreement.

The 1995 Enforcement Agreement consisted of two parts, an exchange of letters containing commitments by both sides on general intellectual property matters, and a State Council Intellectual Property Enforcement Action Plan. The Enforcement Action Plan envisioned, among other things, the establishment of provincial, regional, and municipal working groups to coordinate the implementation of China's intellectual property laws.

Despite China's strong commitments to enforcement, counterfeiting and piracy appeared to be on the increase, and the United States began to doubt Beijing's ability to implement the 1995 Enforcement Agreement. In May 1996, the USTR threatened to impose US$2 billion in trade sanctions against China for failure to comply with the 1995 Enforcement Agreement. China again averted these sanctions by conciliatory actions aimed at effecting the structural changes envisioned by the agreement. Soon thereafter, China issued the Provisional Regulations for the Determination and Administration of Well-known Trademarks, which – in light of China's desire to become a member of the World Trade Organisation – was geared towards bringing China's trademark regime more in line with WTO standards.

THE GATT / WTO AND THE TRIPS AGREEMENT   1.19

On 11 December 2001, China finally joined the world's most important treaty regime dealing with trade and trade related issues – the WTO. The WTO is the product of over five decades of multilateral cooperation in the development of international trade law beginning with the 1947 General Agreement on Tariffs and Trade (GATT).

According to GATT Article XXVIII, the various contracting parties committed themselves to multilateral trade negotiations or 'rounds' on a periodic basis. The original GATT agreement and subsequent negotiation rounds achieved a great deal of success in reducing tariff duty levels on trade in goods, its original purpose. In 1986, the 'Uruguay Round' of trade negotiations began at a Special Session of the GATT Contracting States, and comprised separate negotiations on a wide range of trade related topics, including *inter alia*, non-tariff barriers, agriculture, subsidies and countervailing duties, safeguards, dispute resolution, and intellectual property.

The Agreement Establishing the World Trade Organisation ("WTO Agreement") is a product of the Uruguay Round of GATT negotiations. Annexed to the WTO Agreement are several Multilateral Trade Agreements, including the Agreement on Trade-Related Aspects of Intellectual Property Rights ("TRIPS Agreement"). The TRIPS Agreement establishes minimum standards for the protection of intellectual property rights, and provides basic guidelines and principles regarding the availability, scope and use of such rights.

Section 5 of the Report of the Working Party on the Accession of China to the WTO ("Working Party Report") sets out the various changes China agreed to make to its intellectual property legislation and administrative rules before acceding to the WTO. These commitments mainly involve amendments to laws and regulations that would otherwise bring China's laws in compliance with the TRIPS Agreement and with the national laws of other WTO member states.

As for trademark protection, the TRIPS Agreement requires that all member countries comply with the relevant minimum standards set out in the Paris Convention. The TRIPS Agreement also sets a basic definition of a trademark as "[a]ny sign, or any combination of signs, capable of distinguishing the goods or services of one undertaking from those of other undertakings." The TRIPS Agreement invests owners of such marks with the exclusive right to prevent third parties from using similar marks for goods or services when such use would produce a "likelihood of confusion." Moreover, the TRIPS Agreement requires that exclusive rights to trademarks must last at least seven years after initial registration and be indefinitely renewable for subsequent seven year periods, and that registered marks may be cancelled after three years of continual non-use. Moreover, the TRIPS Agreement requires the elimination of compulsory licenses or the imposition of various restraints on the transferability of marks.

Article 16 of the TRIPS Agreement also extends the protection of well-known marks in various member states to those covering services, and to marks that cover dissimilar goods or services, provided that use of such a mark in relation to those goods or services "would indicate a connection between those goods or services and the owner of the registered trademark and provided that the interests of the owner of the registered trademark are likely to be damaged by such use." Article 13 of China's 2001 Trademark Law tracks the language of TRIPS Article 16, and is one example of the many changes that were made to China's intellectual property laws in preparation for China's accession to the WTO.

Since the early 1980s China has created a sophisticated system for the registration, maintenance and enforcement of trademark rights. At first blush, China's trademark laws are now as nuanced and sophisticated as the laws of the majority of most WTO member states. As will become apparent in subsequent chapters, China's trademark laws continue to be difficult to enforce, and there are numerous inconsistencies between the letter of the law and actual practice. Nevertheless, most legal scholars and practitioners of law in China agree that the development of China's legal system since the early 1980s has been nothing short of astounding, and the area of trademark law is certainly no exception.

CHAPTER 2

CHINESE-LANGUAGE MARKS

INTRODUCTION 2.1

In the process of localising a foreign trademark in China, the most important consideration for the holder, apart from the legal aspects of registering a trademark in China, is the practical aspect of choosing a trademark for use in China. Given the unique characteristics of Chinese culture and language, along with the inherent obstacles in translating a foreign-word mark, there are a number of key factors which must be taken into account to maximise the success of a trademark in China. This chapter addresses these concerns and deals with the intrinsic complexities of the Chinese language, potential cultural implications, marketing realities and the awareness of legal rights.[1]

CHINESE CULTURAL VALUES 2.2

One cannot fully appreciate the technical boundaries of the Chinese language without having an overview of how the Chinese people will react to certain words, names or marks. In a country like China, where the culture is very different from the original foreign market, consumers may interpret international established brands differently from what one would expect, and brands are almost inevitably viewed through the lens of local cultural values. Chinese culture does not only pertain to people in China, Hong Kong and Taiwan, as this Confucian-influenced set of values is shared by most Asian societies. Thus a good understanding of the Chinese consumer behaviour within the Chinese socio-cultural context would be very helpful.

Although many Chinese societies are regarded as modernised, the cultural values accumulated through long history are still deeply embedded. The Chinese are often superstitious about favouring names that convey good health, integrity, longevity, prosperity, good luck, good fortune, and other positive associations. Many Chinese believe

---

1   See generally *Chinese Trademarks*, Baker & McKenzie, 2004.

that a good and well chosen name is likely to pave the way to a life of success and happiness, while a badly chosen one is a curse that may haunt the given person and his family for generations to come. Likewise, in the Chinese business world, consumers react positively to brands that convey good meanings and strong values, with which they are able to associate on a personal and cultural level. They take longer, if at all, to embrace brands that they find to have negative or strange connotations.

2.3 THE CHINESE LANGUAGE

The population of China is made up of a number of indigenous populations, as well as some of the ethnic minorities that inhabit the central and western parts of China, many of which have their own dialects. Fortunately, the Chinese language is based on a unified set of characters even though the pronunciations differ from region to region. Thanks to government initiatives, all schools teach in the standard form of Chinese script, in Putonghua (the official language, which literally means the Common Language). Consequently, Chinese character recognition is widespread, and the use of a Chinese-character trademark will reach a large audience.

2.4 THE CHINESE SCRIPT

To better understand the Chinese language and especially Chinese naming, it is important to understand the linguistic features of Chinese word formation. The Chinese script is over 4,000 years old. Each character represents a syllable of the spoken language, and a large number of Chinese words consist of two-character compounds that are bi-syllabic.

Examples:

1. The word for aeroplane is 飞机 (*fei ji*), a compound of the character meaning to fly, and the character meaning machine.
2. The word for adult is 大人 (*da ren*), a compound of the character meaning big and person.

It is estimated that approximately 5,000 characters are in common daily use, each with a unique, inherent meaning, but there are more than 40,000 characters catalogued in various lexicons published through the ages. This also means that Chinese names cannot be formed as freely as English names. The creation of any Chinese name is restricted to the limited inventory of frequently used characters and the process of compounding. Plainly speaking, the Chinese language does not enjoy the freedom in naming that the English alphabetical system offers.

New characters are rarely created, and cannot be invented for the purposes of developing a trademark. Thus, while languages that are written with alphabets, such as English, permit the creation of new, meaningless words that can be used as trademarks (for example, Exxon or Kodak), this is not possible in Chinese. Moreover, although characters can be combined in an attempt to re-create the sound of a foreign word, each character continues to carry its inherent Chinese meaning. The Trademark Office does not permit the registration of Chinese characters that are fancifully created and cannot be found in a dictionary.

THE CHINESE CHARACTERS 2.5

Traditional Chinese characters are difficult to learn and write. By the end of the six years of primary school, an average student knows only half of the characters commonly used in writing modern Chinese, and even then the student may have difficulty recognising and understanding the characters. Even university graduates, full-time academics and newspaper editors make errors in writing Chinese characters.

The reform

In 1956, a scheme to simplify the traditional form of written Chinese characters was officially adopted within the PRC. The Chinese government hoped that by introducing a simplified writing system, it could facilitate learning, and increase the rate of literacy among the Chinese population. The simplified system did not change all Chinese characters, only the most commonly used and complex ones. Many traditional characters are already quite simple and, therefore, remained unchanged. The simplification process involved the reduction of the number of strokes that make up characters, and standardisation of the method of writing. Unlike Singapore, which adopted the simplified system, Taiwan and Hong Kong still use the traditional script. Simplified characters are largely unrecognised by the Chinese population outside the PRC, and similarly, traditional (or complex) characters are not recognised by the majority of the Chinese population within the PRC.

Everyday use

Use of non-standard Chinese characters, including traditional Chinese characters, is generally not allowed in the PRC. According to official regulations and the attitudes of the relevant authorities, use of Chinese characters in the PRC must be in accordance with the *Simplified Chinese Character Catalogue* (1986). In the *Explanation of the Publication of the Simplified Chinese Character Catalogue*, the State Language Work Committee stated that for those traditional characters that have been simplified and listed in the catalogue, only their simplified versions shall be used. Also, use of popular simplified versions that are not in the catalogue is not permitted.

Traditional characters nevertheless have recently regained popularity in the PRC, and young people, particularly university students, have shown an interest in learning the traditional form of Chinese characters. This perhaps reflects an association made by some between traditional Chinese characters and a higher social class, or more sophisticated lifestyle. On the other hand, many regard traditional characters as old-fashioned, and the authorities have recently been pushing for a more universal use of simplified characters as, for example, on signage, product indications, and labelling.

2.6 ORDER OF CHINESE CHARACTERS

Those unfamiliar with the Chinese language often ask whether Chinese is read from left to right, or from right to left. Traditionally, Chinese was written in vertical columns reading from the right-hand side of the page to the left. Headlines, street names, shop fronts, and similar titles were often written horizontally, reading also from right to left. Taiwan and, to a lesser extent, Hong Kong, have retained the use of this traditional convention, and it can also be found on old street signs and shop fronts in the PRC.

The modern convention, however, is to use horizontal lines reading from left to right, a system that has been in use in the PRC since 1958. The trademark user has a choice of conventions, and therefore must take into account the connotations of using the modern or the traditional. It should also be noted that if a Chinese trademark is used in conjunction with a foreign name, it reads better if the two are written in the same direction.

2.7 THE SPOKEN LANGUAGE

Tones

Chinese is a tonal language, which means that the same sound when pronounced with different tones may signify completely different words.

Example: In Putonghua the sound *fa* can mean 'to issue', 'to punish', 'law', or 'hair', depending on which of the four tones is used.

Homonyms

The Chinese language also contains many homonyms (words with the same pronunciation, including the same tone), which can have completely different meanings. This is similar to groups of words in English such as "two" and "too". The existence of many homonyms only adds to the complexity of the Chinese language. Interestingly, there are many different dialects in the Chinese language and each has its unique sets of homonyms causing even more complications.

Example: In Putonghua the sound of *gong* denotes 官 'palace', 恭 'to greet', and 工 'work'.

To overcome the confusion that this can cause, the Chinese language uses many bi-syllabic character compounds to illustrate meanings that may already be inherent in the single character, but are not evident unless the written character can be seen. For example, although the character *ji* means 'machine', the word *jiqi* is generally used when speaking. Often, the meaning of a character can only be determined from the context. As trademarks or brand names often provide a fairly limited context, it is crucial for marketers to select precise, meaningful names with a relatively limited range of possible meanings, and preferably ones that suggest positive associations.

It is also important for marketers to be aware of words that have homonyms bearing negative or ridiculous meanings in the Chinese languages. This problem exists in any language, but in the case of Chinese, the situation is inherently worse due to the complication of different dialects and the abundance of homonyms in each one. However, for practical considerations, a marketer should focus mainly on Putonghua and Cantonese, which are the two major spoken forms of Chinese.

Example: In Cantonese, the pronunciation of the number four is very close to the word for death or die.

Multiple meanings

Another distinctive aspect of the Chinese language is that the same character can sometimes have more than one meaning. In such cases, the character will be pronounced differently according to the intended meaning.

A good example is the character 行, which when pronounced *xing* means to walk and when pronounced *hang* means a business. However, most characters with multiple meanings have only one pronunciation, and the particular meaning intended must be taken from the context in which it is said or written. Another example is the character 乐, which may be pronounced as *le* or *yue* meaning happiness and music respectively.

Limitations

Every language is made up of a range of sound, so there are bound to be certain sounds in one language that do not exist in another. This inevitably means that it is not always possible to reproduce the sound of a foreign word with Chinese characters. In addition, it is generally preferable for a trademark to have only three, four, or at most, five syllables, with each character representing a single syllable because, from a Chinese speaker's perspective, marks with more than five characters are cumbersome to say and difficult to remember. Thus, when translating polysyllabic, foreign-word marks, it is preferable for the Chinese version to have fewer syllables than the original mark.

Accounting for differences in dialects

Out of the numerous forms of spoken Chinese, the two principal forms are Putonghua, the official spoken language of China, Taiwan, and Singapore, and Cantonese, the predominant dialect in southern China and Hong Kong. The differences in these dialects can be so great that Chinese who do not speak the same dialect cannot understand one another. As the same characters often yield different sounds in different dialects, a particular character that carries an inherently good meaning and sounds appealing in one dialect, may carry negative connotations in another.

2.8 PINYIN: ROMANISATION OF THE CHINESE LANGUAGE

One of the many initiatives taken by the PRC Government in modernising the Chinese language was the introduction of Pinyin, ie romanisation of Chinese words, which can be used as an alternative means of representation. It is inherently inadequate as a complete substitute for the Chinese script as it does not differentiate the many homonyms that exist in the Chinese language. However, its acceptance and popularity in China should not be underestimated. It is regarded as a useful aid which is now widely used in the Chinese education system and as a basis for indexing dictionaries. It is also the basis of one of the most commonly used Chinese input methods for computers. Pinyin, the phonetic alphabet currently in use in China was introduced in 1958.

DEVISING A CHINESE LANGUAGE TRADEMARK

2.9 THE IMPORTANCE OF USING CHINESE-LANGUAGE MARKS

There is no legal requirement to use a Chinese character trademark in China, yet for companies with a vision to penetrate the enormous Chinese-speaking market, a precise translation of their marks into Chinese should be placed high on the agenda. It may seem easy to claim, as the foreign brand is established and has a long history and tradition overseas, that there is no need for a Chinese translation. Adopting only a foreign name might also be a deliberate marketing move for some high-end products, in the hope this will increase their desirability or perceived value. Unlike some westernised Chinese markets (Hong Kong being an example), where certain Western knowledge would be expected from the average consumer, the vast majority of consumers in the PRC, often including the high-end market, have a limited knowledge of foreign languages. This trend is not likely to change as the importance of the Chinese language is only growing. We should not forget that the key to branding is for people to be able to relate to a brand, and a prerequisite to this is that the name is comprehensible by the target audience.

GETTING NICKNAMES   2.10

As the vast majority of PRC consumers have a limited knowledge of foreign languages and will identify products solely by their Chinese name, if the company itself does not develop a Chinese mark, Chinese consumers will usually come up with a Chinese nickname. In some cases, the nickname will be quite innocuous, derived simply from the device used on the products, the shape of the goods or even an absurd association of the mark's pronunciation. The following are some more acceptable examples:

1. Carnation evaporated milk was nicknamed 三花牛奶 (*san hua niu nai*), meaning 'three flowers milk', because of its packaging. Carnation eventually adopted the nickname as its own mark
2. Toblerone became 三角牌 (*san jiao pai*) meaning 'triangle brand', this was also accepted as the official mark.
3. Wrigley's Spearmint was easily nicknamed 绿箭牌 (*lu jian pai*) meaning 'green arrow brand', this was also accepted as the official mark.

In other instances, the nickname that evolves may not be flattering to the product, or in keeping with the company's marketing image. For example:

1. The Quaker Oats logo has become known in the trade as 老人牌 (*lao ren pai*) meaning 'old man brand'.
2. The Polo mark has been termed 三脚马 (*san jiao ma*) i.e. 'three-legged horse'.
3. Salvatore Ferragamo was given the Cantonese nickname in Hong Kong as 飞甩鸡毛 (*fei lat gai mo*), which literally means 'fly off the chicken feather'.

2.11 STAGES OF DEVISING A CHINESE MARK

There are usually four stages involved:

1. compiling a list of possible Chinese versions of the Latin letter word mark. Attention at this stage is given principally to developing marks with a positive connotation and a sound similar to the original Latin letter mark, and is generally not product-specific;
2. review of the marks that have been generated, and those that have either an unpleasant sound or possible negative connotations, are eliminated. In this stage, particular attention should be given to the mark's sound and connotations, in the two major dialects of Putonghua and Cantonese;
3. ranking of the possible marks in terms of their appropriateness to specific products and their market appeal, and clearly inappropriate marks are eliminated;
4. examination in terms of the marks' inherent registrability (this requires legal analysis). Searches for identical or similar trademarks that have already been registered or applied for, also need to be conducted.

2.12 METHODS OF TRANSLATION

There are three general methods of rendering a foreign-word mark in Chinese. These include:

1. literal or conceptual translation;
2. transliteration; and
3. a hybrid form of the literal translation and transliteration, referred to as the phonetic-conceptual method.

When devising a Chinese-language mark, it is advisable to utilise each of these methods in order to determine the best possible translation.

Conceptual method

The literal or conceptual translation of a foreign-word mark approximates as direct a translation as possible of the meaning of the mark. By adopting this method, the Chinese mark's pronunciation would, in most cases, differ radically from its original pronunciation, however characters are selected to convey the exact meaning as the foreign word, or the conceptual quality or feature of the product.

Examples

1. Apple Computers was translated as 萍果 (*ping guo*) in Putonghua, which literally means apple.

28

2. Shell, the oil company, adopted a literal translation 贝壳 (*bei ke*) meaning shell.
3. Nestle, the food producer, was also literally translated in 雀巢 (*que chao*) meaning a nest.
4. Universal, the entertainment company is translated as 环球 (*huan qiu*) meaning 'across the globe'.
5. Palmolive is translated as 棕榄 (*zong lan*), which is a combination of the exact translation for the words palm and olive.
6. Microsoft is translated as 微软 (*wei ruan*), which is also a combination of the exact translation for micro and soft.
7. Lotus, the automobile producer named its Chinese mark 莲花 (*lian hua*), which means lotus.

However, it should be noted that is not always possible to find a concise Chinese equivalent for each foreign term or concept. During the process of finding a proper Chinese substitute, accuracy in meaning may be lost or distorted. Care should also be taken to avoid any Chinese translation that has an unfavourable connotation.

Example

The trademark 'Cannon', for covers and textile articles, is translated in Cantonese as 'big cannon brand'. This is an exact literal translation. The problem, however, is that the first two characters of the trademark have a strong connotation of telling a lie in Cantonese.

Phonetic method

The second translation method is phonetic transliteration. Under this method, Chinese characters are selected to replicate as nearly as possible the sound of the foreign mark in its native language.

Examples

1. McDonald's, the fast food chain, is translated as 麦当劳 (*mai dang lao*) in Putonghua. The meanings of the individual characters are: 'wheat' (*mai*); 'suitable' (*dang*); and 'labour' (*lao*).
2. Sony is translated as 索尼 (*suo ni*). The meanings of the individual characters are: 'cable' (*suo*); and 'nun' (*ni*).
3. Louis Vuitton adopted its Putonghua pronunciation as 路易威登 (*lu yi wei deng*). The meanings of the individual characters are 'road' (*lu*); 'transact' (*yi*); 'mighty' (*wei*); and 'to climb' or 'get on' (*deng*).
4. Ferrari is transliterated as 法拉利 (*fa la li*). The meanings of individual characters are: 'the law' (*fa*); 'pull' (*la*); and 'benefit' or 'profit' (*li*).

5. Cartier uses the Chinese mark of 卡地亚 (*ka di ya*). The meanings of the individual characters are: 'card' (modern meaning) or 'guardhouse' (*ka*); 'earth' (*di*); and 'Asia' or 'second place' (*ya*).
6. Johnson & Johnson is transliterated as 强生 (*qiang sheng*). The meanings of the individual characters are: 'strong' (*qiang*); and 'life' or 'to live' (*sheng*).

In part because such translated names bear absurd literal meanings, it is readily recognised by Chinese consumers as representing a foreign product. This association of the name with an imported product is often one of the company's marketing objectives. Once a Chinese mark becomes established, Chinese speakers generally cease to think about the literal meaning of the characters, and upon seeing the characters together, simply associate with the foreign product. In the above example, instead of registering wheat, suitable, or labour, they simply think of McDonald's. Transliteration is the preferred technique, and the most commonly used when translating surnames.

Although most of the Chinese marks listed above do not bear any meanings at all, it is interesting to note that none of the words used has any inherently bad or negative connotation. It would of course be more desirable if the Chinese characters, though without any meanings in the context, were still inherently suggestive of something good.

Examples

1. Alfred Dunhill was translated as 登喜路 *deng xi lu*). The meanings of the individual characters are: 'to climb' or 'get on' (*deng*); 'happiness' (*xi*); and 'road' (*lu*). Together these words could be interpreted as 'getting on to the road of happiness'.
2. Canon was translated as 佳能 (*jia neng*). The meanings of individual characters are: 'good' or 'outstanding' (*jia*); and 'capable', 'capability' or 'performance' (*neng*). Together these words could mean 'good performance'.

As mentioned earlier, the Chinese language is a tonal language. Tones are related to pitches and are distinguished by their intrinsic sonority. Phonetically, the higher the pitch, the more sonorous it is and for most Chinese speakers, they have a tendency to favour names that can be pronounced sonorously. Therefore, in devising a Chinese name for a brand or a mark, tones are also an important factor and serious consideration needs to be given to these.

Phonetic-conceptual method

This is undoubtedly the most desirable method of all if the circumstance permits. It is a hybrid of the former two methods by producing a Chinese mark that is both phonetically similar to the foreign mark, and at the same time, suggestive of the function or benefits of the product.

Examples

1. The classic example of a hybrid mark is Coca-Cola's Chinese mark. Not only is the Chinese pronunciation, 可口可乐 (*ke kou ke le*) very close in sound to the original mark, but the characters mean 'tasty, happiness producing' or 'permitting the mouth to rejoice'.
2. Pfizer's Viagra is another recent example of hybrid success. Its Chinese name is 威而钢 (*wei er gang*), which is very close to its original English pronunciation and at the same time means 'mighty and strong as steel'.
3. Intel's famous processor "Pentium" is known in Chinese as 奔腾 (*ben teng*), which means "to run fast and free".

GUIDELINES FOR SELECTING A CHINESE-LANGUAGE TRADEMARK   2.13

Precise and professional translation is vital for the accurate reflection of any cultural nuances in the translation and should be carried out by people who have a firm grasp and understanding of each culture and language, as a great deal of implied meaning may be lost if the gap between the two languages is not effectively bridged.

1. The Chinese-language trademark, when pronounced in Putonghua or Cantonese, should be as close as possible to the sound of the original mark.
2. The pronunciation in one dialect should not have a negative connotation in the same or another dialect.
3. The image projected by the Chinese name should be compatible with the product and the company image.
4. Descriptiveness should be avoided, as this generally makes the mark more difficult to register and less distinctive.

CONSISTENCY IN CHINESE CHARACTER TRADEMARKS   2.14

Maintaining a consistent translation and use of Chinese characters is crucial in avoiding many undesirable consequences, which may arise due to the complication of registration and enforcement matters. This is elaborated in Legal factors (paras 2.20–2.22) below.

MARKETING FACTORS

2.15 BREAKING THE CULTURAL BARRIER

Developing an appropriate Chinese trademark requires looking at the characteristics of the specific product and the target market, as well as analysing other marks that have been developed by competitors.

Historically the Chinese people are not known to be open or amenable to change. They are conservative, though perhaps not as true for the new generation of middle class that has quickly emerged from the economic boom during the past decade or so. But the new generation of Chinese are not significant in numbers when compared to the entire population. There is indeed a barrier. This barrier is not entirely impermeable and many internationally recognised brands have strategically paved their way into the China market by localising and understanding the Chinese culture.

Appropriate localisation

The Chinese language is a system entirely different from any European language. For the vast majority of people in China who are not trained in English, a simple word would be impossible to pronounce. Localisation not only provides the locals with a more easily referable name or identity, it also dilutes the undesirable stigma of any cultural imperialism that may be attached. An appropriate degree of localisation closes the gap between a foreign brand and the local consumers, offering the opportunity for an emotional attachment in their everyday lives.

Take a lesson from McDonald's, a very American restaurant that successfully transformed itself into the world's restaurant. Localisation occurs wherever it goes, from its name to its range of food, and China was no exception. A recent market survey revealed that nearly half of the Chinese children under 12 identified McDonald's as a domestic brand. This is a huge success as this literally means McDonald's has totally removed any cultural barrier from half the future generation of its single largest market.

Understanding the culture

In marketing, there is nothing more important than knowing exactly what the consumer wants. By understanding the Chinese culture, one would expect to have a glimpse of what Chinese would generally like, or at least what they would most likely dislike. As mentioned, Chinese tend to favour, and react more positively toward, names that have positive connotations.

Taking Coca-Cola as an example, the unique taste and way of serving Coke was from a different world entirely. By adopting the Chinese

32

name 可口可乐 (*ke kou ke le*), which means 'permitting the mouth to rejoice', Coca-Cola became very acceptable to the Chinese.[2] Another positive example is the brand Alfred Dunhill. The Chinese name chosen was "登喜路" (*deng xi lu*) which bears the Chinese meaning of "getting on a road of happiness".

RULE OF THUMB: GET IT RIGHT UPFRONT   2.16

Many branding professionals and translators will agree that translating and transliterating foreign brands into Chinese is both an art and a science. It is easier said than done. However, endeavours will be rewarded when the right mark is chosen and the adverse consequences, such as getting an inappropriate nickname, are avoided. As mentioned earlier, many internationally established brands have been coined nicknames, some more acceptable than others. Whatever the nickname is, one common feature exists – it is extremely difficult for a company to disassociate with it. The only options are to accept it as official or to launch time-consuming and costly brand transference campaigns with no guarantee as to the result. It therefore makes a lot of sense for companies to plan ahead in developing a Chinese trademark strategy and to register and protect these intangible properties.[3]

Needless to say, if a company does not act quickly in registering a widely recognised Chinese nickname, a third party will move to register it, either to take advantage of the goodwill built up in the name or to attempt to extract a fee from the company to assign the registration.

TRADEMARK RECOGNITION   2.17

A mark's recognition is undoubtedly the very core of every brand's or company's marketing strategy. In the Chinese-speaking market, especially the PRC, Hong Kong and Taiwan, the vast majority of those making the decisions to buy, from the individual end-user to the bulk importer, have a fairly limited command of foreign languages. Consumers, in particular, rely heavily on Chinese character trademarks when making purchasing decisions. Attracting the consumers to a certain brand or label is only the first stage, getting them to remember a mark is another. The consistent use of a single Chinese name can also limit the potential for confusion as the market, and competition, grows.

2 See *Transliteration of Coca-Cola Trademark to Chinese Characters*, HF Allman (former Legal Counsel in China for The Coca-Cola Company).
3 *Chinese Brand Naming: A Linguistic Analysis of the Names of Ten Product Categories*, Business Research Center Papers on China, Allan KK Chan and Yue-Yuan Huang, Hong Kong Baptist University.

It is highly likely that a marketing strategy will require the development of marks that are appealing to the target market. For example, in the case of hair care and cosmetic products (a consumer product rapidly growing in popularity in Asia) the target consumers are women, and the finest quality beauty care and cosmetic products are generally associated with France. For this reason, a Chinese mark for such a product should probably try to convey a foreign flavour. At the same time, the mark should be made up of characters that are still easy for a consumer to recognise, and that will be associated with beauty or elegance. Two examples are the trademarks L'Oreal and Lancôme. It should be noted, however, that an already active and flourishing market in a particular type of product in Asia will usually signify a high level of competition for trademark registration.

2.18 ONE MARK FOR ALL CHINESE-SPEAKING JURISDICTIONS

Ideally, companies should develop trademarks that can be used in all the relevant Chinese-speaking jurisdictions. From a marketing perspective, this is important so that Chinese consumers, no matter where they are located, can easily associate a single Chinese name with the product and the company. For example, a Taiwanese consumer who associates one Chinese character version of a trademark with a product will be confused if, while shopping in Singapore, advertisements for the same product display another Chinese character version of the trademark.

Where products are to be marketed in Taiwan, use of simplified characters is undesirable as the mark will be instantly associated with the PRC, and political tensions between the PRC and Taiwan run high. Only those few characters that were simplified prior to the formation of the PRC in 1949 are acceptable for registration in Taiwan. Hong Kong trademark registration authorities will accept simplified characters for registration, although most trademarks currently used in Hong Kong employ traditional characters.

Hong Kong is now in the seventh year after the handover of sovereignty, but the traditional form of characters are still commonly and widely used in everyday life. However, there are some signs of acceptance of simplified characters, especially in the business world, as China's influence continues to grow at an enormous rate. More and more Hong Kong people are now literate in simplified Chinese. However there are no signs that simplified characters will replace their traditional counterparts in the foreseeable future.

As noted from the various examples given above, even if the simplified characters are used, they are usually those that are less radically different from the traditional form. This may be a very good marketing strategy, as it would surely reduce the chances of any confusion caused to Chinese consumers of different markets.

LOGO IMAGERY
2.19

Successful marketing campaigns in China rarely overlook the importance of the country's unique cultural and linguistic elements. In general, Chinese consumers are more sensitive and perceptive towards brand names and logo imagery than their Western counterparts. This difference is attributed, in large part, to the fact that Chinese characters are inherently meaningful, whereas in the English alphabet, a single letter carries only a sound and no meaning. Native Chinese speakers tend to encode verbal information visually while native English speakers mainly encode phonetically, so the Chinese-speaking consumers tend to judge a brand name on its visual appeal as well. Chinese consumers are also more predisposed towards a name that is considered lucky, or is somehow related to the product benefits.

LEGAL FACTORS

TRADITIONAL OR SIMPLIFIED CHARACTERS?
2.20

Chinese enterprises are already generally prohibited from registering trademarks in traditional characters; an exception is made only in respect of customary stylised forms that have been used for a long time. Foreign enterprises (including enterprises from Taiwan, Hong Kong, and Macau) are at present still permitted to register trademarks using traditional characters, but given the trend towards enforced use of simplified characters, it is probably preferable, in the absence of exceptional circumstances, to use simplified characters when registering a trademark.

It should also be noted that non-standard simplified characters are generally inappropriate where a mark is intended for use throughout China and it is not uncommon for non-standard simplified characters to be mistaken as standard or official. Accordingly, when simplified characters are to be used, it is prudent to enquire whether they are official.

It is reasonable to expect that registration of a mark in China in simplified characters would also protect the same mark in traditional characters, and vice versa. This is similar to the way registration of Roman block capitals protects all forms of a world mark in both China and Hong Kong. However, there is a divergence of opinion on this point among PRC trademark lawyers, and as a matter of prudence, it is advisable to register an important mark in both simplified and traditional characters.

2.21 REGISTRABILITY

There are several major hazards one ought to avoid in devising a translated or transliterated mark. It is not rare for a Chinese mark to be regarded as so laudatory or descriptive of the product that it is incapable of registration. Sometimes it may have been a deliberate marketing decision to opt for a meaningful mark and forego legal protection, but all too often it is done in total ignorance of the law. Another point that is worth noting is that the Trademark Office does not permit the registration of Chinese characters that are fancifully created and cannot be found in a dictionary. The Pinyin for a trademark may also be registered with the Chinese characters in order to provide extra protection against confusion, and to assist those unfamiliar with Putonghua pronunciation. However, the use of Pinyin alone is extremely rare.

2.22 CONSISTENCY IN CHINESE-CHARACTER TRADEMARKS

It is always advisable for applicant companies to develop their own Chinese version of their company name or trademark. Since trademark application forms have to be submitted to the Trademark Office in the Chinese language, if the applicant fails to provide the required information in Chinese, the official agent will translate the application materials and, if necessary, provide a translation or transliteration of the applicant's name. This is not desirable as the Chinese trademark chosen may be unsuitable. There is also a risk that if further applications are made at a later date, a different Chinese language version of the applicant's name will emerge, owing to a different member of staff at the trademark agency dealing with the new filing. Since the Trademark Office maintains files on the basis of an applicant's Chinese name, examiners may then regard the old and the new applications as coming from two separate, unrelated, applicants. Many new trademark applications of foreign companies have been blocked by their own earlier trademark registrations.

Inconsistent use of a company's Chinese name can also create serious problems in the event that infringement actions are undertaken. For example, where the Chinese name of the trademark owner appears in different versions on its trademark certificates, trademark-licensing contracts, company stationery, and business registration certificates, the relevant Administration for Industry and Commerce (AIC) may contest whether the party filing the infringement complaint is in fact the owner of the infringed trademarks. Inconsistent use of Chinese names has been known to result in unnecessary confusion and delay with respect to enforcement.

CHAPTER 3

WELL-KNOWN TRADEMARKS

INTRODUCTION
A trademark enjoys extra protection if it is recognised as a well-known trademark (驰名商标). With its accession to the Paris Convention for the Protection of Industrial Property from 1985 and its membership of the World Trade Organisation ("WTO"), the People's Republic of China ("PRC") is required to provide protection for well-known trademarks whether or not these are registered in PRC. These obligations are fulfilled through the implementation and enforcement of PRC's own trademark legislation. This chapter will illustrate the legal framework for the recognition and protection of well-known trademarks.

3.1

THE RELEVANT INTERNATIONAL CONVENTIONS AND AGREEMENTS

PARIS CONVENTION FOR THE PROTECTION OF INDUSTRIAL PROPERTY ("PARIS CONVENTION")

3.2

Article 6bis of the Paris Convention requires Convention countries to protect well-known trademarks. If a trademark constitutes "a reproduction, an imitation, or a translation" of a well-known trademark "liable to create confusion", and the trademark is used for goods identical or similar to those for which the well-known trademark is used, the Paris Convention requires Convention countries to refuse or cancel its registration and prohibit its use at the request of an interested party (or *ex officio* if their legislation permits). A trademark that is created by adding some elements, or making alterations to a well-known trademark might still come under attack. This is because if the essential part of the trademark constitutes a reproduction of any well-known trademark or an imitation liable to create confusion with any well-known trademark, the owner of the well-known trademark can seek Paris Convention protection.

A period of at least five years from the date of registration of the infringing trademark shall be allowed for requesting the cancellation of it as required by the Paris Convention. Convention countries may provide that the request for the prohibition of use has to be made within a certain period, but no time limit shall be fixed for requesting the cancellation or the prohibition of use of infringing trademarks registered or used in bad faith.

Sometimes the Paris Convention was directly relied upon to give foreign trademarks protection in PRC, especially when the national framework to be discussed below has not been constructed. An Australian company sought to register "PIZZA HUT" in PRC in 1985. Opposition by the genuine owner of the trademark was successful. The Trademark Office ("TMO") directly applied the Paris Convention provisions in relation to well-known trademarks.

3.3 TRADE-RELATED ASPECTS OF INTELLECTUAL PROPERTY RIGHTS AGREEMENT ("TRIPS")

TRIPS itself is Annex 1C of the Marrakesh Agreement Establishing the WTO to which PRC acceded in November 2001. Article 16 of TRIPS extended the protection in Paris Convention given to well-known trademarks in two aspects. First, well-known trademark protection is offered to trademarks used in respect to services also. Second, well-known trademark protection could be sought if the infringing trademark is used on goods or services not similar to those of the registered well-known trademark, provided that the use of the infringing mark would indicate a connection between those goods or services and the owner of the registered well-known trademark, and provided that the interests of that trademark owner are likely to be damaged by such use.

In addition to the extension of protection, Article 16 of TRIPS also provides for determination of well-known trademarks. It requires Member States, when considering whether a trademark is well-known or not, to take account of the knowledge of the trademark in the relevant sector of the public, including knowledge in the Member State concerned which has been obtained as a result of the promotion of the trademark.

THE DOMESTIC LAWS AND REGULATIONS

3.4 PRC TRADEMARK LAW

The general principle and framework of well-known trademarks (驰名商标) protection can be found in the PRC Trademark Law ("Trademark Law"). Provisions in relation to well-known trademarks protection were absent in the Trademark Law before its extensive amendment in 2001.

Implementing Regulations of the PRC Trademark Law ("Implementing Regulations") covers the procedures for well-known trademarks protection and the details of the application of well-known trademark provisions in the Trademark Law. The Implementing Regulations replaced the old Detailed Implementing Rules for PRC Trademark Law in which "trademarks already well-known to the public" (已为公众熟知的商标) were mentioned: registering such trademarks by reproduction, imitation or translation, contrary to the principle of honesty and good faith, would be regarded as obtaining a registration by deceptive or other improper means. Some of the cases referred to below are about "trademarks already well-known to the public".

REGULATIONS ON THE RECOGNITION AND PROTECTION OF WELL-KNOWN TRADEMARKS

3.5

Regulations on the Recognition and Protection of Well-known Trademarks ("Well-known Trademarks Regulations") should also be considered. As its name indicates, Well-known Trademark Regulations provide for, in addition to the extent of protection of well-known trademarks, specific procedures for determining whether a mark is well-known, and relevant materials one needs to submit when requesting recognition of well-known trademarks. The Well-known Trademark Regulations came into force on 1 June 2003, replacing the Provisional Regulations for the Recognition and Administration of Well-Known Trademarks ("Provisional Well-known Trademarks Regulations") promulgated in 1996. As discussed below, the new regulations will substantially change the well-known trademarks recognition system operated under the Provisional Well-known Trademarks Regulations. The full impact of the new Well-known Trademarks Regulations remains to be seen.

WHAT CONSTITUTES A WELL-KNOWN TRADEMARK?

HOW TO DETERMINE WHETHER A TRADEMARK IS WELL-KNOWN

3.6

"Well-known trademark" is not defined in the Trademark Law nor Implementing Regulations. Article 14 of the Trademark Law, though, provides that the following factors shall be taken into account when deciding whether a trademark is well-known:

1. reputation of the trademark to the relevant public;

2. duration of continuous use of the trademark;
3. continuous duration, extent and geographical area of any advertisement of the trademark;
4. records of protection of the mark as a well-known trademark; and
5. any other factors relevant to the reputation of the trademark

Article 14 is always referred to in the Implementing Regulations and the Well-known Trademarks Regulations as the standard or test to be used in determining whether a mark is well known or not. When the Trademark Office ("TMO") or the Trademark Review and Adjudication Board ("TRAB") has to decide whether a mark constitutes a well-known trademark, the relevant provisions almost always state that the relevant authority shall do so "pursuant to the provision of Article 14 of the Trademark Law". But showing the existence of all of the above is not a must. The Well-known Trademarks Regulations provide that, although each of the factors above shall be comprehensively considered by the relevant authority, satisfying all the factors is not a necessary condition for well-known trademark recognition. The Well-known Trademarks Regulations also define "well-known trademark". The term means a trademark that is widely known and has a relatively good reputation among the relevant public in PRC. This "relevant public" is defined as including:

1. consumers of the goods or service;
2. business operators that produce those goods or provide those services; and
3. sellers and related persons that are involved in the distribution channels of such good or service.

Note that the focus is on "relevant public in PRC", thus the mere fact that a trademark is famous outside PRC does not mean that it will necessarily be recognised as a well-known trademark in PRC. However, as will be seen below, foreign well-known status may help in showing that the mark is well known in PRC. In actual practice the PRC TMO has recognised over 200 well-known trademarks under the Provisional Well-known Trademarks Regulations throughout the years and all of them are marks owned by Chinese enterprises. None of the applications for well-known status made by foreign trademark owners under the Provisional Well-known Trademarks Regulations have thus far been processed. *IKEA System BV v Beijing Cinet Information Co Ltd (Gao Zhi Zhong Zi* No 76 of 2000) (the "IKEA Case" – a domain name dispute case), though, shows that it is legally possible for the judiciary to recognise a foreign trademark as a well-known trademark.

The definition above is actually the definition of "well-known trademark" in the Well-known Trademarks Regulations, thus strictly speaking it is not related to the meaning of the term in the Trademark Law and the Implementing Regulations. Well-known Trademarks Regulations will be followed by TMO and TRAB as those are the detailed working and procedural rules made for these authorities, but whether the court will necessarily apply and follow the definitions in Well-known Trademarks Regulations is not clear (as will be discussed below, it is now clear that the courts could on their own recognise well-known trademarks in trial).

PROTECTION OF WELL-KNOWN TRADEMARKS

OPPOSITION TO THE APPLICATION FOR REGISTRATION AND CANCELLATION OF REGISTRATION   3.7

How is a well-known trademark going to be protected in PRC? The owner of the well-known trademark should be able to oppose an application for registration of an infringing mark, or if it is registered, to cancel the registration and stop the use of the infringing mark. Article 13 of the Trademark Law provides for the protection given to well-known trademarks. The treatment of a well-known trademark registered in PRC is different from that of a well-known trademark not registered in PRC.

Well-known trademarks not registered in PRC
Where a trademark is a reproduction, imitation or translation of the well-known trademark and is liable to cause confusion, its application for registration in respect of identical or similar goods or services shall be rejected, and its use shall be prohibited.

Well-known trademarks registered in PRC
Where a trademark is a reproduction, imitation or translation of the well-known trademark and is liable to cause confusion and result in prejudice to the interests of the trademark owner, its application for registration in respect of non-identical or dissimilar goods or services shall be rejected, and its use shall be prohibited.

Thus, in order to obtain protection against use on dissimilar goods or services leading to, for example, dilution or denigration of the well-known trademark, the owner has to register the trademark in PRC first. The two cases below show the protection given to trademarks well known to the general consumers in dissimilar goods situation.

七喜 TMO Decision Shang Biao Yi Zi No 1963 of 2000

The trademark here is identical to the Chinese version trademark of 'SEVEN UP'. The Chinese version has been registered and used by the Opponent, the Concentrate Manufacturing Company of Ireland (a subsidiary of PepsiCo, Inc), in the PRC. The applicant wanted to register the trademark in respect of animal feed. The Opponent argued that its trademark was well known to the general consumers. The TMO held that this was indeed the case as the trademark had been used on soft drinks for many years and SEVEN UP drinks had been widely sold in the PRC. Even though the goods produced by the parties were different, allowing the Applicant to register the trademark would still cause confusion: general consumers would think that the Applicant's goods were produced by the Opponent. The opposition succeeded.

九喜 TMO Decision Shang Biao Yi Zi No 2347 of 2000

The parties were those in the case above, but the Applicant here replaced the Chinese character for seven in the trademark with that for nine (九). The TMO still held that the Opponent's mark was well known to the general consumers but it also held that the Applicant's mark was not similar to the Opponent's mark. Also, the goods (animal feed again) bearing the Applicant's trademark had a function different from the goods of the Opponent. The consumers would be getting respective goods of the parties through different channels and thus there would be no confusion. The opposition failed.

Article 5 of the Implementing Regulations provides that when a dispute arises in the course of trademark registration or trademark review and adjudication, an interested party who believes its trademark constitutes a well-known trademark may file a request with the Trademark Office (TMO) (for opposition) or the TRAB (for cancellation) to establish it as a well-known trademark, and to reject trademark registration applications or to cancel trademark registrations infringing its rights in the well-known trademark. The owner of a well-known trademark needs to submit evidence that its trademark constitutes a well-known trademark. These should be the relevant materials substantiating that its trademark is well known as provided in the Well-known Trademarks Regulations. What these relevant materials include will be dealt with in the section "Recognition of Well-known Trademarks" at paras 3.12 – 3.15 below. The TMO or TRAB will, on the basis of ascertained facts, establish whether the trademark constitutes a well-known trademark. Just like other trademark oppositions, the opposition has to be made within three months from the publication of the preliminarily approved trademark, a limitation period set in the Trademark Law. A request for cancellation, on the other hand, has to be filed within five years from the date of the registration of the infringing trademark, unless the registration of the infringing trademark is made in bad faith in which case there will be no limitation period. These provisions in Article 41 of the Trademark Law reflect the aforementioned provisions in the Paris Convention.

PROHIBITION OF USE   3.8

For prohibition of use, Article 45 of the Implementing Regulations provides that a request has to be made to the Administrative Department for Industry and Commerce for prohibition. Again, when filing the request, one needs to submit evidence that his trademark constitutes a well-known trademark. If the TMO establishes the mark as a well-known trademark, the Administrative Department for Industry and Commerce will order the infringer to cease the use, and confiscate and destroy the representations of the trademark. If it is difficult to detach the representations of the trademark from the goods, both the representations and goods will be confiscated and destroyed. More detailed procedures for prohibition of use are found in Article 5 of the Well-known Trademarks Regulations. It provides that written request for a prohibition of use should be made to the municipal (prefectural) level or higher Administration for Industry and Commerce ("AIC") of the place where the case arose. Again relevant materials substantiating that its trademark is well-known have to be submitted. In addition, the owner of a well-known trademark also needs to send a copy of the request and the materials to the provincial level AIC of the place where it is located. Case materials will be passed to higher level AIC and then to TMO for determination. The administrative authorities have to complete the passing of the case materials by prescribed deadlines.

As readers can see, procedures for requesting well-known trademark protection basically start with seeking recognition of the well-known status of the mark (by submitting relevant materials). Such recognition will be discussed in "Recognition of Well-known Trademarks" at paras 3.12 – 3.15 below.

PROTECTION GIVEN TO 'TRADEMARKS OF SOME   3.9
INFLUENCE'

Article 31 of the Trademark Law may be of assistance to owners of well-known trademarks though strictly speaking it is not about well-known trademarks. The Article provides that an application for registration of a trademark shall not create any prejudice to the prior right of another person, nor shall unfair means be used to pre-emptively register a trademark "of some influence" another person has used. Literally "of some influence" appears to be a lower standard than "well-known". Owners of trademarks not fulfilling the requirement for a well-known status may still be able to rely on Article 31. Article 41 of the Trademark Law on cancellation of registrations of trademarks infringing rights in relation to well-known trademarks (discussed above) applies equally to marks violating Article 31, for the cancellation of registration of such marks. Article 31 seems to go even further and give more protection than what is required in Paris Convention and TRIPS. If TMO continues not to recognise foreign trademarks as well-known trademarks under the Well-known Trademarks Regulations, Article 31 provides an alternate way for foreign well-known trademarks owners to protect their trademarks in PRC.

3.10 PREVENT OTHERS FROM USING A WELL-KNOWN TRADEMARK AS AN ENTERPRISE NAME

Protection of well-known trademarks covers the situation where the well-known trademark is not being used as a trademark but as an enterprise name. Article 53 of the Implementing Regulations provides that the owner of the well-known trademark can file an application with the competent authority for the registration of enterprise names (State AIC and the local AICs at all levels) for cancellation of the registration of the enterprise name if it is likely to deceive or mislead the public. The competent authority for the registration of enterprise names has to handle the matter pursuant to the Regulations for the Administration of Registration of Enterprise Names. The provision is reiterated in Article 13 of the Well-known Trademarks Regulations.

3.11 EFFECTS OF WELL-KNOWN STATUS ON PROTECTION

Article 11 of the Well-known Trademarks Regulations provides that when protecting a well-known trademark, TMO, TRAB or the local AICs are required to consider the distinctiveness and the fame of the trademark. Article 10 of the Interpretations of the Supreme People's Court of Several Issues Concerning the Application of the Law to the Trial of Civil Dispute Cases Involving Trademarks ("the Interpretations") (promulgated on 12 October 2002 and became effective on 16 October 2002) also provides that when considering whether two marks are similar, notoriety of the registered trademark should be considered. The fame / notoriety etc, of a mark is relevant to the question of whether the mark is well known. The effect is that well-known trademarks enjoy a more readily obtainable, and wider, scope of protection. By the same token, owners of a well-known trademark could potentially obtain a larger amount of damages for infringement – Article 16 of the Interpretations provides that the courts shall consider the fame of an infringed mark (together with other factors) when determining the level of damages to be awarded.

Prosecution guidelines issued by the Ministry of Public Security and Supreme People's Procuratorate in April 2001, on the other hand, encourage criminal enforcement authorities to pursue criminal prosecution of trademark counterfeiting cases in which any well-known trademark is involved. (See Li Chiang Ling, "Recognising and Protecting Well-known Trademarks" (September 2003) *Hong Kong Lawyer* 37)

RECOGNITION OF WELL-KNOWN TRADEMARKS

SUBMISSION OF RELEVANT MATERIALS 3.12

As noted above, relevant materials have to be submitted when seeking recognition of a well-known trademark to trigger well-known trademark protection. What are these relevant materials? Article 3 of the Well-known Trademarks Regulations provides that the following materials may serve as evidence that a trademark is well-known:

1. relevant materials which substantiate the notoriety of the trademark among the relevant public;
2. relevant materials which substantiate the trademark's length of use, including materials relating to the history and scope of the trademark's use and registration;
3. relevant materials which substantiate the length of time, extent and geographical scope of any publicity for the trademark, including relevant materials on the means and geographical scope of advertising, publicity and promotion activities, type of advertising media, amount invested in advertising, etc;
4. relevant materials which substantiate the record of protection of the trademark as a well-known trademark, including relevant materials showing that the trademark has been protected as a well-known trademark in PRC or in other countries or regions; and
5. other evidentiary materials which substantiate that the trademark is well-known, including relevant materials which substantiate the levels of production, sales volumes, sales revenues, pre-tax profits, sales territories, etc, during the last three years for the main goods on which the trademark is used.

Submitting materials or evidence of the right kind is very important, as we shall see from the following case.

PENTA & Device, TMO Decision Shang Biao Yi Zi No 1441 of 2002

The opponent filed an opposition against the application for registration of the trademark. It claimed that its trademark "VOLVO" and "VOLVO PENTA" were internationally well-known. In particular, the opponent claimed that it had many sales agents and service centres in PRC. It submitted to the TMO, for example, business registration certificates of companies appointed by it as sales agent and/or operator of the service centres, together with information about the opponent company prepared by the a sales agent. The TMO ruled that those materials failed to establish well-known status. Well-known trademark protection was denied.

It appears that such materials relate more to the activities of the trademark owner rather than the actual reaction of the consumers towards those activities. They could not show directly that the trademark had been made well known to the relevant public. The point in time to which the evidence refers is also very important.

'DOCKERS', TMO Decision Shang Biao Yi Zi No 325 of 2003

The case is not about recognition of well-known trademarks but may be of reference value. In the opposition, the opponent claimed that its trademark "DOCKERS BY GERLI & Device" enjoyed a certain level of notoriety and the applicant's trademark was an imitation and thus the application was contrary to the principle of honesty and good faith. The opponent only submitted a copy of its trademark registration certificate for registration in Korea, the approval date of which was 13 October 1999. TMO held that this piece of evidence was not sufficient to support the bad faith argument as the applicant had already registered the trademark in 1990 in respect of other goods in the same class.

IKEA System BV v Beijing Cinet Information Co. Ltd. ("the IKEA Case"), Beijing Higher People's Court Gao Zhi Zhong Zi No 76 of 2000

This is a domain name dispute case. The Plaintiff wanted to get back the domain name "ikea.com.cn" from the hands of the Defendant. It argued, inter alia, that the "IKEA" trademark was a well-known trademark and the Defendant's act of registering the domain name was contrary to the principle in Paris Convention. The Beijing Second Intermediate People's Court looked into the evidence submitted by the Plaintiff. The court agreed that the trademark had been registered in PRC and many other places and its use had not been interrupted. "IKEA" goods and services were available in 29 countries or regions, giving a huge amount of revenue each year, making it one of the largest furniture retailing companies in the world. A huge amount of investment had been put into advertising and promotion. With the high quality of "IKEA" goods and services, the trademark "IKEA" enjoyed a high level of notoriety and reputation among consumers internationally. In the PRC, the trademark had been made known to the relevant business and consumers through large-scale advertising, IKEA's unique business operation method and its good service. The above were supported by trademark registration certificates for "IKEA" and "宜家" ("IKEA" in Chinese), most valuable trademarks ranking released by INTERBAND on the internet and information about establishment of shops by the Plaintiff in some countries or regions. The defendant submitted no evidence to rebut these. The court concluded that the trademark was well known. However, the Beijing Higher People's Court held in the appeal that the evidence submitted by the Plaintiff was not sufficient to show that the trademark "IKEA" had already become a well-known trademark at the time the Defendant registered the domain name in question.

CHANGING THE DIRECTION IN WELL-KNOWN TRADEMARK PROTECTION   3.13

One point to note is that the present Implementing Regulations and Well-known Trademarks Regulations provide for a system based on a "case by case", "passive protection" rationale. As can be seen from the wording of the relevant provisions, application for recognition of well-known trademarks is a means to obtain well-known trademark protection in situation where someone is trying to register, has registered, or is using an infringing trademark. Recognition is the key to protection and the system basically does not provide for recognition in situations where there is no infringement or likelihood of infringement. This is not what previously took place. The TMO adopted an "active protection" approach and recognised and gazetted a number of well-known trademarks every year with or without infringement or likelihood of infringement. The Provisional Regulations for the Determination and Administration of Well-known Trademarks ("Provisional Well-known Trademarks Regulations"), replaced by the present Well-known Trademarks Regulations, did not mention the situations in which a person could seek recognition of a well-known trademark. Article 4 even provided that the TMO could determine trademarks to be well known, as needed for the registration and administration of trademarks. At the same time, it appears that people are misunderstanding the meaning of well-known trademarks, thinking of them as symbols of high quality goods and services. For enterprises and companies that have had their marks recognised as a well-known trademark, it is common to see the eye-catching phrase "PRC Well-known Trademark" in their advertisement. For those who have not, it is easy to find phrases like

"Strive for a PRC well-known trademark (争创中国驰名商标)" in their advertisements. Some local governments even reward businesses that are able to create trademarks recognised as well known. All of the above seems odd if recognition of well-known trademarks is only required for the battle against infringement or likelihood of infringement. Such misuse of the regime, as reported, has made the issue of recognition of well-known trademarks very sensitive, and makes the TRAB very reluctant to explicitly declare that a foreign mark is well known (instead, it will hold that the mark "had been made well-known to the consumers in China (已为中国广大消费者所熟知)" or "is of certain level of name recognition (有一定知名度)" etc).

Recognition under the replaced Provisional Well-known Trademarks Regulations could last for three years (provided in Article 3). However, relevant factors like reputation of the mark to the relevant public, consecutive time, extent and geographical area of any advertisement of the mark may not be the same at the time of protection, be it a result of the actions of the market forces or trademark owner. The problem of not having a case-by-case system is that a well-known trademark may not really be well known at the time of protection. The Well-known Trademarks Regulations will help in changing the direction.

3.14 PRIOR RECOGNITIONS

Nevertheless, if a trademark has been protected as a well-known trademark before, it may be recognised as a well-known trademark more easily the second time. This is because, as mentioned above, materials showing that the trademark has been protected as a well-known trademark in PRC (or even in other countries or regions) may be submitted to establish that the mark is well known though. Article 12 of the Well-known Trademarks Regulations specifically provides for such kind of materials. Under that Article, records showing that the trademark has previously been protected as a well-known trademark by the relevant responsible authorities in PRC could be submitted for recognition of well-known status. If the scope of protection of the new case is basically identical to that in a previous case where the trademark has been protected as a well-known trademark, the AIC may render a ruling, or handle the case, on the basis of the conclusion stated in the previous record of protection. The AIC will only do so if the opposing party does not dispute the well-known status or, if it does dispute it, fails to submit evidentiary materials showing that the trademark is not well-known. If the opposing party disputes that the trademark is well-known and submits evidentiary materials showing that it is not well-known, or the scope of protection in the new case is different from that in the previous case, The TMO or TRAB will have to carry out a fresh examination of the materials to decide whether the trademark is well-known or not.

Lastly, it has to be mentioned that if a trademark is unfortunately not recognised as a well-known trademark by TMO or TRAB, the trademark owner cannot submit another application for recognition of the same trademark as a well-known trademark on the basis of the same facts and grounds within a year. This is provided by Article 9 of the Well-known Trademarks Regulations.

RECENT RECOGNITIONS OF WELL-KNOWN TRADEMARKS BY TMO

3.15

As reported, 43 trademarks have been recognised as well-known by TMO in trademark dispute cases (ie disputes in application for registration, trademark infringements) by February 2004. Among these 43 trademarks, two ("雪碧" ("Sprite") and "吉列" ("Gillette")) are trademarks owned by a foreign entity (See "Forty Three Trademarks Recognized as Well-known in Trademark", *China Intellectual Property News* 18 March 2004, p 02 and "Recognitions of Well-known Marks are for Protection Purpose, as Pointed out Clearly by the Relevant Person of Trademark Office", *China Industry & Commerce News* 4 March 2004, p 05).

In a more recent trademark opposition (*Shang Biao Yi Zi* No 585 of 2004), the TMO held that "迪士尼" ("Disney") is a well-known trademark and rejected the application for registration of "迪士尼旅游及图" ("Disney Travel & Device"). The TMO noted that Disneyland, with its scale and numerous innovative activities, is widely known worldwide. Especially after it was decided that a Disneyland theme park was to be established in Hong Kong, a Special Administrative Region in PRC, "迪士尼乐园" ("Disneyland") and "迪士尼" ("Disney") became widely known and it enjoys a relatively good reputation among the relevant public in PRC. All of these factors contributed to the decision of the TMO to recognize "迪士尼" ("Disney") as a well-known trademark.

JUDICIAL RECOGNITION OF WELL-KNOWN STATUS

3.16

The above relates to the recognition of well-known trademarks by administrative bodies like TMO. If a case goes to court, can the court determine whether a mark is a well-known trademark? Article 3 of the replaced Provisional Well-known Trademarks Regulations provided that TMO shall be responsible for the determination and administration of well-known trademarks and no other organisations or individuals may determine, or determine by a disguised means, trademarks to be well-known. This appears to say that even the courts cannot recognise well-known trademarks. There is no similar provision in the present

Well-known Trademarks Regulations thus the prohibition does not exist anymore. Actually, even before the replacement of the Provisional Well-known Trademark Regulations, in the IKEA Case it had already been held that the court could decide whether a mark is a well-known trademark as such well-known trademark recognition is a recognition of objective facts.

At the same time, the Interpretations make it clear that the court does have the jurisdiction to recognise a well-known trademark. Article 22 of the Interpretations provides that where a People's Court is trying a trademark dispute case, it may, at the request of a party and in accordance with the actual circumstances of the case, make a determination, to whether the registered trademark in question is well known (note that the Article mentions registered trademarks only). Again, determination of well-known status should be carried out in accordance with Article 14 of the Trademark Law. In Article 22 of the Interpretations, there is a provision similar to Article 12 of the Well-known Trademarks Regulations discussed above, regarding the assistance of previous well-known trademark protection the trademark has been able to obtain. Where a party requests protection in respect of a trademark that has been determined as a well-known trademark previously by administrative bodies or a People's Court and the other party does not dispute the trademark being well-known, the court will not carry out any further examination. If the other party does dispute the trademark being well known, the People's Court has to carry out an examination in accordance with Article 14 of the Trademark Law.

At the same time, in civil dispute cases concerning the registration and / or use, etc, of computer network domain names, the courts may determine according to law whether the registered trademark (note again only registered trademarks are included) involved is well known or not based on a party's request and the actual circumstances of the case, as provided in Explanation of the Supreme People's Court on Several Issues Concerning the Application of the Law to the Trial of Civil Dispute Cases Involving Computer Network Domain Names ("the Explanation"), issued by the Supreme People's Court on 17 July 2001 and effective from 24 July 2001. The question whether a trademark is well known is relevant in domain name disputes because, as provided in the Explanation, one of the criteria to be met for holding that registration and / or use, etc, of a domain name constitutes infringement or unfair competition is that the defendant's domain name or its main part constitutes a copy, imitation, translation or transliteration of a well-known trademark of the plaintiff; or is identical with or similar to a registered trademark, domain name, etc, of the plaintiff to a degree sufficient to cause mistaken identification among the relevant public. Registering another's well-known trademark as a domain name for commercial purposes is also one of the acts that allow the court to hold that the defendant has acted in bad faith. (Bad faith is also required for the defendant's act to be regarded as infringement or unfair competition).

As reported in May 2004, since the coming into force of the Explanation, 11 trademarks (including 'Dupont' and several other Chinese trademarks) have been recognised as well-known by Higher or Intermediate People's Court in various places in the PRC (see "11 Well-known Trademarks have been Recognised by Courts", *People's Daily (Market Edition)* 11 May 2004, p 07).

CHAPTER 4

ADMINISTRATIVE AND ENFORCEMENT FRAMEWORKS

PRC GOVERNMENTAL STRUCTURE

NPC AND STATE COUNCIL   4.1

Many of the characteristics of China's imperial past and the more recent influences of Soviet forms of government persist in China's current governmental structure. One salient and consistent structural feature of China's various governments has been an emphasis on centralised power, usually in a person or close-knit group of persons who head a network of vast government bureaucracies. China's governments have had little tolerance towards organised opposition and open dissent to the prevailing ideology. In this regard, one could say that the structure of government in China has tended to foster general conservatism, and has perhaps stifled China's ability to adapt to rapidly changing social and economic conditions.

But despite the family resemblances discerned in the styles and forms of government in China, the establishment of the PRC in October 1949 marked a stark break from the policies and institutions of the past. Mao Zedong's 'New Democracy' called for the dismantling of feudalism, capitalism and imperialism in China, and the Chinese People's Political Consultative Conference ("CPPCC"), a broad-based organisation composed of politically-minded communists and non-communists alike, was founded to serve as the primary institution of government for the fledgling republic. The CPPCC was the central organ of government until the formal creation of the National People's Congress ("NPC") in 1954, after which the CPPCC receded into the background and assumed a merely ancillary and advisory role.

Every five years the NPC is expected to meet in a plenary session to elect a state president and various members of the State Council. The State Council is composed of a premier, vice-premiers and directors of the various state ministries and commissions. Primary responsibility for the government is delegated to the premier and the Standing Committee of the State Council, a council of elites who oversee the day-to-day workings of the government's enormous administrative network.

ADMINISTRATIVE STRUCTURE OF TRADEMARK AUTHORITIES

4.2 ADMINISTRATIVE AGENCIES

The Chinese government has established a sophisticated network of administrative agencies and authorities to manage the myriad aspects of its current trademark regime. The State Council, as the apex of government in China, is charged with responsibility over the many intellectual property-related administrative agencies. The State Administration for Industry and Commerce ("SAIC") is the supervisory body for all matters concerning trademarks in China. Trademark examination, registration and enforcement are handled through specialised offices under the auspices of the SAIC.

In general the SAIC is responsible for the registration and supervision of the business activities of commercial and industrial entities in China. In addition to developing, disseminating and overseeing the implementation of trademark policy, it also sets the standards and fees for trademark applications, and publishes the table for the classification of goods for trademark registration. Included under the purview of the SAIC are the two primary trademark-related government agencies: the Trademark Office ("TMO") and the Trademark Review and Adjudication Board ("TRAB").

4.3 THE TRADEMARK OFFICE

The TMO is responsible for the administration of trademarks and service marks in the PRC. It examines trademark applications, issues decisions in trademark and service mark oppositions, and processes cancellation actions based on non-use grounds. In addition, the TMO is responsible for processing renewal applications, requests for the transfer of trademark rights, requests for the recordal of trademark licenses, and requests to amend the details of a registered mark or pending application. The TMO also handles lost or damaged trademark registration certificates, processes requests for extension of trademark registrations under the Madrid System, and examines claims for priority rights based on the Paris Convention.

The TMO maintains the Trademark Register in which it records registered trademarks, transfers of trademark rights, and other trademark-related matters. The TMO also publishes the PRC *Trademark Gazette*, the official registry publication, which contains announcements on the preliminary approval, transfer, renewal, cancellation, and license recordal of trademarks in China.

The TMO does not, however, handle the investigation or enforcement of trademark related rights in the marketplace. Such responsibilities are relegated to specific administrative agencies, such as Local Administrations for Industry and Commerce, and the People's Courts. Moreover, since the promulgation of Regulations on the Determination and Protection of Well-known Trademarks in the summer of 2003, the TMO is no longer solely responsible for the determination of well-known marks, and is now one of several administrative organs charged with identifying and determining whether trademarks are well known and otherwise warrant the extended protection afforded such marks. The new procedures for the determination and enforcement of well-known marks is discussed in more detail in Chapter 3.

THE TRADEMARK REVIEW AND ADJUDICATION BOARD 4.4

The TRAB is primarily responsible for reviewing disputes or specific petitions relating to the registration and ownership of trademark rights. Before the promulgation of the 2001 Trademark Law, the TRAB had exclusive and final jurisdiction over such matters, but its decisions are now subject to review by the People's Courts.

The TRAB handles appeals from the TMO, including cases where the TMO has rejected an application to register, renew, or assign a mark. The TRAB also reviews appeals to TMO decisions on opposition matters and on matters involving non-use cancellations. In addition, the TRAB directly handles cancellation actions based on grounds of improper registration.

On 17 October 2002, a new set of procedural rules governing all matters before the TRAB came into effect – the *Rules for the Review and Adjudication of Trademarks* ("TRAB Rules"). These rules set out the procedures for submitting materials and evidence in support of cases before the TRAB, including foreign-sourced evidence, and otherwise anticipate greater judicial scrutiny of the TRAB decisions. In brief, the TRAB rules set out the following:

1. materials and evidence filed by parties in support of a case before the TRAB must be listed, their source declared, and the facts they support should be summarised in table form;
2. for evidence in support of a case that has been sourced outside the PRC, the evidence should be both notarised (ie by a notary public) in the country of origin, and then legalised by the Chinese embassy or consulate in the same country; and
3. all documents submitted in a language other than Chinese, must be translated, and only translated materials will be considered.

Although in practice, the TRAB has occasionally treated points 2 and 3 above as optional, strict compliance with the TRAB rules is the best way to guarantee that foreign-sourced or non-Chinese language evidence will be considered in a case before the TRAB.

4.5 LOCAL ADMINISTRATIONS FOR INDUSTRY AND COMMERCE

Local AICs have been established as part of the basic government administration at all regional levels under policy guidance from the SAIC. Currently, AICs have been set up in China's twenty-three provinces, five autonomous regions, in the municipalities under the central government (ie Beijing, Chongqing, Shanghai, Tianjin), and at the municipal, prefecture, county, and rural levels. In addition, AICs in large cities in China are often subdivided into specific district-level bureaus.

In general, local AICs are responsible for the enforcement of China's trademark laws in the market. This function is described in more detail in paras 4.8 – 4.12 below.

4.6 TECHNICAL SUPERVISION BUREAU

Technical Supervision Bureaus ("TSB"s) operate under the auspices of the State General Administration for Quality Supervision, Inspection and Quarantine ("AQSIQ"), and are in charge of enforcing China's Product Quality Law ("PQL") at the local level. As certain forms of trademark infringement may also be actionable under the PQL, trademark owners may choose to take action through the local TSBs. Because TSBs have many of the same inspection and seizure powers of the AICs, they provide another viable enforcement option for certain trademark owners.

4.7 FAIR TRADE BUREAU

China has established a Fair Trade Bureau under the auspices of the SAIC. The Bureau is charged with the coordination of unfair competition work, including matters pertaining to the Anti-unfair Competition Law, which in turn includes certain trademark related offences, such as the passing off of a registered trademark. The Fair Trade Bureau is also responsible for drafting rules concerning fair trade, and dealing with certain cases involving unfair trade practices. At the local levels, however, the Anti-unfair Competition Law is enforced primarily by the AICs.

ENFORCEMENT STRUCTURE OF TRADEMARK AUTHORITIES

ENFORCEMENT INFRASTRUCTURE   4.8

China's trademark enforcement infrastructure provides recourse to both administrative and judicial options. The authorities charged with the enforcement of China's trademark laws include the AICs, the People's Courts, the People's Procuratorates, and PRC Customs authorities. The general framework for handling enforcement actions, and the jurisdictional limitations and remedies of the various authorities responsible for trademark enforcement are set out below. The specific procedures for bringing an enforcement action, and practical considerations for selecting a specific enforcement remedy are discussed in detail in Chapter 11 below.

ADMINISTRATIVE ENFORCEMENT: THE AICS   4.9

AICs are charged with the administrative enforcement of China's trademark laws in the marketplace. Depending on their size, local AICs usually have separate departments for handling trademark matters, although in many instances, this same department will also handle the enforcement of China's advertising laws as well.

Either the rights holder (ie the registrant of the infringed mark) or an interested party may file trademark infringement complaints with the AIC. Once a complaint is lodged, the AIC will generally proceed with an investigation into the alleged infringing activity. In cases where infringement is determined, the AIC may seize infringing goods, destroy infringing trademark representations, issue stop-orders, and/or require the payment of an administrative fine.

Although under the 2001 Trademark Law, AICs no longer have the authority to award compensation to an aggrieved party, administrative enforcement continues to be the most cost-effective enforcement alternative for most right holders, particular in cases involving small-scale infringements. Nevertheless, rights owners who find themselves the victims of large-scale infringement, or otherwise wish to pursue compensation for damages, may choose to bring a civil action in the People's Courts in conjunction with or in lieu of AIC involvement.

THE PEOPLE'S COURTS   4.10

Civil litigation in China is governed primarily by the Civil Procedure Law, which sets forth the jurisdictional limits for People's Courts at various levels in China's court system. In brief, China's court system consists of four levels of courts and a number of specialised tribunals that may serve as a court of first instance, depending on the nature of a particular case.

China's highest court is the Supreme People's Court, which has jurisdiction over civil and criminal cases of major significance, but generally operates in its capacity as an administrative organ in charge of managing the judicial affairs of the lower People's Courts, the military courts and special tribunals. Part of its administrative role involves issuing interpretations regarding the application of laws and regulations by the People's Courts. The president of the Supreme People's Court is elected by the NPC, and is responsible to, and makes regular reports to the NPC on the work conducted by the Court.

The Higher People's Courts are located at the provincial level, in autonomous regions, and in municipalities directly under the central government. The Higher People's Courts have original jurisdiction over civil and criminal cases deemed of great importance, but usually act in their capacity as an appellate level court for the courts at lower levels, and will retry cases in which a judgement of a lower court is disputed by the procuratorate.

The Intermediate People's Courts are established in the prefectures and in major cities throughout China. Intermediate People's Court's serve as courts of first instance for cases involving foreign nationals, cases in areas over which the court exercises jurisdiction, and other cases as determined by the Supreme People's Court. The Intermediate People's Court also serves as an appellate level court for cases tried in the Basic Level People's Courts, and when the People's Procuratorate disputes a judgement at the trial level.

The Basic Level People's Courts are established at the county, city, autonomous county, and district levels, and handle civil cases at the trial level, common criminal cases, and oversee the activities of the local people's mediation committees. Such courts cannot, however, hear cases involving foreign parties.

4.11 THE PEOPLE'S PROCURATORATES

The People's Procuratorates are charged with the investigation and prosecution of criminal cases on behalf of the State, and are divided into four levels. The Supreme People's Procuratorate is the highest procuratorial body in China, followed by procuratorates at the provincial, municipal and county levels. The People's Procuratorates have considerably wider investigative powers than either the People's Courts or the AICs, and include the power to search and confiscate property, intercept communications, and arrest and detain suspects.

CUSTOMS AUTHORITIES

4.12

PRC Customs authorities are empowered to confiscate products that infringe registered trademarks, copyrights and patents upon their import or export from the PRC and, until most recently, to impose administrative fines. New PRC Regulations for Customs Protection of Intellectual Property Rights became effective on 1 March 2004, and superseded previous regulations issued in 1995.

The new regulations set out a system whereby trademark owners can apply to have their trademark rights recorded at the General Administration of Customs in Beijing. According to the new regulations, customs enforcement is not contingent on customs recordal, but in practice it is unlikely that Customs will notify brand owners of suspect shipments unless trademark rights are recorded and otherwise inserted into the Customs watch list. Customs recordal in China is valid for 10 years, and can be renewed for additional 10-year periods.

Unlike the 1995 regulations, the current regulations do not include provisions granting customs the power to impose administrative fines against offenders, but it is hoped that future implementing rules will contain provisions that will be consistent with the 2001 Trademark Law, ie by providing for fines up to three times the illegal business amount. Details of these new regulations and their effect on customs enforcement procedures will be discussed in Chapter 11 below.

AGENTS, INVESTIGATORS AND LAWYERS

CHINA COUNCIL FOR THE PROMOTION OF INTERNATIONAL TRADE

4.13

The China Council for the Promotion of International Trade ("CCPIT") was established in 1952. It functions as a quasi-governmental body comprised of enterprises and organisations representing the economic and trade sectors in China. CCPIT is also known as the China Chamber of International Commerce ("CCOIC"), and is one of the largest and most active institutions involved in the promotion of foreign trade in China. Its activities involve, *inter alia*, trade consultation, the sponsoring of exhibits, and the provision of legal assistance.

In 1963, CCPIT became the only organisation in China with the power to process foreign applications for trademark registration. Current trademark law requires that trademark applications involving foreign parties are processed through officially designated trademark agents, but the CCPIT is no longer the sole agent responsible for processing trademark applications for foreign parties. In 1988, the CCPIT's monopoly was revoked, and the SAIC was granted the power to appoint other organisations to represent the interests of foreign trademark owners and applicants in China.

4.14 TRADEMARK AGENTS

Trademark agents must be approved by the SAIC, and provide agency services related to applications for trademark registration, general legal consulting, and advice relating to trademarks and trademark related matters. Certain trademark agents have been designated by the SAIC to deal with only foreign trademark applications and other matters involving foreign trademark applicants or holders of trademark rights. Foreign parties must use these specially designated trademark agencies for filing trademark applications, and for determining trademark rights before the TMO or TRAB, as well as for filing trademark infringement and related complaints with the AICs.

Currently, most trademark agencies that deal with foreign trademark applications and related issues are independent SAIC designated trademark agencies. However, several agencies, such as the CCPIT Patent and Trademark Law Office, and its affiliate, the China Patent Agent (HK) Ltd. in Hong Kong, operate under the aegis of CCPIT. In recent years, the number of independent official agents has expanded considerably.

All SAIC designated trademark agencies in China are subject to the guidance and supervision of the AICs. In several large cities in China, such as Beijing, Shanghai and Shenzhen, AICs have even established subsidiary trademark agencies under their direct supervision. The competition is keen and the quality of the agencies vary from city to city.

OTHER ORGANISATIONS

4.15 MINISTRY OF COMMERCE

The State Economic and Trade Commission ("SETC") and the Ministry of Foreign Trade Economic Cooperation ("MOFTEC"), two government organisations dealing with trade related issues, were merged in March 2003 to establish the Ministry of Commerce ("MOFCOM"). MOFCOM, like its predecessor, MOFTEC, is involved in the prevention of trademark counterfeiting at the point of export-by-export enterprises.

CONSUMER COUNCILS AND OTHER CONSUMER ORGANISATIONS 4.16

China's Consumer Protection Law provides the legal basis for the establishment of consumer protection organisations. The China Consumer Association was established in 1984 to provide consumer information and consultant services, to supervise commodities and services, and to otherwise protect consumers' interests in the marketplace. Currently, there are more than 3222 consumer associations at or above the county level, 31 of which operate at the provincial level (or at the level of autonomous regions or municipalities directly under the Central Government). The consumer associations oversee the work of community centres, which conduct publicity campaigns and handle consumer complaints, including those related to products and services sold or marketed under infringing or counterfeit trademarks.

CHAPTER 5

TRADEMARK REGISTRATION

GENERAL OVERVIEW 5.1

Under the current PRC Trademark Law ("Trademark Law") (revised on 27 October 2001), individuals, companies or any other organisations may apply for trademarks in the PRC and where preferred, applications may be made jointly by more than one applicant. Trademark registrations may be obtained for goods and / or services and the PRC Trademark Office ("TMO") also accepts applications for collective and certification marks.

The trademark registration process in the PRC is relatively straightforward. Upon filing a trademark application, the TMO will proceed to examine the application under principles set out in the Trademark Law. If no objection is raised by the TMO upon preliminary examination, an application will receive preliminary approval and is subsequently published for opposition purposes in the PRC *Trademark Gazette* (see Chapter 6 for discussions on trademark opposition proceedings). Where objections are raised against an application, whether in whole or in part, the TMO will issue a notice to the applicant explaining the grounds of objection. The applicant has the opportunity to appeal against the TMO's rejection to the PRC Trademark Review and Adjudication Board ("TRAB"), whose decision may in turn be appealed to the People's Court.

A general account of the steps involved in the trademark application process is set out in this Chapter.

THE IMPORTANCE OF TRADEMARK REGISTRATION IN THE PRC 5.2

Although the use of unregistered trademarks is generally permitted in the PRC, the Trademark Law does not confer users exclusive right to use the unregistered marks. Limited protection of unregistered trademarks is instead offered indirectly under Article 31 of the Trademark Law (see Chapter 6 at para 6.8 for discussion on the provision) and the Anti-Unfair Competition Law of 1993 (see Chapter 14 at para 14.41 for more detailed discussions of the law). It is therefore preferable to register a trademark in the PRC to ensure its adequate protection under the Trademark Law.

(An exception to the above is the broad protection afforded to well-known marks. Under Article 13 of the Trademark Law, the owner of a well-known trademark that has not been registered in the PRC is afforded protection against the registration and use of copies or imitations of the well-known mark where consumer confusion is likely – see details on well-known marks in Chapter 3).

Furthermore, China adopts a "first-to-file" system, ie prior right subsists in the application of a trademark, rather than its first use (unless the mark in question is well-known). The date of a trademark application is therefore of paramount importance in China. While the TMO and the TRAB are generally receptive to oppositions and cancellations if there is clear evidence that the prior marks have been applied for in bad faith, the safest course of action for a trademark owner is always to register its mark as early as possible. For foreign applicants, trademark applications should really be filed prior to the intended use in the PRC where possible.

5.3 WHAT MARKS ARE REGISTRABLE IN THE PRC?

The Trademark Law allows the registration of visual marks that are comprised of words, devices, letters, numbers, three-dimensional marks or any combination thereof. Furthermore, trademarks can be in colour or in black and white.

Trademarks can be obtained for services as well as goods. The TMO also accepts applications for collective and certification marks.

Previously, only two-dimensional marks were registrable. Under the current Trademark Law, three-dimensional marks are registrable provided that they are not simply the shape of the goods covered or the shape as is necessary to fulfill the desired technical effects or function of the goods covered.

Although there are now examples of registered three-dimensional marks, the practical value of registering such marks remains debatable due to the uncertainties surrounding the exact scope of protection afforded to three-dimensional marks.

It is currently not possible to register sound or smell marks in the PRC.

REGISTRABILITY OF TRADEMARKS UNDER THE TRADEMARK LAW

5.4 GROUNDS OF OBJECTION OF TRADEMARK APPLICATIONS

In general, trademarks are only registrable in the PRC if they have distinctive characteristics and are easy to distinguish, and they do not conflict with prior rights lawfully obtained by a third party, including trademark rights and copyright rights.

The Trademark Law prescribes various grounds of objection of trademark applications and some of the more frequently encountered grounds are discussed below.

DISTINCTIVENESS   5.5

Article 11(3) of the Trademark Law prohibits the registration of trademarks that lack distinctiveness.

The logic of this distinctiveness requirement is apparent when consideration is given to the function and use of trademarks. In very simple terms, trademarks are unique markings on goods or used in association with services that enable consumers to distinguish the sources of goods or services. By the same token, trademarks also enable mark owners to develop goodwill through consumers' recognition and support of its brands. Clearly, a mark that lacks distinctiveness cannot reasonably fulfill such functions.

It is for the same reasons that the Trademark Law also prohibits the registration of marks that consist exclusively of the generic name, shape or model number of the goods or services concerned (Article 11(1)).

For example, applications for marks that are comprised of simple one or two alphabets (such as 'AB'), numbers (for example '99') or simple surnames should in theory be rejected for registration because the marks are non-distinctive. It appears, however, that the trademark authorities are rather lenient in allowing such marks to be registered as long as they are accompanied by a degree of stylisation or elements of design features, and provided that they are not generic terms for the goods or services covered.

TRAB Decision [2000] No 712

The applicant applied to register the 'Mrs Cheng's / Mrs Cheng's in Chinese (*cheng shi*)' mark in Class 30. The TMO rejected the application on the ground that the mark lacked distinctiveness.

The TRAB stated that although the mark consisted only of a common Chinese surname, the stylisation of the mark, together with the additional English element in the mark (ie Mrs Cheng's), enabled the overall mark to serve to distinguish the source of goods. In addition, the mark is not a generic term for the goods covered by the application. The TRAB therefore overturned the TMO's rejection and granted preliminary approval to the application.

Similarly, marks that may be seen as advertising slogans, which are common to the goods or services offered, will be rejected by the TMO for lack of distinctiveness.

TRAB Decision [2001] No 4264

The applicant applied for the "BODY TOUCHES BY DELICATES" mark in Class 4. The TMO rejected the application because it considered the mark as a common advertising slogan, which lacked distinctiveness.

The TRAB overturned the TMO's rejection on the basis that the mark was distinctive for the goods designated (ie candles etc). The application was granted preliminary approval.

Under the Trademark Law, a non-distinctive mark can be registered if it can be proved that the mark has acquired secondary meaning through use. Currently, however, there are no published guidelines on the level of use required to show such 'acquired distinctiveness'.

TRAB Decision [2001] No 2985

Applicant applied to register the '501' mark in Class 14. The TMO rejected the application on the basis that the mark lacked distinctiveness. The TMO stated that the mark is composed of plain numbers without any stylisation, and as such is likely to be confused as the model number of the goods covered.

On appeal, the TRAB accepted the applicant's argument that the '501' mark, although composed only of plain numbers, had acquired distinctiveness due to extensive and long-term use. The TRAB overturned the TMO's rejection and granted preliminary approval to the application.

5.6 DESCRIPTIVENESS

Article 11(2) of the Trademark Law prohibits the registration of marks that are exclusively and directly descriptive of the quality, main raw materials, function, use, weight, quantity or other characteristics of the goods (or services). This means, for example, the mark 'banana' cannot be registered in respect of 'banana shake', the mark 'cleaners' cannot be registered by a company offering cleaning services and the wording 'long lasting' cannot be registered for batteries.

Next to rejections based on prior conflicting applications or registrations (see para 5.8 below), this is perhaps the most frequently encountered ground of rejection in TMO's rejection notices. On the other hand, there have been many examples of marks that are descriptive, which have been approved of registration. Where an application is rejected on descriptiveness grounds, consideration should be given to appealing the TMO's rejection with the TRAB where appropriate – the TRAB appears to be interpreting 'exclusively and directly descriptive' more narrowly than the TMO.

TRAB Decision [2000] No 1949

Applicant applied for the 'SECURI – DAB' mark in Class 37 for computer installation services. The TMO rejected the application on the ground that the mark had the meaning of 'security', and therefore was directly descriptive of the nature and characteristics of the services provided.

The TRAB overturned the TMO's rejection. It stated that the wording 'SECURI' in the mark did not have the meaning of 'security'. Further, there was no evidence demonstrating that the mark was directly descriptive of the services covered. The application was granted preliminary approval by the TRAB.

TRAB Decision [2000] No 4830

Applicant applied for the 'TURBO' mark in Class 2. The TMO rejected the application because the mark means 'turbine engine' and as such, the mark was directly descriptive of the objects on which the goods were to be used.

The TRAB disagreed. It stated that even though the Chinese meaning of the mark is 'turbine engine', this was not a valid basis for concluding that the goods covered are to be used exclusively on turbine engines. The TRAB therefore overturned the TMO's rejection and granted preliminary approval to the application.

Registration of a descriptive mark may be approved by the TMO where it can be proved that the mark has acquired secondary meaning, so as to enable it to be distinguished from other trademarks.

OTHER SPECIFIC STATUTORY PROHIBITIONS   5.7

Article 10 of the Trademark Law sets out categories of marks that cannot be registered, or even used, as unregistered marks. These include marks that are:

1. identical or similar to the state name, national flag, national emblem or military flag of a foreign country, unless approved by the government of that country;
2. identical or similar to the name, flag or emblem of an intergovernmental international organisation, unless consented by that organisation or unless doing so would not likely confuse the public;
3. the names of PRC administrative districts at or above the county level and commonly-known foreign place names, unless such names have other meanings;

4. identical or similar to the name or mark of the "Red Cross" or the "Red Crescent";
5. of a racially discriminatory nature;
6. of a deceptive nature and which promote in an exaggerated manner; or
7. detrimental to socialist morality or customs or that have other adverse effects.

5.8 CONFLICT WITH PRIOR IDENTICAL OR SIMILAR MARKS

Because of China's first-to-file rule, a trademark application will be rejected by the TMO if there are prior registrations or applications for identical or similar marks covering identical or similar goods / services (Articles 28 and 29 of the Trademark Law). This is the most frequently invoked ground of objection by the TMO in rejecting trademark applications.

Same-day filing

Although evidence of prior use is in general irrelevant in view of the first-to-file rule, where two applications for identical or similar marks in respect of identical or similar goods / services are filed on the same day, preliminary approval will be granted to the mark that has been used first.

Similar marks?

A number of factors are important in assessing whether two trademarks are similar, such as the inherent meaning, pronunciation, design, overall visual effect, and the composition (ie whether they are word marks, device marks or composite marks containing both word and device elements) of the marks. Where the marks to be compared are composed of various elements, the TMO will usually identify the most distinctive element in each of the marks – where the distinctive elements are found to be similar, the marks will be considered similar by the TMO despite differences in the other elements of the marks.

Identical or similar goods / services?

A background introduction to China's system of classification of goods and services is necessary here.

The PRC adopted the International Classification of Goods and Services formulated under the Nice Convention in 1988. With effect from 1 January 2002, the PRC has adopted the new classes (43–45) under the World Intellectual Property Organisation ("WIPO") Classification of Goods and Services.

Under the TMO's Internal Classification of Goods and Services ("Internal Classification"), however, the 45 international classes are further divided into smaller subgroups, each of which contain goods and services that the TMO considers to be similar ('similarity subgroups'). Generally speaking (there are numerous exceptions), items of goods or services that fall within the same similarity subgroup will be considered similar; if they fall within different similarity groups, however, they will be considered dissimilar.

The TMO allows similar and even identical marks to coexist within the same international class, provided that they cover goods or services considered dissimilar by the TMO.

In deciding whether two trademarks cover identical or similar goods / services, therefore, the TMO will primarily follow its Internal Classification. In the preamble of this guide, however, it is expressly stated that the Internal Classification need not be followed strictly – considerations must also be given to the similarity between the relevant goods or services, such as their raw material, function and use, distribution channels and targeted consumer base.

Effect of coexistence agreements

It remains highly questionable whether coexistence agreements are helpful in overcoming citations of prior marks. Although the TRAB has recently expressed willingness to take coexistence agreements into consideration, it is still not clear at present whether the TMO will do the same in conducting preliminary examination of trademark applications. Even if coexistence agreements are considered, it is important to note that consumer interest is paramount – if consumer confusion is likely, the TMO or TRAB may still reject the application despite the coexistence agreement between the applicant and the owner of the prior conflicting mark.

PRE-FILING CONSIDERATIONS

THINKING AHEAD – IMPORTANT ISSUES TO BE CONSIDERED   5.9

Before trademark applications are filed, there are a number of important issues that need to be addressed. For example, which marks should be registered? Is the proposed mark available for registration in the classes of interest? Is it inherently registrable? What should be the specification in each relevant class? Should a word mark be applied in plain letters or in stylised form? Who should be the applicant?

Discussions on each of these important issues are set out below.

5.10 TRADEMARKS TO BE PROTECTED

Chinese language marks

Many foreign entities entering the Chinese market underestimate the importance of Chinese language marks.

Too often, trademark pirates succeed in pre-emptively registering the Chinese counterpart of a foreign language mark and thus blocking the rightful trademark owners' later applications. The mark owner is then forced to either negotiate for a purchase of the pirated mark or to commit large financial resources in a long legal battle for the removal of the pirated mark.

From a commercial prospective, consumers in the PRC tend to identify products by their Chinese names due to limited knowledge of foreign languages. If a Chinese language mark is not devised and actively promoted in association with the foreign entity and its foreign language counterpart, therefore, it is most likely that various versions of the Chinese mark will end up being used in the market (whether by businesses or consumers). When this happens, the mark owner will have no say in the choosing of its preferred Chinese mark and there is a danger of trademark dilution. Although marketing campaigns (whether to unify the brand or to launch a new brand) are possible, such exercises are always very expensive.

It is therefore advisable to devise a Chinese mark and apply for trademark registration as early as possible before entering into the Chinese market (see Chapter 2 for a detailed discussion on Chinese trademarks).

Composite marks

Where a trademark is composed of different elements (such as a Chinese element, an English element and a device element), consideration should be given to filing an application for each of the elements as standalone marks where possible, in addition to registering the composite mark.

The need to do so is derived from the difficulties faced by the PRC administrative authorities in determining what constitutes 'substantially similar' trademarks when enforcing trademark rights. There have been examples where the administrative authorities refused to take enforcement actions because the infringing marks are identical to only a portion of the trademark owner's registered composite mark – it would appear that the authorities did consider the marks to be substantially similar in those cases.

In addition, enforcement actions against counterfeiting in the PRC are only possible where there has been unauthorised use of marks that are identical to the registered marks (see Chapter 10 for discussions on anti-counterfeiting in the PRC).

Registering both the composite mark and the different elements in the mark would ensure better protection against trademark infringement and counterfeiting in the PRC.

PRE-FILING AVAILABILITY SEARCH   5.11

Prior to filing a trademark application, consideration should be given to conducting a pre-filing availability search to flush out prior marks that might be cited by the TMO in rejection of the application under Articles 28 and/or 29 of the Trademark Law.

Pre-filing availability searches against word and Chinese character trademarks are conducted by a service centre attached to the TMO ('Tongda') based on the TMO's trademark database. The search results are therefore subject to the TMO's official records and to the subjective judgement of the search clerk conducting the search. A further limitation is that recent applications (filed within 1-3 months prior to the search date) will generally not be revealed by the official search.

Despite the limitations, a pre-filing availability search is still advisable so that a filing strategy can be formulated to avoid TMO's rejection due to prior conflicting marks. Foreign parties who wish to carry out official trademark searches via Tongda must file their requests through PRC trademark agents.

The service centre can also conduct trademark proprietor searches. As the consent of the relevant proprietor is not required for such searches, it is a good way to identify trademark pirates.

INHERENT REGISTRABILITY   5.12

Some thought must be given to the inherent registrability of the proposed mark prior to filing an application. For example, is the mark sufficiently distinctive? Does it merely provide a direct description of the characteristics of the goods or services covered? Is the mark one that is prohibited for registration under the Trademark Law (eg it contains the name of a commonly known foreign place such as London or Paris)?

Where a mark is likely to be rejected because it is non-distinctive or descriptive, one or more of the following ways of overcoming the rejection may be applicable.

Secondary meaning

As discussed above, non-distinctive or descriptive marks that have acquired secondary meaning through use can be registered. Where applicable, therefore, evidence of use should be submitted to the TMO to support the assertion that the mark has acquired distinctiveness (although as mentioned above, there are no published guidelines on the level of use required in such cases).

Addition of a more distinctive element

The introduction of a more distinctive element in a mark is a useful tactic in improving the overall distinctiveness of a mark, thereby lowering the risk of rejection by the TMO because the mark is either non-distinctive or descriptive.

Disclaimers

A rejection on descriptiveness or lack of distinctiveness ground may be avoided, where appropriate, by disclaiming the exclusive right of use of the generic or descriptive wording in the trademark.

The Trademark Law and its accompanying Implementing Regulations do not provide for the disclaimer of generic, non-distinctive or descriptive elements in trademarks. However, it has been the TMO's policy to accept disclaimers of such elements in trademark applications, provided that they do not form the main part of the applied marks and that the use of the disclaimer will not render the mark deceptive.

An important point to note when applying for a trademark that contains generic, non-distinctive or descriptive wording, is the question of its effective enforcement. Article 49 of the Implementing Regulations provides that where descriptive or generic wording is registered as a trademark, the owner of the mark in question cannot stop third parties from making bona fide use of the said wording. Even if registered without disclaimers, therefore, the value of trademarks containing generic or descriptive wording is somewhat limited.

5.13 CLASSES AND SPECIFICATION

Foresight must be applied in deciding the relevant Classes to be covered and the precise items of goods or services within each Class to allow for possible development of the brand coverage in the future. For example, many fashion brands start off by focusing on clothing or fashion accessories only (Class 25), but often extend the range of products later to cosmetics in Class 3 and even high fashion eyewear in Class 9. Given the first-to-file rule, it is clearly more advantageous to secure registration of the trademark in all classes, and for all goods or services of interest, from the outset.

In addition, as mentioned above, the TMO allows similar or even identical marks to coexist in the same class provided that the goods or services covered are considered dissimilar by the TMO. From a defensive point of view, therefore, it is necessary to select at least one item of goods or services from each of the similarity subgroups in a given class to prevent the registration and use of identical or similar marks on dissimilar goods or services within a given class.

There is no limit as to the number of designated items of goods or services per application. However, the official fee charged by the TMO per application per class covers only ten items of goods or services and each additional item will incur a surcharge (currently US$12.50).

A further point to note in deciding the specification is that the TMO will generally only allow the designation of goods and services specifically listed in the WIPO's Classification of Goods and Services. Where an item of goods or services has not been so listed, explanation on the nature of that item of goods or services should be provided at the time of application.

At present, it is impossible to register service marks for services relating to the commercial sale of goods across the different levels of distribution (ie wholesale, retail or franchise) in the PRC. Protection against non-authorised use of a registered trademark for these types of service therefore needs to be afforded indirectly. This can generally be achieved by registering the mark for the relevant goods sold by the applicant, as well as for services that are necessary for conducting commercial sale activities, such as advertising and sales promotional services in Class 35. However, protection for these services should not be regarded as equivalent to protection for retail services per se.

Finally, where pre-filing availability searches have been conducted, the specification should be tailored so as to minimise the risk of rejection by the TMO due to citations of prior conflicting registrations or applications revealed in the search.

SPECIMEN   5.14

Applications should always be filed for marks in the exact form as they are used in practice. This is for the following reasons.

First, the Trademark Law prohibits the 'unilateral modification' of PRC-registered trademarks. The use of an unregistered variant of the registered mark could in theory lead to cancellation of the registered mark (see Chapter 7 for more detailed discussion on trademark cancellations).

The Trademark Law also prohibits misrepresentations that an unregistered mark has been registered. If the ® symbol is used next to the variant of a registered mark, there is a risk that the use will be viewed as a misrepresentation that the variant – which is clearly unregistered – is a registered mark. Fines of up to 20 per cent of the turnover for the goods using the offending mark may be imposed.

A further risk is that use of the unregistered variant mark may not be considered as use of the registered mark. The registered mark will thus be vulnerable to cancellation on non-use grounds if only its variant has been used for the goods or services covered by that registration.

The risk of any of the above happening depends on the extent of the modification to the registered mark – where the modification is not significant, the risks are clearly much lower.

Finally, consideration should be given to whether the mark to be registered will provide adequate protection against third parties from making unauthorised use of modified versions of the mark (see para 5.10 above).

For the above reasons, it is best to register a mark in the same form as it is used in practice. In addition, where there is a change to the wording or design of a registered mark, a new application should be filed.

5.15 APPLICANT

Any individual or legal entity from a country that has diplomatic relations or reciprocal agreements with the PRC can file trademark applications in the PRC. Under the current Trademark Law, joint application for a single trademark by two or more natural persons, legal persons or other organisations is also permissible. One of the joint owners may be elected as the representative and so stated on the trademark application form. If no election is made, the applicant whose name appears first will be deemed the representative by default.

Applications for identical or similar marks in respect of identical or similar goods should always be filed in the name of the same entity in the PRC. This is to avoid the TMO's rejection of later applications due to citations of prior applications or registrations held in the name of different entities.

Where an applicant's affiliates or group companies hold prior conflicting marks, it is advisable to unify the ownership of the relevant trademarks, rather than relying on coexistence agreements (which, as discussed under para 5.8 above, are unlikely to assist in overcoming the citations). This can be achieved by either (a) assigning the prior conflicting marks to the intended applicant of the new application, or (b) filing the new application in the name of the owner of the prior conflicting marks and then arrange for licensing of the new mark (see Chapter 8 on the assignment and licensing of trademarks).

5.16 ADMINISTRATIVE REQUIREMENTS OF TRADEMARK APPLICATIONS

A separate application is required per mark per Class, eg three separate applications need to be filed for the same mark in each of Classes 1, 2 and 3 if protection in all three classes is desired.

The application must be filed in Chinese, and as such, a Chinese language name and address must be devised for a foreign applicant. The Chinese name and address used for filing trademark applications in the PRC must be consistent – the TMO will reject later applications for identical or similar marks by the same applicant if a different Chinese name and address were used for prior registrations or applications.

A foreign applicant must execute a power of attorney in favor of a PRC trademark agent for filing a trademark application in the PRC.

Finally, 10 specimens of the mark applied for (where colors are applied for, it is necessary to provide two additional black and white specimens) should be submitted to the TMO, together with the trademark application and the executed power of attorney.

Where an application complies with the formality requirements and is accepted by the TMO, the TMO will issue a filing receipt, which provides the number and date of the application.

It is important to note that substantive amendments to an application, ie a change to the representation of the mark itself (eg by removing the device element in a composite mark), or a widening of the specification, are not permitted post-filing. Instead, a fresh trademark application is required. Applications to amend the applicant's name, address or the appointed trademark agent, or to delete items of designated goods or services, however, are permissible.

PRIORITY APPLICATIONS   5.17

As discussed above, China follows the first-to-file system and the application date is of great importance. The Trademark Law permits filing of priority applications in accordance with international treaties or interstate agreements to which China is a party. A trademark applicant may claim priority for its PRC application if it is filed within six months of the filing date of the first application outside PRC ('base application').

The PRC priority application must be identical to the base application in all respects, including specimen of mark applied for and the goods or services designated. Although it is possible to edit the specification so that the terminology of the goods or services designated is acceptable to the TMO, it would not be possible to widen the specification in any way. Certified copy of the application documents for the base application must be submitted within three months' of filing the PRC application; if not, the priority claim is deemed to have never been made, ie the application is reduced to an ordinary application for which no priority date may be claimed.

Up until now, priority applications are mainly filed to claim US filing date as priority date. Following the accession of the US to the Madrid Protocol (which took effect November 2003), the importance of priority applications is expected to diminish somewhat.

5.18 INTERNATIONAL REGISTRATION

China is a member of both the Madrid Agreement and Madrid Protocol. An owner of a registered international trademark can secure trademark protection in the PRC by applying to extend the validity of that registration to the PRC.

The application to extend the validity of an international registration to the PRC needs to be filed through the International Bureau of WIPO, which in turn transfers the application to the TMO for preliminary examination. The examination standards applied by the TMO in processing extension applications should be the same as those applied to national trademark applications. However, it appears that the standards for international marks are somewhat lower and many marks of doubtful registrability have been successfully extended to the PRC via the Madrid Agreement and Protocol (see Chapter 1 at paragraph 1.16 for more information).

5.19 APPLICATION FOR COLLECTIVE AND CERTIFICATION MARKS

Under the Trademark Law, a 'collective mark' is defined as a sign that has been registered in the name of a group, association or other organisation and that is intended to be used by the members of the organisation in their commercial activities in order to indicate the user's status as a member of the organisation.

'Certification marks' are defined as signs that are controlled by an organisation, which has a supervisory capacity over certain goods and services, and that are used by units or individuals (other than the organisation that owns the mark) to certify the origin, raw materials, manufacturing method, quality or other special qualities of the relevant goods and services.

The registration and administration of collective and certification trademarks, whether used on goods or on services, are governed by the revised Measures for the Registration and Administration of Collective Trademarks and Certification Trademarks (effective 1 June 2003).

When applying for collective and certification trademarks, the rules for the administration of the use of the mark ('Use Rules') and documents supporting the applicant's eligibility to apply must be submitted. An applicant essentially needs to show that it has the necessary qualification, as well as the capacity, to inspect and certify the special qualities that the goods or services using that mark are supposed to have.

Any changes to the Use Rules are subject to approval by the TMO and will take effect only upon its publication.

PRELIMINARY EXAMINATION BY THE TMO

OBJECTIONS TO SPECIFICATIONS BY THE TMO 5.20

Where the TMO decides that items of goods or services specified by the application do not conform to the TMO's standard terminologies for filing purposes, the TMO will issue a Notice of Amendment requiring the applicant to amend the specification. An application will be deemed to have been abandoned if no response is filed with the TMO within 30 days of receipt of the notice.

If there are no further objections, the TMO will preliminarily examine a trademark application based on the criteria set out in para 5.3.

IN THE CASE OF AN APPROVAL 5.21

Where the TMO preliminarily approves an application in whole, the applicant will not be notified of the TMO's decision and instead, the application will proceed to be advertised in the PRC *Trademark Gazette* for opposition purposes (please see Chapter 6 for discussions on trademark oppositions).

If no opposition is raised against the advertised mark during the statutory opposition period of three months, the mark will become registered on the day after the expiry of such period. There is one exception to this general rule – once successfully extended to China, a trademark filed through the Madrid Agreement or the Madrid Protocol will be deemed retroactively effective from the date of filing for the extension, rather than the final date of approval by the TMO.

The time from application to advertisement varies according to the TMO's current caseload and can take more than one year, even where the application is straightforward. Where no opposition is filed against the advertisement mark, the registration certificate can normally be expected within six to nine months of the publication date of the advertisement.

IN THE CASE OF A REJECTION 5.22

Previously, the TMO would issue an 'Opinion Upon Examination' if it considers an application objectionable unless certain goods or services are deleted or a disclaimer offered. The applicant, upon receipt of such an Opinion, may elect to accept the TMO's suggestions or to refuse to comply, and is thus given an opportunity to affect the outcome of its application.

Under the current Trademark Law, the TMO no longer issues Opinions prior to making its final determinations.

Where the TMO considers that the trademark applied for is not registrable, the TMO will issue a notice of rejection to the applicant, setting out the grounds of objection and where prior marks are cited, provide the details of the cited marks. The applicant is then given the opportunity to appeal to the TRAB against the TMO's rejection within 15 days of receipt of the notice of rejection. This deadline is final and no extension of time is allowed (in contrast to the single extension of thirty days permitted previously).

Under the new Implementing Regulations, any supplementary submission in support of an appeal must be filed within three months of filing the original appeal submission. Where a party wishes to file a supplementary submission, it must clearly state so in the initial appeal submission or it will lose its right to do so. It remains unclear whether parties will be able to file supplemental arguments or evidence after the three-month deadline, even in cases where new evidence, simply not available prior to the supplementary submission deadline, comes to light.

Under of the Rules of Trademark Review and Adjudication ("TRAB Rules"), effective 17 October 2002, which govern trademark disputes before the TRAB, it is necessary to provide notarised and legalised versions of all evidence that originates outside the PRC (Article 81, TRAB Rules). Where the evidence submitted is in a foreign language, the relevant portions should be translated into Chinese (Article 82, TRAB Rules). Evidence that does not fulfill these evidential requirements will not be considered by the TRAB. These requirements clearly have great impact on foreign parties and careful consideration must be given to the time and cost of the evidence collection exercise required to support an appeal.

Where the TMO's rejection of an application is overturned on appeal, the application is returned to the TMO for publication in the PRC *Trademark Gazette*. Assuming that the application is then unopposed within the statutory three-month opposition period, the mark in question will become registered.

The TRAB's decision in the application can be further appealed to the People's Court within 30 days of receipt of the TRAB's decision. This deadline is again final and cannot be extended.

Where prior marks are cited against an application in the TMO's notice of rejection, consideration should be given to filing oppositions or cancellation applications against the cited marks where applicable.

If oppositions or cancellations have been or are to be filed, a request for the TRAB to suspend its review of the case pending the outcome of the related opposition or cancellation proceedings can be made in the appeal submission – from experience, such requests are almost always entertained by the TRAB.

TRAB Decision [2000] No 1206

The applicant applied for the 'STAR WARS' mark in Class 28. The TMO rejected the application due to a citation of the prior application for the 'Star Wars in Chinese (*xing ji da zhan*)' mark by a PRC company.

The applicant appealed against the TMO's rejection on the basis that the applicant in fact had prior right to the 'STAR WARS' mark and that an opposition had been filed against the cited mark.

The TRAB suspended its review of the appeal until the TMO issued a decision in the opposition. The TRAB noted that the cited mark had been successfully opposed by the applicant. Since the applied mark no longer conflicted with any prior marks, the TRAB granted preliminary approval to the application.

IN THE CASE OF A PARTIAL REJECTION   5.23

Under the current Trademark Law, the TMO is able to partially reject an application, ie rejecting the mark for only the portion of goods or services that are considered identical or similar to those covered by a prior conflicting mark. Previously, such partial approvals were only possible with respect to international registrations extended to the PRC under the Madrid Agreement or the Madrid Protocol.

Where an application is partially rejected, the applicant is given the same opportunity to appeal against the TMO's partial rejection with the TRAB within a non-extendable 15-day statutory time limit.

Careful consideration must be given in deciding whether an appeal against the partial rejection is warranted. The main drawback in filing an appeal is that the advertisement of the partially approved application in the PRC *Trademark Gazette* (and therefore registration) could be delayed by as long as two to three years. This is because under the current TMO policy, the TMO will only publish the application after the TRAB has issued a decision in the appeal against the partial rejection of the application.

Where the items of goods or services that are left after the partial rejection are in fact useful and / or the chances of successfully overcoming the partial rejection is low, it is therefore advisable to refrain from filing an appeal, to ensure an early gazettal of the partially approved application. If no opposition is filed within the opposition period, the application will become registered for the items of approved goods or services.

If protection for the partially approved mark needs to ultimately extend to the rejected items of goods or services, oppositions or cancellations against the cited marks may be filed – if such proceedings are successful, a new application covering the goods that were rejected the first time can then be made.

MAINTENANCE OF A REGISTERED MARK

5.24 RENEWAL

The owner of a registered trademark enjoys the exclusive right to use the mark and may enforce against any unauthorised use, as provided under the Trademark Law (see Chapter 11 for more details on trademark enforcement in the PRC). The owner also has the right to use the symbol ® or the wording 'registered trademark' (in Chinese) to indicate the registered status of its mark.

The validity period of a registered mark is 10 years from the date of registration (although international registrations extended to the PRC may have renewable terms of 20 years). Thereafter, a renewal application must be filed on a 10-yearly basis to ensure that the mark remains registered.

A renewal application should be filed at least six months before the validity period expires. There is, however, a grace period of six months (upon payment of fees) so that an application can be filed within six months after the registration expires.

Where no renewal application is filed within the prescribed statutory time limits, the registration of the mark will be cancelled and the priority date of the mark is lost. In addition, the TMO will reject an application for a trademark that is identical with or similar to the lapsed mark within one year of its expiry date.

5.25 CHANGE OF NAME OR ADDRESS APPLICATIONS

Where there has been a change to the name or address of the owner of a registered mark, applications to record such changes in respect of all registered trademarks held by the same owner must be filed with the TMO. Failure to do so may result in the cancellation of the registered marks (Article 44(2), Trademark Law).

An application to record change of name or address needs to be accompanied by documentary evidence, for example, an extract of the company register certified by the relevant registry. Such documents do not need to be translated, legalised or notarised.

Where no supporting documentary evidence is submitted, whether at the time of filing or within three months of the original filing date, the application is deemed to have been withdrawn.

LOSS OF OR DAMAGE TO REGISTRATION CERTIFICATE   5.26

If the registration certificate is lost or damaged, an application should be made to the TMO for a replacement.

Where the certificate is lost, a notice to that effect should be published in the PRC *Trademark Gazette*. If the certificate is damaged, the original needs to be returned to the TMO before a replacement certificate can be issued.

There are criminal penalties attached to forging or altering trademark registration certificates.

USE OF REGISTERED TRADEMARKS AND NON-USE CANCELLATIONS   5.27

Under Article 44(4) of the Trademark Law, a registered mark is susceptible to cancellation if it has not been used for a continuous period of three years.

The requirements of use and the filing of non-use cancellations are detailed in Chapter 7.

VOLUNTARY CANCELLATION OF A REGISTERED MARK   5.28

It is possible for the owner of a registered mark to voluntarily cancel the mark, either in whole or with respect to a portion of the designated goods or services. An application, together with the original registration certificate of the mark to be cancelled, needs to be filed with the TMO.

The exclusive right to use the subject mark is terminated from the date of receipt of the voluntary cancellation application by the TMO.

CHAPTER 6

TRADEMARK OPPOSITIONS

GENERAL REMARKS   6.1

After a trademark registration application receives preliminary approval by the PRC Trademark Office ("TMO"), it will be published in the PRC *Trademark Gazette* (Article 27, Trademark Law). Within a period of three months starting from the publication date, any individual, company or other organisation can file an opposition to the application (Article 30, Trademark Law; Article 23, Implementing Regulations). It is important to note that since an opposition can be filed by anyone, and not just by the parties who perceive their rights as being infringed, oppositions can essentially be filed anonymously via seemingly unconnected third parties. Indeed, filing through a third party is often preferred where the interested party intends to negotiate a settlement on an anonymous basis so to reserve a better bargaining position.

The statutory opposition period of three months is non-extendable and if no opposition is filed, a trademark will become registered upon the expiry of the opposition deadline. Thereafter, any party wishing to remove a trademark must file cancellation applications instead, which is discussed in Chapter 7.

It is always preferable to object to trademarks at the opposition stage where possible, as cancellations tend to be more difficult, time-consuming and expensive than oppositions.

POSSIBLE OUTCOME OF AN OPPOSITION   6.2

Where an opposition is successful, a public notice will be published in the PRC *Trademark Gazette* stating that the mark is refused registration due to a successful opposition. The opposed mark will be deemed to have never been registered. Details of the opponent or the grounds of opposition, however, will not be disclosed.

If an opposition fails, the opposed mark will be deemed to have been registered upon expiry of the opposition period, ie the day after the opposition period runs out. Note, however, that a trademark owner cannot pursue third parties for the bona fide use of its mark between the deemed registration date and the date of the final opposition decision as issued by the relevant authority (the TMO, TRAB or People's Court).

GROUNDS OF OPPOSITION

6.3 POSSIBLE GROUNDS OF OPPOSITIONS

The grounds of oppositions in general mirror the grounds of rejection during the trademark application examination process as discussed in Chapter 5. The idea is that if a trademark violates any of the principles of registrability under the Trademark Law, or indeed conflicts with third parties' prior marks, it should not have been granted preliminary approval.

The different grounds of opposition are not mutually exclusive and it is advisable to put forward multiple grounds in an opposition submission where applicable.

6.4 CONFLICT WITH PRIOR REGISTRATIONS OR APPLICATIONS

As discussed in Chapter 5, China adopts the 'first-to-file' principle of trademark registration. An opposition is therefore often based on prior registrations or applications for identical or similar marks in respect of identical or similar goods / services.

The TMO generally allows similar or even identical marks to coexist provided that they cover goods or services considered dissimilar by the TMO (ie they do not fall within the same 'similarity subgroups'). Where the prior mark and the opposed mark cover goods or services that are considered dissimilar by the TMO, therefore, arguments should be made to persuade the TMO to accept the goods as similar if in fact they share common distribution channels, targeted consumer base, function, use and raw materials etc.

TMO Opposition Decision, No 2687 of 2001

The opponent filed an opposition against the 'Peace in Chinese (*he ping*) & HP Device' mark in Class 16 based on its prior registration for the 'HP' mark. The goods covered by the opposed mark include "mimeograph apparatus and machines; inking ribbons for computer printers".

The TMO concluded that the opposed mark and the opponent's prior mark constituted similar marks because the distinctive element in the opposed mark was the "HP Device". Furthermore, the TMO considered selected items of the goods covered by the two marks were 'closely connected', because they shared common target consumers, functions, use and distribution channels. The TMO concluded that the registration and use of the opposed mark was likely to cause consumer confusion and refused its registration.

In all oppositions based on prior registrations or applications, it is advisable to provide the TMO with evidence of fame and use of the relevant prior marks in the PRC. The likelihood of consumer confusion is the deciding factor in such opposition proceedings, and the TMO often takes into account the distinctiveness and fame of the prior mark in question when assessing this likelihood.

TMO Opposition Decision, No 2163 of 2001

The opponent filed an opposition against the 'DULUX / DULUX in Chinese (duo le shi)' mark in Class 3 for polishing wax and parquet floor wax. The opposition was based on the basis of the fame and use of the opponent's 'DULUX' and 'DULUX in Chinese' marks in respect of paints and varnishes.

The TMO concluded that the opponent's 'DULUX' and 'DULUX in Chinese' marks both enjoyed a certain level of fame in the PRC due to extensive use and promotion. Even though the goods covered by the opposed mark were polishing wax and parquet floor wax in Class 3, given the similarity between the marks and level of fame of the opponent's marks, the TMO concluded that consumer confusion was likely and rejected the registration of the opposed mark.

Applicant's mark is inherently not registrable 6.5

Opposition applications can rely on the same principles used to assess the inherent registrability of a trademark, as set out in Chapter 5. The most commonly encountered grounds of an opposition targeting the inherent registrability of a trademark are that the mark (a) lacks distinctiveness, (b) is descriptive of the goods or services it covers, (c) promotes in an exaggerated manner and is deceptive or (d) is generic in nature.

Oppositions of such nature are much less common than those filed on the basis of prior conflicting marks.

CONFLICT WITH WELL-KNOWN TRADEMARKS 6.6

The Trademark Law offers special protection for well-known trademarks under Article 13 and an opposition can be filed where the registration and use of a trademark is liable to violate this provision.

Previously an opposition relying on Article 13 needed only be supported by evidence of fame of the mark copied or imitated without a formal request for recognition of its well-known status by the TMO. The recently issued Regulations of the Recognition and Protection of Well-known Marks (the "Regulations"), effective 1 June 2003, now prescribes the formal procedural rules in making applications for recognition of the well-known status of trademarks in the PRC. Under the new law, a formal request is necessary where an opposition is filed on the basis of Article 13. Although neither the Implementing Regulations nor the Regulations detail the consequences for non-compliance of such procedural rules, it is likely that the TMO will not decide on the contravention of Article 13 in the absence of a formal request.

Please see Chapter 3 for a detailed discussion on well-known trademarks.

6.7 CONFLICT WITH PRIOR LAWFUL RIGHTS OF OTHERS

The Trademark Law provides that any trademark for which registration is applied may not conflict with or prejudice prior lawful rights of any third party (Article 9 and Article 31). Whilst the Trademark Law and the Implementing Regulations do not provide an exhaustive list of such 'prior lawful rights', examples would include civil rights in personal, enterprise and corporate names, portraits, industrial designs, copyright, famous product trade dress and domain names.

In practice, however, it is often difficult to rely on any such prior rights to oppose trademarks because the TMO is reluctant to make determinations on the validity and subsistence of the other prior rights alleged. It is advisable that proper supporting evidence (such as a copyright or design right registration certificate) be supplied to strengthen oppositions of such nature.

6.8 PRE-EMPTIVE REGISTRATION OF A THIRD-PARTY'S UNREGISTERED MARK

The Trademark Law expressly prohibits the pre-emptive registration by improper means of a third-party's trademark that is already in use and that has a certain degree of influence (Article 31, Trademark Law).

This is a new ground of opposition introduced in the revised Trademark Law and it has been subject to much debate amongst practitioners and legal academics alike. The inclusion of Article 31 was prompted by the need to better protect unregistered trademarks in the PRC, given that its legal system does not encompass the common tort of 'passing off' ('passing off' is generally provided under the principles of unfair competition). The language of Article 31 as it stands, however, is ambiguous. To successfully oppose a trademark under Article 31, the only requirements are that the unregistered mark is 'in use' (there is no guidance whether 'use' is limited to goods or services that are identical with or similar to those covered by the opposed mark) and that the mark has a 'certain degree of influence' (contrast the higher standard for recognition as 'well-known' under Article 13). The result – most likely unintended – is that Article 31 provides wider protection against improper registration to unregistered marks, than Article 13 provides for well-known marks.

Article 31 is most likely to be revised in the next round of reform to the Trademark Law. Nevertheless, an opposition relying on Article 31 is justified in the meantime, where it is clear that the applicant has copied / imitated and pre-emptively applied to register in bad faith a famous mark that is in use in the PRC.

PARTIAL OPPOSITIONS 6.9

Previously, where the TMO approves an opposition application, the opposed mark is rejected for registration in respect of all goods or services designated in the application. Under Article 23 of the revised Implementing Regulations, the TMO is now able to approve oppositions partially, so that the opposed trademark is rejected for registration in respect of only a portion of the designated goods or services that are deemed to conflict with prior marks.

By the same token, a partial opposition can be filed against a trademark for selected items of designated goods or services. However, since partial oppositions do not in fact confer any benefits over ordinary oppositions, they are almost never filed in practice.

IMPORTANT STATUTORY TIME LIMITS

Note: Following the revision of the Trademark Law and the Implementing Regulations, all statutory deadlines imposed are final and no extension of time is allowed.

FILING OF DEFENSE AGAINST AN OPPOSITION RAISED 6.10

Under the Implementing Regulations, the TMO is required to serve a copy of the opposition on the applicant in a timely manner and the applicant has the opportunity to file a defense within 30 days from the receipt of the notification of opposition (Article 22). However, no adverse inferences may be drawn by the TMO from the applicant's failure to file a defense – the TMO will simply proceed to review the opposition based on the evidence presented before it.

The applicant's defense will not be made available to the opponent to raise further counter-arguments.

FILING OF SUPPLEMENTARY EVIDENCE 6.11

If a party needs to submit relevant supplementary evidence in support of its opposition or defense submission, it must state so clearly in the opposition or defense submission. The statutory time limit for submitting supplementary evidence is three months from the date on which the opposition or defense was filed. For example, supplementary evidence must be filed on or before 18 April 2004 in support of an opposition filed on 19 January 2004. If the supplementary evidence is not submitted within the time limit, the party will be deemed to have abandoned its right to submit supplementary evidence.

Any evidence that is in a foreign language should be submitted together with its Chinese translation. Where no Chinese translation is provided, the evidence will be deemed to never have been submitted.

6.12 FILING OF APPEAL

The Trademark Law provides that an appeal against the TMO's decision in opposition proceedings can be made to the TRAB within 15 days of the receipt of the TMO decision.

The procedural rules governing the review and adjudication by the TRAB are set out in the Rules for the Review and Adjudication of Trademarks ("TRAB Rules"), effective 17 October 2002. Upon receipt of the appeal submission, the TRAB will forward a copy of the appeal to the opposed party. The opposed party is given 30 days from the receipt of the notification of appeal to file a defense. If no defense is filed, the TRAB will proceed to review the opposition appeal based on the evidence presented before it and no adverse inference will be drawn from the opposed party's failure to respond.

Where a defense is filed, the submission, together with its supporting evidence (if any), will be forwarded to the applicant of the appeal for the raising of counter-arguments. Such exchange of documents was not routine practice in the past.

Similar to the filing of supplementary evidence before the TMO, a supplementary submission may be filed with the TRAB within three months of filing the appeal and the defense submission. Again, a declaration of the intention to file a supplementary submission must be made in the original submission or else the right to do so will be lost. It is important to note, however, that no supplementary submission can be filed in support of the applicant's counter-arguments to a defense – counter-arguments are subject to one time filing.

It is important to bear in mind that under the TRAB Rules, evidence that originates from outside the PRC needs to be notarised and legalised, and where evidence in a foreign language is submitted, translation into Chinese is necessary. Failure to comply with these evidential requirements means that the evidence will not be considered by the TRAB.

If dissatisfied with the TRAB's decision, a further appeal to the People's Court can be filed within 30 days of receiving the TRAB's decision.

TRADEMARK WATCH SERVICE   6.13

Under the current Trademark Law, PRC individuals can apply to register trademarks, whereas previously they were prohibited from doing so. This has caused a flood of new applications for pirated marks.

It is always advisable for trademark owners to retain a trademark watch service, to actively monitor the PRC *Trademark Gazette* for advertisements of marks applied for by third parties that are likely to be detrimental to their exclusive right to use prior marks.

Where the trademark owners are alerted to preliminarily approved marks that are of potential concern, the most important information to ascertain is the opposition deadline. Since the deadline is final and no extension of time is allowed, it is imperative that legal opinion is sought as soon as possible, regarding the feasibility of opposition and chances of success.

CHAPTER 7

TRADEMARK CANCELLATIONS

GENERAL OVERVIEW 7.1

A registered trademark can only be removed by cancellation.

The Trademark Office ("TMO") can cancel registered trademarks under several provisions of the Trademark Law and these generally relate to the failure to duly maintain registered marks or their misuse. In addition, the TMO can cancel registered marks that are inherently unregistrable (see Chapter 5 for detailed discussion on the registrability of trademarks).

Third parties can also file cancellation applications to remove registered marks. With the exception of cancellations on the basis of continuous non-use for three years, cancellation applications are made to the PRC Trademark Review and Adjudication Board ("TRAB"). Cancellations are generally filed on the basis that the registration of the subject marks is in violation of the Trademark Law. The statute of limitation for filing such a cancellation application is five years from the registration date of the subject mark, except where there is bad faith involved or where the application is made by the owner of a well-known mark (Article 41, Trademark Law).

The TMO processes non-use cancellation actions. Because the burden of proof of trademark use is on the registrant, non-use cancellations are normally straightforward to file.

It is important to note that if an opposition has been unsuccessfully raised against a registered mark, a cancellation application against the same mark based on the same grounds will not be accepted by the TRAB (Article 42, Trademark Law).

GROUNDS OF CANCELLATION

POSSIBLE GROUNDS OF CANCELLATION 7.2

Depending on the circumstances, a registered mark may be cancelled by the TMO on its own initiative, or alternatively, by the TRAB at the request of third parties. A cancellation by the TMO is never subject to statutory time limits, although time limits may apply where cancellation applications are filed by third parties.

The most common ground relied on in cancellation applications is that the subject should not have been registered at all, either because it violates provisions of the Trademark Law or because it was registered in bad faith, ie the trademark was improperly registered. The available grounds for cancellation provided in the Trademark Law are discussed in detail below.

Improperly Registered Trademark

7.3 VIOLATION OF ARTICLES 10–12 OF THE TRADEMARK LAW

As discussed in detail in Chapter 5, trademarks that:

1. contain prohibited wordings or devices;
2. are generic;
3. lack distinctiveness;
4. are wholly descriptive; or
5. do not fulfill the requirements of a registrable three-dimensional mark

cannot be registered.

Where such an inherently unregistrable trademark somehow became registered, the TMO can initiate a cancellation, or alternatively, any other third party can file an application to the TRAB to cancel the registered mark. There is no time limit for filing a cancellation application on such grounds.

7.4 REGISTRATION BY DECEPTIVE, OR OTHER IMPROPER MEANS

Neither the current Trademark Law nor the Implementing Regulations provide guidance as to what constitutes acts of 'deceptive or improper means'. However, an elaboration on the topic can be found in the old Implementing Regulations of April 1994. Under the old regulations, obtaining registration by any of the following acts amounts to registration by deceptive or other improper means:

1. fabricating facts, withholding facts or forging documents;
2. copying, imitating, translating, etc, of another's famous trademark, in contrary to the principles of honesty and trustworthiness;

3. registering a principle's trademark in the agent's own name without authorisation;
4. infringing upon another's lawful right of priority;
5. any other improper means.

Apart from "fabricating fact, withholding facts or forging documents", every single other act listed above is now specifically prohibited under the current Trademark Law (Articles 13, 15 and 31 respectively, see below). It would appear therefore that registration by deceptive or other improper means in the context of cancellation proceedings refers to obtaining registration by fabricating or withholding facts, or by forging application documents.

Again, the TMO can, on its own initiative, cancel a registered mark obtained on this deceptive basis. Alternatively, any third party may file an adjudication request for the mark to be cancelled by the TRAB. As with cancellations on the basis that the registered trademark is inherently unregistrable, there is no time limit for filing an application to cancel a mark registered by deceptive or other improper means.

VIOLATION OF ARTICLES 13, 15, 16 AND 31 OF THE TRADEMARK LAW   7.5

Common to all four provisions of the Trademark Law is perhaps a degree of bad faith on the part of the registrant in registering its trademark. Cancellations of registered trademarks that contravene these provisions can only be filed by prior right holders or other interested parties with the TRAB.

The time limit to file cancellation applications of such nature is five years from the registration date of the marks to be cancelled, except where there is bad faith involved, or where the application is made by the holder of a well-known mark. In such cases, cancellations are not subject to time limits at all.

Article 13 provides protection in the PRC for well-known marks, whether registered or unregistered. When filing a cancellation based on Article 13, it is necessary to make a formal request in the cancellation submission for the TRAB to recognise that the prior mark relied on is a well-known mark (the background to well-known applications has been briefly discussed in Chapter 6 at paragraph 6.6; see Chapter 3 for a detailed discussion on well-known trademarks).

Article 31 protects prior rights and prohibits the pre-emptive registration of another's trademark, which is in use and which has a certain degree of influence in the PRC. A detailed account of this provision is provided in Chapter 6 at paragraphs 6.7 and 6.8.

Cancellation applications on the basis of violations of Articles 15 (agent's registration of its principle's trademark without authorisation) or 16 (false and misleading indication of geographical origin) are rare.

7.6 CONFLICTING WITH PRIOR REGISTRATIONS OR APPLICATIONS

Where a mark owner considers that a registered mark conflicts with its prior registrations or applications in respect of identical or similar goods or services, but that the protection of well-known marks is not applicable, a request for adjudication can be filed with the TRAB to cancel the registered mark.

A cancellation of such nature must be filed within five years of the registration date of the mark to be cancelled.

7.7 PROCEDURAL RULES

As mentioned above, cancellations against improperly registered trademarks are filed with the TRAB.

The significance of having to make cancellation submissions to the TRAB, as with all appeals against the TMO's decisions as discussed in Chapters 5 and 6, is that the TRAB's evidentiary requirement is much more stringent than that expected by the TMO. Under of the Rules of Trademark Review and Adjudication ("TRAB Rules"), foreign entities wishing to submit evidence that originates from outside the PRC, must first arrange for the evidence to be notarised and legalised; translation into Chinese is also necessary for evidence presented in foreign language.

7.8 FILING OF RESPONSE AGAINST A CANCELLATION

Upon receipt of a cancellation application, the TRAB will give notice to the owner of the registered mark subject to cancellation and request a response within 30 days of receipt of the notice. Failure to respond to the cancellation submission, however, will not affect the adjudication, as the TRAB will proceed to review the proceedings based on the evidence already presented before it.

7.9 FILING OF SUPPLEMENTARY EVIDENCE

Similar to the procedures for filing supplementary evidence in opposition proceedings,[1] if a party needs to submit supplementary evidence in support of its cancellation application or response, it must state so

---

1 See Chapter 6 on PRC Trademark Oppositions.

clearly in the relevant submission. The statutory time limit for submitting supplementary evidence is three months from the date on which the cancellation application or response was filed.

If the supplementary evidence is not submitted within the time limit, the party will be deemed to have abandoned its right to submit supplementary evidence.

FILING OF APPEAL 7.10

The Trademark Law provides that an appeal against the TRAB's decision in cancellation proceedings can be made to the People's Court within 30 days of receipt of the TRAB decision.

Three Years' Continuous Non-use of a Registered Mark

GENERAL PROCEDURE FOR NON-USE CANCELLATIONS 7.11

The Trademark Law provides that the TMO may request rectification or cancel a registered trademark if the mark has not been used for a continuous period of three years (Article 44(4), Trademark Law).

In addition, anyone may apply to the TMO to cancel a registered mark on the basis of non-use for three years (Article 39, Implementing Regulations). Upon receipt of a non-use cancellation application, the TMO will give notice to the registrant of the subject mark and request for evidence of use, or legitimate reasons for not having used the registered mark, to be furnished within two months of receipt of the notice. Failure to respond to the TMO's notification within the time limit will result in the cancellation of the registered mark.

FILING A NON-USE CANCELLATION 7.12

Before filing, it is important to ensure that the registered trademark to be cancelled has been registered for more than three years so that a non-use cancellation is prima facie applicable.

On-site investigation against the owner of a registered mark is often necessary so that preliminary information on the use of the mark may be gathered. Where the investigation reveals that the mark has in fact not been used by the owner or its authorised users, a market survey should be conducted so that the survey results can be used to support a non-use cancellation. Although the burden of proof regarding use falls on the owner of the registered trademark, it is a requirement under the Implementing Regulations to include an "explanation of the relevant situation" in a cancellation application submission.

Where the investigation and / or market survey reveal that the subject mark has not been used for more than three years in respect of only a portion of the designated goods or services, a partial-cancellation application may filed to cancel the mark only in respect of that portion of the specification.

A very common outcome of on-site investigations is that the owner of the subject mark cannot be found at the address as shown on the TMO record and that it cannot be located after further investigation efforts. Where the application for the subject mark was not filed through a trademark agent (this can be verified by looking at the PRC *Trademark Gazette* advertisement of the mark) and there has been no subsequent assignment of the mark recorded at the TMO, chances are that the owner will not receive the notice of cancellation from the TMO and therefore not be in the position to provide evidence of use – a non-use cancellation would therefore be worth a try.

7.13 DEFENDING AGAINST A NON-USE CANCELLATION

Trademark use is defined under Article 3 of the Implementing Regulations to include use of trademarks on goods, on the packing or containers for goods, on trade documents for goods, as well as use of trademarks in respect of advertisements, promotions, exhibitions and other commercial activities. Evidence of use includes materials that demonstrate the use of the mark by the trademark owner itself, and by those who are authorised to use the mark.

Where evidence of trademark use of the above nature can be provided to the TMO timely, a non-use cancellation will fail either in part or in whole.

Previously, the use requirement could be satisfied by placing a simple advertisement setting out the registration details of a registered mark in one of the national newspapers approved by the TMO (such as *China Trade News* or *China Consumers Daily*). Although the current Implementing Regulations do not specifically exclude the use of such non-commercial advertisements, there appears to have been a change to TMO policy, as evident from recent decisions issued. It now appears that a non-commercial advertisement is no longer sufficient in defending against a non-use cancellation.

Clearly, the TMO now expects advertising to have greater commercial characteristics. Just how far such advertisements must go remains unclear. There is yet no clear TMO policy in this regard, and since decisions of the TMO and TRAB can now be appealed to courts in Beijing, perhaps new policies will be generated over time through court decisions.

In the absence of legal certainty on this topic, it is advisable to place an advertisement with a strong commercial emphasis if it is intended as a defense against a non-use cancellation. Details of the mark, including an indication of as many of the goods or services covered as possible, the name and contact details for the trademark owner, an invitation to traders to make commercial enquiries regarding the product or services concerned and perhaps a brief introduction to the trademark owner and its fame, should be included.

Without actual commercial activities, however, there can be no guarantee that a commercial advertisement of such nature can successfully defend a trademark registration against cancellations for non-use.

Where there is no real commercial use of a registered trademark, therefore, the best course of action is to file a new application for the mark in question when faced with a non-use cancellation.

FILING OF APPEAL 7.14

Only the registrant of the cancelled mark can appeal the TMO's decision in non-use cancellation proceedings; the party who filed the non-use cancellation has no right to appeal to the TRAB against the TMO's decision. An appeal must be filed with the TRAB within 15 days upon receipt of the TMO decision. If dissatisfied with the TRAB's decision, the registrant can file a further appeal to the People's Court within 30 days of receipt of the TRAB decision.

Death or Termination of Trademark Registrant

RELEVANT LEGAL PROVISION 7.15

If a trademark registrant dies or is terminated, and there has been no assignment of the subject trademark within one year after the date of death or termination, anyone may apply to the TMO for the deregistration of the trademark (Article 47, Implementing Regulations).

Evidence of the death or termination of the trademark registrant should be submitted to support such an application.

EVIDENCE REQUIRED IN SUPPORT OF THE 7.16
CANCELLATION

Where the registrant is a legal entity rather than a natural person, it is in reality very difficult to produce sufficient evidence to convince the TMO that the registrant no longer exists. Although any corporate entity engaged in business activities is required to register with the relevant local Administration for Industry and Commerce ("AIC"), registration records held by the AIC are often outdated or incomplete. It is understood, at present, that only where a business has been delisted from the AIC business register for more than two years will the TMO consider a registrant terminated for the purpose of Article 47 of the Implementing Regulations. Such policy is of course liable to change without notice in the future.

If a registrant is terminated but there is no concrete evidence to support such, where possible, it is better to file a non-use cancellation at the appropriate time – clearly, a registrant that is no longer operational will not be able license its mark or provide evidence of its use.

When a trademark registration is cancelled because of the death or termination of the registrant, the exclusive right to use the mark is terminated from the date of the registrant's death or termination.

Cancellations by the TMO on Administrative Grounds

7.17 SPECIFIC GROUNDS

The TMO can cancel registered trademarks on the following grounds:

1. unilateral modification of a registered mark (Article 44(1), Trademark Law);
2. failure to file applications with the TMO to record change of trademark owner's name or address (Article 44(2), Trademark Law);
3. failure to file applications with the TMO to record the assignment of a registered trademark (Article 44(3), Trademark Law); and
4. passing off goods of poor quality that bear the registered trademark as superior goods, with an aim to deceive the consumers (Article 45, Trademark Law).

7.18 FILING OF APPEAL

Upon receipt of the TMO's decision to cancel the registered trademark, the registrant has 15 days within which to appeal the TMO's decision to the TRAB. If dissatisfied with the TRAB's decision, a further appeal to the People's Court may be filed within 30 days of receipt of the TRAB decision.

CONSEQUENCES OF CANCELLATION

7.19 ON GROUNDS OF IMPROPER REGISTRATION

If a registered mark is cancelled because it was improperly registered, the exclusive right to use the mark will be deemed to have never existed. The TRAB's decision to cancel the mark, however, does not have retroactive effect on the validity of infringement decisions made by the People's Court or the administrative authorities. Likewise, the cancellation decision will not affect the validity of any assignment or licensing agreements previously entered into by the registrant. If a party has suffered any loss as a result of the registrant's bad faith in registering the cancelled mark, the registrant is liable to compensate such loss.

ON OTHER GROUNDS   7.20

Where a registered mark is cancelled on grounds other than improper registration, the exclusive right to use the mark is terminated from the date the TMO issues a decision to cancel the mark.

CONSEQUENCES OF A SUCCESSFUL CANCELLATION   7.21

The TRAB or the TMO may cancel a registered trademark in whole or in part.

Regardless of the grounds, cancellation of registered trademarks will be published in the PRC *Trademark Gazette*. If a registered mark is cancelled wholly, the original registration certificate becomes invalid. Where a registered trademark is partially cancelled, the original registration certificate must be returned to the TMO so that the TMO can either provide a statement to that effect in the original registration certificate, or to issue a replacement certificate.

Finally, where a registered trademark is successfully removed (whether by cancellation or deregistration), the TMO will not approve applications for identical or similar marks covering identical or similar goods / services within one year of the date of cancellation or deregistration (Article 46, Trademark Law).

CHAPTER 8

TRADEMARK LICENSING AND ASSIGNMENT

TRADEMARKS AS VALUABLE PROPERTY RIGHTS   8.1

As mentioned in previous chapters, trademark rights are valuable property rights. Trademark owners can transfer such rights in return for consideration by way of license, assignment or franchise.

A trademark owner may wish to license the use of its trademark to another party, say a distributor for promotional purposes. Assignment of a trademark may occur when a trademark owner transfers its trademark together with its other corporate assets to another party. An entity that wishes to open a chain of operations in the PRC would need to provide the use of its trademark and trade name to its franchisee(s), which makes entry into a franchise arrangement necessary.

TRADEMARK LICENSING AGREEMENT AND RECORDAL   8.2 PROCEDURES

Trademark licenses are governed by the Trademark Law, the Implementing Rules and the Trademark Licensing Contract Recordal Measures (the "Recordal Measures") promulgated by the State Administration of Industry and Commerce ("SAIC") and effective from 1 August 1997.

Article 40 of the Trademark Law requires the licensor and the licensee to enter into a trademark license contract. The license contract clearly delineates the respective rights and obligations of both parties, and the scope of the license. For example, the scope of the license may only extend to one English trademark. If the trademark owner subsequently develops another, say Chinese trademark, then this Chinese mark will not be within the scope of the trademark license contract.

A trademark licensor who licenses its registered trademark to another entity is required, under Article 43 of the Implementing Rules, to deliver a duplicate trademark license contract to the Trademark Office for recordal within three months after the date of execution of the license contract.

Further, under Article 6 of the Recordal Measures, the SAIC requires the trademark license contract to include the following information:

1. identification of the mark(s) being licensed for use and its registration(s);
2. the scope of the goods being licensed;
3. the term of the license;
4. the method in which the licensed trademarks is to be provided to the licensee;
5. clauses providing that the licensor will supervise the quality of the commodities on which the licensee uses the registered trademarks; and
6. a clause requiring the licensee to indicate its name and the place of origin of the goods

Failure to include information may result in the Trademark Office refusing recordal. The following documents are needed for the license recordal of a registered trademark:

1. original or notarised copy of the trademark license contract. Where multiple trademarks have been licensed, separate applications for recordal should be filed by the licensor. However, only one of the applications for recordal needs to be submitted with the original or notarised copy of the trademark license agreement, the remaining license agreements may be photocopies. If the original license contract is not in Chinese, a Chinese translation of the license agreement must be submitted;
2. duly completed standard recordal form;
3. standard power of attorney in favour of an official PRC trademark agent; and
4. a copy of the Trademark Registration Certificate for the licensed trademark.

The Trademark Office may refuse recordal of a trademark license contract where there are discrepancies against the trademark registration certificate in the identity of the licensor, the term of the license, the scope of goods, etc.

Unsuccessful applications for recordal will be returned by the Trademark Office, together with reasons for rejection. Where the application is rectifiable, the licensor has up to one month to amend the application in accordance with the Trademark Office's recommendations and resubmit the application for approval.

Upon recordal by the Trademark Office, it will issue a notice to the successful applicant and publish the recordal in the second issue of the PRC *Trademark Gazette*.

The licensor and licensee have a continuing obligation to notify the Trademark Office and the local Administration of Industry and Commerce ("AIC") where there is a change in the name of the licensor or licensee, and upon early termination of the license contract. Fresh recordal applications have to be filed where there are changes in the scope or term of the licensed goods.

Note that the SAIC allows any unit or individual to conduct a search on the recorded trademark license contract upon written enquiry and payment of a prescribed fee under Article 17 of the Recordal Measures.

SUBLICENSING CONTRACTS   8.3

Sublicensing of trademarks is within the ambit of the recordal process under Article 8 of the Recordal Measures. A valid trademark sublicense contract must contain either provisions permitting the licensee to grant the right to use the licensed trademark to a third party; or letters of authorisation from the licensor permitting the licensee to sublicense to third parties.

The State Administration for Industry and Commerce Regulations Concerning the Administration of Trademarks in Foreign Trade, effective from 1 August 1995 ("Foreign Trade Regulations"), states in Article 6 that entities participating in foreign trade should comply with the Trademark Law and relevant laws and regulations. So although Article 9 of the Foreign Trade Regulations provides that "licensees may not sublicense registered trademarks to others", this should be reconciled with a relevant regulation of the Trademark

Law, namely the Recordal Measures, which contemplates the recordal of sublicense contracts. In other words, trademark sublicense contracts are permitted unless expressly prohibited under the main trademark license contract.

8.4 ASSIGNMENT ISSUES

Where the trademark owner wishes to sell its trademark outright, and transfer all its interest, the transfer will take the form of an assignment.

Assignments and registration procedures

The principal rules governing assignments of registered trademarks are found in Article 39 of the Trademark Law, and Article 25 of the Implementing Rules. The basic framework set out in the mentioned legislation to carry out a trademark assignment includes the following procedures:

1. the joint filing of an application for assignment of a registered trademark by the assignor and the assignee with the Trademark Office;
2. completion of application procedures by the assignee;
3. issuance of appropriate certification by the Trademark Office after examination and approval; and
4. publication of the assignment.

The assignment does not become effective until publication of the approval by the Trademark Office.

Note also that for trademark assignments, the assignee must guarantee the quality of the goods under the registered trademark; and that the assignor must simultaneously assign the same or similar trademarks registered for the same or similar goods.

The Trademark Office will reject applications for assignment that it considers may cause mistaken recognition, or confusion, or have other negative effects.

8.5 FRANCHISING ISSUES

Under a franchise arrangement, an entity may transfer the use of its trademark and / or trade name to its franchisee(s).

The Ministry of Internal Trade (now the Ministry of Commerce) published the Administrative Measures for Commercial Franchising (Trial) ("Franchising Measures") on 14 November 1997. The Franchising Measures contain 19 articles and is the first attempt by China to regulate franchising.

The Franchising Measures define 'franchising' as the arrangement whereby a franchiser by an agreement authorises a franchisee to use its trademark, trade name, products, patents, know-how and business systems. The franchiser must be an independent legal entity with an excellent business performance record for more than one year; the franchisee can be any legal or natural person with the ability and resources to manage the franchise.

The franchiser has the right to monitor and supervise the operations of the franchise, levy franchise fees and terminate the franchise if the franchisee breaches the franchise contract. Its obligations include providing the franchisee with the necessary operation manuals, initial training and long-term guidance and operational advice and support.

The franchisee, on the other hand, is obliged to operate the franchise in strict compliance with the franchise contract, observe the guidance and supervision of the franchiser, make timely payments in accordance with the franchise contract, and preserve the goodwill and uniformity of the franchise.

The terms of the franchise contract are also detailed under the Franchising Measures. Note that an initial franchise fee, an utilisation fee and a guarantee fee are all allowed under the Franchising Measures. Other fees may also be agreed between the parties.

The Measures for the Administration of the Recordal of Commercial Franchises (Trial) came out in January 2000 ("Franchising Recordal Measures"). Under the Franchising Recordal Measures, the applicant must fulfil the criteria for a franchiser as outlined above, and submit the following documents to the China Chain Store and Franchise Association: (a) a recordal application form; (b) a copy of an enterprise legal person business license; (c) a copy of a legal person code certificate and photo of the legal representative; (d) a copy of the trademark registration certificate for the licensed trademark; (e) a copy of the national patent certificate (if applicable); (f) relevant franchisee recruitment materials; a 1,000 word business summary; photos of the exterior and interior of the main branch and two or more franchised stores, together with other relevant information. The China Chain Store and Franchise Association will notify the applicant of the results of its application within one month of receiving the above documents. The recordal fee is RMB500 and the recordal lasts for one year.

It is expected that Regulations on Commercial Franchising will also be issued before the end of this year. These regulations would include detailed guidelines on the qualification of franchise store operators and franchise brand owners, and the format and contents of franchise agreements. Emphasis will be on, information availability, advertising issues, ways to avoid fraud, and punishment for violators of the relevant rules.

8.6 VALUATION AND CAPITAL CONTRIBUTION

When establishing a foreign investment enterprise, a foreign investor will want the license of its trademark to the foreign investment enterprise to constitute part of the investor's contribution towards registered capital. In such cases, the parties will have to agree on the appropriate value of the contribution on the basis of fairness and reasonableness, or agree to have a third party make a valuation. In addition, the valuation is subject to verification by the official appraisers. Needless to say, the value of the use of a trademark may become a point of controversy.

Similarly, there will be cases where part of the Chinese party's contribution will be the license (or assignment) of its own Chinese trademark which may have acquired some reputation, at least in the Chinese party's locality. Such transfers of state-owned assets have, in recent years, attracted the attention of the Chinese authorities, who are concerned about widespread transfers of state-owned assets to foreign interests at artificially low values. As a consequence, in 1991 and 1992, China introduced a regulatory framework for compulsory valuations of state-owned assets prior to transfer.

The main legislation governing this valuation requirement, and the valuation process, are the Measures for the Administration of State Asset Valuation effective 16 November 1991, and the Detailed Implementing Rules for the Measures for the Administration of State Asset Valuation effective 18 July 1992. State-owned assets under these regulations are broadly defined, and will include trademarks. The regulations do not mandate that the transfer of the asset in question must be made at a price equal to the valuation arrived at, but in practice it will be very difficult to transfer at a price much different from the authorised valuation.

CHAPTER 9

TRADEMARK INFRINGEMENT

WHAT IS TRADEMARK INFRINGEMENT? 9.1

Trademark infringement can assume myriad forms, but it generally entails the unauthorised use of the same or a similar trademark on goods or services in a manner that is deemed likely to mislead or otherwise confuse consumers as to the source, affiliation, or sponsorship of the goods or services in question. Such unauthorised use entails a violation of the 'exclusive right' to use a trademark. According to Article 51 of the Trademark Law, this exclusive right is limited to the goods or services on which a trademark is registered. In certain circumstances, however, the unauthorised use of a well-known trademark on goods that are dissimilar to those for which the mark is registered may also constitute trademark infringement. The expanded protection provided to well-known marks is discussed in brief in the current chapter, and in more detail in Chapter 3.

It is important to note that it may be difficult for a rights holder to enforce exclusive rights to registered trademarks that contain generic or descriptive elements. Article 49 of the Implementing Regulations stipulates that registered marks containing generic names, devices, model numbers or other descriptive elements are not enforceable against third parties who make legitimate use of such elements.

THE SCOPE OF TRADEMARK INFRINGEMENT UNDER 9.2 THE CURRENT TRADEMARK LAW

Article 52 of the Trademark Law enumerates five primary acts of trademark infringement. These five acts of infringement include:

1. the unauthorised use of a trademark that is the same as or similar to a registered trademark on the same or similar goods for which it is registered;
2. the sale of goods that infringe the exclusive right to use a registered trademark;

3. the forgery or unauthorised manufacture of representations of another's registered trademark, or sale of representations of a registered trademark that were forged or manufactured without authorisation;

4. substituting the trademark of a trademark registrant without consent and returning to the market goods bearing a substituted trademark; or

5. causing 'other harm' to a third party's exclusive right to use a registered trademark.

According to Article 50 of the Implementing Regulations, the term 'other harm' (qita sunhai) set out in Article 52(5) of the Trademark Law includes:

1. use as the name or trade dress of goods, of a sign which is the same as or similar to a third party's registered trademark for the same or similar goods, thereby misleading the public; or

2. intentionally providing conditions that facilitate the infringement of a third person's exclusive right to use a trademark such as by storing, transporting, mailing or concealing infringing goods.

In addition to the provisions provided above, the Supreme People's Court issued the Interpretation on Several Issues Concerning the Application of the Law to the Trial of Civil Disputes Involving Trademarks ("SPC Trademark Interpretation"), a binding judicial interpretation intended to assist the People's Courts in dealing with trademark infringement disputes. The interpretation became effective on 16 October 2002, and specifies three additional circumstances that may be considered infringements despite their conspicuous absence from the Trademark Law and Implementing Regulations. The three circumstances entail:

1. the 'prominent' use of a registered trademark within a trade name in relation to goods that are similar or identical to those for which the mark is registered;

2. the use of a registered trademark that is a reproduction, imitation or translation of a well-known mark for goods that are dissimilar to those for which the trademark is registered; and

3. the registration and use of a domain name which is similar to a registered trademark where such use is made in relation to goods that are similar to those for which the trademark is registered.

The SPC Trademark Interpretation also provides guidelines for the People's Courts when discerning identical and similar marks in the context of trademark infringement suits. The interpretation defines 'identical' marks as those that are essentially without difference in the way they appear visually. Marks that are 'similar' are those that bear visual, aural, or conceptual resemblances in the wording, composition or colour, or overall structure of the combined main elements of the mark in question. Most important, perhaps, is that such resemblances are determined to easily lead the relevant public to mistake the source of the products or to otherwise believe that their source has a certain connection to the products of a third party rights holder. When determining whether marks are similar, the SPC Trademark Interpretation requires courts to consider the following:

1. the 'ordinary powers of observation' of the relevant public should be the standard for determining similarity;
2. the important elements of the mark should be compared separately, as opposed to side-by-side; and
3. the distinctiveness and notoriety of the marks of the aggrieved party should be taken into consideration when determining similarity.

The final consideration mentioned above suggests that marks that are deemed famous or well known may engender a wider scope of protection against infringements.

In addition to determining whether a mark is identical or similar per se, enforcement authorities must also discern whether a certain mark is used on identical or similar goods or services in order to gauge the relevance of an infringement claim. In general, the Nice Classification Index and China's own Classification of Similar Goods and Services (see Chapter 5) is used as a reference for determining the similarity of goods and services for infringement purposes. The SPC Trademark Interpretation stipulates that similarity may be found if the relevant public would normally think a certain connection existed between the goods and services. This is arguably a flexible approach to determining the similarity of goods and services, but administrative authorities and indeed even the courts are likely to adopt more conservative approaches in hard case scenarios.

COMMON FORMS OF TRADEMARK INFRINGEMENT

OVERVIEW
9.3

Acts of trademark infringement can assume many forms, but actions most commonly considered infringement fall into three categories:

unauthorised use, acts of counterfeiting (ie specific acts of infringement that may invoke criminal liability), and other violations. This third category is, of course, a catch-all category that includes certain acts that do not fit squarely into the confines of Article 52 of the Trademark Law, the most common of which is the act of filing an application to register an existing trademark.

9.4 PIRATE APPLICATIONS OF EXISTING TRADEMARKS

Pirate applications or third-party applications to register existing trademarks are a common problem for trademark owners in China. Pirate applications are generally of two types, either applications for a trademark identical to a mark registered in the PRC on dissimilar goods, or applications for the marks of foreign entities that have not obtained registration in China. In light of China's first-to-file rule, both types of pirate applications may result in the pre-emptive registration of an existing trademark, consequently blocking a later application by the original owner of the trademark on goods or services covered by the pirate application.

As the issue of prior rights is generally disputed in cases involving pirate applications, such acts are not considered infringement per se, and are normally adjudicated at the trademark registry in the context of opposition or cancellation proceedings. In other words, the remedies available in common infringement cases are not available in cases involving pirate applications. The desired remedy in such cases is the rejection of the disputed application or cancellation of the registration in question.

9.5 UNAUTHORISED USE

Perhaps the most common forms of trademark infringement in China entail actions that fall into the general category of unauthorised use. Actions that fall into this category include almost any action that is contemplated by the language of Article 52 of the Trademark Law discussed above, including acts of label replacement or 'reverse passing off'. The most common forms of infringement include the unauthorised use, sale or manufacture of goods bearing a mark identical or similar to a trademark registered on identical or similar goods, which includes acts of trademark counterfeiting.

In the context of unauthorised use infringements, right holders have recourse to administrative and civil remedies. In addition, where acts of counterfeiting meet relevant liability criteria, infringers may be prosecuted according to China's criminal law. Such remedies are discussed in more detail in Chapters 11 and 12, and in the following section.

PRODUCING COUNTERFEIT GOODS 9.6

As suggested above, trademark counterfeiting is a specific kind of trademark infringement, which entails the production or use of an identical representation of a registered trademark, as opposed to the production or use of a representation that is merely similar. Traditionally, right holders have sought relief against counterfeiters and other trademark infringers almost exclusively through the Administration of Industry and Commerce ("AIC"s) and Technical Supervision Bureaus ("TSB"s). As suggested in Chapter 2 above, increased involvement of Public Security Bureaus ("PSB"s) in enforcement work is now widely accepted by government authorities and industry alike as the key to bringing China's counterfeiting problem under control.

In the PRC, cases against counterfeiters are routinely brought under one of two sets of provisions of the Criminal Code: Articles 140 to 149 relating to the sale of fake or substandard goods, and Articles 213 to 215 relating to crimes involving the counterfeiting of registered trademarks.

Articles 140 to 149 specifically prohibit the sale of "fake and or inferior goods" and acts of "passing off a fake product as a genuine product." The word 'fake' in this context refers not to the affixation of trademarks but rather the accuracy of key product descriptions on product packaging (eg selling products without an effective ingredient, etc), and the word 'inferior' refers to products that fail to meet relevant quality standards. Although Articles 140 to 149 do not address trademark infringements per se, cases involving counterfeit trademarks may, depending on the circumstances, be prosecuted under these provisions of the Criminal Code, just as cases involving trademark infringements may be dealt with as product quality offences and handled on the administrative level by local TSBs.

Articles 213 to 215 relate to crimes involving the counterfeiting of registered trademarks. Acts that may be prosecuted under these provisions of the Criminal Code include the following:

1. the unauthorised use of a trademark identical to a registered trademark on the same type of goods;
2. the sale of goods with the knowledge that they bear a counterfeit registered trademark; and
3. the unauthorised forging or manufacture of representations of the registered trademark of a third person, or the sale of representations of a registered trademark that has been forged or manufactured without authorisation.

Until recently, local PSBs have been reluctant to involve themselves in counterfeiting cases, mainly on account of the absence of detailed standards for determining whether an infringer's actions constitute a crime under the Criminal Code. Because of this, right holders have traditionally been forced to contend with counterfeiters much the same way they would contend with ordinary infringers, ie by recourse to administrative and civil remedies.

In April 2001, the Supreme People's Court, Supreme People's Procuratorate and Ministry of Public Security issued prosecution guidelines to assist PSBs and prosecutors with determining whether cases involving trademark counterfeiting may be pursued under the Criminal Code. Article 213 of the Criminal Code provides for prison terms of up to three years in cases where a counterfeiter's acts create conditions that are serious or where sales are deemed relatively large. Prison terms of three to seven years may be imposed in cases where conditions are extremely serious or where sales are determined to be huge. These terms are not defined in the Criminal Code, and the new prosecution guidelines were to provide much needed, albeit limited, interpretive guidance.

Although the prosecution guidelines do not define the operative terms of Articles 213 mentioned above, they do however provide minimum standards for serious conditions and relatively large sales. These minimum standards establish, albeit indirectly, basic criteria for PSB and prosecutorial handling of investigations and criminal prosecutions against suspected counterfeiters. In summary, the guidelines provide that criminal liability may be sought when:

1. individuals are involved in counterfeiting activity and the value of fake products seized and / or sold exceeds RMB100,000;
2. companies or enterprises are involved and the minimum value of fake products seized and / or sold is RMB500,000;
3. there is suspicion that vendors of counterfeit goods knowingly sell fakes over these same values;
4. offenders that have been penalised on two or more occasions by administrative authorities are involved in counterfeit activity and the value of the relevant counterfeit goods is at least 80 per cent of the minimum standards set out above;
5. well-known trademarks have been counterfeited;
6. counterfeit trademarks are used in relation to pharmaceuticals for human use; and
7. 'very bad influences' are caused.

Regrettably, the above standards have been difficult to rely on for most brand owners, largely because of the lack of a definition for 'illegal business amount'. At the time this book went to press (July 2004), the Supreme People's Court was considering the issuance of further opinions or regulations to address this and other ambiguities in the April 2001 rules.

In addition to the prosecution guidelines discussed above, in July 2001, the State Council introduced regulations intended to facilitate the transfer of cases involving serious violations of laws from administrative enforcement authorities to the PSBs. While the regulations do not refer specifically to trademark counterfeiting, it is widely understood that the regulations were issued mainly to increase the number of counterfeiting cases transferred from AICs and TSBs to the police.

The regulations require administrative enforcement authorities to establish committees to evaluate whether a given case meets relevant standards for criminal investigation. After gathering and reviewing relevant evidence, the administrative authorities must reach a decision on transfer within three days. Once transferred, the police are required to either accept or return the case to the relevant administrative bureau within three days. In addition, the new regulations introduce various procedures for appealing determinations by administrative authorities and the police, and give local prosecutors overall power to supervise transfers.

Where PSBs are unable or unwilling to handle individual counterfeiting cases, Chinese law permits right holders to pursue criminal enforcement through the filing of private criminal prosecutions. To date, private prosecutions are very rare, but a few cases have recently been pursued with positive results by foreign and local brand owners.

A notice issued in September 2001 by judicial authorities in Fujian Province suggests that private prosecutions may be pursued even in cases where the minimum standards for public prosecution have not been satisfied. Given the ambiguities and fairly high standards for public prosecution set out in the April 2001 guidelines discussed above, trademark owners may find private prosecutions to be a critical tool for deterring smaller offenders. However, it remains unclear whether national and other local authorities will adopt the aggressive stance taken in Fujian, and what the minimum standards will be for pursuing private criminal prosecutions against counterfeiters.

THE CONTROVERSY OVER PARALLEL IMPORTS 9.7

There are currently no laws in China that deal directly with the act of parallel importing or the sale of grey market goods. Grey market goods are goods that are legally marked with a trademark registered in China and sold into a foreign market. After such goods are initially released into a foreign market, they are then imported into the PRC for resale at a price that is generally lower than the average Chinese market-price for the same product. After the Asian financial crisis in the late 1990s, the number of grey market goods sold into Chinese markets increased considerably, particularly from countries in South Asia, and parallel imports became a hot topic for domestic and foreign brand owners in China almost overnight.

In late 1999, the Guangzhou Intermediate People's Court ruled that an import company's unauthorised import of soap products bearing a trademark registered in China constituted an infringement of the exclusive rights of the plaintiff to manufacture, import and sell products bearing the mark in question. The court, however, refused to comment on the parallel import issue altogether. Most practitioners and scholars in China consider this case somewhat of an anomaly, and because court cases in China have no real precedence value, the legality of parallel imports in China is unresolved and will likely remain so until the issue of parallel imports is addressed by the Supreme People's Court or by Chinese lawmakers. (See *Shanghai Lever Co Ltd v Commercial Import and Export Trading Company of Guangzhou Economic Technology Developing District*, Hui Zhong Fa Zhi Chu Zi (1999) 82.)

9.8 UNFAIR COMPETITION AND PASSING OFF

APPLICABILITY OF UNFAIR COMPETITION LAWS

There is considerable overlap between provisions of China's Anti-unfair Competition Law and the Trademark Law, both of which prohibit the act of passing off (ie counterfeiting) PRC registered trademarks. In light of this overlap, the Anti-unfair Competition Law specifically refers back to the Trademark Law in its provisions dealing with punishments for acts of passing off.

China's current Anti-unfair Competition Law was promulgated on 2 September 1993, and entered into effect on 1 December 1993. The Anti-unfair Competition Law provides legal protection to unregistered trademarks, as well as packaging and trade dress. The law also prohibits measures taken by monopolies or cartels to effect control of market prices, and extends protection to confidential information and business and trade secrets.

The law defines Anti-unfair competition as the actions of business owners that are prohibited by the Anti-unfair Competition Law and otherwise injure the lawful rights and interests of other business operators and disrupt the social and economic order. Article 5 of the Anti-unfair Competition Law provides that business operators may not engage in the following acts:

1. passing off of the registered trademark of a third party;
2. unauthorised use of the name, packaging or trade dress peculiar to

well-known merchandise or use of a name, packaging or trade dress similar to that of well-known merchandise, thereby causing confusion with the well-known merchandise of a third party, and otherwise causing purchasers to mistake the merchandise for such well-known merchandise;

3. unauthorised use of the enterprise name or personal name of another party, thereby causing people to mistake the merchandise for that of another party; or

4. use on merchandise of quality marks such as certification marks, marks of fame and marks of excellence that are counterfeit or used without authorisation, falsification of the place of origin or the making of misleading false statements as to the quality of the merchandise.

In addition, Article 9 of the Anti-unfair Competition Law prohibits business operators from making misleadingly false publicity (eg via advertising) regarding the quality, manufacturing components, functions, uses, producers, period of validity, place of origin, and other aspects of the merchandise in question.

In general, acts of counterfeiting a registered trademark also constitute acts of unfair competition in contravention of the Anti-unfair Competition Law. In addition to protecting registered trademarks, the Anti-unfair Competition Law provides protection for unregistered marks, packaging and trade dress, provided that such marks are considered famous, and the packaging and trade dress unique to or similar to well-known merchandise.

In July 1995, the SAIC promulgated Several Regulations on the Prohibition of Acts of Unfair Competition Involving the Passing Off of a Name, Packaging or Trade-dress Peculiar to Well-known Merchandise ("Unfair Competition Regulations"). The Unfair Competition Regulations define 'well-known' merchandise as "merchandise which has achieved a certain level of name recognition in the market, and which is known to the relevant public."

THE ROLE OF THE AICS   9.9

AICs above the county level are empowered to inspect acts of unfair competition, and according to Article 17 of the Anti-unfair Competition Law, may exercise the following functions and powers:

1. make inquiries of the business operators, interested parties and witnesses, and require them to provide evidence or other information concerning the alleged act of unfair competition, in accordance with prescribed procedures;

2. inquire about, and duplicate agreements, account books, bills, receipts, documents, records, business letters, business telegrams, business telexes, business facsimiles and other materials related to the alleged act of unfair competition; and

3. examine property connected with acts of unfair competition and, when necessary, order the relevant party under examination to provide details as to the source and quantity of the merchandise, to suspend sales, and pending examination, remove, conceal or destroy such property.

The penalties that AICs can impose depend on the nature of the act of unfair competition. For example, in cases where a business operator has passed off the name, packaging or trade dress of well-known merchandise of a third party, AICs have the power to:

1. order the business operator to cease the act in question;
2. confiscate the illegal income;
3. impose a fine of up to three times the illegal income; and
4. revoke the business license of the business operator.

As AICs do not have power to award compensation in unfair competition cases, aggrieved parties must seek compensation by bringing a civil action in the People's Courts. Business operators may be liable for damages calculated on the basis of the profit derived from the activities in question, and may also be liable for the reasonable expenses incurred by the aggrieved party. As the current Anti-unfair Competition Law does not contain provisions providing for statutory damages; in cases involving the passing off of a registered trademark, the statutory damage provisions of the Trademark Law will apply.

PRODUCT QUALITY VIOLATIONS

9.10 APPLICABILITY OF PRODUCT QUALITY LAW

There is considerable overlap between China's Product Quality Law and Trademark Law, and strict product quality violations often coexist with trademark violations as well. The Product Quality Law specifically prohibits manufacturers and traders from engaging in the following activities:

1. counterfeiting or passing off quality marks, such as certification marks, marks of fame, and marks of excellence;
2. falsifying the place of origin of products and falsifying or passing off the name and / or address of another factory;

3. adulterating products or mixing improper elements in their production;
4. passing off fake products as genuine; and
5. passing off products of poor quality as quality products.

As mentioned in Chapter 4 above, the TSBs are in charge of enforcing China's Product Quality Law at the local level. As certain forms of trademark infringement may also be actionable under the Product Quality Law, trademark owners may choose to take action through the local TSBs, which have many of the same inspection and seizure powers of the AICs.

CHAPTER 10

TRADEMARK COUNTERFEITING

INTRODUCTION

10.1

The biggest problem intellectual property holders face today in China is the exponential growth of trademark counterfeiting,[1] a problem that far from being assuaged, has been exacerbated by China's entry into the World Trade Organisation ("WTO").[2] Counterfeiting is rampant in China. In the United States, US$48.6 million in infringing goods emanating from China were seized in the 2002 financial year ("FY"), in a total of 1488 shipments seized – actually up from the US$26.4 million and 807 shipments that were captured in FY 2001.[3] Chinese-made infringing products have been found all over the world, including Brazil, India, Germany, Japan, Russia, Saudi Arabia, the United Kingdom and the Philippines.[4] The scale and scope of production of counterfeited goods is staggering: in April 2002, the American news channel, ABC News, reported that in the Chinese town of Shenzhen, counterfeit versions of just about every well-known consumer product, software, DVD movies and medications were available. As was reported, "they even sell fake Viagra".[5]

---

1   While the term 'counterfeiting' is often used interchangeably with 'piracy', here counterfeiting refers to the copying of a product's trademark or its trade dress. See Black's Law Dictionary 7th edn (West Publishing Company, 1999), p 354.
2   See The Economist Intelligence Unit, China Hand (2003), ch 10, p 1.
3   See Submission of the International Anti-counterfeiting Coalition Inc to the US Trade Representative, Special 301 Recommendations, 13 February 2003.
4   Very recently, Analog Digital, a leading US chip maker, was awarded an injunction by an Indian court, preventing an Indian distributor of Chinese-made counterfeit chips from selling them in India. See "Analog Acts to Enforce IP Rights", *Financial Times*, 22 January 2004.
5   Mark Litke, "Faking it: China Manufacturing Huge Amounts of Knockoffs", ABC News.com, http://abcnews.go.com/sections/wnt/DailyNews/China_ Counterfeits 020418.html (21 April 2002), cited in Amanda S Reid, "Enforcement of Intellectual Property Rights in Developing Countries: China as a Case Study", (Spring 2003) 13 J Art & Ent Law 63, 67. A very recent CBS broadcast found the situation unchanged: fake Callaway golf clubs could be had for US$275, the genuine ones retailing for US$3000. The fake Viagra was still there, offered to young and old alike. Bob Simon, "The World's Greatest Fakes", CBS News, www.cbsnews.com/stories/2004/01/26/ 60minutes/main595875.shtml (28 January 2004).

10.2 LEGISLATIVE DEVELOPMENTS

The Chinese government has been responsive to this problem.[6] Since China's accession to the WTO in December 2001, it has enacted significant reforms to its laws and regulations in order to comply with the requirements of WTO's Agreement on Trade-Related Aspects of Intellectual Property Rights ("TRIPS"). The amendment of the PRC Trademark Law in late 2001 now gives trademark owners access to the same tools and remedies relied upon by their counterparts in other major countries, including preliminary injunctions, statutory damages and compensation for enforcement expenses. Meanwhile, under the new Implementing Regulations to the Trademark Law, which entered into effect on 15 September 2002, the maximum fines for trademark infringement have been increased to a level six times higher than under earlier regulations. In addition, the new regulations indicate that in cases where the scope of a counterfeiter's prior transactions is unclear, local administrative authorities will have the discretion to impose fines up to RMB100,000.00 (US$12,000.00).

ADMINISTRATIVE ENFORCEMENT

10.3 THE ADMINISTRATION FOR INDUSTRY AND COMMERCE

The administrative body charged with enforcement of anti-counterfeiting laws and regulations is the Administration for Industry and Commerce ("AIC"). Local branches of the AIC are responsible for administrative enforcement of trademarks, trade dress, registration and monitoring of businesses, eradication of those that operate without a license, preventing illegal business practices and other general duties relating to commercial activity. Since administrative enforcement has hitherto been the primary means of combating counterfeiting, AICs have so far been at the forefront of any enforcement policy.

In October 2001, the National People's Congress ("NPC"), enacted significant amendments to the PRC Trademark Law in order to bring the law into compliance with the minimum requirements of TRIPS. The new Implementing Regulations to the Trademark Law entered

---

6   China seized 177 million pirated and smuggled audio-visual products and 6.99 million pieces of pirated computer software in 2003, as part of its campaign against counterfeiting. See Xin Dingding, "Piracy smashed at Record Pace", *China Daily*, 16 January 2004.

into effect on 15 September 2002. Under the revised Trademark Law and new Implementing Regulations, administrative penalties that may be imposed on violators by local AICs include (a) the confiscation and destruction of infringing products seized from violators; (b) the imposition of a fine up to three times the infringer's 'illegal business amount'; and (c) in cases where it is impossible to determine the 'illegal business amount', a discretionary fine up to RMB100,000.00 (US$12,000.00).

While these administrative penalties are clearly a step in the right direction, and demonstrate the desire of the Chinese government to tackle the problem, the new law and regulations require supplementation by the Trademark Office in order to facilitate their implementation by local AICs, many of whom are understaffed, under funded and under trained. Among the key questions that need to be addressed are the following.

CONFISCATION AND DESTRUCTION 10.4

The law and regulations leave unclear whether confiscation and destruction of counterfeits must take place in all cases involving counterfeiting of registered trademarks or whether removal of trademark representations will be acceptable in certain circumstances. The Trademark Law suggests that all goods must be destroyed, but in many instances, local AICs are merely ordering the removal of trademark representations from counterfeit goods, with the goods then being returned to violators.[7]

BASIS FOR CALCULATING FINES 10.5

The new regulations fail to provide a clear basis for calculating 'illegal business amounts', which are themselves the basis for calculating administrative fines. To date, most AICs have relied upon the counterfeiter's declared price, without requiring supporting evidence in the form of contracts and receipts. Given that any reasonable counterfeiter

---

7 China's State Council recently issued regulations, effective 1 March 2004, that will replace earlier regulations from 1995 on the protection of IP rights by local Customs offices. Under the new Regulations, Customs officials have the right to dispose of counterfeit products in four ways: (a) via donation to a charity after all counterfeit labels have been removed; (b) through sale to the legitimate brand owner; (c) through auction, again after all labels have been removed; and finally (d) through destruction, but only if the counterfeit marks cannot be effectively removed from the product. For more elaboration on these new Regulations, please refer to Chapter 11. Thus, while the Trademark Law seems to call for destruction of the counterfeit goods, the new Customs regulations mandate destruction only in narrow circumstances. This is illustrative of an underlying problem – that of inconsistency within the laws and regulations themselves.

would deflate the declared prince to a minimum, any fine imposed under the regulation as written, would be a mere "slap on the wrist".

10.6 MINIMUM FINES

The Implementing Regulations provide maximum fines up to three times the infringer's turnover, but they fail to provide any minimum fines or other standards that would ensure appropriate penalties are in fact being imposed by local AICs. Without minimum standards, enforcement of the penalties becomes more difficult, especially given the lack of records, and portable nature, of most counterfeiting enterprises.

10.7 STATUTORY FINES

The implementing Regulations permit local AICs to impose fines up to RMB100,000.00 in cases where it is "impossible to determine the illegal business amount". However, the regulations fail to clarify the type of situations in which such discretionary fines might be imposed, and in what amounts.

Again, it is of some comfort that the appropriate regulations are being passed, and that the Chinese government is taking notice of this enormous problem. But it is also becoming clear to both the government and foreign intellectual property holders operating in the PRC that the stringent imposition of criminal liability would be the only effective method of stemming counterfeiting in the country.[8]

CRIMINAL LIABILITY FOR COUNTERFEITING

10.8 NEW STANDARDS FOR CRIMINAL ENFORCEMENT

Chinese authorities established new standards in April 2001 for determining the circumstances that warrant criminal enforcement. These developments were followed in July 2001 by regulations issued by the State Council that establish procedures to facilitate the transfer of serious cases from administrative enforcement authorities to the Chinese police, the Public Security Bureaux (PSBs).

---

8   It is an interesting commentary on the Chinese view of intellectual property rights (as discussed in Chapter 1), that while embezzlement of funds is a crime punishable by death (see *South China Morning Post*, 2 February 2004), a short term of imprisonment is the strictest liability available for egregious counterfeiting.

ARTICLES 213 TO 215 OF THE CRIMINAL CODE   10.9

Articles 213 and 214 of the Criminal Code provide for prison terms up to three years for the counterfeiting of registered trademarks that results in 'serious conditions' or where the sales made by counterfeiters are 'relatively large'. Prison terms of three to seven years are imposed where conditions are deemed 'extremely serious' or sales are determined to be 'huge'. The April 2001 prosecution guidelines do not explicitly define any of these terms. However, they appear to indirectly define an offence as causing 'serious' conditions or constituting 'relatively large' sales if it meets the following criteria for prosecution:

1. where an individual is responsible for the counterfeiting of registered trademarks, and the 'illegal business amount' exceeds RMB100,000.00, prosecution is applicable. Where the counterfeiter is an organisation, the illegal business amount needed to make criminal prosecution applicable is RMB500,000. Vendors, who knowingly distribute counterfeit goods having the same value, can also be prosecuted under this scheme;

2. repeat offenders, those who have been administratively penalised at least twice, and where the value of the goods seized is at least 80 per cent of the minimum value (ie RMB80,000.00 for an individual and RMB400,000.00 for an organisation) can also be criminally prosecuted;

3. when the mark that has been counterfeited is a well-known (chi ming) trademark.[9]

---

9   China's State Administration for Industry and Commerce ("SAIC") recently issued Regulations on the Recognition and Protection of Well-known Trademarks intended to widen protection for marks deemed to be well-known (chi ming). The new regulations replace regulations issued in 1996 and provide more detailed procedures regarding both the filing of applications for well-known status and petitions for relief against infringements. The new regulations define well-known trademarks as marks "that are widely known to the relevant public in China and that enjoy a relatively high reputation." The 'relevant public' is defined to include consumers of the goods or services covered by the trademark, as well as relevant producers and distributors. The new regulations clearly limit the application of well-known status to those marks that have achieved a high degree of fame inside China. The new regulations set out a list of materials that may be submitted to support claims of well-known status. These include materials proving: (a) the trademark's recognition level among the relevant public; (b) the trademark's length of use, including materials relating to the history and scope of the trademark's use and registration; (c) the length of time, amount spent, extent and geographical scope of any advertising for the trademark; (d) the trademark's history of protection as well-known, inside or outside of China; (e) other materials proving that the trademark is well-known, including materials showing levels of production, sales volumes, sales incomes, pre-tax profits, and sales territories during the last three years for the main products bearing the trademark. The new regulations do not apply to China's civil or criminal courts' deliberations.

4. counterfeiting of brands used on pharmaceuticals for human use can be prosecuted without need for a showing of minimum value; or

5. cases in which 'very bad influences' are caused. Again, what 'very bad influences' are is not defined, but it is generally understood to mean cases in which the Chinese government perceives a threat to public health, morals or socialist principles.[10]

Again, while these regulations are a creditable attempt at addressing the counterfeiting problem, they have left several critical issues unresolved. Some of these issues are:

Illegal business amounts
The standards do not include a clear definition of the procedures for calculating 'illegal business amounts', and more specifically, whether such amounts should be calculated based upon the infringer's declared price or the wholesale or retail value of the legitimate product. Stocks held by violators are intentionally kept low in order to avoid criminal penalties under the rule concerning 'illegal business amounts'.

Repeat offenders
The requirement in the standards that 80 percent of the 'illegal business amount' be satisfied, has created a near-complete barrier to reliance on this standard, and it thereby undermines the purpose of imposing criminal liability for repeat offenders.

Well-known marks
The standards do not provide procedures for determining what constitutes a well-known trademark for the purposes of criminal enforcement. While the regulations issued by the SAIC clarify the standards for determining a well-known trademark, these regulations do not apply to criminal and civil courts and are purely administrative in nature (see Chapter 3 for more information).

Underground factories
The standards do not contain any provisions that would mandate criminal enforcement against operators of unlicensed 'underground' factories, or factories that operate without business licenses and any

---

10 One might argue that socialist principles decree free sharing of intellectual property with the public, but given China's accession to the WTO, and the sweeping amendments made to Chinese intellectual property laws, such an interpretation is presumably incorrect.

other required permits. Such operators leave no paper trail, and their operations are easily movable. They thus normally flee after being detected, and do not leave sufficient evidence for prosecution.

COUNTERFEIT LABELS AND PACKAGES 10.10

Corresponding criteria provided for counterfeit labelling and packaging include the following:

1. three-time offenders;
2. offenders that are proven to have generated revenues above RMB200,000 (US$24,000) or profits above RMB20,000 (US$2,400);
3. production / sale of more than 20,000 sets of unauthorised trademark representations; and
4. any number of labels bearing well-known trademarks.

The lack of clarity regarding the law and its enforcement only adds to the circumstances hampering enforcement. With a number of bureaucracies sharing responsibility for enforcement, and a lack of clear guidelines regarding the circumstances under which each agency will or should act, coupled with fines that amount to "the IP equivalent of a parking ticket",[11] it is no small wonder that counterfeiting continues unabated.

JUDICIAL INTERPRETATION OF ARTICLES 140 TO 149 OF THE CRIMINAL CODE 10.11

China is unusual in that a key method of prosecuting counterfeiters is via product quality provisions in the Criminal Code. The Supreme People's Court (the highest court in the land) and the Supreme People's Procuratorate (the highest prosecutorial body) jointly issued a judicial interpretation of product quality law provisions in the Criminal Code, which took effect on 10 April 2001. The interpretation provides a clearer definition of the types of products that qualify as 'fake or inferior' under Article 140 of the Criminal Code. It states that a 'fake' product is one that does not meet the specifications or description provided on the packaging while an 'inferior' product is one that does not meet relevant quality standards.

---

11 Joseph T Simone, a partner at Baker & McKenzie Hong Kong, quoted in Ralph Cunningham, "Maintaining the Anti-Counterfeiting Momentum" in *Managing Intellectual Property*, (June 2003) pp 26, 28.

Once a product is determined to be fake or inferior, the interpretation provides guidelines for judging liability based on the value of the seized products, and sets out commensurate punishments:

1. the threshold for criminal prosecution is sales in excess of RMB50,000 (US$6,000);
2. punishment ranges from no more than 2 years in jail and / or a fine, to 15 years to life imprisonment and confiscation of assets, depending on the amount of product sold;
3. if a violator has been caught on multiple occasions either producing or selling fake or inferior products, the value of products involved in each prior case may be added together for the purpose of determining criminal liability; and
4. the method for valuing product seized and / or previously sold depends on the 'indicated price' of the infringer, or if this is difficult to determine, the median market price for similar products in the local market. The interpretation provides for appraisals by government appraisal institutions in cases where the value is still difficult to determine.

Most noteworthy among the improvements in this area is the stipulation that liability may be established against a violator based on the value of offending products seized, rather than merely the value of products proven to have been sold. Although it has been quite common for brand owners to orchestrate large seizures of fake or inferior products, it has been far more difficult to prove past sales, since counterfeiters seldom keep records of their transactions.

The interpretations also establish and increase criminal liabilities in several other important areas:

1. liability is established for accomplices to product quality crimes. Examples include the provision of capital, credit, and documentation;
2. harsher penalties for producers or vendors of fake or inferior drugs and other potentially harmful products such as food and agricultural products; and
3. prison terms of up to five years for local government and enforcement authorities who "practice favouritism and malpractice and fail to perform their duties under the law."

Even with clarification of these issues, brand owners, local police and administrative authorities will continue to look to the trademark counterfeiting provisions of the Criminal Code as a basis for pursuing offenders, since the procedures for determining whether a product is fake or inferior will not be practical for most trademark owners and enforcement authorities.

TRANSFER OF CASES 10.12

On 9 July 2001, the State Council issued regulations to promote the transfer of counterfeiting cases from administrative bodies to the Public Security Bureaus. The Rules Regarding the Transfer of Suspected Criminal Cases by Administrative Law Enforcement Organisations state that when an administrative body discovers that the details of a case meet the standards for criminal liability, the case must be promptly considered and then transferred to the responsible PSB. The PSB will then have three days to examine the case and determine whether it will investigate. Should the PSB decide to investigate, the administrative body submitting the case will have three days to transfer all related evidence. The rules also allow any entity or individual to file a complaint with the People's Procuratorate or another higher-level administrative law enforcement organisation if they feel that an administrative enforcement authority has failed to transfer a case that meets the requirements for criminal liability.

Chinese police are gradually becoming more interested and involved in handling counterfeiting cases. The overall trend and direction are positive in this regard. Clearly, though, further measures need to be taken to increase manpower, financial support and training of all levels of police organs. The Ministry of Public Security has designated two different departments – the Social Order Division and the Economic Crimes Investigation Division – to deal with product quality and trademark counterfeiting violations, respectively. Most regional PSB offices maintain the same division of labour in the handling of these two types of counterfeiting offences. If this division of responsibility is to continue, both divisions will need to be provided adequate resources and training. However, the transfer of cases to the PSBs is likely to continue to be hampered in the future due to local protectionism, lack of education in the law, the lack of clear understanding by local authorities of relevant criminal liability standards and the self-interest of local administrative authorities that prefer to assess fines (a major source of income) rather than transfer cases to the police.

GAPS IN ENFORCEMENT 10.13

China's revised trademark law is one of the most comprehensive in Asia, and affords intellectual property rights holders an impressive array of protection. But there is a yawning gap between the law as written and as actually enforced. China's enforcement system fails to provide effective means of deterring counterfeiters. The combination of geographic size, difficulties in administration, cultural hang-ups and local protectionism[12] continues to hamper enforcement efforts. The problems arise first of all, from the ambiguity in the Chinese Criminal Code as to the types of activities that warrant criminal enforcement, as opposed to administrative penalties. These new laws, regulations and standards attempt to fill gaps in the existing legal regime for criminal prosecution of counterfeiters under China's Criminal Code. However, they still leave several critical issues unresolved. These unresolved issues may pose a barrier to prosecution in the majority of cases in which criminal penalties are appropriate, thereby frustrating the government's key objective of creating real deterrence against counterfeiting. Added to this are the laughably low administrative penalties, and the lack of implementing rules that set out guidelines for fines and other punishments. Moreover, there is a lack of cooperation between the various authorities charged with enforcement, some arising out of bureaucratic rivalry, but much of it arising from the fragmented regulatory environment. The Chinese police are also not as trained or well-equipped as they need to be in dealing with this sensitive area, although that is probably a function of the relative novelty of China's enforcement efforts and should improve. Finally, the fact remains that China is, by and large, a poor nation, and while the situation is improving rapidly,[13] most genuine goods remain far out of reach of the average consumer. Much more vital is the fact that many of the counterfeiters provide employment on a large scale, often in remote and otherwise undeveloped areas. As a consequence, many local bureaucrats and enforcement officials are liable to ignore the counterfeiting – weighing the needs of their people with the intellectual property interests of far-off foreign corporations and often finding the latter wanting.

---

12 The South China Morning Post recently reported that a Chinese software company would soon be the first domestic firm to compete with Microsoft in the domestic Chinese market. The company, Evermore Software has its main development centre in Wuxi, which enjoys heavy investment from the local government. See Danyll Wills, "China Software Maker Set to Compete with Microsoft", *South China Morning Post*, 3 February 2004. While Evermore Software is unlikely to commit any acts of infringement, it is a clear example of the vested interests local governments have in domestic enterprises, even the less savoury ones.

13 See Allen T Cheng & Jane Cai, "US$1000 signals rise of the consumer class", *South China Morning Post*, 21 January 2004.

CHAPTER 11

ENFORCEMENT OF TRADEMARK RIGHTS

GENERAL ENFORCEMENT CONCERNS 11.1

Trademark owners face a variety of challenges in the PRC, ranging from trademark piracy (the pre-emptive registration of trademarks that are identical with or similar to trademarks belonging to third parties) to the rampant infringement or blatant counterfeiting of registered trademarks. In fact, the inability of brand owners to adequately enforce intellectual property rights was the focus of trade-related 'sabre rattling' between the United States and China during the 1990s, and resulted in two landmark agreements: the 1992 MOU and 1995 Enforcement Agreement discussed in Chapter 1.

Inadequate IP enforcement remains a primary concern for brand owners in China, and continues to colour trade relations between the United States and other World Trade Organisation ("WTO") Member States following China's accession to the WTO in December 2001. The United States' Trade Representative's *2003 Report to Congress on China's WTO Compliance* referred to China's efforts to bring its framework of laws, regulations and implementing rules into compliance with the TRIPS agreement as "satisfactory," but considered efforts to enforce intellectual property rights as "ineffective." The report underscored the need for China to take immediate and substantial steps towards compliance with "its critical TRIPS Agreement obligation to maintain effective enforcement mechanisms." Some current concerns include the following:

1. administrative fines remain extremely low, and administrative enforcement generally has very little deterrence value;
2. administrative authorities rarely forward administrative cases to the Public Security Bureau ("PSB") for criminal investigation, even for commercial-scale counterfeiting;
3. administrative protectionism at the local level hinders effective enforcement against trademark infringers and inhibits the collection of relevant evidence to support judicial actions; and

4. PSBs are often poorly funded, officials lack adequate training, and there are currently no clear standards for determining criminal liability and the orderly transfer of serious counterfeiting cases from administrative authorities to the PSBs.

11.2 SMALL STEPS FORWARD: RECENT EFFORTS TO ADDRESS ENFORCEMENT CONCERNS IN THE PRC

Since the early 1990s, the Chinese government has responded to calls from both foreign and local brand owners to take steps to address its enforcement problems, particularly through greater reliance on criminal enforcement. Campaigns against counterfeiting have been pursued by the SAIC as part of a recent program for 'market rectification' and also by the State General Administration for Quality Supervision, Inspection and Quarantine. The campaigns have aimed to increase the effectiveness of IP enforcement in general, to bring criminal penalties against large-scale counterfeiters, and to target protectionism by local authorities.

In October 2003, the PRC created the IPR Leading Group, chaired by Vice Premier Wu Yi, signalling a more focused and sustained effort by China to tackle its myriad IPR enforcement issues. During an IPR conference in November 2003, Vice Premier Wu remarked that China would work with "consistent determination" to solve its IP enforcement problems and pursue adequate penalties for infringers of IP rights. Despite great strides over the last 20 years in creating a trademark regime that meets, and in some respects even exceeds international standards for the recognition of trademark rights, brand owners and top-level governmental officials tend to agree that the relative effectiveness of administrative, judicial, and criminal enforcement of such rights continue to be inadequate.

INFORMAL ACTIONS

11.3 WHEN AND WHY?

In conjunction with or in lieu of pursuing infringers through formal administrative, civil, or criminal action, brand owners also have recourse to a number of informal enforcement options as well. The effectiveness of informal enforcement measures is often contingent on a brand owner's ability to convincingly threaten recourse to formal options if an infringer refuses to cooperate. Although the success of informal actions is largely a reflection of the degree of general deterrence value associated with would-be formal sanctions, it is also, perhaps, a reflection of what is arguably a general historical preference for informal mechanisms of dispute resolution in China. Informal methods are often preferred when brand owners are contending with current or potential business partners, or in contexts where formal enforcement options may not be cost-effective due to factors such as protectionism and lack of relevant evidence.

INFORMAL ACTIONS IN PERSPECTIVE   11.4

The most common informal actions employed by brand owners in China are sending warning letters, requesting letters of undertaking, and conducting direct and informal negotiations. When contacted informally, an infringer may be more inclined to negotiate and otherwise resolve the matter amicably. But even if an infringer ultimately refuses to cooperate, informal contact may provide the aggrieved party with access to information that could prove useful in the event a formal complaint is later filed.

There are, of course, risks involved in adopting informal methods to enforce trademark rights against infringers. Brand owners run the risk of alerting a recalcitrant infringer to possible formal action, and inciting informed defensive measures, which ultimately complicate efforts to obtain relevant evidence of infringement. As a general matter, infringers often ignore warning letters, and admittances or replies are rare. In addition, it is often difficult to monitor the success of warning letters and compliance with undertakings and negotiated settlements. In short, informal actions are usually most efficient when employed in conjunction with enforcement strategies that involve formal administrative or judicial components.

STRATEGIC PUBLICITY   11.5

Another informal option available to aggrieved parties prior to or after adopting formal enforcement measures is the use of media campaigns to raise public awareness of infringing activities. A common form of publicity used by brand owners in China is the publication of warning notices in newspapers and trade magazines calling attention to the reputation of the marks in question, and threatening legal action in cases involving the unauthorised use of the relevant marks. Another common form of publicity is post-enforcement publicity, generally geared towards raising public awareness and enhancing the deterrence effect of exemplary enforcement actions taken by administrative or judicial organs.

ADMINISTRATIVE ACTIONS

11.6 GENERAL OVERVIEW

The vast majority of trademark infringement cases in China are dealt with administratively, usually through actions initiated by local AICs. In some circumstances AIC actions are a precursor to the filing of a civil suit, and on rare occasion, the basis for transfer to the PSB for prosecution under China's Criminal Code. One advantage of pursuing administrative action is that such an approach is comparatively non-adversarial, and otherwise amenable to traditional cultural preferences of avoiding direct confrontation when resolving disputes. A brand owner that institutes a civil suit without first attempting to settle the matter through a more informal route may run the risk of attracting negative publicity. An administrative action, by contrast, can be undertaken with little if any fanfare, and is typically far less obtrusive than a court action. Such concerns, however, are likely to become less relevant to brand owners as China becomes more litigious over time.

Enforcement actions by the AIC generally proceed in four stages. First, the brand owner conducts an investigation to collect relevant evidence of the nature and extent of the infringement in question. The brand owner then submits a formal complaint to the AIC for consideration. If the brand owner is a foreign entity, the complaint must be filed via an official trademark agent but may be filed by either the registrant of the infringed mark or an interested third party. After reviewing the complaint, the AIC may conduct its own investigation, and depending on the evidence submitted and the results of the investigation, the AIC may proceed to impose a wide range of penalties on the infringer, including the imposition of fines, confiscation of goods, and issuance of official orders to stop relevant infringing acts.

11.7 INVESTIGATIONS OF INFRINGING ACTIVITIES

Administrative authorities and local governments do not provide investigation services to brand owners on a commercial basis. Brand owners must therefore collect initial evidence of infringements, and usually employ the services of private investigation firms, many of which specialise in providing IP-related intelligence. Because private investigation firms are not permitted to operate in China, most firms are registered as consultancy companies or 'business service providers'. Many of these companies generate business by providing pro-bono 'sighting reports' to brand owners or their attorneys, and occasionally brand owners will initiate enforcement actions on the basis of such reports.

The purpose of such investigations is to collect evidence establishing a prima facie case of infringement. Such evidence may include:

1. product samples, receipts of sale, and other relevant documents;
2. product labels or packaging with infringing trademark representations;
3. advertisements that display infringing representations, etc.

SUBMISSION OF A FORMAL COMPLAINT   11.8

A formal complaint will usually include copies of relevant trademark certificates, and evidence supporting the infringement claim in question. If the rights holder is a foreign party, the complaint must be submitted by a trademark agent. Upon review of the complaint, the AIC may request additional materials, commence its own investigations, or make a determination that the complaint establishes a prima facie case of trademark infringement.

When investigating suspected trademark infringement cases, AICs may exercise the following powers:

1. questioning the relevant parties and investigating the circumstances connected with the alleged infringement;
2. consulting and copying relevant contracts, invoices, account books and other materials connected with the infringement;
3. conducting an on-site inspection of the premises where the concerned parties are suspected of being or having been engaged in infringing activities;
4. inspecting articles connected with the infringing activities and sealing up or impounding items or representations that infringe a third party's trademark rights.

AIC investigations usually entail an on-site visit to the infringer's premises to collect or confirm relevant evidence. The trademark agent will usually accompany the AIC officials on such visits, and representatives of the brand owner and / or its attorney may also be present at well, but entirely at the discretion of the AIC officers in charge.

AIC ENFORCEMENT POWERS   11.9

If, after investigation, the AIC determines that an infringement has occurred, it may impose the following remedies:

1. order the infringer to immediately cease the acts of infringement;
2. confiscate and destroy the tools of infringement and the tools used to manufacture the infringing goods or forge the representations of the trademark in question;
3. impose a fine upon the infringer.

Fines imposed may be up to three times the infringer's 'illegal business amount' – up six-fold from the maximum set out in earlier regulations. In cases where it is impossible to determine the illegal business amount, AICs may impose a discretionary fine up to RMB100,000 (US$12,000). Current regulations do not, however, provide standards for the imposition of minimum fines, nor do they provide detailed guidelines for the imposition of fines against repeat infringers, or dealers in counterfeit goods. Absent specific guidelines on the application of current standards, AICs have been hesitant to impose maximum fines and have generally adopted conservative interpretations of the relevant or illegal business amount.

Under the 2001 Trademark Law, AICs may no longer award compensation to an aggrieved party. While AICs had this right under the old Trademark Law, it was seldom exercised and trademark registrants seeking compensation generally had to initiate actions in the People's Courts. AICs are now encouraged to assist parties in trademark disputes to reach settlement through mediation. It may therefore be possible for brand owners to obtain compensation from infringers via negotiated settlements brokered by AICs.

If a party is dissatisfied with an AIC's decision or handling of an infringement matter, it may, within 15 days of the date on which the relevant party receives notification of the decision, initiate administrative proceedings in a People's Court according to the Administrative Procedure Law of the PRC.

CIVIL ACTIONS AND CRIMINAL PROCEEDINGS

11.10 CIVIL ACTIONS BEFORE THE 2001 TRADEMARK LAW

Civil litigation against trademark infringers in the People's Courts has always been possible, but in the past brand owners have tended to avoid litigation due to the cost of attorneys and investigators, conservative attitudes of courts in the calculation of compensation, the lack of access to preliminary injunctions and delays in the issuance of decisions. In many cases, foreign plaintiffs have had to wait over a year for Chinese courts to issue a decision – much longer than the six-months that is the maximum period for disputes involving domestic litigants.

11.11 THE 2001 TRADEMARK LAW – A TURNING POINT

The 2001 Trademark Law contains a number of provisions that have increased the appeal of civil actions for both foreign and domestic parties. In particular, preliminary injunctions and statutory damages are now available in cases involving infringements of registered trademarks. Furthermore, courts are empowered to compensate trademark owners for enforcement related expenses, ie legal and investigation costs.

In China's major cities, Chinese civil courts are now quite experienced with handling trademark infringement suits. Intellectual Property Tribunals were originally set up in the Beijing Intermediate Courts and Higher People's Court. Currently, specialised tribunals are operative in a number of other Chinese cities, including Shanghai, Fuzhou, Haikou, Guangzhou, Shenzhen, Zhuhai and Shantou.

CRIMINAL AND CIVIL ENFORCEMENT   11.12

As discussed in detail in Chapter 10, certain acts of trademark counterfeiting may constitute a crime punishable by terms of imprisonment determined by virtue of the circumstances and amount of sales. Such cases may be dealt with directly by the PSB, transferred to the PSB from an administrative agency (ie AIC or TSB), or pursued as a private criminal prosecution. The procedures associated with both criminal and civil litigation of trademark offences, as well as relevant remedies and sanctions will be discussed in more detail in Chapter 12.

CUSTOMS PROCEEDINGS

THE 2004 REGULATIONS   11.13

As discussed in Chapter 4, PRC customs authorities are empowered to confiscate products that infringe registered trademarks at the point of import or export from the PRC. New PRC Regulations for Customs Protection of Intellectual Property Rights became effective on 1 March 2004, and superseded previous regulations issued in 1995.

Features of the current customs enforcement regime include the following:

1. the recordal of trademark rights for customs protection is valid for 10 years, renewable for additional 10-year terms, but ultimately contingent on the status of the trademark rights on which the recordal is based;
2. holders of trademark rights may submit an application to customs requesting the seizure of suspected infringing goods regardless of whether the trademark rights in question have been recorded with the General Administration of Customs in Beijing;
3. holders of trademark rights who request customs to seize suspect shipments shall provide customs with a bond not exceeding the

value of the goods in question, which shall be used to compensate for losses which may arise for the consignee and consignor for an improper application, or for storage fees and other relevant costs;

4. customs shall immediately notify the holders of trademark rights recorded with customs of any shipments suspected of containing infringing items, and shall provide the rights holder with three working days from issuance of the notice to provide the relevant bond;

5. if customs notifies a holder of recorded trademark rights that it has discovered a suspected infringing shipment, and the rights holder subsequently requests customs to seize the goods in question, customs shall investigate and determine whether the seized goods do in fact infringe the relevant trademark rights within 30 days of the seizure;

6. after the holder of trademark rights applies to customs for protective measures, he or she may apply to a People's Court for a preliminary injunction against the infringement for preliminary preservation of property, in accordance with the provisions of the 2001 Trademark Law;

7. if, in the course of protecting trademark rights, Customs discovers a suspected criminal case, it shall refer the case to the relevant PSB for further handling; and

8. where seized shipments are determined to be infringing, the goods shall be confiscated and used for the public welfare (ie, donated), sold to the infringer, auctioned (after infringing representations are removed), or destroyed.

Unlike the 1995 regulations, current regulations do not include provisions granting customs the power to impose administrative fines against offenders, but it is hoped that future implementing rules (expected in 2004) will contain provisions that will be consistent with the 2001 Trademark Law, ie by providing for fines up to three times the illegal business amount.

There is language in the new regulations that suggest that IP owners may provide bonds in the form of a bank guarantee or other surety. The General Administration of Customs is currently considering the matter, and it is hoped that the right to provide bonds other than in the form of cash will be clarified in the future implementing rules.

Under both the 1995 and current regulations, brand owners are required to pay for the cost of destruction and storage of seized goods, and there are no provisions in the current regulations that would require infringers to pay these costs. The cost of destruction and storage should, however, be recoverable through separate civil actions.

CHAPTER 12

CIVIL LITIGATION

CIVIL PROCEEDINGS

PRIMARY PROCEDURAL LAWS AND ACTIONS 12.1

Trademark rights holders (including trademark registrants and licensees) are entitled to institute civil proceedings with the People's Court. The rules of procedure for civil litigation are set forth in the Civil Procedure Law (effective April 1991). The Opinion of the Supreme People's Court on Several Issues Concerning the Application of Civil Procedure Law (issued 14 July 1992) is another important source of civil procedure law.

There are generally three types of civil actions with respect to trademark rights, namely, trademark infringement, unfair competition and contractual disputes.

Types of Actions

TRADEMARK INFRINGEMENT 12.2

Trademark infringement proceedings are mainly governed by the Trademark Law (amended October 2001), its Implementing Regulations (effective September 2002) and relevant judicial interpretations issued by Supreme People's Court.

Infringing acts defined

According to the above laws, the following acts are defined as infringing:

1. where a registered trademark (or one similar thereto) is used without the trademark registrant's permission on same or similar goods;
2. where a well-known trademark, or its main part, is reproduced, imitated or translated and then used as a trademark on non-identical or dissimilar goods;

3. where another has forged, manufactured or sold another's registered trademark without authorisation;
4. where a registered trademark is placed on goods without the registrant's consent;
5. where a domain name is registered using words that are identical or similar to another's registered trademark and then that domain name is used to carry out electronic commerce in related goods;
6. where a business name is worded in the identical or similar language of another's registered trademark which is then displayed prominently on identical or similar goods; and
7. where a person causes harm to another's exclusive right to use a registered trademark.

12.3 UNFAIR COMPETITION

The Anti-unfair Competition Law in the PRC (effective December 1993) covers a number of different illegal business activities from bribery to dumping. In the intellectual property arena, the law is mostly used against others who use, without authorisation, the name, packaging or trade dress peculiar to well-known merchandise, thereby causing confusion, and causing purchasers to mistake the merchandise as well-known. In other words, this law often comes into play against counterfeit products. In addition, the principle of 'honesty and trustworthiness' set forth in Article 2 is applied from time to time by the People's Court to deter unfair acts that are not covered by more specific legal provisions.

12.4 CONTRACTUAL DISPUTES

Contractual disputes regarding trademark assignments, licensees or other such transactions constitute the third type of civil action. The Trademark Law contains few, if any, substantive provisions regarding contractual disputes. Therefore the Contract Law (effective October 1999) is the fundamental governing law in this area.

Specific Procedures for Foreign-related Cases

12.5 FOREIGN-RELATED CASES DEFINED

Special procedural provisions for foreign-related cases are set forth in Part IV of the Civil Procedure Law. In general, foreign-related cases are defined to include those where:

1. one or both parties is a foreigner, foreign enterprise or organisation;

2. the contract, or other matter in dispute, was established, modified, or terminated in a foreign country; or
3. the object of the action is located in a foreign country.

SAME RIGHTS AND OBLIGATIONS 12.6

Foreign nationals, enterprises, and organisations are guaranteed the same rights and obligations in the People's Courts as PRC citizens, enterprises, and organisations. The Civil Procedure Law also ensures that international treaties to which China has acceded shall prevail if they conflict with provisions of the Civil Procedure Law, except those treaties where China has acceded and reserved certain rights.

LEGAL REPRESENTATION 12.7

A foreign national or entity suing or being sued in China that wishes to appoint a lawyer must appoint a lawyer admitted to practice law in the PRC. A foreign lawyer may assist a Chinese lawyer, and may attend hearings but he or she cannot act directly in the capacity of a lawyer.

A foreign party may appoint a Chinese lawyer by executing a power of attorney, in which the scope and length of the appointment should be clearly specified. This power of attorney must comply with certain certification formalities set forth below.

CERTIFICATION FORMALITIES 12.8

Powers of attorney, as well as evidence formed in another country, must be notarised in that country and then authenticated by the Chinese embassy stationed there in order to be admissible in the People's Courts. Alternatively, such documents can also be admitted if they comply with the certification formalities set forth in relevant treaties concluded between the PRC and the other country. Such certification formalities also apply to powers of attorney and evidence formed in Hong Kong, Macau or Taiwan.

Documents written in a foreign language must be accompanied by Chinese translations. Such translations should be performed by a reputable or approved translation company. One should check first to make certain that the court will accept a translation from the company chosen.

Commencement of a Civil Action

FILING A LEGALLY SUFFICIENT COMPLAINT 12.9

Litigation in the People's Republic of China ("PRC") commences with the filing of a written complaint in a court having jurisdiction over the matter. Once a complaint is received, the case-filing division of the court reviews it and determines whether four conditions have been satisfied. First, the plaintiff must be a citizen, legal person, or other organisation with a direct interest in the case. Second, there must be a specific defendant. Third, there must be a specific factual basis and specific legal grounds supporting the action. Finally, the case must fall within the jurisdiction of the court in which it is filed. A case that meets the above criteria will be placed on the court's trial docket. The plaintiff is then notified of the case's acceptance and the defendant is notified of the complaint and is summoned to answer by a certain deadline. If the court rejects the complaint, it will dismiss the action and issue a written order to the plaintiff. This order can be appealed.

12.10 STATUTE OF LIMITATIONS

Normally, the statute of limitations for bringing an infringement action is two years starting from the date that the trademark rights holder knew or should have known about the infringement. However, if the infringement is still continuing at the time the suit is brought, and the exclusive right to use the registered trademark is still valid, even if the plaintiff brings a suit after more than two years, the People's Court will still issue a judgement stopping the infringement. However, the measure of damages should be calculated by reckoning back two years from the date the suit was brought.

Actions taken by a rights holder to stop the infringement cause the statute of limitations to begin anew. Such actions may include filing a court action, taking administrative action or even sending a cease and desist letter.

12.11 JURISDICTION

The PRC court system has four levels, namely the Supreme People's court, higher courts at the provincial level, intermediate courts at the municipal level and district courts at the county level.

With respect to subject matter jurisdiction, first-instance trademark civil proceedings are normally held before an Intermediate People's court or above. District People's Courts can hear such cases if they have first been approved by the Supreme People's Court. However, District People's Courts are excluded from hearing foreign-related cases. For cases in which the value of the claim is high, or the impact will be great, the Higher People's Court may have original jurisdiction.

With respect to personal jurisdiction, trademark cases fall under the jurisdiction of the People's Court of the place where (a) the infringer is domiciled; (b) where an act of infringement occurred; or (c) where the infringing products have been stored, sealed or detained. The place 'where the infringing products have been stored' means the place where large quantities of the infringing products have been stored or hidden, or the place where they are regularly stored or hidden. The place where they are 'sealed or detained' means the place where an administrative body such as Customs, or the Administration for Industry and Commerce, have sealed up or detained the infringing products.

With respect to a contract dispute, jurisdiction falls to the People's Court where the defendant is domiciled or where the contract is performed. Parties are free to designate the forum by contract but are limited to (a) where the contract is signed, (b) where the plaintiff is domiciled; or (c) where the object of the action is located.

SERVICE OF PROCESS 12.12

Under the Civil Procedure Law, the People's Court is responsible for serving process on the defendants. In general, process documents are required to be delivered to the person being served, who then must acknowledge receipt by signing a document. In cases where the recipient is a legal person or other organisation, the documents must be served on its legal representative, the organisation's leadership, or the relevant person in charge of receiving documents.

Where direct service is difficult, the People's Court may serve process by mail or through the assistance of another tribunal. If the whereabouts of the person to be served are unknown or the other methods of service have been exhausted, the documents may be served by public announcement.

Parties located in foreign countries may be served in accordance with relevant judicial assistance treaties to which China is a party. But if the foreign party has entrusted a local lawyer within the territory of China, the documents will be served directly to that local lawyer.

The complaint must be forwarded for service by the court within five days of the case being docketed. A defendant must file a defence within 15 days (or 30 days if the defendant has no PRC domicile) from receipt of the complaint. When the defendant files a defence, the People's Court must send a copy of it to the plaintiff within five days from its receipt. Failure to file a defence will not result in a default judgement and will not prevent the case from being tried.

CASE ACCEPTANCE FEE 12.13

Upon acceptance of a case, the plaintiff is required to pay a case acceptance fee to the court. The fee is levied on a sliding scale according to the value of the claim. The fee ranges from 4 per cent to 0.5 per cent depending on the value – the higher the value the lower the percentage. Above RMB1,000,000, the fee is 0.5 per cent. Details are set out in the Measures for the Charging of Court Costs by the People's Court, issued by the Supreme People's Court in 1989 and amended in 1999.

Although the case acceptance fees are payable in advance by the plaintiff, the imposition of fees will ultimately be decided by the judgement. Normally the losing party will bear all the fees, but if the claiming party is also found to be at fault, such as by claiming an unreasonably high amount of compensation, the People's Court may divide the fees between both parties.

Pretrial Procedure

12.14 NO REGULARISED EVIDENCE DISCOVERY PROCESS

Pretrial procedure, at least as that term is understood in the United States, is much more simplified in the PRC. This is mainly because pretrial in the United States is largely devoted to the discovery of otherwise hidden evidence prior to trial. With one notable exception discussed below, pretrial discovery procedure does not exist in the PRC. There is no serving of interrogatories, requests for production of documents, or the taking of depositions. All discovery work should be accomplished, usually using stealthy means, prior to the formal initiation of the action.

Presently, the PRC court system is in transition away from a civil law inquisitorial system, in which the judge actively investigates a case, towards an adversarial system, in which the parties are responsible for the investigation. Unfortunately, the evidence collection mechanisms currently available to parties remain undeveloped. These are likely to increase over time as pressures mount on PRC courts to more efficiently redress risks and losses.

As the system currently exists, plaintiffs have an advantage in simple contract disputes because, usually, most of the relevant evidence exists with the plaintiffs and not the defendants. However, for fraud matters – which predominate in the intellectual property area – the lack of pre-trial discovery gives many defendants a decided advantage. This is because usually most of the relevant evidence exists with the defendants and not the plaintiffs. For instance, a plaintiff may discover that a defendant is producing counterfeit items, but unless that plaintiff can review that defendant's books and records, it is difficult to show the volume of counterfeiting and the actual amount of damages. At present, unusual amounts of creativity, diligence and patience are required from plaintiffs in order to mount successful actions that truly remedy the level of harm caused.

12.15 EVIDENCE COLLECTION

As mentioned above, many parties are forced into employing stealthy means to collect the evidence they need to sustain their cases. However, before describing some current investigation techniques, it is important to keep in mind another key difference between litigation practice in the US and the PRC. In the PRC, most evidence will not formally be confronted and challenged at trial. As described later, trials in the PRC are more akin to closing arguments in the US, but with the parties and the judge asking questions. For the most part, witnesses are not called and are not cross-examined. Their testimony is usually by way of letter or affidavit to the court.[1] Similarly, exhibits are not authenticated and then moved into evidence.[2] All of this does not mean the evidence comes in unexamined. Rather, such examination is theoretically incorporated in the manner in which evidence is thought best collected – under the supervision of a notary.

In the US, where the confrontation of evidence is a constitutional right, notarisation is nearly meaningless. As a practical matter, notarised documents in the US are not legally more significant than other non-notarised documents. However, in other countries, including the PRC, notaries play a far greater role in vouching for the validity and truthfulness of evidence. In the PRC, notaries are supposed to be neutral observers of actual evidentiary events who then objectively report their observations back to the court. An example is set forth below.

NOTARISED TRAP PURCHASES   12.16

One of the most important investigation techniques in the PRC is the so-called 'notarised trap purchase'. In the US, if someone knows that a shop is selling counterfeit goods, an ordinary person – or even a party – can go into the shop, make a purchase and then testify about it in court. Nothing more is required, and it is up to the judge or jury to determine if the person is telling the truth. In the PRC, such testimony is unlikely to even be allowed in court – especially from a party – unless the purchase was observed and reported by a notary. In such a case, the notary's report will be considered by the court as reliable. It is practically unheard of that the notary would actually appear in court, testify and be cross-examined. The notary's bestowed neutral status vouches for his or her reliability.

---

1   Mo Zhang and Paul J Zwier, "Burden of Proof: Developments in Modern Chinese Evidence Rules", (Spring 2003) 10 Tulsa J Comp & Int'l L 419, 468–469 (describing the extremely low appearance rate of witnesses in Chinese courts).

2   The process of authentication is described at Fed R Evid 901 – 902. Generally, for something to be admitted as evidence in trial, evidence must first be presented showing that the item in question is what the proponent claims. For instance, in a telephone call, in order to claim that person X made a statement during a call, the witness must first provide evidence showing how he or she is familiar with person X's voice. This is called 'authentication'.

Not all evidence, and not all investigations, can be notarised. In such instances, it is critical that measures such as tape recording or videotaping, are employed to allow for independent verification. Although PRC courts are trying to encourage witness testimony, the general attitude remains that witnesses are subject to powerful personal interests and external pressures that cause them to bend the truth and lie. All non-notary witnesses' statements are viewed with great suspicion. Unless there is an independent means for confirming what is represented, such representations are very likely to be ignored or heavily discounted by the court.

12.17 EVIDENCE PRODUCED BY GOVERNMENT AGENCIES

Another important investigation technique (strategy actually) is to plan for government agencies to produce the evidence to the court. This also provides the inherent indicia of reliability that the court looks for in all evidence. For instance, in a counterfeit case, if the relevant governmental agency, such as the Administration for Industry and Commerce ("AIC"), can be persuaded to conduct a raid, it is in a party's best interest to work closely with the AIC to make sure it seizes and then stores as much relevant evidence as possible – especially documents. If the AIC (as opposed to a party) then produces the evidence to the court, its validity is practically unquestionable.

Besides the seizure of physical evidence and documents, AIC officials are also empowered to conduct investigations – which include the taking of witness statements. Working with the AIC, and other government agencies, to collect such statements prior to filing a court case can be an effective means for solidifying facts and eliminating possible bogus defences. The inability to conduct formal discovery prior to trial in China makes it nearly impossible to collect inconsistent statements for impeachment. However, with careful planning and a close working relationship with government officials, similar kinds of statements can be collected early on, which then limits an opponents' ability to 'spin' or even lie about the facts of the civil matter.

12.18 EVIDENCE PRESERVATION

In some circumstances, parties may apply *ex parte* to the court for the preservation of evidence.[3] This is the one notable pretrial discovery

---

3   Evidence preservation rules can be found in various laws. For instance, the Trademark Law of the People's Republic of China contains such a provision at Art 58; China's Civil Procedure Law contains such provisions at Arts 93–96 and 99; and finally the Provisions from the Supreme People's Court Concerning Evidence in Civil Matter contains such provisions at Arts 17–19.

device mentioned above. The required written application must include the following:

1. sufficient information identifying the person or entity holding the evidence;
2. the specific subject matter and scope of the application;
3. the relevance of the evidence for which the application is made and for which preservation is requested; and
4. the cause of the application, including a specific statement that the evidence is likely to be destroyed or hard to obtain, or the interested party cannot collect the evidence on its own for 'objective reasons'.

The phrase 'objective reasons' is not further defined. This allows for flexibility, which can be helpful in unusual circumstances where the judge is ultimately cooperative. It can also prove difficult in antagonistic situations where a judge can allege that no 'objective reason' was provided.

At least in trademark matters, an application to preserve evidence can be filed even prior to the initiation of formal proceedings, although such proceedings must follow within 15 days or the preservation order is discharged. Courts in trademark cases must rule on evidence preservation applications within 48 hours. In non-trademark matters, courts are not so constrained.

Where an evidence preservation order may cause a loss to the opponent, the court may require the applicant to provide a financial guarantee. The amount of the guarantee is not specified in the law, but typically an applicant should expect to post a guarantee equal in value to the material to be seized (and often in cash – although this is changing). Anecdotally, some courts have found guarantees sufficient where they are a small percentage of the total value – but this is the exception rather than the rule.

PRELIMINARY INJUNCTIONS 12.19

Beyond evidence preservation matters, affected parties may also apply *ex parte* for injunctions to immediately halt infringing or damaging acts. Such applications may be made even prior to the initiation of formal proceedings.

Similar to evidence preservation matters, preliminary injunction applications must be in writing and contain the following information:

1. sufficient information identifying the person or entity to be enjoined;
2. the specific subject matter and scope of the injunction; and

3. the cause of the application, including a specific statement that failure to promptly suspend the damaging activity will cause irreparable injury to the legitimate rights and interests of the applicant.

In addition to the above, the applicant must also show a reasonable probability of success on the merits and post a financial guarantee. The reasonable probability of success standard is for most Chinese judges very high – similar to the beyond a reasonable doubt standard found in the US. Once again, if possible, every effort should be made to make certain that the evidence supporting the pretrial injunction is collected in the presence of Chinese notaries or it can be independently verified through the review of photographs, audio or video tapes. As in evidence preservation matters discussed above, an applicant should expect to have to post a significant financial guarantee equal in value to the loss that might be suffered by the opposing party. This can prove to be a significant hurdle in many cases, especially since often the guarantee required is a cash bond. Once again, however, this practice seems to be changing.

12.20 THE *ZHI ZHENG* PROCESS

At the same time the court notifies the plaintiff it has accepted the case and the defendant of its duty to answer, it simultaneously gives the parties notice of their duty to exchange evidence before the trial. This evidence exchange process is called *zhi zheng*.[4] The parties may agree on when the evidence will be exchanged, but if they cannot agree, then the court will set a deadline. Typically the exchange deadline is very short. At present, it is usually the thirtieth day following the first notices to the parties.

On the evidence exchange deadline, the parties meet at court. The original evidence is tendered to the court and copies are provided to opposing parties. The court issues a receipt noting the date the evidence was produced, and the producing party then briefly introduces the evidence. The opposing parties are then allowed to briefly raise questions. Throughout this process the court takes notes. The official presiding over the exchange may be the trial judge, but it is often some other official within the court.

If evidence is not submitted during this *zhi zheng* process it cannot be later introduced and considered at trial unless it is new or rebuttal

---

4   Further information concerning the Zhi Zheng Process can be found in Paul J Schmidt, "A Review of China's New Civil Evidence Law", 2 Pacific Rim Law & Policy Journal, 291–313 (March 2003).

evidence or if all the parties agree to allow it in. New evidence is evidence discovered after the exchange deadline or evidence that could not have been produced earlier due to 'objective reasons'. Unfortunately, the phrase 'objective reasons' is not further defined.

As discussed later in greater detail, trials in the People's Republic of China are very short usually lasting less than one or two days – even in complex matters. In large measure this is because much of the evidence review occurs during the *zhi zheng* process and thereafter by the court outside of the parties' presence. If the trial judge is not present during the exchange, it is even more critical that the parties carefully weigh their actions and statements during the exchange. The notes taken by the attending official are likely to play an important role in the court's review. It is important that the significance of the evidence be stated succinctly and clearly by the introducing party. Objections must be equally well thought out and delivered. Rambling statements are likely not to be recorded clearly and therefore are not likely to influence or help direct the review.

Court of First Instance

TRIAL PROCEDURE   12.21

Civil cases are tried in public unless state secrets, business secrets, or issues of personal privacy are involved. Simple cases may be heard by a single judge, but that rarely happens in intellectual property cases. Typically, the case is heard before a collegiate bench consisting of an odd number of judges (normally three). Parties are entitled to apply for the withdrawal of any judge in the panel or other court personnel that are involved in the case.

Under the PRC's Civil Procedure Law, judges consider evidence in the following order: (a) presentation of statements by the parties; (b) testimony by witnesses and the reading of statements by absentee witnesses; (c) presentation of documentary and material evidence; (d) reading of expert witness reports; and (e) reading of inspection reports.[5]

Following the presentation of evidence, the next trial stage is the debate. Here each party first gives a statement of its view. Following that, they then debate with each other, often with continued questioning by the court. To conclude, each party is allowed to present its final opinion concerning the case.[6]

---

5   Civil Procedure Law of the People's Republic of China, Art 124.
6   *Ibid*, Art 127.

Once the debate has ended, the court is required to issue its judgement without delay – unless a mediated settlement is still possible.[7] In general, courts are required to conclude cases within six months from the date they are docketed.[8]

12.22 JUDGEMENT

Under Article 134 of the Civil Procedure Law, a judgement must be announced publicly by the court. It must detail the subject matter of the action, the claims, the facts in dispute, the facts and reasons for the judgement, the assessment of court costs, the appropriate court for filing an appeal and the time limit for filing.

With respect to judgements entered in trademark infringement cases, the court will normally order the immediate cessation of the infringing acts, compensation for damages and a public apology.

Pursuant to the Civil Procedure Law, the People's Court should conclude a domestic case within 6 months after docketing the case, or 12 months where an extension of the period is necessary. Further extension is allowed, but must be reported to the People's Court at the next highest level for approval. With respect to foreign-related cases, no such time limits are provided for by the law.

12.23 DAMAGES: THREE FORMULAS

In trademark matters, damages are awarded to injured parties under three different formulas: (a) infringer benefits; (b) losses suffered; and (c) statutory damages. An injured party may elect between formulas one and two, but only the court can impose formula three – statutory damages. An injured party can request statutory damages but it remains at the court's discretion.

The **infringer benefits formula** is calculated by multiplying the number of infringing product sales by the unit of profit for each sale. Where it is difficult to ascertain the unit of profit, an injured party's own profit margin may be applied. So, for instance, if a party knows that an infringer sold 10,000 infringing products, and the profit for each is US$5, the total damage award should be US$50,000. The calculation is simple enough, but the problem with it is that, most often, it is impossible to ascertain infringing product sales numbers. Unless there is careful planning early on to seize documents and records containing these numbers, it is generally impossible to apply this formula.

---

7   *Ibid*, Art 128.
8   *Ibid*, Art 135.

The **losses suffered formula** is calculated by reference to the reductions in sales suffered by an affected party by the infringement, or it can be calculated, once again, by multiplying the number of infringing product sales by the unit of profit for the genuine product. So, under this scenario, if a party knows that his or her sales were reduced by 10,000 because of the infringement, and the profit for each sale is US$5.00, the total damage award should be, once again, US$50,000. The main difficulty with this formula is the problem in showing a causal connection between the sales lost and the infringement. The defending party can always claim that the drop was caused by other factors such as a poor economy, bad weather or a general decline in sales.

Finally, if it is still difficult to determine damages, the court can elect to award up to RMB500,000 (US$60,000) in **statutory damages**. Factors that a court should consider in making such an award include the nature of the infringement, the period and consequences of the infringement, the reputation of the trademark, the amount of trademark licensing royalties, the types, periods and scope of trademark licenses for the mark, and the reasonable expenses incurred in stopping the infringement.

EXPENSE AWARDS

12.24

In calculating any damage award, a People's Court is required to include "the reasonable expenses incurred by a party in stopping the infringement." The Supreme People's Court has interpreted this phrase as including the reasonable expenses of the rights holder or an appointed agent in investigating and collecting evidence. Awarding of such expenses is mandatory, according to the Supreme People's Court. However, an award of attorney's fees is discretionary.

Court of Second Instance

CASE REVIEW PREFERRED OVER CASE FINALITY

12.25

Every country's legal system must strike a balance between case finality and case review. Stated one way, how often and how easy is it to appeal an alleged error made in a court below? Stated another way, at what point is the decision final, and thus able to be relied upon by the victorious party? In the PRC, it can take a great amount of time for a judgement to become final and non-appealable. First, a dissatisfied party can appeal the matter to the court of second instance. Even a decision from this body is not necessarily final because it too can be amended or set aside through the trial supervision procedure also discussed below.

12.26 PERIOD FOR FILING AN APPEAL

A party dissatisfied with either a judgement or a written order from a court of first instance has the right to appeal to the court at the next higher level. The period for filing an appeal against a judgement is 15 days from service. The period for filing an appeal against an order is 10 days from service. For a foreign party (who has no domicile within the PRC), both periods are 30 days.

12.27 SCOPE OF TRIAL

Chinese law does not restrict the court of second instance to matters of law only. Appellate courts review matters of both facts and law. New evidence that was not presented in the court of first instance can nevertheless be reviewed in a court of second instance. Fortunately, however, the Supreme People's Court has restricted the definition of 'new evidence' to essentially that evidence discovered only after the conclusion of the first instance trial.[9] Further, new claims will not be admitted in the court of second instance, except by the parties' mutual agreement.

In the typical case, the scope of trial at the second instance is limited to those issues appealed. Nevertheless, courts are empowered to review other matters outside the appeal if necessary.

12.28 PROCEDURE

The procedures at the court of second instance are generally identical to those procedures at the court of first instance – with a few exceptions. For example, second instance cases cannot be heard by a single judge, which may have been possible in the court of first instance.

In general, judgements in second instance trials are to be delivered within three months from the date of appeal, but this period can be extended and it is not applicable to foreign-related cases.

12.29 JUDGEMENT

After trying a case of second instance, the court may dispose of the appeal in three ways:

1. reject the appeal and affirm the original judgement;
2. amend the original judgement by issuing a new judgement; and

---

9 Several Provisions of the Supreme People's Court on Evidence in Civil Actions, Art 41.

3. set aside the original judgement and remand the case back to the lower court for retrial.

Trial Supervision Procedure

APPLICATION FOR RETRIAL BY A PARTY 12.30

If a party is dissatisfied with a final judgement or written order made by a court of second instance, and it can show there is error, the party can apply to either the same court or to the court at the next higher level for a retrial. However, execution of the judgement or order will not be suspended.

Application for a retrial made by a party must be submitted within two years of the effective date of the judgement or written order.

The court that accepts the retrial application will review the case. If the judgement or written order is found to be in error, the court will order a new trial. Execution of the original judgement or order is suspended.

There is no time limit set on the reviewing court. Normally the process is lengthy, and only a few cases are ever retried under this provision.

RETRIAL INITIATED BY THE COURT OR PROCURATORATES' OFFICE 12.31

Apart from the party concerned, the court that made the decision and higher-level courts may launch a retrial if they find definite error in an earlier decision. However, such events are extremely rare. A high level People's Procuratorate can also lodge a protest to a judgement or order. Such protest commences a retrial.

DEBATES 12.32

This trial supervision procedure has been the subject of much debate over the past few years. Many legal professionals and scholars believe this procedure undermines the certainty and authority of court decisions, and contributes to an already aggravated court workload. But others in favour of the retrial system think it is a necessary procedure to correct mistakes.

Enforcement of Judgements

TIME PERIOD AND RESPONSIBLE AUTHORITY 12.33

There is a separate department called the Execution Office or the Execution Division in every court at each level. This department is responsible for the enforcement of court decisions.

A winning party has up to one year to apply for execution of a court judgement by a People's Court. However, in cases where both parties are legal persons or other organisations, a six-month limit applies. The original court of first instance is responsible for enforcement of the decision. If the object of enforcement is located outside the jurisdiction of the original court, the People's Court in that location may be entrusted to enforce the decision. Courts entrusted to enforce a decision are required to commence execution within 15 days of receipt of a written request from the respective court.

12.34 SETTLEMENT AGREEMENT DURING EXECUTION

A settlement agreement post judgement is acceptable if the parties become reconciled on their own initiative. But if either party fails to fulfil the settlement agreement, the People's Court may, at the request of the other party, resume the execution of the original judgement.

12.35 NON-PARTY'S OBJECTION

During execution, a person that is not party to the action has the right to raise an objection. Such objection may be referred, at the discretion of the execution officer, to the president of the court. Based upon the reasonable objection of a non-party, the court may grant a stay of execution.

12.36 COMPULSORY MEASURES

In executing a judgement, the execution officer notifies the relevant party to perform within a stipulated time period. If a party fails to comply with the judgement, measures for compulsory enforcement will be applied. The compulsory measures include: (a) freezing and transferring a deposit; (b) withholding or withdrawing the income; (c) sealing up, distaining, freezing, selling by public auction, or selling the property. Before such compulsory measures are taken, a notice for assistance in execution will be issued to relevant organisations if necessary. An organisation that fails to fulfil its assistance obligations may be fined and the responsible person may be disciplined.

JUDICIAL REVIEW

12.37 JUDICIAL REVIEW OF TRAB DECISIONS

Judicial review for decisions made by the Trademark Review and Adjudication Board ("TRAB") is a new regime introduced by the 2001 amendments to the Trademark Law. In the past, decisions issued by the TRAB were final. Now a party that is dissatisfied with a TRAB decision may appeal to the People's Court for review. In such matters, the TRAB is always the defendant. The governing law is the Administrative Procedure Law (effective October 1990) and relevant judicial interpretations issued by the Supreme People's Court. In general, an administrative trial is similar to that of a civil trial.

PARTIES INVOLVED

12.38

All decisions made by the TRAB can be reviewed. With respect to decisions concerning trademark applications, only two parties will be involved – the complaining trademark applicant and the defending TRAB. For decisions regarding trademark oppositions and cancellations, since these concern disputes between two competing parties besides the TRAB, the other party concerned will be informed by court and allowed to participate in the litigation as third party.

JURISDICTION

12.39

Judicial review of TRAB decisions is the exclusive domain of the No 1 Beijing Intermediate People's Court. Any party, either the plaintiff, the TRAB or a third party (if any) can appeal to this court for review.

There are two divisions within the No 1 Beijing Intermediate People's Court that may hear the review, namely the Administrative Division and the No 5 Civil Division (also known as the Intellectual Property Division).

JUDGEMENT

12.40

The time period for concluding a judicial review is generally three months after docketing the case. The corresponding period for an appeal of the review is two months. Both periods are extendable. However, if a foreign party is involved, there is no such time limitation.

Pursuant to Article 54 of the Administrative Procedure Law, the reviewing court will either: (a) affirm the TRAB decision; or (b) set aside the TRAB decision and order it to issue a new decision. The court is not allowed to directly alter the TRAB decision. The court can do so only when it reviews a punishment decision that is obviously unfair.

CHAPTER 13

DOMAIN NAMES AND THE INTERNET

DEFINING DOMAIN NAMES

OVERVIEW

13.1

The PRC was officially linked to the internet in 1994. Three years later, the PRC had its first domain name regulations. In the same year, the China Internet Network Information Center ("CNNIC") conducted a survey and reported 620,000 internet users in China. A similar CNNIC survey done in July 2003 reported a total of 68 million PRC internet users, a hundred-fold leap from the figure reported six years ago.

Currently, domain names in the PRC are governed by the Measures for the Administration of China Internet Domain Names, effective from 30 September 2002 ("Administration Measures"), and the Detailed Implementing Rules of the CNNIC for the Registration of Domain Names ("Registration Rules"), effective from 1 December 2002. The Administration Measures prevail in the event of inconsistency with other regulations.

Domain names need to be registered before they can be used. The Administration Measures and the Registration Rules no longer specifically require a local presence and a local server for applicants to register a .cn (the country code for China) domain name. In other words, foreign entities, regardless of their geographical location, can now also apply for second level and third level .cn domain names. The total number of registered ".cn" domain names jumped from 4066 to a staggering 250,651 between 1997 and 2003. About half of all ".cn" registrations in 2003 were for ".coms and most registrations were in Beijing.

Trademark owners often register the primary part of their domain names as their trademarks. Registrations are based on a first-come-first-served basis. In other words, a domain name cannot be registered if the same name has previously been registered. The rapid increase in domain name registrations also includes registrations by unrelated third parties who pre-empt the trademark owner in registering their trademarks as domain names, in anticipation of selling the domain names back to the trademark owner for a profit. These unconscionable entities are called cybersquatters. Trademark owners who do not wish to pay off the cybersquatter may file a complaint with a domain name dispute resolution provider to have the domain name transferred.

In the first part of this chapter, the concept of domain names in China will be introduced – what they are and the different types. Then domain name registration, the relationship between domain names and trademarks, cybersquatting and domain name dispute resolution will be discussed. Next, the other methods in which intellectual property rights may be affected by the use of the internet will be considered – such as framing, linking, caching and internet keywords. The second part of this chapter traces the development of domain name dispute resolution in the PRC with a summary of landmark cases and their significance.

13.2 WHAT IS A DOMAIN NAME?

A domain name is an alphanumeric name that corresponds to an Internet Protocol address. An Internet Protocol address is a routing address on the Internet, made up of a string of numbers. For example, the domain name www.internic.net corresponds to the Internet Protocol address of 192.0.34.161. Domain names are used because they are easier for humans to remember than a string of numbers.

Domain names consist of a sequence of letters or numbers separated by dots. The group of letters after the last dot is called the top level domain ("TLD"). Moving backwards, the penultimate group of letters preceding the last dot is the second level domain ("SLD") and so on. For example, in the domain name www.abc.com, '.com' is the TLD, and 'abc' is the SLD.

13.3 PRC DOMAIN NAMES

A "ccTLD" is a country code top-level domain name. It generally consists of two letters representing the name of a country, territory or other geographical location. For example .cn represents China. In the PRC, .cn SLDs are divided into 'category domain names' and 'administrative division domain names'.

The different category domain names and their meanings are illustrated in the table below.

Table 1: Category domain names

Domain Name Type	Meaning
.com.cn	Enterprise of industry, business, finance etc.
.net.cn	Network information centre or network operation centre
.org.cn	Non-profit organisation
.gov.cn	Government
.ac.cn	Institution of science and research
.edu.cn	Institution of education
.cn	China
.aadn	Administration area domain name

There are 34 .cn administrative division domain names, which are applicable to PRC's provinces, autonomous regions, municipalities directly under the central government and special administrative regions. These are:

AH – Anhui Province
BJ – Beijing Municipality
CQ – Chongqing Municipality
FJ – Fujian Province
GD – Guangdong Province
GS – Gansu Province
GX – Guangxi Zhuang Autonomous Region
GZ – Guizhou Province
HA – Henan Province
HB – Hubei Province
HE – Hebei Province
HI – Hainan Province
HK – Hong Kong
HL – Heilongjiang Province
HN – Hunan Province
JL – Jilin Province
JS – Jiangsu Province
JX – Jiangxi Province
LN – Liaoning Province

CHINESE-LANGUAGE DOMAIN NAMES   13.4

Chinese-language domain names contain Chinese characters, and may also contain roman letters, numerals or hyphens. Chinese-language domain names can be registered in both simplified and traditional

Chinese characters. Simplified characters are used in mainland China whereas traditional characters are used in both Taiwan and Hong Kong. Registration in one version will permit visitors who input the other version to access the same site. It will also block third parties from registering the other version. Visitors may access sites using either of the prevailing input methods (GB or Big5).

There are now six separate and competing registries aiming to facilitate registration and use of Chinese-language domain names. It is uncertain how many of these six will survive in the future, therefore trademark owners should consider filing for domain names containing their Chinese-language trademarks under each of the six systems because names registered in each system can ultimately be linked to one Chinese-language website.

Note also that CNNIC uses different protocols and software from the other registries, and Chinese-language domain names registered with CNNIC are not interchangeable with those registered in other registries. For example, the name '大友.公司' (pronounced *da you.gong si*, corresponding to *da you*.com) is not interchangeable with '大友.com' (pronounced *da you*.com), and companies should register both '大友.公司' and '大友.com'.

13.5 WELL-KNOWN MARKS AND NAMES

According to the amended Trademark Law, no mark, for the same or similar product, which is a copy, limitation, or translation of another's well-known mark not registered in China, and is likely to cause confusion, shall be registered or used. Furthermore, any mark of a different or dissimilar product, which is a copy, imitation or translation of another's well-known mark registered in China, and is so misleading to the general public that the interest of the well-known mark registrant is likely to be harmed, shall not be registered or used. While these provisions are regarded as directly applicable to curb cybersquatting, China at present does not have an anti-dilution law to protect famous marks against dilution.

Another piece of legislation that has been used primarily to address cybersquatting practices in China is the Anti-unfair Competition Law of China ("UCL"). Adopted in September 1993, the UCL is aimed at promoting competition and protecting consumers by establishing principles of fairness and good faith, and by adhering to commonly accepted business ethics. Under Article 5 of the UCL, a business operator is prohibited from exploring any of the following illegitimate means to harm its competitor:

1. counterfeiting a registered trademark of another person;

2. using a distinctive name, package, or design of a famous product without authorisation, or using the name, package or design similar to that of a famous product which causes confusion about the product or misleads purchasers;

3. using the name of another person or enterprise without authorisation, thereby causing the public to mistake its product for that of said person or enterprise; or

4. forging or counterfeiting product quality marks such as authentication marks or 'famous and excellent' product marks on its product, making a false and misleading representation of the quality of its product, or forging origin of its product.

CNNIC has reserved well-known Chinese marks and names, as set out in the PRC Trademark Office's List of Major Trademarks which are to Receive Nationwide Protection, for registration by their owners with '公司' ('.com' in Chinese) and '网络' ('.net' in Chinese) suffixes. This practice of reserving Chinese domain names was challenged in court in the ALIBABA Chinese-language domain name case. CNNIC has, as of November 2001, stopped this practice, and adopted another practice which has similar effects. CNNIC now requires applicants of such domain names to show evidence that the applicants have rights to the domain names before registration.

Registration

FRAMEWORK

13.6

Protection for .cn domain names is generally through registration. The PRC's domain name registration system follows a first-to-file rule, that is, the first applicant to file an application will pre-empt all later applicants. Although registration of domain names incorporating third party names or marks is prohibited, in practice, CNNIC does not check this prior to allowing registration.

The PRC Ministry of Information Industry ("MII") is in charge of the administration of internet domain names in China. The setting up of domain name root servers and the establishment of domain name root server operators in the PRC must be authorised by the MII. It also oversees domain name registration services, and is responsible for the international coordination of domain names.

The operation and administration of the ".cn" ccTLD and the Chinese domain name system is managed by the China Internet Network Information Center ("CNNIC"), a non-profit organisation. CNNIC is also responsible for "IP address distribution, autonomous system codes distribution, and so on", and provides registration services for Chinese domain names (see www.cnnic.org.cn).

13.7 REGISTRARS

Domain name registration and related services are provided by registrars accredited by CNNIC. To date, 23 registrars have been accredited, 21 of them located in mainland China, one in Hong Kong – Chinese Domain Name Corporation, and one in the United States – NeuStar.

13.8 APPLICATION FOR DOMAIN NAME REGISTRATION

The applicant for a domain name must be an organisation that has been lawfully registered and is independently capable of bearing civil liability. The applicant may be from within or outside the PRC.

The Administration Measures provide that domain name registration applicants must abide by PRC State laws, administrative regulations and rules as regards the internet and observe the regulations relating to the registration of domain names formulated by the domain name registration administrator (ie CNNIC). Applicants must also provide true, accurate, and complete domain name registration information. A domain name registrar is given the power to cancel a registration if the domain name registration information submitted by the domain name owner is untruthful, inaccurate, or incomplete.

When applying to register a domain name, an applicant can deliver its domain name application form and submit its registration to an appointed domain name registrar and execute a domain name registration agreement with the registrar via online registration, e-mail, etc.

An application for the registration of a domain name must include the following particulars:

1. the domain name applied for;
2. the host names and IP addresses of the primary domain name server and secondary domain name server;
3. the name, person in charge, industry, correspondence address, postal code, e-mail address, telephone number and facsimile number of, and certification information on, the unit which is the domain name owner; and
4. the names, units, correspondence addresses, postal codes, e-mail addresses, telephone numbers and facsimile numbers of the contact persons for technical aspects, administration and payment of fees in respect of the domain name and the person handling the application for the domain name.

In the domain name registration agreement, the applicant must warrant that:

1. it will abide by relevant internet laws and regulations;

2. it will abide by the Measures for the Administration of China Internet Domain Names and other relevant regulations of the competent authorities;
3. it will comply with such relevant regulations formulated by CNNIC as the Detailed Implementing Rules for the Registration of Domain Names, Measures for the Resolution of Domain Name Disputes, etc, and amended versions thereof; and
4. the domain name registration information it submits is true, accurate and complete.

Domain name registrars are given the power to delete domain names that violate the relevant regulations. In practice, however, domain name registrars do not normally exercise this power. If a domain name applicant or owner is dissatisfied with the domain name registrars' deletion of its domain name, it may petition the authority in charge of domain names for a review.

When applying to register a third level domain name under the second level domain name '.gov', the applicant must submit the following written documentation:

1. a domain name registration form bearing the applicants official seal; and
2. relevant documentation certifying that the applicant is a government organisation.

Each item of information entered in domain name registration application forms by applicants must be included in the publicly searchable database and other publications by the domain name registration administrator or domain name registrar, unless the non-disclosure thereof is expressly stated by the applicant. The data also forms part of the search services offered to internet subscribers by the domain name registration administrator or the domain name registrar.

Applicants need not have corresponding roman-letter domain names for the purpose of filing Chinese-language domain names.

REGISTRATION ISSUES 13.9

It is possible to register an unlimited number of domain names. The CNNIC has no obligation to check potential infringements. As registration is on a first-come-first-served basis, PRC enterprise names or trademarks registered by others cannot be registered. This is why cybersquatting (considered in the next section) is a big issue to trademark owners. Nor does the CNNIC have a mediating or adjudicating role regarding domain name disputes. 'Oppositions' are available only during the initial 30-day application period.

13.10 CAN DOMAIN NAMES BE ASSIGNED?

A domain name registrant may assign its .cn domain name by submitting to the domain name registrar a domain name assignment application form that bears the applicant's official seal or that has been notarised. Upon approval by the domain name registrar, the assignment is effected and the domain name made available for use.

13.11 TRADEMARK VERSUS DOMAIN NAMES

Although one might reasonably expect a domain name consisting of a trademark to be associated with the owner of that trademark, sometimes this is not the case because domain names differ from trademarks in both their nature and the rights they confer.

Each domain name is unique and can only be allocated to one entity in the world. Therefore, unlike trademarks where it is possible for different owners to register and use identical trademarks, only one unique domain name can be registered under each TLD, regardless of the registrant's location or business type. Note, however, that it is possible for the same name to be registered by different entities under different top-level domains. Domain names, per se, do not attract rights that can be protected. Under the existing ccTLD registration systems (which differ from one country to another), they are granted quite liberally, on a first-come-first-served basis. Furthermore, what humans may consider as confusingly similar variations of a domain name can coexist because of the way computers interpret alphanumeric names.

Cybersquatting

13.12 DEFINITION

Despite the difference between domain names and trademarks, domain name disputes often arise from a third party taking a well-known trademark or name and registering it as a domain name with a view to selling it back to the trademark owner for a profit, using it to increase hits to the registrant's site, or using it to ride on the goodwill built up by the well-known marks. Such practices are known as cybersquatting.

A lot of websites are found by intuitively guessing the addresses. One of the first addresses to guess is the name or house mark of the company. If the domain name registered by a cybersquatter uses such a name or mark or its shorthand version, customers and clients who use the name or house mark trying to find the website of the company may be misdirected to the cybersquatter's site.

Typosquatting, a variation of cybersquatting, is the bad faith registration of domain names that are intentional misspellings of distinctive or famous names.

IDENTIFYING CYBERSQUATTERS 13.13

Trademark owners can use the WhoIs system to identify cybersquatters because an active SLD registered with the CNNIC can be located on the WhoIs system, which provides the following information:

1. domain name;
2. Internet Protocol address;
3. host names of the primary and secondary name servers for the domain name;
4. identity of the registrar;
5. dates on which the domain name was created and when it expires;
6. details of the registrant; and
7. details of the administrative and technical contacts.

Note, however, that it is not possible to search by the name of the registrant. This poses a problem to trademark owners, given that one of the key elements in proving the bad faith of a registrant is the establishment of a pattern of cybersquatting by that registrant. Additionally, WhoIs services generally do not provide for Boolean[1] searching. Trademark owners are therefore not able to easily search for domain names held by unauthorised third parties that are similar but not identical to trademarks in which they have rights.

REMEDIES FOR CYBERSQUATTING 13.14

The activities of cybersquatters have led trademarks owners and others prejudiced by their activities to take action to establish their rights in respect of the domain names registered by cybersquatters. Domain name disputes can either be initiated in the courts or by the dispute resolution procedures provided for in the contract between the domain name owner and the registrar.

The only remedy available as a result of dispute resolution is the cancellation or transfer of the subject domain name. Where a plaintiff is seeking more than that (eg damages), he or she must bring an action for trademark infringement or passing off in the courts.

---

1 Boolean searching, named after British mathematician George Boole, is a method of searching the internet database according to logical relationships among search terms. Boolean logic consists of three main logical operators, 'or', 'and' and 'not'. For example, a Boolean search for 'internet and crime' would display all sites containing both the word 'internet' and the word 'crime'; a Boolean search for 'internet or crime' would display all sites containing the word 'internet' or the word 'crime'; and a Boolean search for 'internet not crime' would display sites containing only the word 'internet' and not the word 'crime'.

13.15 PENDING APPLICATION

If a pirate application is discovered (such as through monitoring CNN-IC's website) prior to the domain name being registered, an objection may be raised with CNNIC, supported by evidence such as copies of the relevant PRC Trademark Registration Certificates of the third level domain name. CNNIC has rejected quite a number of pirate applications through this informal opposition system.

13.16 AFTER REGISTRATION

Once a domain name is registered, CNNIC however refuses to be involved in disputes between the pirate and the right-holder.

13.17 INVESTIGATION

A trademark owner whose mark has been filed as a domain name by a third party without authorisation may wish to investigate the third party. For example, if evidence can be obtained of the third party demanding a ransom for the return of the domain name, or the third party intentionally passing itself off as the trademark owner through the use of the domain name, a strong case can be built against the third party.

There are a number of PRC and Hong Kong investigation firms that offer investigation services with respect to intellectual property infringement. Legally speaking, investigation, including investigation of cybersquatting, in the PRC requires government approval. PRC courts may refuse to admit evidence collected outside the legitimate channels.

If the investigator does not have experience with the cyber world, the right-holder will need to train the investigator.

The types of permissible evidence that litigants may present to court are documentary evidence, physical evidence, audio-visual material, live testimony of witnesses, statements by interested parties, and expert opinions.

A PRC court should take legal acts, legal facts and documents notarised pursuant to legal procedures as a basis for ascertaining facts, except where contrary evidence is sufficient to invalidate the notary certification. Notarisation by a PRC notary public is not only a verification of the authenticity but also of the legality of the subject matter being notarised.

Evidence for court proceedings should preferably be notarised if possible. This means involving a PRC notary public in the process of evidence collection, such as having a PRC notary public accompany the investigator on the investigation.

Investigations may also uncover other infringing evidence. For example, if the investigation shows that the infringer is using a mark similar to the trademark of the right-holder on its products, a raid may be organised against the infringer and such information could be used in support of the domain name case against the infringer.

ENFORCEMENT 13.18

The right-holder may try to negotiate with the cybersquatter for deregistration of the domain name (usually by paying the cybersquatter off). If negotiation fails, the right-holder may lodge a complaint under the Procedural Rules for the Measures for the China Internet Network Information Centre for the Resolution of Domain Name Disputes, which are a domain name dispute resolution mechanism similar to the Internet Corporation for Assigned Names and Numbers' Uniform Domain Name Dispute Resolution Policy. Rulings under these Rules relate solely to change of information concerning the ownership of the disputed domain name. If a right-holder seeks further remedies, it may commence a court action.

Consultation

If the right-holder wishes to resolve the dispute without resorting to legal actions, or the domain name dispute resolution mechanism, it may wish to send warning letters to and / or meet with the cybersquatter and ask the cybersquatter to stop the infringement and deregister or assign the domain name. Well-known mark owners have paid cybersquatters in order to take back their domain names. Such actions were particularly evident prior to the availability of the domain name dispute resolution mechanism.

WHAT CAN BE DONE IF A DOMAIN NAME IS PIRATED? 13.19

Domain name piracy is rampant in the PRC. One notorious PRC cybersquatter was reported to have registered 10 per cent of all .cn domain names, among which many were pirate registration of internationally well-known marks and names, including ikea.com.cn, olay.com.cn, whisper.com.cn, dupont.com.cn, amex.com.cn, bacardi.com.cn, boss.com.cn, cartier.com.cn, carlsberg.com.cn, hertz.com.cn, polo.com.cn, and rolex.com.cn. In a count taken on 18 December 1999, the cybersquatter was found to have registered 3,510 .cn domain names.

In 1999, when Procter & Gamble applied to CNNIC for registration of whisper.com.cn as a domain name, the application was denied because the domain name was already registered in August 1998 by a Chinese company named Beijing CINet Information Co Ltd ("Guowang"). It was also found that from 1996 to 1998, Guowang registered with CNNIC more than 2,000 domain names, many of which were for globally famous trademarks and service marks, including: 'amex', 'bacardi', 'boss', 'carlsberg', 'ikea', 'cola', 'dunhill', 'hertz', 'lancome', 'lv', 'marriott', 'omega', 'phillips', 'polo', 'rolex'. The first domain name dispute was heard in a people's court in Beijing in April 1998, and as of July 2001, there had been more than forty domain name related cases litigated in the people's courts in Beijing, Shanghai and other cities. We will consider these cases in "Domain Name Cases" at paras 13.46 – 13.55 below.

Domain Name Dispute Resolution

13.20 APPLICABLE RULES

To implement the Administration Measures, three sets of rules were issued on 25 September 2002, including the Measures of the China Internet Network Information Centre for the Resolution of Domain Name Dispute, ("CNNIC Measures"), the Procedural Rules for the Measures of the China Internet Network Information Center for the Resolution of Domain Name Disputes, ("CNNIC Procedure Rules") and the CIETAC Supplemental Rules relating to the CNNIC Domain Name Dispute Resolution Policy ("CIETAC Supplemental Rules"). These are now the main legislation governing disputes involving the registration or use of .cn ccTLDs and Chinese domain names. The Domain Name Dispute Resolution Centre ("DNDRC"), established by the China International Economic and Trade Arbitration Commission ("CIETAC"), is currently the sole domain name dispute resolution provider for .cn ccTLDs.

Any organisation or individual that feels that the domain name registered by a third party conflicts with their legitimate rights and interests may file a complaint with a dispute resolution institution appointed by CNNIC, including CIETAC and the Hong Kong International Arbitration Centre ("HKIAC"). Note that the HKIAC has its own supplemental Rules to the CNNIC Domain Name Dispute Resolution Policy.

13.21 COMPLAINT REVIEWED BY A PANEL OF EXPERTS

After accepting a complaint, the dispute resolution institution organises a panel of one or three experts who have a thorough knowledge of the internet and its related laws, sound professional ethics and the ability to render the domain name dispute ruling in an independent and neutral manner to resolve the dispute. The dispute resolution institutions provide a list of the experts online from which complainants and respondents can select. The panel of experts renders a ruling within 14 days after the date of its formation.

If the complainant or the respondent believes that a member of the panel of experts has a material interest in the opposite party that could prejudice an impartial ruling in the case, the complainant or the respondent, as the case may be, can file a challenge against the relevant expert. The challenge must be filed with the dispute resolution institution, before the ruling in the dispute is rendered by the panel of experts, by stating the specific facts and grounds on which the challenge is based, and presenting evidence in support. The challenge is to be decided by the dispute resolution institution.

The language used in domain name dispute resolution procedures is Chinese, unless the complainant and the respondent agree otherwise or the panel of experts decides to adopt another language.

The complainant and the respondent are responsible for presenting evidence to support their assertions.

CRITERIA FOR COMPLAINANT'S SUCCESS 13.22

To succeed, the complainant must satisfy all three conditions below:

1. the disputed domain name is identical with or confusingly similar to the complainant's name or mark in which the complainant has civil rights or interests;
2. the disputed domain name holder has no right or legitimate interest in respect of the domain name or major part of the domain name; and
3. the disputed domain name holder has registered, or is using, the domain name in bad faith.

The owner of the disputed domain name is deemed to have registered or be using the domain name in bad faith if:

1. it registered or accepted the assignment of the domain name in order to sell, lease or otherwise transfer the same in order to obtain improper benefits;
2. it has on numerous occasions registered, as its own domain names, the names or marks in which third parties have legitimate rights and interests, so as to prevent such third parties from using those names or marks as domain names on the internet;
3. it has registered or acquired the domain name in order to damage the reputation of the complainant, disrupt its normal business activities or confuse the distinction with the complainant in order to mislead the public; or
4. it has otherwise acted in bad faith.

If a complainant disputes multiple domain names owned by the same complainant, the complainant or the respondent may petition the dispute resolution institution to consolidate all these disputes under one case to be handled by the same panel of experts. The panel of experts decides whether to consolidate the disputes.

The panel of experts renders its ruling on the dispute based on the facts and on evidence presented by the complainant and the respondent. The panel may either decide to uphold the complaint and rule to cancel the registered domain name or to transfer it to the complainant; or the panel may not uphold the complaint and rule to reject the complainant's complaint.

13.23 THE RULING

Prior to the filing of a complaint, while the dispute resolution procedure is pending or after the panel of experts has rendered its ruling, either party may institute legal proceedings in respect of the same dispute with a PRC court of the place where the CNNIC is located or, on the basis of an agreement, submit the same to a PRC arbitration institution. When a dispute resolution institution rules to cancel a domain name or to transfer the same to the complainant, the domain name registrar must implement the same within 10 days after the date of publication of the ruling. However, if within 10 days after the date of publication of the ruling the respondent submits valid proof that the competent judicial authority or arbitration institution has accepted the relevant dispute, implementation of the ruling of the dispute resolution institution must be suspended.

Depending on circumstances, the domain name registrar handles suspended rulings as follows:

1. if there is evidence to show that the parties to the dispute have reached a settlement, it must implement the settlement agreement;
2. if there is evidence to show that the relevant legal action or arbitration application has been rejected or withdrawn, it must implement the ruling of the dispute resolution institution; or
3. if the relevant judicial authority or arbitration institution has rendered a judgement or award that has become legally effective, it must implement the judgement or award.

The domain name owner may not apply to transfer or deregister a disputed domain name while the domain name resolution procedure is pending or within 10 days after the publication of the ruling, unless the transferee agrees in writing to be bound by the dispute resolution ruling.

AMENDMENTS TO DISPUTE RESOLUTION RULES · 13.24

CNNIC may amend the dispute resolution rules. The amended rules will not apply to domain name disputes submitted to dispute resolution institutions prior to the amendment. The amended rules will, however, automatically become part of the domain name registration agreements already existing between domain name owners and domain name registrars. If a domain name owner refuses to be bound by the dispute resolution rules or their amendments, it must notify its domain name registrar in good time. After receipt of the notice, the domain name registrar will continue to provide domain name services to it for 30 days. Thereafter, the relevant domain name will be deregistered.

Domain Name Litigation

DISPUTES ACCEPTABLE FOR LITIGATION · 13.25

Domain name disputes are also governed by the Explanation of the Supreme People's Court on Several Issues Concerning the Application of the Law to the Trial of Civil Dispute Cases Involving Computer Network Domain Names, effective from 24 July 2001 ("Domain Name Judicial Interpretation").

According to the Domain Name Judicial Interpretation, the causes of action for internet domain names and related cases acceptable by the courts include disputes concerning the registration and use of internet domain names. Moreover, according to a newspaper interview with a Judge of the Supreme People's Court, disputes concerning the registration and use of internet domain names include the following:

1. disputes between domain names and 'famous trademarks';
2. disputes between domain names and registered trademarks;
3. disputes between domain names and trade names;
4. disputes between domain names and special names for famous commodities;
5. disputes between domain names; and
6. disputes between domain names and names of individuals, etc.[2]

It is obvious that the Interpretation adopts an aggressive approach, including not only disputes between domain names and trademarks, but also other kinds of disputes concerning domain names that have emerged from use of cyberspace.

---

2 V Wang and R Cai, "Domain-Name Dispute-Resolution: Alternative Resolution vs Litigation", Davis Wright Tremaine LLP 2001, available at: http://www.dwt.com/practc/sha_chi/articles/domaindisputes.htm (visited 27 August 2002).

Disputes involving infringement of domain names are resolved by Intermediate People's Courts located either at of the 'place of infringement' or the place of the defendant's domicile. Where the place of the infringement and the place of the defendant's domicile are difficult to determine, the location of the equipment, such as a computer terminal through which the plaintiff discovered the domain name may be regarded as the place of the infringement.

13.26 CRITERIA FOR INFRINGEMENT OR UNFAIR COMPETITION

The defendant's registration and / or use, etc, of a domain name constitutes infringement or unfair competition if each of the following conditions are satisfied:

1. the civil rights or interests for which the plaintiff seeks protection are legitimate and effective;
2. the defendant's domain name or its main part constitutes a copy, imitation, translation or transliteration of a well-known mark of the plaintiff; or it is identical with or similar to a registered mark, domain name, etc, of the plaintiff to a degree sufficient to cause mistaken identification among the relevant public;
3. the defendant does not enjoy rights or interests to the domain name or its main part, and has no justification to register and / or use the domain name; and
4. the defendant's registration and / or use of the domain name is in 'bad faith'.

Courts are to find that 'bad faith' will be found to exist if the defendant's conduct constitutes any one of the following:

1. for commercial purposes, registering another's well-known mark as a domain name;
2. for commercial purposes, registering and / or using a domain name that is the same as or similar to the plaintiff's registered mark, domain name, etc, and deliberately causing confusion with the product and / or services provided by the plaintiff or with the plaintiff's website in order to mislead network users into accessing one's own website or another online site;
3. having offered to sell, lease or otherwise transfer the domain name at a high price and obtained unfair benefits;
4. neither using nor intending to use the domain name after registration, but intentionally preventing the registration of the domain name by the right-holder; or
5. otherwise involving bad faith.

If the defendant produces evidence that the domain name gained a certain degree of notoriety before the dispute occurred, and is distinct from the plaintiff's registered mark, domain name, etc, or if there are other circumstances sufficient to show that it has not acted in bad faith, the court is not required to determine that the defendant acted in bad faith.

The Domain Name Judicial Interpretation confirms that courts have the power to determine whether the marks involved were well known. Recently, however, the courts have been very conservative in making such determinations. See section on 'Domain Name Cases'.

The Supreme People's Court for the first time empowers People's Courts to determine whether a trademark is a well-known trademark upon the disputing parties' request.

Once a court finds infringement or unfair competition, it may order the defendant to cease the infringement and / or deregister the domain name, or, at the request of the plaintiff, order that the domain name be registered and used by the plaintiff. If the conduct has caused actual damage to the holder of the rights, the court may order the defendant to pay damages.

DOMAIN NAME JUDICIAL INTERPRETATION   13.27

The Domain Name Judicial Interpretation has a significant influence on domain name disputes in China. First, the Domain Name Judicial Interpretation takes into consideration disputes regarding internet domain names other than domain name / trademark conflicts. It classifies the content for People's Courts to determine bad faith, and well-known marks. Awards for damages may be granted if the rightful owner has so requested. This will discourage cybersquatting, registering another's trademark as domain names, and unfair competition activities. However, courts still lack the discretionary powers to award damages to actively discourage cybersquatting and other infringement acts.

FRAMING, LINKING AND CACHING

DEFINITIONS   13.28

A link is an embedded electronic address (or HTML tag) which allows users of one website to jump to another website. There are two types of linking: external links and internal links.

Internal linking is also termed framing. This allows an internet user to visit a website while viewing the content of a second website within a smaller frame. This often obscures the URL and some of the content on the framed site.

Caching is the temporary storage of website material on a local network to reduce the delay in accessing the website.

13.29 ISSUES

There is potential for copyright infringement from linking, framing and caching.

The content of the linked / framed sites are reproduced and distributed through linking and framing, placing burdens on traffic to the linked / framed websites and confusing internet users as to the sponsorship or source of the linked or framed content.

Caching involves copying the content of the cached sites and infringes the following copyrights:

1. The right to copy or reproduce
2. The right to publicly distribute
3. The right to public performance
4. The right to digital performance
5. The right of transmission
6. The right to access

Harm done to the cached websites includes: providing outdated information to internet users which is especially an issue with time-sensitive materials; hindering the site owner's ability to keep track of hits, hence affecting advertising; and rendering a loss of control of the website.

INTERNET KEYWORDS

13.30 WHAT ARE INTERNET KEYWORDS?

Internet keywords refer to websites made up of Chinese characters, English letters (A–Z, a–z, without distinguishing capitalisation), numbers (0–9) or denotations (-, !), and can have a maximum of 31 characters. Each component is regarded as a character.

Internet keywords lead customers and clients to the websites of companies as they are essentially domain names without any suffixes. For example, whereas abc.com.cn is a domain name, 'ABC' may be an internet keyword. The 'ABC' internet keyword may be set to point to ABC Co Ltd's website so that when an internet user types 'ABC' at the Uniform Resource Locator ("URL") bar of the Internet Explorer of his or her computer, the relevant search engine will take the user to ABC Co Ltd's website at abc.com.cn.

Internet keywords are easier to remember than domain names and should enable easier access by internet users to websites. Currently, however, the technology with respect to internet keywords is not yet up to standard and internet keywords are not very user friendly.

Internet keywords may not contain information that:

1. contradicts the basic principles of the PRC Constitution;
2. compromises PRC State security, discloses PRC State secrets, incites the subversion of PRC State Power or damages PRC national unity;
3. harms the reputation or interest of the PRC State;
4. incites ethnic hatred or ethnic discrimination or damages inter-ethnic unity;
5. undermines PRC State religious policy or propagates evil cults or feudal superstitions;
6. disseminates rumours, disturbs the social order or aims to destabilise society;
7. disseminates obscene or pornographic information or information on gambling, violence, murder or terror or incites the commission of crimes;
8. insults or slanders a third party or infringes upon the lawful rights and interests of a third party;
9. contains other information that is prohibited by laws or administrative regulations.

Internet keywords may be assigned and the assignment may be recorded with the registrar with which the internet keyword was maintained.

INTERNET KEYWORD REGULATIONS 13.31

The major regulations governing internet keywords in the PRC include the Measures for the Registration of Internet Keywords ("IR Registration Measures") and the Measures for the Resolution of Internet Keyword Disputes ("IR DR Measures") (both effective from 4 August 2001), and the Measures for the Designation of Internet Keyword Registrars.

INTERNET KEYWORD REGISTRATION 13.32

To make use of internet keywords, they must be registered with internet keyword registrars. At the present time, there is no one single and uniform system for the administration and registration of internet keywords. For example, CNNIC, CommonName and Netpia are different systems for the administration and registration of internet keywords.

Furthermore, as the technology is not yet up to standard, the internet user needs to have the relevant version of Internet Explorer and the relevant software, in order to use internet keywords. The internet user can usually download the required software from the website of the relevant internet keyword registrar. Such services are usually provided by internet keyword registrars free of charge.

For example, with respect to the internet keyword 'ABC' registered with CNNIC, an Internet user who wishes to access ABC Co Ltd's website using the internet keyword 'ABC' needs to have Chinese Internet Explorer as well as specific software downloaded from CNNIC or an internet keyword registrar designated by CNNIC.

13.33 INTERNET KEYWORD REGISTRATION WITH CNNIC

There are three levels in the internet keyword registration system: registry, registrar and reseller. CNNIC manages the internet keyword system, internet keyword registration and the internet keyword central database in China. It also provides service attestation and technical permission to internet keyword registrars.

Internet keyword registrars are responsible for accepting registration applications based on the contract with CNNIC, and on an impartial and first-come-first-served basis. These registrars transmit the registration information to the CNNIC internet keyword central database to complete the registration.

The resellers accept registration applications of internet keywords under the authorisation of the registrars. After choosing one of the CNNIC appointed registrars to register an internet keyword, this can be available 24 hours later after the registration. (See www.cnnic.net.cn/cnaddr/e-agen.shtml).

The following discussions focus only on the internet keyword system administered by CNNIC.

13.34 HOW CAN PROTECTION FOR INTERNET KEYWORDS BE OBTAINED?

Protection for internet keywords is obtained through registration with one of the registrars designated by CNNIC. The registrars are to accept applications in accordance with the principle of fairness and the first-to-file principle.

There are no restrictions on applicants. Both PRC and foreign companies and individuals may register internet keywords.

CNNIC reserves certain internet keywords for registration by their rightful holders. For the present time, internet keywords that are the same as the marks on the List of Major Trademarks that are to Receive Nationwide Protection are reserved for registration by their rightful holder.

When applying to register an internet keyword, the applicant must submit an application form and an application agreement. The applicant must warrant that:

1. in registering and using the internet keyword it will abide by the laws and regulations concerning the Internet;
2. it will abide by the relevant regulations formulated by the CNNIC, including the Measures for the Resolution of Internet Keyword Disputes;
3. the registration information that it submits is true, accurate and complete; and
4. the registration of the internet keyword is not done in bad faith or for any illegal purpose.

The application form for the registration must include the following information:

1. the internet keyword;
2. the uniform resource locator ("url") to which the internet keyword resolves;
3. the applicant's contact details, including its name, correspondence address, postal code, telephone number, facsimile number and e-mail address, and information on the contact person; and
4. authentication method and password.

An application for registration may be submitted by such means as online registration, e-mail, etc. For internet keywords reserved by CNNIC, the applications must be signed by authorised representatives of the right-holder but may be faxed to the registrars. A copy of the business license of the applicant and a copy of the relevant Trademark Registration Certificate must also be submitted with respect to such an application.

The date on which CNNIC receives the first valid application for registration is deemed the application date.

Unless an applicant states otherwise, the information entered into an internet keyword registration application form may be entered by CNNIC or the registrars into the publicly searchable database at www.cnnic.net.cn.

HOW CAN PROTECTION FOR INTERNET KEYWORDS BE MAINTAINED? 13.35

An internet keyword registration is maintained by the payment of annual fees.

If there is a change to the internet keyword registration information, the registrant must promptly notify the change to the registrar who registered the internet keyword.

A registrar must deregister a registered internet keyword if:

1. the registrant or its agent applies to deregister the internet keyword;
2. the registration information submitted by the applicant is false, inaccurate or incomplete, or the applicant fails to amend the same in a timely manner after a change;
3. the registrant fails to pay the relevant fees;
4. deregistration is required pursuant to a judgement or award rendered by a competent court, arbitration institution or internet keyword dispute resolution institution; or
5. a violation of the Measures for the Registration of Internet Keywords or related laws and regulations is committed.

13.36 INTERNET KEYWORD POLICY

On 4 August 2001, the CNNIC adopted the Internet Keyword Dispute Resolution Policy[3] ("IKDRP"). Internet keyword is a newly arisen technique for visiting network names, and a convenient way for the browser to visit by establishing a corresponding relationship between the internet keyword and the uniform resource locator[4] ("url"). Normally, an internet keyword is part of a domain name. The main distinctions between the CNNIC Procedure Rules and the IKDRP lie in two areas; one is subject matter; the other is the scope of the complaints. The IKDRP only applies to internet keyword disputes (however, an internet keyword may be a trademark). In compliance with the rules of the IKDRP, the complainant shall submit that:

1. he has the legitimate right or interest under Chinese laws;
2. the disputed keyword is identical or confusingly similar to a name in which the complainant has rights;

3   Internet Keyword Dispute Resolution Policy, available at http://www.cnnic.net.cn/cnaddr/e-5.shtml (visited 27 August 2002).
4   An url is an address of a web page or a file of information, such as www.cnnic.net.cn. You only need to use the language you are familiar with to tell the browser the address of the internet keyword you want to go to. If you want to register an internet keyword, you must first register your domain name, then direct the internet keyword to the url which is based on the domain name, and then submit it to the registrar. The internet keyword will then point to the website you provide. Only a registered internet keyword can point to its corresponding website. Available at http://www.cnnic.net.cn/cnaddr/e-faq.shtml (visited 27 August 2002).

3. the registrant has no rights or legitimate interests in respect of the keyword, or a major part thereof;

4. the keyword has been registered and is being used in bad faith.[5]

After promulgation of the IKDRP, the CNNIC again delegated the CIETAC as administrator. The CIETAC Domain Name Dispute Resolution Centre therefore, in August 2001, became the sole arbitral forum dealing with internet keyword disputes under the .cn ccTLD. According to CIETAC's Rules of Internet Keyword Dispute Resolution Policy, they shall use online facilities and the dispute will usually be decided within 14 working days.[6] To date, 19 cases have been decided under the CNNIC Procedure Rules and ten decided under the IKDRP and published online.[7]

The above-mentioned realities illustrate that China has adopted independent dispute-resolution methods, modelled on international practices. However, it does appear that there are some problems. First, except for the subject matter and the scope of the complaints, the CNNIC Procedure Rules and the IKDRP have similar procedures. Although they may supply more specific rules for the correspondent complaints, it is uneconomic and complicated to apply them. Second, the idea behind the administrative procedures is to deal with the most egregious types of cybersquatting, leaving other disputes to the courts.[8] But the IKDRP is intent on covering a wide scope of disputes, and this will inevitably cause some delay in the proceeding when deciding complex disputes. Third, because the CNNIC Procedure Rules only deal with conflicts between Chinese-language domain names and those trademarks protected by Chinese law, and the IKDRP only deals with internet keyword dispute in cyberspace, China still needs a dispute resolution policy concerning English and Chinese pronunciation (or Pinyin) domain names and the protected trademarks.

Keyword Cybersquatting

DEFINITION

13.37

The importance of internet keywords can also be seen in the case of cybersquatting. Cybersquatters register others' well-known marks and

---

5   See IKDRP, above at n 3, Art 4.
6   CIETAC's Rules of Internet Keyword Dispute Resolution Policy, Rules 29 and 32, available at http://www.cietac.org.cn/cd18/cd18_13.htm, (visited 27 August 2002).
7   See the Reports, available at http://www.cietac.org.cn/cd18/cd18_11.htm and http://www.cietac.org.cn/cd18/cd18_20.htm, (visited 27 August 2002).
8   M Muller, "Rough Justice: An Analysis of ICANN's Uniform Dispute Resolution Policy, Section 1: ICANN and UDRP" available at http://dcc.syr.edu/roughjustice.htm, (visited 27 August 2002).

names as internet keywords, preventing the right-holders from registering and using the internet keywords themselves. Furthermore, the cybersquatters may also be using such internet keywords to ride on the goodwill built up by the well-known marks. Many websites are found by intuitively guessing the address – one of the first addresses guessed is the name or house mark of the company. If the internet keyword registered by a cybersquatter uses such a name or mark or its shorthand version, customers and clients who use the name or house mark to try to find the website of the company may be misdirected to the cybersquatter's site.

13.38 WHAT CAN BE DONE IF AN INTERNET KEYWORD HAS BEEN PIRATED?

To combat cybersquatting of internet keywords, a trademark owner can choose one or a combination of the following courses of action: investigation and / or enforcement through consultation, litigation or alternative dispute resolution.

13.39 INVESTIGATION

A trademark owner whose mark has been filed as an internet keyword by a third party without authorisation may wish to investigate the third party.

If evidence of the third party demanding a ransom for the return of the internet keyword or the third party intentionally passing itself off as the trademark owner through the use of the internet keyword can be collected, a strong case can be built against the third party.

There are a number of PRC and Hong Kong investigation firms that offer investigation services with respect to intellectual property infringement. Legally speaking, investigation in the PRC, including investigation of cybersquatting, requires government approval. PRC courts may refuse to admit evidence collected outside of the legitimate channels.

The types of permissible evidence that litigants may present to court are documentary evidence, physical evidence, audio-visual material, live testimony of witnesses, statements by interested parties and expert opinions.

A PRC court should take legal acts, legal facts and documents notarised pursuant to legal procedures as a basis for ascertaining facts, except where contrary evidence is sufficient to invalidate the notary certification. Notarisation by a PRC notary public is not only a verification of the authenticity but also of the legality of the subject matter being notarised.

Evidence for court proceedings should preferably be notarised. This means involving a PRC notary public in the process of evidence collection, such as having a PRC notary public accompany the investigator on the investigation.

Investigations may also uncover other infringing evidence. For example, if the investigation shows that the infringer is actually also using a mark similar to the trademark of the right-holder on its products, a raid may also be organised against the infringer and such information may also be used in support of the internet keyword case against the infringer.

The trademark owner and the cybersquatter can try to resolve the dispute themselves. The right-holder may also take the cybersquatter to court or submit the dispute to CIETAC under the Measures for the Resolution of Internet Keyword Disputes.

CONSULTATION 13.40

If the right-holder wishes to resolve the dispute privately, it may wish to send warning letters to and / or meet with the cybersquatter and ask the cybersquatter to return the internet keyword. In cases where the right-holder wishes to avoid the cost involved – in litigation, for instance – the right-holder may consider resolving the dispute with the cybersquatters directly. Instead of taking the them to court or to CIETAC, well-known mark owners have paid cybersquatters in order to take back their domain names.

LITIGATION 13.41

It is expected that pending the issuance of similar guidelines for adjudicating internet keyword cases, PRC courts will use the Domain Name Judicial Interpretation as a reference in adjudicating internet keyword cases.

The general rule on presentation of evidence is that the party asserting an allegation bears the burden of proof. The plaintiff needs to collect sufficient evidence for discharging the burden of proof.

It should be noted that evidentiary requirements in PRC lawsuits are very strict. However, the Civil Procedure Law of the People's Republic of China provides that if a party is unable to obtain evidence due to objective reasons or if a court considers certain evidence to be of relevance to a case, the court may itself collect the evidence from relevant entities and individuals must provide such evidence.

INTERNET KEYWORD DISPUTE RESOLUTION 13.42

The internet keyword dispute resolution mechanism under the Measures for the Resolution of Internet Keyword Disputes is applicable to resolve disputes arising in the course of registration and use of internet keywords under the CNNIC system.

The dispute resolution mechanism is done online, supplemented with submission of original documents. The process is very efficient.

Complaints may be lodged with an internet keyword dispute resolution institution. CIETAC is currently the only organisation that has been designated by CNNIC as an internet keyword dispute resolution institution. CIETAC has issued rules governing the filing and handling of such complaints,

When CIETAC accepts a complaint, CIETAC organises a panel of expert(s) (which may consist of only one expert) within the prescribed time, and the dispute is dealt with by this panel of expert(s). CIETAC has also issued rules about the appointment of experts onto panels of expert(s).

If the complainant makes the following four claims to a dispute resolution institution, the internet keyword registrant must accept the jurisdiction of the dispute resolution proceeding:

1. the complainant enjoys rights or legitimate interests protected under PRC law;
2. the internet keyword which is the subject of the complaint is identical with or similar to a name in which the complainant enjoys rights or interests;
3. the internet keyword registrant against whom the complaint is filed does not enjoy rights or legitimate interests in the internet keyword or the substantive part thereof; and
4. the internet keyword registrant against whom the complaint is filed has registered or is using the internet keyword in bad faith.

The complainant bears the burden of proof in respect of its claims. However, the internet keyword registrant bears the burden of proof of its rights or legitimate interests in the internet keyword or the substantive part thereof.

The panel of experts responsible for deciding a dispute has the authority to determine whether the internet keyword registrant against whom the complaint is filed has registered or is using the internet keyword in bad faith. If the internet keyword registrant against whom the complaint is filed is characterised by any of the circumstances set forth below, such circumstance constitutes evidence of its registration or use of the internet keyword in bad faith:

1. the main objective of registering or acquiring the internet keyword is to sell, lease or otherwise transfer the internet keyword in order to obtain illegitimate gains;
2. the registrant has on numerous occasions registered names in which third parties enjoy legitimate rights and interests as its own internet keywords and the objective of registering such internet keywords was to prevent others from using, in the form

of internet keywords on the internet, the names in which they enjoy legitimate rights and interests;

3. the objective of registering or acquiring the internet keyword is to damage the complainant's reputation, undermine the complainant's normal business activities, or obscure the distinction between the registrant and the internet keyword owner and thus mislead the public;

4. other manifestations of bad faith.

Based on the evidence presented by the parties and all of the facts involved in the case, the panel of experts has the authority to determine whether the respondent had a legitimate reason to register or has a legitimate reason to use the internet keyword.

If the complainant disputes more than one internet keyword owned by the same respondent, either party has the right to request the dispute resolution institution that the disputes be consolidated into one case and be dealt with by one panel of experts.

While a dispute is pending before a panel of experts, if either party is of the opinion that any of the experts on the panel of experts has a material interest in the opposite party which could have an effect on the rendering of an impartial decision in the case, it has the right to challenge such expert before the dispute resolution institution.

The relevant internet keyword registrar is obliged to provide information on the registration and use of the internet keyword at the request of the dispute resolution institution.

The internet keyword registrar and CNNIC will otherwise not participate in any capacity or manner in the internet keyword dispute resolution proceeding.

If the panel of experts upholds the complaint, it may only decide the internet keyword dispute in one of the ways set forth below:

1. that the registered internet keyword be deregistered; or

2. that the registered internet keyword be transferred to the complainant.

Dispute resolution through CIETAC normally takes around 45 days from the day the complaint is submitted.

Before a party files a complaint with a dispute resolution institution, or during the dispute resolution proceedings, or after the panel of experts has rendered its decision, either party may institute an action concerning the same dispute with the court or, on the basis of an agreement, submit the dispute to an arbitration institution for arbitration.

If the dispute resolution institution decides that the internet keyword shall be deregistered or transferred to the complainant, the internet keyword registrar will wait 10 working days before enforcing the decision. If during such waiting period, the internet keyword registrant against whom the complaint is filed submits valid proof that a competent judicial institution or arbitration institution has accepted the relevant dispute, the internet keyword registrar will not enforce the decision rendered by the dispute resolution institution and will decide on subsequent measures according to the following circumstances:

1. if there is evidence establishing that the parties have reached a settlement, it shall enforce such a settlement agreement;
2. if there is evidence establishing that the relevant legal proceeding or arbitration has been rejected or withdrawn, it shall enforce the dispute resolution institution's decision;
3. if the relevant judicial authority or arbitration institution has rendered a judgement or award and such judgement or award has become legally effective, it must enforce such judgement or award.

CIETAC has established a dedicated website at www.cietac.org.cn to receive complaints and to publish information related to them. However, at the request of a party, CIETAC may decide not to publish materials and information that it considers may be prejudicial to the interests of the party if published.

While a judicial proceeding, arbitration proceeding or dispute resolution proceeding is pending in an internet keyword dispute, the internet keyword registrant may not transfer the disputed internet keyword unless the transferee agrees in writing to be bound by the judicial judgement, arbitration award or dispute resolution decision.

CNNIC may amend the Measures for the Resolution of Internet Keyword Disputes from time to time. Amended versions of the Measures will be published on CNNIC's website and be implemented 30 days after the date of publication. Internet keyword disputes submitted to the internet keyword dispute resolution institution prior to the amendment of the Measures will not be governed by the amended version of the Measures.

The amended version of the Measures will automatically become a part of internet keyword registration agreements already in existence at such time. If an internet keyword registrant does not agree to be bound by the dispute resolution measures or an amended version thereof, it should promptly notify the internet keyword registrar thereof. The internet keyword registrar will maintain the internet keyword services for such registrant for 30 days after the receipt of such notification, and the relevant internet keyword will be deregistered after the passage of the 30 days.

Although there are also many difficulties with the Measures for the Resolution of Internet Keyword Disputes, the Measures generally deals with the straightforward cybersquatting cases fairly effectively and economically.

TIPS AGAINST CYBERSQUATTING 13.43

As there is no single and unified body that administers and registers internet keywords, registration of an internet keyword under one system does not prevent the registration of the same internet keyword by a third party under another system. If possible, it is advisable for rightholders to try to register their marks and names under all of the internet keyword systems as soon as possible.

ALIBABA (CHINA) NETWORK TECHNOLOGY CO LTD V GUANGZHOU QINJIAYUAN SCIENCE AND TECHNOLOGY INDUSTRIAL CO LTD 13.44

The respondent Guangzhou Qinjiayuan Science and Technology Industrial Co Ltd registered the internet keyword 'Alibaba' (in Chinese characters) with CNNIC through one of the registrars designated by CNNIC on 4 August 2001. The complainant Alibaba (China) Network Technology Co Ltd lodged a complaint with CIETAC under the Measures for the Resolution of Internet Keyword Disputes, requesting the return of the internet keyword.

The panel found the following:

1. *The complainant enjoyed rights or legitimate interests protected under PRC law.* The complainant registered the 'Alibaba' (in Chinese characters) and 'Alibaba' domain names.

   The panel found that the complainant's website name registrations and PRC trademark registration for 'Alibaba' (in Chinese characters) were later in time than the respondent's registration of the internet keyword 'Alibaba' (in Chinese characters), and took the position that therefore the complainant may not rely on such registrations to establish that it enjoyed rights or legitimate interests at the time the internet keyword 'Alibaba' (in Chinese characters) was registered.

   The complainant was established in September 1999 and the registered name was Alibaba (Hangzhou) Network Technology Development Co Ltd (in Chinese). On 6 July 2000, the PRC State Administration for Industry and Commerce approved the registered name change to Alibaba (China) Network Technology Co Ltd (in Chinese). The panel found that the complainant enjoyed protection under PRC law for the 'Alibaba' (in Chinese) trade name.

The panel took the position that the evidence submitted by the complainant showed that 'Alibaba' (in Chinese characters) had become the name of a well-known service. The panel took the position that a well-known service should be protected like a well-known product under the Anti-unfair Competition Law. Under Article 5(2) of the Anti-unfair Competition Law,

"Business operators may not engage in market trading and harm competitors by the following unfair methods:
(2) unauthorised use of the name, packaging or trade dress peculiar to well-known merchandise or use of a name, packaging or trade dress similar to that of well-known merchandise, thereby causing confusion with the well-known merchandise of another party and causing purchasers to mistake the merchandise for such well-known merchandise".

The panel therefore took the position that the complainant had rights to the 'Alibaba' (in Chinese characters) domain name, trade name and name of a well-known service.

2. *The 'Alibaba' (in Chinese characters) internet keyword was identical with or similar to the 'Alibaba' (in Chinese characters) name in which the complainant enjoyed rights or interests.*
3. *The respondent did not enjoy rights or legitimate interests in the internet keyword or the substantive part thereof.*
   The respondent argued that the registration agreement between the registrar and the respondent with respect to the registration of the 'Alibaba' (in Chinese characters) internet keyword created for it rights or interests in the internet keyword protected by law. The panel disagreed and held that the rights created by the registration were not the rights or interests on which the respondent may rely in defence against a complaint under the Measures for the Resolution of Internet Keyword Disputes.
4. *The respondent had registered or was using the internet keyword in bad faith.*
   The panel found that the establishment of the complainant company and the running of its business, together with advertising and creation of the complainant website, had resulted in its 'Alibaba' name and service being well known. The respondent had also acknowledged the fame of the complainant in its own advertisement, which stated that the complainant was a well-established strategic partner. The panel held that the respondent's registration of 'Alibaba' (in Chinese characters) as an internet keyword, knowing that the complainant had legitimate rights to

the name and that the name was well known, constituted bad faith registration.

The complainant and the respondent entered into a cooperation agreement on 18 June 2001, prohibiting either party from using the marks, etc, of the other party without authorisation. The panel found that the respondent registered the complainant's 'Alibaba' (in Chinese characters) mark and name as its own internet keyword one month after the execution of the cooperation agreement. The panel found that such conduct of the respondent constituted bad faith registration.

The panel found that the circumstances of the case, including the fact that the respondent had not used the 'Alibaba' (in Chinese characters) internet keyword for seven months after registration, showed that the respondent had registered the internet keyword in bad faith.

The panel therefore ruled that the 'Alibaba' (in Chinese characters) internet keyword should be transferred to the complainant. The panel's ruling was dated 19 March 2002.

SUPOR GROUP CO LTD V ZHEJIANG JINGDE ADVERTISING DESIGN CO LTD

13.45

The respondent Zhejiang Jingde Advertising Design Co Ltd registered the internet keywords 'Supor' (in simplified and traditional Chinese characters) and 'Supor' on 17 October 2001 with CNNIC through a registrar designated by CNNIC. The complainant Supor Group Co Ltd lodged a complaint with CIETAC under the Measures for the Resolution of Internet Keyword Disputes, requesting the return of the internet keyword.

CIETAC organised a panel for the adjudication of the dispute. The panel found the following:

1. *The complainant enjoyed rights or legitimate interests protected under PRC law.*

   The complainant registered the 'Supor' (in simplified Chinese characters) mark and the 'Supor' mark in the PRC in 1996 and 1997 in Class 21. Therefore, the panel found that the complainant enjoyed registered trademark rights protected under PRC law.

2. *The 'Supor' (in simplified and traditional Chinese characters) and the 'Supor' internet keywords were identical with or confusingly similar to the 'Supor' (in simplified Chinese characters) mark and the 'Supor' mark in which the complainant enjoyed rights or interests.*

3. *The respondent did not enjoy rights or legitimate interests in the internet keyword or the substantive part thereof.*

   The respondent did not respond to the complaint and did not submit any evidence to refute the claim by the complainant that the respondent did not enjoy rights or legitimate interests in the "Supor: (in simplified and traditional Chinese characters) and the "Supor" internet keywords. The panel therefore held that the respondent did not enjoy rights or legitimate interests in the "Supor" (in simplified and traditional Chinese characters) and the "Supor" internet keyword

4. *The respondent had registered and was using the internet keyword in bad faith.*

   The panel found that:

   (a) the complainant's 'Supor' (in simplified Chinese characters) and 'Supor' marks had been determined well known by the PRC Trademark Office;

   (b) the marks had also been determined famous by the Zhejiang Province Administration for Industry and Commerce;

   (c) according to the statistics of the China Industry Enterprise Information Dissemination Center, the volumes of sales of the complainant's products in 1999 and 2000 came first for the whole of the PRC; and

   (d) the complainant also advertised in the PRC Central Television Station (which is an official television station and which is one of the major television stations in the PRC).

   The panel therefore found that the complainant's 'Supor' and 'Supor' (in Chinese characters) pressure-cooker products were well-known products in the cookery industry.

   The panel also found that the 'Supor' (in simplified and traditional Chinese characters) and 'Supor' internet keywords were all pointed to a chat room. The panel was of the opinion that confusion involving the complainant was therefore very likely, misleading network users and affecting the normal business of the complainant.

   The panel found that as 'Supor' and 'Supor' (in Chinese characters) were well-known marks, the registration and use of the 'Supor' (in simplified and traditional Chinese characters) and 'Supor' internet keywords by the respondent were done in bad faith.

The panel therefore issued a ruling on 8 May 2002 ordering the transfer of the 'Supor' (in simplified and traditional Chinese characters) and 'Supor' internet keywords to the complainant.

DOMAIN NAME CASES

INTRODUCTION

13.46

Cases were brought by a number of trade mark owners against China's notorious cybersquatter, Beijing Cinet Information Systems Co, which on appeal in late 2001 returned the disputed domain names to the trade mark owners: Ikea v Beijing Cinet Information Systems Co, El Du Pont v Beijing Cinet Information Systems Co, Cartier International v Beijing Cinet Information Systems Co, and The Procter & Gamble Co v Beijing Cinet Information Systems Co.

THE KELON CASE

13.47

The first cybersquatting case in China was Guangdong Kelon (Rong Sheng) Group Ltd v Guangdong Yong An Clothing Manufacturing Company, (the "Kelon Case"), heard in the Beijing Haidian District Court in March 1998. The domain name in question was kelon.com.cn. Kelon claimed that it was the owner of the registered trademark, 'Kelon', and had used the mark since 1992. Kelon further claimed that its mark was distinctive and well known to the public. When Kelon attempted to register a website under its name with the CNNIC in 1997, it discovered that the defendant, Yong'an had registered kelon.com.cn as its domain name but the website was empty. When Kelon consulted with Yong'an and filed a complaint with the CNNIC, the defendant offered to transfer the domain name kelon.com.cn to the plaintiff for, initially RMB1,000,000, which was then revised to RMB800,000. Kelon refused and filed a lawsuit in the District Court, claiming Yong'an registering the trademark 'kelon' as a domain name constituted infringement of Kelon's trademark and demanded that Yong'an immediately discontinue his use of the domain name. The defendant asserted that 'kelon' meant 'clone' in Chinese, that his domain name registration was conducted by legal means and that the domain name registration certificate was issued. Later on, Yong'an offered not to use the domain name if Kelon paid him the registration fee of RMB2,000 and the first annual administrative fee of RMB300, which is about US$277 in total. Kelon refused and persisted in its trademark infringement claim. In March 1999, three days prior to the day of trial, the defendant voluntarily applied for a cancellation of the domain name with CNNIC. Kelon then withdrew its lawsuit against Yong'an. After reviewing Kelon's demand for withdrawal of litigation, the Judges issued a Civil Order for the permission, in which it was also concluded that the defendant registered the domain name for the purpose of exacting payment by intentional acts of bad faith. Such acts are prohibited.

This case is significant because the Court used its discretionary powers to return a trademark registered as a domain name to its rightful owner. Secondly, the Court stated that registration of domain names for extorting financial reward is acting in bad faith and is forbidden in China. Thirdly, as there was no fine attached to the Order, other enterprises may decide that cybersquatting is worth the risk because the worst-case scenario will be the loss of one domain name. Thus, the decision did nothing to discourage other enterprises from abusing legitimate trademarks.

13.48 IKEA

The first important case regarding a foreign trademark owner and a local domain name registrant, decided by the Beijing No 2 Intermediate People's Court, involved Inter IKEA System BV and Beijing Cinet Information Co. Ltd.[9] When IKEA applied for domain name registration in China, the CNNIC reported that the defendant had pre-emptively registered the domain name ikea.com.cn. The mark is a distinctive mark[10] and has been used as the name of 155 specialist chain stores in 29 countries, including 2 specialist stores in China, in Beijing and Shanghai. During the hearing, the plaintiff further pointed out that Cinet had registered several thousand domain names, including some brands well known worldwide, such as 'Boss', 'Cartier', 'Du Pont', 'Phillips', 'Polo', 'Omega', 'Rolex' and 'Carlsberg', and they had not been put into active use. The plaintiff requested the Court to order an injunction, cancel the domain name and order payment of the court fee by the defendant.

The defendant argued that:

1. the registration of IKEA was legitimate because the name was self-created, from a combination of "i" for internet and 'kea' for a kind of tropical parrot widely recognised as birds capable of voice imitation, and they intended to use the domain for offering a voice-mail service over the internet;
2. domain names and trademarks are two different subject matters, and that protection for trademarks under the current law should not be extended to domain names;
3. the trademark IKEA was not recognised as a well-known mark in China;

---

9   Judgement of *Inter IKEA System BV v Beijing Cinet Information Co Ltd* decided by an appellate court, the Beijing Higher People's Court, available at http://www.cnnic.net.cn/policy/35.shtml, (visited 27 August 2002).
10 The mark was originated by a Swede, Ingvar Kamprad in 1947. IKEA is an acronym of his name and his home town Elmtaryd Agunnaryd.

4. the domain name was duly registered with CNNIC; and
5. IKEA should bring an administrative proceeding rather than legal proceedings.

Although it is not clear which regulations should cover the procedure for resolving disputes between domain names and trademarks, exercising its discretionary powers, the Court adjudicated the IKEA dispute. The Court stated that Inter IKEA System BV was the owner of the registered trademark IKEA in over ninety countries including China[11] and the mark is distinctive as it is a created name. Because the defendant was unable to provide viable evidence, the Court rejected its arguments that the name IKEA was of its own creation and that they had devoted much effort and cost in designing, promoting and developing the website and the proposed voice-mail services. Due to the fact that IKEA spends a great deal of money in advertising worldwide and is known by a relatively wide public in China, the Court declared that the trademark IKEA is a well-known mark.[12] The defendant's illegitimate use of the well-known trademark would mislead general consumers to assume that the defendant was the owner of the mark, or that some form of cooperation existed between the defendant and the mark owner. This would further mislead consumers, causing them to visit the defendant's website for information related to IKEA's goods and services. The Court stated that, in this way, the defendant would take unfair advantage of the goodwill and high reputation associated with the famous mark, thus harming the legitimate rights and interests of the trademark owner.

Due to the uniqueness of the assignation of domain names, Cinet's registration could block the legitimate owner of the trademark from registering it as a domain name and thus deprive the owner of doing business on the internet through the trademark. This could jeopardise fair competition in the market and harm the legitimate rights and benefits of the trademark owner. The Court also considered the defendant's registration of the domain names of a large number of other

---

11 According to the judgement, IKEA was first registered in China in 1983 and was re-registered for more classes in 1994 and 1996 respectively, by Inter IKEA System BV, see n 9.
12 The judge of the case, Fanwu Wang, said: "According to relevant provisions, the State Trademark Bureau is the only administrative organ being authorised to make such determinations. However it cannot exclude People's Court the right to determine a renowned trademark during the trial of an individual case. Judicial power is theoretically higher than executive power. As long as there are no forbidding provisions in law and regulations, People's Courts shall have the right to make such judgements." N Wei and S Wei, "Registration of Domain Names and Protection of Renowned Trademarks" available at http://www.lawinfochina.com/legalforum/hottopics/displaycontent.asp?id=15, (visited 27 August 2002).

famous names as strong proof of bad faith. The Court, however, did nothing about the defendant's argument of regarding the CNNIC. After ruling that the act of cybersquatting of well-known marks violates the principles of honesty and credibility in market competition upheld by the Chinese Anti-Unfair Competition Law and therefore should be stopped, the Court ordered that use of the name be stopped immediately and the registration be cancelled within 10 days of the Judgement becoming effective in June 2000. The Court Fee of RMB1,000 (US$120) was to be borne by the defendant. Cinet appealed.

The Appellate Court stated that Cinet's use of the registered trademark IKEA could confuse general consumers. As a network information company, the defendant should have known the possible interests of a registered mark holder in cyberspace. Because there were no legitimate interests in the mark and because the domain name was not used after registration, the obvious intention of blocking the trademark owner's registration of the domain name, for financial gain, constituted bad faith. The defendant's act violated the principles of honesty and credibility in market competition under the Chinese Anti-Unfair Competition Law. The Court confirmed that People's Courts are competent to determine whether a mark is renowned or not. The Higher Court held that there was no evidence that IKEA had become a famous mark at the time when the defendant registered ikea.com.cn. The Higher Court further held that since IKEA was not a famous mark, the defendant's conduct did not constitute an infringement on the plaintiff's exclusive right of the registered trademark IKEA. However, the Higher Court ruled that the third-level domain 'ikea' as registered by the defendant was identical to the plaintiffs registered trademark and therefore would sufficiently cause confusion among the public.

The Higher Court found that the defendant not only failed to prove that it had a legitimate right to the name 'ikea' and a reasonable ground to register it as its domain name, but that the defendant also had never actually used the domain name after its registration. The Higher Court then concluded that as a provider of online services, the defendant should have known the importance of a domain name. Therefore, the defendant's intentional use of the plaintiff's registered mark for commercial purposes clearly indicated that the defendant was trying to prevent the plaintiff from registering 'ikea' as its domain name in bad faith. Based on this analysis, the Higher Court determined that the defendant violated the fairness and good faith principles of Article 2 of the UCL and held the defendant liable for unfair competition. The Court ordered that the infringement be stopped immediately and the registration of ikea.com.cn be cancelled within 10 days of the judgement becoming effective. The Court Fee of RMB2,000 (US$240) for the two instances was to be borne by both IKEA (5 per cent) and Cinet (95 per cent).

Effect of IKEA Case

1. Cases not heavily relied on as precedents in the PRC.
2. Need for specific laws and regulations dealing with cybersquatting.

The case is significant for several reasons. Firstly, it was not clear what the applicable law was and therefore there was chaos in deciding the cybersquatting case. The Intermediate Court held the same view as is widely accepted in the international arena – that the protection for well-known marks should be extended to the field of domain name registration.[13] The Appellate Court, however, considered only Cinet's infringement under the Chinese Anti-Unfair Competition Law, not infringement of trademark, but reached a similar result in considering that IKEA is not a well-known trademark in China. Secondly, as confirmed by the Appellate Court, the courts are capable of determining, without authorisation, whether a mark is well known or not. But this will not help future cases where determination of well-known marks is needed, because Chinese law is based on the civil law model, and where legislation is not clear, courts need not follow precedents; thus different courts may have different interpretations. Thirdly, the case took from September 1999 to June 2000, plus the appellate period, for a decision. The slowness of the litigation decision in and of itself may encourage more cybersquatting. Finally, the courts did not set punishments or award damages in the IKEA case, which would actively discourage the infringement of trademarks as domain names.

Well-known mark determination

The case of ikea.com.cn was the first where a PRC court made a determination of well-known mark status. Before that, the PRC Trademark Office was the exclusive authority for determining well-known marks as stated in the Provisional Regulations for the Determination and Administration of Well-known Trademarks. The court, although asserting that it has such a power, seems to have retracted that liberal move, and the determinations made previously, including that made in the IKEA case, were quashed by the appeal court.

The PRC is party to the Paris Convention and is committed to implementing TRIPS. Both the Paris Convention and TRIPS contain provisions on the protection of well-known marks. Protection under

---

13 J Ling, "Protecting Famous Trademarks in Domain Names, S Rouse & Co International (2000), available at http://www.domainnotes.com/news/print/0., 5281_440001,00.html, (visited 27 August 2002).

the Paris Convention has been cited in court judgements, in trademark prosecution decisions and in local AIC punishment decisions against trademark infringement.

A formal framework for the recognition of well-known marks was created with the PRO State Administration for Industry and Commerce's promulgation, on 14 August 1996, of the Provisional Regulations for the Determination and Administration of Well-known Trademarks. The Regulation defines well-known marks as registered marks that enjoy a relatively high reputation in the market and are familiar to the relevant public.

The Trademark Office has, to date, issued over 200 determinations of well-known trademark status, but only in respect of marks owned by Chinese enterprises. The Regulation, however, does not exclude foreign marks, and foreign owners have filed numerous applications. Unfortunately, none of these applications have thus far been processed.

Under the revised Trademark Law of the People's Republic of China, which came into effect on 1 December 2001, enhanced protection is provided to well-known marks. The revised Trademark Law stipulates that when recognising a well-known mark, the following factors should be considered:

1. the degree of notoriety of the mark among the relevant public;
2. the length of continuous use of the mark;
3. the continuous length, degree and geographical scope of the publicity for the mark;
4. the record of protection of the mark as a well-known mark; and
5. other factors associated with the mark's being well-known.

Both PRC and foreign marks should be eligible to be recognised as a well-known mark on a case-by-case basis under the revised Trademark Law. The courts' refusals to make well-known mark determination in the domain name cases should not prevent the marks from obtaining such status, either by the PRC Trademark Office or in subsequent court judgements. The court's determinations were based on the evidence of fame at the time the cybersquatters registered the domain names. Determinations made in the future should be independently assessed on fresh evidence of fame.

13.49 SHIJIAZHUANG FULANDE DEVELOPMENT CO V BEIJING MITIAN JIAYE TECHNOLOGY & TRADE CO LTD (THE "PDA CASE")

The defendant registered pda.com.cn in 1998 to advertise and sell laptop computers. The court ruled in favour of defendant because (a) registration of another's trademarks as domain names was not an act of trademark infringement; and (b) there was no evidence that "pda" was a well-known mark. In other words, it is essential to establish a mark as a well-known mark in cybersquatting cases.

DUPONT.COM.CN 13.50

The court found that the disputed domain name was identical to the Du Pont registered marks, trade name, and domain name; that the plaintiff Du Pont had legitimate and valid trademark rights, including valid PRC trademark registrations; the Du Pont mark was also its trade name and domain name; and that the defendant did not enjoy rights or interests to the third-level domain name and had no justification to register and / or use the domain name.

The lower court determined the mark well known. The appeal court concurred. This is the only such determination in the latest PRC domain name cases, probably due to the evidence submitted showing that Du Pont entered the PRC market fairly early.

The court then went on to state that in accordance with the relevant provisions of the Paris Convention for the Protection of Industrial Property ("Paris Convention"), a higher level of protection should be provided to well-known marks. The unauthorised use of a well-known mark is infringement. The unauthorised use or registration of a well-known mark as a domain name is infringement of the well-known mark. The protection for the Du Pont mark, a well-known mark, is extended to the internet. The unauthorised registration of the dupont.com.cn domain name by the defendant was a reproduction of Du Pont's well-known mark. Such reproduction could cause confusion for the relevant public. Beijing Cinet Information Co Ltd, being an Internet service provider, should know the function and value of domain names but nevertheless, registered the domain name without authorisation. Therefore, it obviously had a commercial purpose. The court also found that the defendant Beijing Cinet Information Co Ltd did not use the domain name after registration, but prevented the registration of the domain name by the legitimate owner. The court found that because Beijing Cinet Information Co Ltd did not heed the requests and warnings from Du Pont to stop the infringement prior to the litigation, there was obviously bad faith.

The court also found that Beijing Cinet Information Co Ltd infringed the Du Pont registered mark and well-known mark, violated the principle of honesty and trustworthiness, and engaged in unfair competition.

The appeal court therefore upheld the judgement of the lower court. The defendant was ordered to deregister the domain name and pay the plaintiff's expenses incurred for collecting evidence for the litigation (in the sum of RMB2,700 – approximately US$337.50) and the case acceptance fees in the first and second instances (in the total of RMB2,000 – approximately US$250).

13.51 TIDE.COM.CN

Another interesting case worth noting is *The Procter & Gamble Company v Beijing Tiandi Electronic Group* (IP Decision 27 of 2001 by the Higher People's Court). The defendant in this case was a Chinese company incorporated in 1988 that started using the name Tide on its '386' PC in 1993. In June 1997, the defendant adopted Beijing Tide Electronic Group as its English name. Then, on 9 April 1998, the defendant registered the domain name tide.com.cn. Finally, on 7 September 1997, the plaintiff registered the trademark Tide in China with the Trademark Bureau of China, State Administration of Industry and Commerce. Notably, the word Tide was first registered as a trademark in China by P&G AG (the Swiss company) on 10 May 1976, and the registered trademark Tide was transferred to the plaintiff on 10 August 10 1992. Indeed, the plaintiff registered the domain name tide.com on 30 July 1995.

On 14 October 1999, the plaintiff wrote to the defendant, claiming that the defendant's use of the word 'tide' in its domain name infringed on the plaintiff's trademark right. P&G also asked the defendant to amend or cancel the registration of tide.com.cn. In its reply on 9 November 1999, the defendant expressed its willingness to give up the name on the condition that the plaintiff pay the defendant Chinese RMB708,300 (or about US$86,378). This amount mainly included RMB184,000 for damages from changing the domain name and RMB300,000 to cover the fees to change the domain name and possible business losses. In response, P&G rejected the offer and brought a lawsuit in Beijing against the defendant for trademark infringement.

The Beijing No 1 Intermediate People's Court granted P&G's request and ordered the defendant to stop using the domain name tide.com.cn. The court held that registering another person's famous trademark as a domain name, without authorisation of the mark holder, undoubtedly damaged the legitimate right of the mark holder. Therefore, the court held that such conduct would be deemed trademark infringement. In reaching its decision, the court reasoned that the defendant was fully knowledgeable about the famous nature of the plaintiff's mark Tide and that the defendant's registration of the domain name tide.com.cn had caused confusion among the public as to the origin of products associated with the mark. The court further held that the defendant's use of the word 'tide' as its domain name would unreasonably prevent the plaintiff from using its own famous mark on the internet for business activities, which would consequently dilute the value of the mark.

The judgement was reversed on appeal. The Beijing Higher People's Court held that a key factor in favour of the defendant in this case was that since the defendant first used the word Tide in its business in 1993, a reasonable relationship between the defendant and the name Tide was established. Therefore, there was a justifiable basis for the defendant to register the domain name tide.com.cn and use it reasonably. Pursuant to this 'justifiable basis' test, the Higher Court rejected the lower court ruling that the defendant had infringed on the plaintiff's famous mark and had committed unfair competition practices. The Higher Court opined that because of the existence of the justifiable basis, the defendant's registration of tide.com.cn did not offend the plaintiff's trademark right, and consequently did not fall within unfair competition.

THE PROCTER & GAMBLE COMPANY V BEIJING CINET INFORMATION CO LTD   13.52

The defendant registered whisper.com.cn as its domain name. The Beijing No 2 Intermediate Court rendered a judgement against the defendant on trademark infringement grounds. The court held that the registration of a domain name identical to a well-known trademark belonging to another person is an infringement on their exclusive right of use. The court found that the defendant's conduct clearly infringed on the plaintiff's right of exclusive use of the mark Whisper because the mark was proven to be a famous mark.

The Beijing Higher People's Court disagreed, finding that the defendant did not infringe the plaintiff's trademark because the evidence was not sufficient to prove that the mark Whisper was well known at the time of defendant's registration of whisper.com.cn. The Higher Court ruled, however, that since the third-level domain 'whisper' was identical to the plaintiff's registered mark Whisper, it would inevitably cause confusion to the public. The court also ruled that the defendant Beijing Cinet Information Co Ltd's action violated the principle of honesty and trustworthiness. The court ordered the defendants to cease the infringement or unfair competition, and to deregister the domain name.

THE PROCTER & GAMBLE COMPANY V SHANGHAI CHENGXUAN INTELLIGENCE TECHNOLOGY DEVELOPMENT CO LTD   13.53

In May 1976, the plaintiff registered Safeguard as its trademark for soap and related products. On 18 January 1999, the defendant, an electronic service company in Shanghai, registered safeguard.com.cn as its domain name. The plaintiff then sued the defendant for trademark infringement on several grounds, including: (a) 'safeguard' was a well-known mark of the plaintiff; and (b) the defendant registered its domain name using 'safeguard' in bad faith.

The court noted that the resolution of a dispute over a domain name requires a "balancing of interests" among the trademark owner, the domain name holder, and the general public because a domain name, in addition to its technical function, may serve as an indicator of the origin of certain products or services. The court then held that the defendant should have known at the time of registering the domain name that the trademark Safeguard had a good reputation and already enjoyed wide public awareness. The court concluded that the defendant registered 'safeguard' as its domain name in bad faith because the defendant's main purpose was to take advantage of the plaintiff's trademark for its own unjustified business interest. In ruling against the defendant, the court directly applied Article 10bis(1)–(2) of the Paris Convention, in addition to Article 4 of the General Principles of Civil Law of China ("China Civil Code") and Article 2 of the UCL.

13.54 KFC.COM.CN AND PEPSI.COM.CN

The domain names kfc.com.cn and pepsi.com.cn were pirated by the defendant Guangzhou Yuejing Information Network Co Ltd ("Guangzhou Yuejing"). Kentucky Fried Chicken International Holdings Inc and PepsiCo Inc were the plaintiffs. Besides kfc.com.cn and pepsi.com.cn, Guangzhou Yuejing also registered cocacola.com.cn and nike.com.cn.

The judgements closely followed the guidelines set out in Articles 4 and 5 of the Domain Name Judicial Interpretation. Firstly, the court found that the plaintiff foreign trademark owners had legitimate and valid trademark rights, including valid PRC trademark registrations, in the marks used in the third-level domain names. Some of the marks involved were also the trade names and .com domain names of the plaintiffs and their affiliates.

The court also found that the third-level domain names were identical with the relevant registered marks, trade names, or domain names, sufficient to cause confusion among the relevant public.

The court also found that the defendants did not enjoy rights or interests in the third-level domain names and had no justification to register and / or use the domain names.

The court also found that the defendants had, for a commercial purpose, registered and / or used the domain names. In the case of pepsi.com.cn, the court found that the registration and use of the pepsi.com.cn domain name were done in bad faith, injuring the interests of the plaintiff as well as the public.

The court also found the serial piracy of the defendants sufficient to establish that the registrations were done for a commercial purpose, or in bad faith.

The court therefore found that the defendants' registration and / or use of the domain names were in bad faith, and that the defendants had engaged in infringement or unfair competition in violation of the first paragraph of Article 2 of the Anti-unfair Competition Law. Article 2 of the Anti-unfair Competition Law provides that:

"In the course of market trading, business operators must observe the principles of voluntariness, equality, equitability, honesty and trustworthiness and abide by generally accepted business ethics.

For the purposes of this law, the term unfair competition" shall mean business operators' acts that violate this law by injuring the lawful rights and interests of other business operators and disrupting the social and economic order.

For the purposes of this law, the term business operators "shall mean legal persons, other economic organisations and individuals that deal in merchandise or are engaged in the provision of services for profit (the term "merchandise" shall include services)."

The court therefore ordered the defendants to cease the infringement or unfair competition and deregister the domain names. In the pepsi.com. cn case, besides ordering that the domain name should be registered in the name of PepsiCo Inc, the court ordered that the defendant issue a public apology to PepsiCo Inc.

No compensation was awarded in the kfc.com.cn case. The court awarded damages in the sum of RMB5,060 in the pepsi.com.cn case.

In cases where the plaintiffs requested the court to make well-known mark determinations with respect to the marks in question, the court asserted that it had the power to make such determinations, but declined to make such determinations based on the evidence submitted, although acknowledging that the marks had a certain degree of fame.

RETRIAL   13.55

A party dissatisfied with any of the appeal judgements may still petition the court which originally heard the case or a court at a higher level for a retrial, but presentation of the petition does not suspend the execution of the judgement. There are, however, limited grounds for the court to accept a petition for retrial. The grounds are:

1. there is new evidence which is conclusive enough to repudiate the original judgement or ruling;

2. the main evidence on which the facts were ascertained for the original judgement or ruling was insufficient;
3. there was a definite error in the application of the law in the original judgement or ruling;
4. a violation of the legal procedure of the court may have affected the correctness of the judgement or ruling; or
5. while hearing the case, judicial personnel committed embezzlement, accepted bribes, practised favouritism for personal benefit, or perverted the law.

A court must reject an application that does not meet any of these grounds.

A petition for a retrial must be submitted within two years of the effective date of the relevant judgement or ruling.

CHAPTER 14

OTHER INTELLECTUAL PROPERTY RIGHTS AND RELATED AREAS OF LAW

OVERVIEW

Rights other than trademark rights may come into play even if an infringement appears to be a trademark infringement. Sometimes, exercising these rights may give additional protection to the trademark, or if trademark protection is futile in a particular situation, exercising these rights could be an alternative way to safeguard a trademark owner's interest. Of course, effectiveness of rights enforcement is one of the most important factors to consider when making the choice. Effectiveness relates not only to the legal framework of a particular kind of right but also the actual practice of the relevant authorities in upholding those rights. At the same time, attention has to be paid to the term of the intellectual property right. While a trademark registration could be renewed, copyright and patent will expire after a certain period of time. This chapter will give an introduction to the following intellectual property right regimes:

1. copyright;
2. computer software;
3. patents; and
4. enterprise names.

The sections below will deal with each right individually. Important details will be highlighted and the relevant enforcement mechanisms and penalties available will be discussed.

We will then discuss the following areas of law:

1. unfair competition;
2. product quality and consumer protection;
3. advertising; and
4. customs recordal of intellectual property rights.

Customs recordal of intellectual property rights is itself a mechanism to facilitate the enforcement of trademark rights. Unfair competition claims are an additional way, or an alternative, to combat trademark infringement. Product quality and consumer protection laws are designed, inter alia, to lay down sanctions against fake and substandard products, which might at the same time be an infringement of a trademark. The use of trademarks in advertising may also be subject to regulations, thus the relevant provisions in the advertising laws and regulations will have to be considered by trademark owners and advertisers.

COPYRIGHT

14.2 LEGAL FRAMEWORK

The laws which govern the general protection of copyright in China are the Copyright Law of the PRC (the "Copyright Law"), effective from 1 June 1991, and with amendments effective from 27 October 2001 and the Implementing Regulations for the Copyright Law of the PRC (the "Copyright Implementing Regulations"), which became effective from 1 June 1991, with amendments effective from 15 September 2002.

The Copyright Law now provides explicit recognition for the protection of rental rights in respect of films (cinematographic works) and software (except where the software is not the essential object of the rental), the right of public performance of works in the public (including the presentation of films), and the right to distribute works via the internet. The Copyright Law specifically permits the full or partial assignment of economic rights in copyright subject matter. The restriction in the earlier Copyright Law that copyright licences be limited to 10 years has been removed. The Copyright Law also provides explicit protection for databases, ie original compilations of works, or information that does not qualify for copyright protection.

14.3 SCOPE OF APPLICATION

Article 3 of Copyright Law

Article 3 of the Copyright Law provides that works of Chinese citizens and legal entities, whether published or not, are eligible for protection. Such works include literary, artistic, natural science, social science and engineering technology works, etc, created in any of the following forms:

1. written works;
2. oral works;

3. musical works, operatic and dramatic works, works of *quyi*, choreographic works and acrobatic works;
4. works of fine art and architectural works;
5. photographic works;
6. cinematographic works and works created by a process analogous to cinematography;
7. graphics works such as drawings of engineering designs, drawings of product designs, maps, schematic drawings, etc, and three-dimensional model works;
8. computer software;
9. other works as stipulated in laws and administrative regulations.

Article 5 of Copyright Law

Definitions for 'architectural works', 'graphic works' and 'model works' were newly introduced under the Copyright Implementing Regulations. Article 5 of the Copyright Law, however, expressly excludes the following subject matter from copyright protection:

1. laws, regulations, resolutions, decisions and orders of government organs, other documents of a legislative, administrative or judicial nature, and their official translations;
2. news of current events; and
3. calendars, numerical tables in common use, forms in common use and formulas.

Works that are banned from publication or distribution under other laws are also excluded.

Article 10 of Copyright Law

Under Article 10 of the Copyright Law, the term 'copyright' includes the following rights:

1. the right of publication, ie the right to decide whether or not to make a work available to the public;
2. the right of attribution, ie the right to affix one's name to a work in order to indicate the author's identity;
3. the right of revision, ie the right to revise or authorise others to revise one's work;
4. the right of integrity, ie the right to protect one's work against misrepresentation and distortion;
5. the right of reproduction, ie the right to make one or more copies of one's work through such means as printing, photocopying, making a rubbing, making a sound recording, making a video recording, duplicating a recording, reproducing by photographic or cinematographic means, etc;

6. the right of distribution, ie the right to provide originals or reproductions of one's work to the public by means of sale or gift;

7. the right of rental, ie the right to permit others to temporarily use one's cinematographic work, work created by a process analogous to cinematography or computer software for consideration, unless the computer software itself is not the essential object of the rental;

8. the right of exhibition, ie the right to publicly display the original or a reproduction of one's work of fine art or photographic work;

9. the right of performance, ie the right to publicly perform one's work and to publicly broadcast by any means a performance of one's work;

10. the right of projection, ie the right to publicly show the original or a copy of one's work of fine art, photographic work, cinematographic work or work created by a process analogous to cinematography by means of such technical equipment as a movie projector, slide projector, etc;

11. the right of broadcast, ie the right to publicly broadcast or communicate one's work by means of wireless transmission, to communicate one's broadcast work to the public by wire transmission or rebroadcast, and to communicate one's broadcast work to the public through a loudspeaker or any other analogous instrument transmitting symbols, sounds or images;

12. the right of communication via an information network, ie the right to make one's work available to the public by wire or by wireless means, enabling members of the public to access the work at a time and from a place individually chosen by them;

13. the right of cinematisation, ie the right to fix a work in a medium by a cinematographic process or a process analogous to cinematography;

14. the right of adaptation, ie the right to change one's work thereby creating an original, new work;

15. the right of translation, ie the right to convert one's work from one language to another language;

16. the right of compilation, ie the right to cause one's work or extracts of one's work to become a new work through selection or arrangement and assembly; and

17. other rights to which a copyright owner is entitled.

The rights in points 5 to 17 above can be licensed or assigned. The Copyright Implementing Regulations require exclusive licence agreements to be in writing, and they also provide for voluntary recordal of licences, as well as assignments.

Copyright Implementing Regulations

The Copyright Implementing Regulations also provide that if an exclusive licence agreement is silent or unclear, then an exclusive licensee will be deemed to have the power to exercise his rights to the exclusion of all other persons, including the copyright owner. Further, the Copyright Implementing Regulations indicate that, unless otherwise agreed, an exclusive licensee must obtain the copyright owner's consent in order to issue sublicences to third parties.

Clarification of rights of co-authors

Where a jointly created work cannot be used by dividing it and the co-authors cannot reach agreement on the terms for their separate uses of the work, the Copyright Implementing Regulations permit each co-author to exercise his rights freely, absent 'proper cause' from the other co-author. The Copyright Implementing Regulations further suggest that a co-author may not grant any exclusive licence to third parties without consent from the other co-authors.

The Copyright Implementing Regulations require the agreement of all co-authors, however, in cases where one of them wishes to assign his rights to another party. Consent from all co-authors is clearly required for assignment of the entire copyright of the work to another party. The Copyright Implementing Regulations also require a co-author to account for and share any gains obtained through his separate use of the work with the other co-authors.

Extended protection for foreign works

Consistent with China's commitments under the WTO, the Copyright Implementing Regulations explicitly recognise protection for performances and sound recordings produced or distributed by foreigners and stateless persons. Likewise, protection is explicitly recognised for rights in radio and television programs broadcast by foreign radio and television stations. These provisions of the Copyright Implementing Regulations render China's copyright legislation into compliance with Article 14 of the TRIPS Agreement.

Works by foreigners will enjoy protection if (a) they were first published in China; or (b) the work was published outside China but there exists an international treaty acceded to by both the foreigner's country of habitual residence and China; or (c) the work was first published in a country which is a signatory to an international treaty which China has acceded to, or is simultaneously published in a signatory country and a non-signatory country.

In compliance with Article 3 of the Berne Convention for the Protection of Literary and Artistic Works (the "Berne Convention") (1971), the Copyright Implementing Regulations clarify that works created by a foreigner or stateless person that are published in China within 30 days after first publication outside China will be deemed to have been simultaneously published in China. Under the old Regulations, such works were regarded as having been first published in China.

14.4 TERM OF PROTECTION

Under the Copyright Law, most copyrights are protected for the life of the author plus fifty years. In cases of copyrights originally vesting in a legal person, and copyrights in cinematographic, television, and photographic works, and video and sound recordings, the duration of protection is fifty years from the date of first publication.

14.5 INTERNATIONAL CONVENTIONS

China acceded to several important international copyright conventions. These include: the Berne Convention, as from 15 October 1992; the Universal Copyright Convention, as from 30 October 1992; and the Convention for the Protection of Producers of Phonograms Against Unauthorised Duplication of their Phonograms, as from 30 April 1993.

Implementation of international copyright treaties acceded is done through the Regulations for the Implementation of International Copyright Treaties (the "Treaties Regulations"), which came into effect on 30 September 1992. The Treaties Regulations stipulate that upon the effective date of these international copyright treaties, works not yet in the public domain in their country of origin will be protected for the period of time specified in the Copyright Law and the Copyright Implementing Regulations. As expressly stated in the Treaties Regulations, international copyright treaties to which China has acceded prevail over the Treaties Regulations in cases where the two are in conflict.

14.6 REGISTRATION

Unlike the trademark system, registration is not a prerequisite to the enjoying of copyright protection in China. However, if there is a copyright registration system, resolution of disputes over ownership of copyrights could be facilitated. The registrations themselves may also be used as preliminary evidence to facilitate the resolution of copyright disputes in general. These are the objectives of the voluntary registration system of literary and artistic works in China.

The system is laid down in the Trial Measures for the Voluntary Registration of Literary and Artistic Works ("Voluntary Registration Measures"), issued by the National Copyright Administration (the "NCA") on 31 December 1994, and which came into effect on 1 January 1995. As registration is not compulsory, the Voluntary Registration

Measures state that failure to register will not affect the automatic protection of copyrights in accordance with Chinese laws. Note that the Voluntary Registration Measures apply to literary and artistic works, and also audio and video products (see Article 14). Although computer software is not within the scope of this registration system, computer software can be registered in accordance with the relevant regulations to be discussed below.

Some kinds of work are not registrable under the Voluntary Registration Measures. These include works that are not protected by Chinese copyright law, works for which the copyright protection period has expired, and works for which publication or broadcasting are prohibited. If a work of these kinds is registered, the registration is prone to cancellation. A registration will also be cancelled if the details of the registration do not accord with the facts, if the original applicant requests cancellation, or if the registration duplicates an earlier registration.

Authors, other individuals, or legal persons holding copyrights, owners of exclusive rights, or their agents are eligible to register the copyright works. Foreign parties (and parties from Hong Kong, Taiwan, and Macau) are not barred from the system, but they have to go to NCA in Beijing for registration. Local parties are required to go to Provincial-level Copyright Bureaux, which are responsible for the registration within their own territorial jurisdictions. Individuals must submit an application to the local Copyright Bureau in their place of residence. If there are co-authors or multiple persons holding the copyright, the place of residence of the person entrusted with the registration has to be looked at in deciding which Copyright Bureau to go to. Enterprises and other units should apply to the Copyright Bureau in their place of business.

Materials or documents to be submitted for an application include proof of identification, evidence of copyright ownership (such as duplicates of cover pages, copies or photos of original manuscripts, models, copies of contracts for entrustment or exclusive rights, etc). There is a prescribed application form for local parties and another prescribed form for works involving foreign parties. There is also an application fee. Registration authorities will examine and decide on an application within one month of submission. If the registration is successful, a certificate will be issued. The registration number will be consisted of the code referring to the region, year, the code referring to the type of work, and a serial number. Registration records are open to public inspection, though those who want to inspect the records have to fill in a registration form and pay a fee.

As a matter of practice, it is generally easier to convince the copyright agencies and the courts that copyright subsists in a foreign work if the copyright owner is able to produce a Copyright Registration Certificate.

14.7 OWNERSHIP

In general, the Copyright Law regards the individual author of a work to be the copyright owner. Exceptions to this rule include cinematographic and television works, and video and sound recordings. Copyright for those kinds of work vests in the producers. If the creation of the work is sponsored by a legal person (eg a company) or other organisation and represents the will of such legal person or other organisation, and responsibility for the work is borne by that legal person or other organisation, that legal person or other organisation will be deemed to be the author (thus copyright owner) of the work in question.

For occupational work, the situation is a little bit more complicated. A work created by a citizen in order to accomplish a task assigned to him by a legal person or other organisation (eg an employer) is an occupational work. The copyright of such work will be vested in the author, but the legal person or other organisation shall have the right of priority in using such work within its scope of business. At the same time, until two years after the completion of the work, the author may not authorise third parties to use such a work in the same way as that in which it is used by the unit without the consent of such unit. The above is the general position. The position of some of the occupational works is different. For the following two kinds of occupational work, the right of attribution will be vested in the author, and the other copyright rights will be vested in the legal person or other organisation:

1. drawings of engineering designs, drawings of product designs, maps, computer software, etc, created mainly by using the material and technical resources of a legal person or other organisation and the responsibility for which is borne by such legal person or other organisation;
2. occupational works in which the copyright vests in a legal person or other organisation pursuant to the provisions of a law, administrative regulation or contract.

For commissioned works, the ownership of the copyright in a commissioned work has to be decided according to the contract between the commissioner and the commissioned party. If the contract does not expressly provide for ownership or if no contract has been concluded, copyright will be vested in the commissioned party.

INFRINGEMENT 14.8

Infringement of copyright occurs when a party, without the consent of the copyright owner, commits any of the acts set out in Articles 46 and 47 of the Copyright Law.

Copyright infringements under Article 46:

1. publication of a work without permission from the owner of the copyright therein;
2. publication of a joint work as a work created solely by oneself, without permission from the other co-authors;
3. affixing one's name to another's work in pursuit of fame and profit where one has not participated in the creation of such work;
4. distortion and mutilation of a work;
5. plagiarising of another's work;
6. unless this Law provides otherwise, use of a work in ways such as exhibiting, cinematising or treating by a process analogous to cinematising, or use of a work through adapting, translating, annotating, etc, without permission from the copyright owner;
7. use of another's work without paying remuneration when re-muneration should be paid;
8. unless this Law provides otherwise, rental of a cinematographic work, work created by a process analogous to cinematography, computer software or sound or video recording without the permission of the owner of the copyright or neighbouring rights therein;
9. live broadcast of a performer's performance, or public transmission of his live performance or record his performance without his permission;
10. other infringements of copyright or neighbouring rights; or
11. use, without the permission of the publisher, of the layout of a book or periodical published by it.

Copyright infringements under Article 47:

1. reproducing, distributing, performing, projecting, broadcasting or compiling a work or communicating the same to the public via an information network, without permission from the owner of the copyright therein, unless this Law provides otherwise;
2. publishing a book in which another person has the exclusive right of publication;
3. reproducing and/or distributing a sound or video recording of a performance or communicating the same to the public via an information network without permission from the performer, unless this Law provides otherwise;

4. reproducing and/or distributing a sound or video recording or communicating the same to the public via an information network without permission from the producer thereof, unless this Law provides otherwise;

5. broadcasting or reproducing a radio or television broadcast without permission, unless this Law provides otherwise;

6. deliberately circumventing or cracking the technical measures taken by a copyright owner or owner of neighbouring rights to protect his copyright or neighbouring rights in a work, sound recording, video recording, etc without the permission of such copyright owner or owner of neighbouring rights, unless otherwise provided in laws or administrative regulations;

7. deliberately removing or modifying the electronic rights control information contained in a work, sound recording, video recording, etc without the permission of the copyright owner or the owner of neighbouring rights, unless otherwise provided in laws or administrative regulations; or

8. producing or selling a work on which another's signature is passed off.

The Copyright Law does not expressly prohibit the manufacture or trade in circumvention devices, components, services, etc. Lobbying efforts have been directed at defining in the revised Copyright Implementing Regulations 'technological measures' to include both 'copy-control' and 'access controls'. Meanwhile, the PRC Criminal Law has not been amended to provide for criminal penalties for circumvention violations, and there do not appear to be plans to amend the Code in this regard in the near future.

14.9 ENFORCEMENT AND PENALTIES

Copyright infringement will lead to civil liability. The infringer may be ordered to cease the infringement, eliminate its effects, make a public apology, and / or pay damages. If his act is one of those listed in Article 47, in addition to the civil liability, he may be subjected by a copyright administration department to an (a) order to cease the infringing act; (b) confiscation of unlawful income; (c) confiscation and destruction of the infringing reproductions and (d) the imposition of a fine, if his act also prejudices the public interest. If the circumstances are serious, the copyright administration department may also confiscate the materials, tools, equipment, etc, used mainly in the manufacture of the infringing reproductions; if a criminal offence is constituted, the criminal liability shall be pursued in accordance with the law.

Article 48 of the Copyright Law provides that when copyright or neighbouring rights are infringed upon, the infringer shall pay damages based on the actual losses of the right-holder. If the actual losses are difficult to calculate, the damages paid may be based on the illegal income earned by the infringer. The measure of damages shall also include the reasonable expenses incurred by the right-holder in halting the infringing act. If neither the actual losses of the right-holder nor the illegal income earned by the infringer can be determined, the People's Court shall, depending on the circumstances of the infringing act, render a judgement awarding damages not exceeding RMB500,000.

There are also provisions in the Copyright Law for a preliminary injunction against the act and an order of preservation of property (Article 49), and preservation of evidence prior to the institution of proceedings (Article 50). If a copyright owner or an owner of neighbouring rights has evidence showing that another person is carrying out or about to carry out an act of infringement upon his rights and that failure to immediately halt such act would cause damage to his lawful rights and interests which would be difficult to remedy, he may, prior to instituting an action, apply to a People's Court for a preliminary injunction against the act and an order of preservation of property. A copyright owner or an owner of neighbouring rights may, with the object of halting infringing conduct, apply to a People's Court for the preservation of evidence prior to the institution of proceedings, if such evidence might be destroyed, lost or difficult to obtain later. The People's Court must render a ruling within 48 hours of acceptance of the application. The implementation of preservation measures shall commence promptly upon the rendering of a ruling adopting such measures. The People's Court may order the applicant to provide security. If the applicant fails to provide security, his application shall be rejected. If the applicant fails to institute proceedings within 15 days after the People's Court takes preservation measures, the People's Court shall terminate such preservation measures.

When hearing a case, a People's Court may confiscate the illegal income, the infringing reproductions and property used in the commission of illegal activities, of the party that has infringed upon copyright or neighbouring rights.

Articles 36 and 37 of the Copyright Implementing Regulations provide that for acts of infringement which violate Article 47 of the Copyright Law and prejudice the public interest, the copyright administration department may impose a fine of not more than three times the amount of the illegal turnover or, if the amount of the illegal turnover is difficult to calculate, a fine of not more than RMB100,000, and the acts of infringement shall be investigated and dealt with by the copyright administration department of the local People's Government. Infringing acts that have a serious impact nationwide may be investigated and dealt with by the copyright administration department of the State Council.

Under Article 55 of the Copyright Law, a party who objects to an administrative penalty may institute proceedings in the People's Court within three months from the receipt of the written decision on the penalty. Where a party has neither instituted proceedings, nor performed in accordance with the decision by the expiry of the time limit, the Copyright Administration Department may request the People's Court to enforce the decision.

14.10 ADMINISTRATIVE AUTHORITIES

The National Copyright Administration ("NCA") itself is responsible for the nationwide administration of copyright, while there are Copyright Administration Departments ("CAD"s) under People's governments in provinces, autonomous regions, and municipalities directly under the central government, responsible for the administration of copyright in their respective administrative districts. The promulgation of the Implementing Measures for Administrative Penalties in Copyright Matters in 28 January 1997 (amended version came into force on 1 September 2003) makes it possible for foreign complainants to bring complaints to local copyright administration departments. It is believed that this will give a greater protection to copyright owners and speed up the process of undertaking enforcement.

The Copyright Implementing Regulations have eliminated the previous requirement that foreigners file complaints for administrative enforcement solely with the NCA, ie at the central government level. The Copyright Implementing Regulations now explicitly permit foreigners to seek relief directly from local copyright bureaux in cases where "harm is done to the social and public interests". NCA will only be involved in cases that have serious impact nationwide.

At the same time, China Copyright Consulting Centre was established in September 1998. This Centre is an investigative agency looking at copyright infringements. The Centre can be contacted through the NCA. Sometimes NCA will require foreign complainants obtain supplementary evidence on the alleged infringement through the Centre before it will proceed further with its investigations. As there is a shortage of personnel, NCA generally encourages complainants to use the People's Courts to combat infringements.

14.11 COMPLEMENTARY ROLES OF THE NCA AND ADMINISTRATION FOR INDUSTRY AND COMMERCE

There are situations where an act infringes trademark rights and copyright at the same time. For example, a pirated Windows OS is a copyright infringing item. When you run it, the Windows trademark will appear on the screen, making it a trademark infringing item also. Some trademarks are a copyrighted work themselves. Best examples are those cartoon characters registered as trademarks. The cartoon characters should be works of fine art enjoying copyright protection. Where the trademark constitutes part of a design on packaging, which may be protected by a patent, a multiple infringement is also possible. It is possible for a trademark owner to seek protection of its trademark by enforcing its copyright, but the reality is that enforcement under the Copyright Law is more difficult than under Trademark Law. This is because NCA is understaffed and underfunded, and the powers of its officers are not as clearly defined as that of Administrations for Industry and Commerce ("AIC"s), the administrative body combating trademark infringement. AIC officers have the power to enter premises, seize accounts and records, seal and destroy goods, impose fines and award compensation, and destroy infringing materials, under the relevant laws and regulations.

Sometimes it is possible to mobilise more than one administrative department, for a joint action. Involvement of more than one department is justified theoretically if more than one kind of IP right is being infringed. For example, a trademark and company name infringement associated with copyright infringement should be able to trigger the action of NCA, the Fair Trade Bureau ("FTB") of the State AIC ("SAIC") and other local AICs. The Notice Concerning a Decisive Crackdown on Piracy and Other Acts of Copyright Infringement issued by the SAIC and the NCA on 28 February 1995 gives AIC a formal role to play in enforcing copyright. Local AICs are required by the Notice to work with CADs to raise the awareness of copyright protection. Local AICs are also required to monitor piracy activities. Local AICs are given power to impose penalties of up to 5 times the total price of the illegal products, or 5 to 10 times the illegal income; revoke the infringer's business licence; issue a warning; order the cessation of the sale, the rental, or the screening of the illegal products; and confiscate the illegal products and illegal income. The principle of "the first to put a case on the docket shall handle it" would be adopted for the coordination between CADs and AICs.

CRIMINAL SANCTIONS AGAINST COPYRIGHT INFRINGEMENT

14.12

Apart from incurring civil liability, an infringer may, in serious cases, face criminal prosecution.

Article 217 of Criminal Law

The Decision of the Standing Committee of the NPC Concerning Punishment of the Crime of Copyright Infringement, was promulgated on 5 July 1994, and came into effect on the same date. The Decision was repealed by the PRC Criminal Law when the latter was amended in 1997. The Criminal Law now provides for offences of copyright infringement. Article 217 of Criminal Law provides that copyright infringement in any of the following ways is an offence, if the infringement is for the purpose of obtaining profit:

1. reproduction and distribution of another person's written work, musical, cinematographic, television or videographic work, computer software or other work without the permission of the owner of the copyright therein;
2. publication of a book to which another person enjoys exclusive publishing rights;
3. reproduction and distribution of an audio or video recording without the permission of the recording's producer; or
4. production and sale of a work of art passed off under another person's signature.

If the amount of illegal income is relatively large or there are other serious circumstances, the offender will be sentenced to a fixed term imprisonment of not more than three years or criminal detention, and / or a fine. If the amount of illegal income is very large or there are other exceptionally serious circumstances, the offender will be sentenced to a fixed term imprisonment of not less than three years and not more than seven years, and a fine.

Meaning of terms like "amount of illegal income is relatively large", "other serious circumstances" etc, in relation to illegal publications, are provided by the Interpretation of the Supreme People's Court of Several Issues Concerning Specific Application of the Law in the Trial of Criminal Cases of Illegal Publications, promulgated on 17 December 1998 and effective from 23 December 2003, summarised as follows:

Amount of illegal income is relatively large:
1. more than RMB50,000 (offender is an individual)
2. more than RMB200,000 (offender is an unit)

Other serious circumstances:
1. Offender has been investigated more than twice for administrative or civil responsibility for copyright infringement, and carried out again within two years, one of the acts of copyright infringement specified in Article 217 of the Criminal Law;
2. amount involved in the illegal operation exceeds RMB200,000 (offender is an individual) / RMB1,000,000 (offender is an unit); or
3. other serious consequence has been caused.

Amount of illegal income is very large:
1. more than RMB200,000 (offender is an individual);
2. more than RMB1,000,000 (offender is an unit).

Other exceptionally serious circumstances:
1. amount involved in the illegal operation exceeds RMB1,000,000 (offender is an individual) / RMB5,000,000 (offender is an unit); or
2. other especially serious consequence has been caused.

At the same time, according to Article 218 of the Criminal Law, it is also an offence for a person to knowingly sell an infringing reproduction as specified in Article 217 for the purpose of obtaining profit. If the amount of illegal income is very large, the offender will be sentenced to a fixed term imprisonment of not more than three years or criminal detention, and / or a fine. If the offender is an individual and the illegal gains exceed RMB100,000 or if the offender is a unit and the illegal gains exceed RMB500,000, the offender will be convicted and punished for a crime of selling works reproduced by infringement on copyright in accordance with the provisions of Article 218 of the Criminal Law, according to Supreme Court's Interpretation just referred to.

Punishments

Prison terms of up to three years with possible fines may be imposed on individuals and organisations for cases involving 'relatively large amounts' of illegal income, that is, profits obtained in the range of RMB20,000 and RMB100,000, or 'other serious factors', where:

1. literary, musical, film, television, video recording, computer software, or other copyrighted works are reproduced, and distributed for profit, without the permission of the copyright holder;
2. books for which others hold exclusive publishing rights are published for profit;
3. audio or video recordings produced by other parties are copied, or distributed for profit, without permission of the producer; or
4. counterfeits of others' famous works of fine art are made or sold.

Other serious factors exist in cases where:
1. an infringer infringes copyright again, after being held liable for administrative or civil liabilities in more than two prior cases;
2. the amount of illegal business operated by an individual exceeds RMB100,000, and the amount of illegal business operated by an unit exceeds RMB500,000; or
3. other serious consequences are caused, or there are other serious circumstances.

Where the above infringements involve an amount between RMB 100,000 and RMB500,000, or other especially serious circumstances, an infringer could receive a three to seven year prison term, together with fines.

Before the promulgation of the monetary criteria mentioned above, enforcement of copyright through the criminal route appear to be quite uncommon, and few copyright owners have resorted to the Criminal Law when combating counterfeiting. A procuratorial official in Shenzhen has reported that his office had only handled eight criminal cases involving counterfeit trademarks in 1983-1993. Nevertheless, as prompted by the WTO accession, China is putting more and more efforts into combating the piracy problem.

14.13 QUESTIONS UNANSWERED

The Copyright Implementing Regulations fail to address a number of critical issues raised under the revised Copyright Law, such as:

1. whether works of applied art will be protected under the Copyright Law. For now, only foreign works of applied art are protected in China, via the Berne Convention, the Universal Copyright Convention and Treaties Regulations. It is believed that the case "胡三三诉裘海索和中国美术馆" (Beijing Higher People's Court *Gao Zhi Zhong Zi* No 18 of 2001) shows that applied art is protected under the Copyright Law.
2. whether unauthorised three-dimensional reproduction of two-dimensional works will be considered as infringement.
3. whether circumvention or sabotage of technological measures such as 'copy control' and 'access control' and the trade in or manufacture of circumvention devices will be considered as infringing acts.

COMPUTER SOFTWARE RIGHTS

14.14 LEGAL FRAMEWORK

Regulations for the Protection of Computer Software (the "Software Regulations"), which came into effect on 1 October 1991, with amendments effective from 1 January 2002, and the Measures for the Registration of Computer Software (the "Software Registration Measures"), which took effect on 18 April 1992, with amendments effective from 20 February 2002, offer the legislative framework for software copyright protection, together with the Copyright Law, the Copyright Implementing Regulations, and the Treaties Regulations.

SCOPE OF APPLICATION 14.15

Computer software under the Software Regulations covers computer programmes (including 'source code programmes' and 'object code programmes') and related documentation. Only software that is independently developed by the creator is protected. Protection is available only if the software is stored onto a tangible medium. Ideas, processing methods, operation methods or mathematical concepts used in the development of the software are expressly excluded from protection.

Rights of software copyright holders include: (a) right of publication; (b) developer's right of authorship; (c) right of revision; (d) right of duplication; (e) right of distribution; (f) right of rental (except where the software is not the essential object of the rental); (g) right of publication over networks; (h) right of translation (the right to convert the software from one natural language to another natural language); (i) other rights which should be enjoyed by the copyright holder.

EXCLUSIVE RIGHTS 14.16

Under the prior regulations, the right to exploit copyright in software excluded uses that might harm the public interest. This limitation has been removed in the new Software Regulations. However, it remains in Article 4 of the Copyright Law, and thus it would be prudent to assume the removal of the relevant language from the Software Regulations is just a cosmetic change.

The revised Software Regulations accord protection for new types of uses of software, including rental rights and the right to authorise "distribution over information networks," which ostensibly includes the internet. Consequently, online distribution of software without authorisation (whether for profit or otherwise) is considered a prohibited form of reproduction under the new Software Regulations. The provisions on network infringements in the new Regulations follow the issuance in December 2000 of an interpretation by the Supreme People's Court, which sets out in detail the conditions for pursuing civil liability against network pirates.

Further, the new Software Regulations provide explicit protection against activities that attempt to circumvent or sabotage technological measures used by software copyright owners. Likewise, the regulations outlaw the removal or alteration of electronic rights management information incorporated into works to facilitate copyright protection.

TERM OF PROTECTION 14.17

Under the prior regulations, copyright in software is vested upon creation and extended 25 years from the date of first publication, subject to a right of renewal for another 25 years. Foreigners were exempt from this renewal requirement under the Treaties Regulations, which were themselves drafted to facilitate implementation of the Berne Convention and Universal Copyright Convention.

The revised Software Regulations have removed the 25-year limitation on duration, and essentially provide local copyright owners with the same rights as foreigners. Thus, in the case of software owned by legal persons and other organisations, the period of protection is now 50 years, ending on 31 December of the fiftieth year after the work was published. If the software is not published within 50 years after its creation, no protection is to be afforded.

Article 14 of the Software Regulations lays down the term of protection. For copyright software of a natural person, the protection period is consisted of the natural person's lifetime and 50 years after his death, and ending on 31 December of the fiftieth year after his death. If the software was jointly developed, protection shall end on 31 December of the fiftieth year after the death of the last surviving natural person. The software copyright of a legal person or other organisation shall be protected for a period of 50 years and end on 31 December of the fiftieth year after the software was first published. However, if the software is not published within 50 years after the date of completion of the development thereof, it shall no longer be protected.

Article 5 of the Software Regulations extends protection to foreign works that are either 'first distributed' in China, or that are created by citizens of countries that acceded to an international treaty also acceded to by China (eg the Berne Convention and the Universal Copyright Convention).

14.18 OWNERSHIP

The copyright in computer software vests in the developer who organises and carries out the development work, provides working conditions for such development and bears responsibility for the software. The developer is the legal person or other organisation that actually organises and directly carries out the development work and bears responsibility for the finished software, or a natural person who independently completes development of the software on the strength of his own conditions and bears responsibility for such software. In general, software companies and individual software developers are allowed to determine ownership in accordance with development contracts. If there is no agreement on the issue, where the software was developed by a natural person during his term of service with a legal person or other organisation, the copyright in such software shall be owned by the employer, if:

1. the software was developed to achieve an expressly designated development objective forming part of the developer's job;
2. the software developed by him is a foreseen or natural result of the activities performed as part of his job; or
3. the software was mainly developed using such material and technical resources of the employer as its funds, dedicated equipment, unpublished specialised information, etc, and for which the legal person or other organisation bears responsibility.

The employer may reward the developer. If the development of software was commissioned, the copyright ownership vests in the commissioned party, unless otherwise provided for by written agreement.

REGISTRATION 14.19

As a result of China's accession to the Berne Convention, foreign computer software is protected as literary work without the need for registration. Under the prior Software Regulations, registration of software copyrights was voluntary, although for local rights owners, registration was a precondition for the filing of administrative or judicial complaints against infringers. The new regulations still permit registration for the purpose of providing *prima facie* evidence of ownership and validity of software, although registration is no longer a condition for effective enforcement and assignment of rights. Foreign parties who wish to register their software copyright should go to the detailed provisions of the Software Registration Measures.

FAIR USE 14.20

The prior regulations set out a range of exceptions on the exclusive rights in software by permitting use of small quantities of unauthorised copies in a broad range of situations. These included use for non-commercial purposes such as classroom teaching, scientific research, carrying out of official duties by State organisations, etc. This particular provision has been removed in the revised Software Regulations. Meanwhile, the new Regulations eliminate the odious Article 13, Section 2 in the prior Regulations, which permitted the equivalent of compulsory licensing of software developed by state-owned entities in cases where required for the national interest or public interest.

The Software Regulations provide broad privileges to persons holding lawful copies of software. Such persons may perform the following without the need for consent of the software copyright owner:

1. install the software in devices which have information processing capabilities, such as computers, etc, as required for use;

2. make backup copies as a precaution against damage to the original copies; such backup copies may not be made available to others by any means and the owners shall be responsible for destroying such copies once they lose lawful ownership of the original copies; and

3. make necessary modifications to the software in order to use it in the actual computer application environment or to improve its functions or performance, provided that, unless otherwise specified in the contract, the modified software is not furnished to any third party without the permission of the software copyright owner.

Article 17 of the revised regulations also allow the use of software for the purpose of "study and research on design ideas and theory of the software through installing, displaying, transmitting or storing the software or any other means of use" without authorisation of the copyright owner. That said, officials with the NCA in Beijing, which sets government policy in relation to copyright matters and is influential with Chinese courts, have informally confirmed that reverse engineering of software will be prohibited under the new Regulations.

14.21 INFRINGEMENT, ENFORCEMENT AND PENALTIES

The following acts constitute copyright infringement under the Software Regulations:

1. publication or registration of software without the permission of the software copyright owner;
2. publication or registration of the software of another as one's own software;
3. publication or registration of jointly developed software without permission from the other co-developers as software solely developed by oneself;
4. affixing one's name to another's software or changing the attribution on another's software;
5. modification or translation of software without the permission of the software copyright owner; or
6. other infringements of software copyright.

The infringer would need to undertake civil liability by ceasing the infringement, eliminating the effects, apologising, paying damages, etc, depending on the circumstances. If the infringement also prejudices the public interest, the infringer may, by a copyright administration department, be subject to an order to cease the infringing act, confiscation of unlawful income and confiscation and destruction of the infringing copies, and / or a fine may also be imposed on him. If the circumstances are serious, the copyright administration department may also confiscate the materials, tools, equipment, etc, mainly used in the manufacture of the infringing copies; if a violation of criminal law is constituted, his criminal liability under the criminal law provisions concerning the crime of copyright infringement or the crime of selling infringing copies shall be pursued:

Commission of the acts under points 1 and 2 above may be punished by the imposition of a fine of RMB100 per item or of not more than five times the value of the goods. Commission of the acts described under points 3, 4 and 5 may be punished by the imposition of a fine of not more than RMB50,000.

The following are discussions of specific issues in infringement.

Reproduction

Under the revised Software Regulations, administrative and civil liability for infringement by reproducers of software appears to be provided on a strict liability basis, and reproducers will only be able to avoid liability if they can prove that they were lawfully authorised.

Distribution

Parties that are accused of distributing or renting software can be pursued if they are unable to provide evidence that the software was from a 'lawful source'. However, the Software Regulations do not define 'lawful source' or provide examples of the types of evidence that would satisfy this requirement. (Interestingly, Article 56 of the recently revised Trademark Law likewise removes liability for compensation for vendors of products that infringe registered trademarks, provided the vendor is "able to prove that he obtained the same lawfully and identifies the supplier").

End-user liability

The prosecution of end-users may be hampered by Article 30 of the Software Regulations, as it provides that if the holder of a copy of a piece of software was unaware, and there was no legitimate reason why he should be aware, that the piece of software was an infringing copy, he shall not bear liability for compensation. However, he will have to cease the use of and destroy the infringing copy. If ceasing the use of and destruction of the infringing copy would cause material loss to the user of such copy, he may continue the use after paying a reasonable fee to the software copyright owner. The impact of this restriction on the scope of exclusive rights will depend in large part on the interpretation of "reasonable grounds to know software was infringing" by the courts and administrative enforcement authorities.

221

14.22 ADMINISTRATIVE ENFORCEMENT

The revised Software Regulations still permit rights holders to file complaints with either civil courts or administrative enforcement authorities. Under the prior Copyright Implementing Regulations, foreigners were required to file complaints with the NCA in Beijing, whereas local copyright owners were empowered to file complaints directly with local copyright bureaux which operate under NCA's supervision. In practice, NCA and local Copyright Bureaux have removed this restriction on complaints by foreigners. It is likely that this practice will be codified in the future Implementing Rules to ensure compliance with the principle of 'national treatment' under the WTO.

The State Council transferred the responsibility for the enforcement of copyrights in computer software from the Ministry of Electronics Industry to NCA in 1995. NCA is quite effective in enforcing software copyrights. As reported, it took just three months for the NCA to conclude the complaint by Sega with an order and a fine. Sega filed a complaint in May 1994, claiming that a state-owned enterprise in Shenzhen was manufacturing and exporting video game machines containing built-in copies of Sega's game programmes. Sega hired the China Copyright Consulting Centre for investigation and preparation of a consultation report. In August 1994, the NCA delivered a decision to the Guangdong Copyright Bureau, ordering the infringer to stop sales and production of the infringing items, to hand over all infringing game cards, and to pay a fine of RMB30,000.

PATENTS

14.23 LEGAL FRAMEWORK

Patent protection in China is provided by the Patent Law of the PRC (the "Patent Law"), second revised version effective from 1 July 2001 and the Detailed Implementing Rules for the Patent Law of the PRC (the "Patent Implementing Rules"), major revisions effective from 1 July 2001 (further revisions of provisions on international registration effective from 1 February 2003).

According to the Transitional Measures for the Implementation of the Revised Patent Law and its Implementing Regulations, for any patent application filed on or after 1 July 2001 where the patent right is granted on the basis of the application, the provisions of the revised Patent Law and its Implementing Regulations will apply; for any patent application filed before 1 July 2001 where the patent right is granted on the basis of the application, the provisions of the revised Patent Law and its Implementing Regulations will also apply on or after 1 July 2001, except where otherwise provided for.

China became a member of the Patent Cooperation Treaty on 1 January 1994. The PRC Patent Office can now receive international applications filed by applicants in any contracting state of the treaty.

SCOPE OF PROTECTION   14.24

The Patent Law grants protection to 'invention-creations'. There are three kinds of invention-creations: inventions, utility models and designs. An invention is any new technical solution relating to a product, a process, or an improvement thereof. A utility model means any new technical solution relating to the shape, structure, or the combination of shape and structure of a product, which is fit for practical use. A design is any new design of the shape, pattern, colour, or their combination, of a product that creates an aesthetic feeling, and is fit for industrial application. The term of protection available to inventions is different from the other two invention-creations. A patented invention enjoys 20 years of protection, while a patent for utility model or design lasts for 10 years.

SCOPE OF APPLICATION   14.25

To be eligible for patent, an invention or utility model must be novel, must involve an inventive step and must be useful. The term 'novel' means that, prior to the date of application, no identical invention or utility model was publicly disclosed in a domestic or foreign publication, or was publicly used or otherwise known to the public in China, and that no one had filed an application with the Patent Office for an identical invention or utility model and that it was not described in any patent application document published after the date of application. On the other hand, prominent substantive distinguishing features and marked progress, when compared with prior art existing before the date of application, are required for an 'inventive step' for an invention patent. In the case of utility model patent, substantive distinguishing features and progress (not marked progress) is required. An invention or utility model is 'useful' if it can be manufactured or used and is capable of producing a positive result.

There are fewer hurdles for designs. To be eligible for patent, a design must not be identical or similar to any design publicly disclosed in a domestic or foreign publication or publicly used in China prior to the date of application, nor may it conflict with the prior legitimate right of any third party.

Some matters are not eligible for patent, as provided by Article 25 of the Patent Law:

1. scientific discoveries;
2. rules and methods for intellectual activities;
3. methods for the diagnosis and treatment of diseases;
4. animal and plant varieties (processes used in producing animal and plant varieties, however, may be patented in accordance with the Patent Law); and
5. substances obtained from the use of nuclear transformation.

Prior to the revisions to the Patent Law, food, beverages, flavourings and pharmaceutical products, and substances obtained by means of a chemical process could not be patented, although the processes used in producing such products could. The revisions make it possible to obtain a patent for products such as pharmaceuticals and agricultural chemicals, along with the process for the same. The revised law has extended patents that protect a process, to products obtained directly by using the process. Administrative protection is also available for foreign pharmaceutical products patented by the US, Japanese, and European Community companies in their respective jurisdictions between January 1986 and January 1993. (For details, see Regulations for Administrative Protection of Pharmaceuticals).

14.26 OWNERSHIP

The inventor has the right to file for patent registration in general. An exception to this rule, as for copyright, is where the invention-creation is created in the execution of the duties of the creator or the invention-creation is created mainly using the material and technological conditions of a unit to which the creator belongs (collectively referred to as 'work-related invention-creation'). Rights to apply for the patent will be vested in that unit in such cases, but entitlement to right to apply for a patent and patent right can also be provided in a contract in the second situation. Other than that the creator of a non work-related invention-creation has every right to apply for a patent, and the Patent Law expressly provides that no entity or individual can prevent him from doing so. The Patent Law also requires the enterprise to remunerate the inventor for his work-related invention-creation and award him bonuses. Prescribed minimum amount of remuneration and bonuses can be found in Article 74 of the Patent Implementing Rules (for state-owned enterprises and state-run units) and the Regulations Concerning the Allocation of Bonuses and Rewards to Inventors or Creators of Work-related Invention-creations Patent.

In cases where two or more units or individuals have cooperated in the completion of an invention-creation, or where a unit or individual has completed an invention-creation upon acceptance of a commission from another unit or individual, the right to apply for a patent shall vest in the unit or individual who completed or jointly completed the invention or creation, unless otherwise agreed upon.

PRINCIPLES OF PATENT PROTECTION 14.27

If two or more applicants separately apply for patents for an identical invention-creation, the patent rights shall be granted to the person who applied first, according to Article 9 of the Patent Law. Thus the system is one of 'first-to-file'. Having said that, applicants may be able to rely on the Paris Convention to claim priority. Pursuant to that Convention, if a patent application for an invention or utility model is first filed in another Convention member country within 12 months before the PRC application, the prior filing date will be regarded as the filing date in China. An applicant in a design patent application cannot claim that much time – the PRC application must be filed within six months of the first Convention filing date in order to claim priority.

PATENT COOPERATION TREATY 14.28

China acceded to the Patent Cooperation Treaty and became a member with effect from 1 January 1994. The Patent Office can now receive international applications filed by applicants in any contracting state of the Patent Cooperation Treaty. Regulations Concerning China's Implementation of the Patent Cooperation Treaty govern the international application in China.

According to the Regulations, international applications filed with the Patent Office have to be in Chinese or English. Applicants in an international application can claim priority for an invention patent that has been applied for in a Paris Convention Member State. The applicant must furnish a Chinese translation of the international application to the Patent Office and pay the prescribed fees (eg fees for patent search). The application has to be made through a prescribed patent agency (see below).

In an international application, a Chinese patent will be granted only after the applicant goes through the procedures before the Patent Office. Yet the time needed might be not be too long, as the international application is likely to have already gone through the formal examination, international search and international publication.

PATENT AGENTS 14.29

Article 19 of the Patent Law requires that foreigners, foreign enterprises, or other foreign organisations having no habitual residence or business office in China have to appoint a patent agency designated by the State Council to act as its agent in their patent application or to carry out other patent-related matters in China. Such designated agents include: China Patent Agent (HK) Limited, CCPIT Patent and Trademark Law Office, Liu, Shen & Associates, NTD Patent and Trademark Agency Limited, and Shanghai Patent Agency. The full list of designated agents is available at the website of the State Intellectual Property Office, www.sipo.gov.cn.

14.30 APPLICATION, EXAMINATION AND TIMING

Since the PRC patent application system is based on the first-to-file principle, it is important that patents are filed as early as possible.

Inventions and utility models

Certain documents are required for a patent application for an invention or utility model, as provided by Article 26 of the Patent Law. These include: (a) a request; (b) a description of the invention or utility model; (c) an abstract of the descriptions; and (d) the claims. An application should be limited to a single invention or utility model, but if two or more inventions or utility models belong to one general inventive concept, a single application may be filed to cover them all. The applicant can amend the application documents, but the amendments cannot exceed the scope in the original specifications and claims. Once a patent application is received by the Patent Office, the Patent Office will carry out a search of prior art. This is not a formal requirement, as the obligation to identify relevant prior art rests on the applicant.

A preliminary examination carried out by the Patent Office will follow, and this is a process that is more concerned with formality than substance. After the preliminary examination confirms that the application is in conformity with the formal requirements of the Patent Law, it will be published within 18 months from the date of application. The Patent Office may, upon the request of the applicant, publish such application earlier. For an invention patent application, under Articles 35 and 36 of the Patent Law, the Patent Office may, upon a request made by the applicant at any time within three years after the date of application for an invention patent, conduct a substantive examination of the applicant's application. The application shall be deemed to have been withdrawn should there be no request from the applicant within the time limit, without just cause. The Patent Office, though, may conduct the substantive examination of an invention patent application on its own initiative if it deems necessary. When an applicant for an invention patent requests a substantive examination, he shall provide reference materials in relation to his invention prior to the date of application.

If an application for an invention patent has been filed in a foreign country, the Patent Office may require the applicant to submit the documentation used by the foreign country to conduct any search in connection with the examination of the applicant's application, or the documentation concerning the results of such examination, within a prescribed period of time. If the applicant fails to submit such documentation within the prescribed period of time without just cause, his application shall be deemed to have been withdrawn.

Under Articles 37 to 39 of the Patent Law, if the Patent Office finds that an invention patent application fails to conform herewith after conducting the substantive examination, it shall notify the applicant and require him to state his comments or amend his application within a prescribed period of time. If the applicant fails to respond within the prescribed period of time without just cause, his application shall be deemed to have been withdrawn. If the Patent Office still finds that the invention patent application fails to conform to the Patent Law after the applicant has stated his comments or made amendments thereto, it shall reject the application. If, after substantive examination, there are no grounds for rejecting an invention patent application, the Patent Office shall render a decision to grant invention patent rights, issue an invention patent certificate and register and gazette the patent. The invention patent rights shall enter into effect on the gazette date.

There is no substantive examination for utility model patent applications. If the Patent Office finds, after a preliminary examination, that there is no cause for rejecting the application for a utility model patent, the Patent Office will render a decision to grant utility model patent rights, and issue the appropriate patent certificate and register and gazette the patent. The utility model patent rights shall enter into effect on the gazette date.

Designs

As required by Article 27 of the Patent Law, the application for a design patent should be accompanied by a request, drawings or photographs of the design, and an indication as to the product incorporating the design, and the class to which that product belongs. There is also no substantive examination for applications for design patents. Just like a utility model patent application, if the Patent Office finds, after a preliminary examination, that there is no cause for rejecting the application for a design patent, the Patent Office will render a decision to grant design patent rights, and issue the certificate and register and gazette the patent. The gazette day will be the day the design patent rights enter into effect.

RE-EXAMINATION

14.31

If an application is rejected, the applicant may submit a request for re-examination to the Patent Re-examination Board within three months after the date of receipt of the notice, as provided by Article 41 of the

Patent Law. After the re-examination, the Patent Re-examination Board shall render a decision and notify the patent applicant. If the re-examination decision is still not in his favour, the applicant can resort to the People's Court. He may institute an action in a People's Court within three months after the date of receipt of the notice on the result of the re-examination.

14.32 INVALIDATION

Invalidation procedures are also available under the Patent Law. Articles 45 to 47 of the Patent Law provide that any unit or individual that considers the grant of patent rights not to be in conformity with the relevant provisions hereof may, after the date on which the Patent Office publicly announces the granting of the patent right, submit a request to the Patent Re-examination Board to declare the relevant patent right invalid.

The Patent Re-examination Board shall timely examine and render a decision on the request to declare the patent rights invalid and notify the petitioner and the patentee. The Patent Office shall register and gazette decisions to declare patent rights invalid. If a party is dissatisfied with the decision of the Patent Re-examination Board to declare the patent right invalid or to uphold the patent right, he may institute an action in a People's Court within three months after the date of receipt of the notice. The People's Court shall notify the other party to the invalidation procedure to participate in the action as a third party.

Patent rights that have been declared invalid shall be deemed void *ab initio*. Decisions declaring patent rights invalid shall not have retroactive force on patent infringement judgements and rulings which were rendered and enforced by People's Courts, decisions on the handling of patent infringement disputes which were performed or enforced, or patent licensing contracts and patent transfer contracts which were performed, before the patent rights were declared invalid. However, if a third party incurred losses due to bad faith on the part of the patentee, the patentee shall compensate such third party. If failure to refund the royalties or the patent right transfer fee by the patentee or patent right transferor to the licensee or patent right transferee is a clear violation of the principle of fairness, the patentee or the patent right transferor shall refund all or part of the patent royalties or patent transfer fee to the licensee or patent right transferee.

Article 64 of the Patent Implementing Rules provides that anyone requesting invalidation or part invalidation of a patent right in accordance with the provisions of Article 45 of the Patent Law shall submit a request and the necessary evidence in two copies. The request for invalidation shall state in detail the grounds for filing the request, making reference to all the evidence as submitted, and indicate the piece of evidence on which each ground is based. Article 64 also provides the grounds for invalidating a patent, including: (a) no novelty, no inventive step or no usefulness (for inventions or utility models); (b) published or used, or contrary to prior rights (for designs); (c) specification not clearly and completely written (for inventions or utility models); (d) not within the definition of invention, utility model or design in Article 2 of the Patent Implementing Rules, etc.

DESIGN PATENT AND TRADEMARK PROTECTIONS 14.33

Designs that can be registered include boxes, bottles, bags, labels, and designs which may be represented in two or three dimensions, and may contain generic elements. As mentioned above, the protection period of a design patent is 10 years. Design patent is a useful supplement to trademark protection. Despite the fact that a design patent is not perpetual, it can still offer some form of protection to elements in boxes, bottles, etc, which are not registrable as a trademark. That design patent registration should not be ignored is evidenced by the fact that Chinese entities have started to apply for patents for designs which are, in fact, label or device trademarks owned by other parties, including owners of some famous foreign trademarks. This will create problems in the enforcement of the trademark even if the mark in question is registered in China by the foreign entity. Confusion among the various enforcement and official bodies may result, making it very difficult for the foreign trademark owner to take quick and efficient action against the infringer. The Opinion Concerning the Question or the Handling of Conflicts of Rights Between the Exclusive Right to Use Trademarks and Design Patent Rights issued by the SAIC on 7 December 1995 provides, to a limited extent, some guidance regarding this issue. The Opinion provides that where the date of gazetting the initial examination and approval of a trademark is made prior to the date of application for the relevant design patent, and before the design patent is cancelled or declared invalid, the AIC will handle the trademark infringement case in accordance with the Trademark Law. Nevertheless, as the Opinion was issued by SAIC, whether the Patent Office is bound by it is open to question. To play it safe, foreign trademark owners should register trademarks both under the Trademark Law and as design patents wherever possible.

COMPULSORY LICENSING 14.34

Article 48 of the Patent Law provides that if a unit, which possesses the conditions to work a patent, submits a request to the patentee of an invention or utility model for a licence to work his patent, offers reasonable conditions, but fails to obtain such licence within a reasonable length of time, the Patent Office may, upon application by the unit, grant it a compulsory licence to work the patent for the invention or utility model. The Patent Office may also grant such a compulsory licence if a national emergency or other extraordinary circumstance arises, or if it is in the public interest, according to Article 49 of the Patent Law.

The patentee will be notified of the decision of the Patent Office in cases where a compulsory licence is granted. Such a decision will be registered and announced by the Patent Office. The compulsory licensee does not have an exclusive right to exploit the patent, nor does it have the right to authorise exploitation by third parties. It must also pay the patentee reasonable royalties for using the patent.

14.35 INFRINGEMENT, ENFORCEMENT AND PENALTIES

Infringement of a patent means the working of a patent without a licence from the patentee. What is the scope of the patent then? For an invention or utility model, the scope of patent rights is determined by the contents of the claims, and the description and drawings may be used to interpret the claims. For a design patent, the scope will be determined by the product incorporating the patented design depicted in the drawings or photographs.

Patent holders are given the right to prevent any other person from importing, without authorisation, the patented product or the product directly obtained by the patented process, for the purposes of making, using, or selling the patented product, using the patented process, or using or selling the product directly obtained by the patented process for production or business purposes.

Article 63 of Patent Law

Under Article 63 of the Patent Law, infringement of patent rights shall not be deemed to have occurred in any of the following circumstances:

1. the patented product manufactured or imported by, or manufactured or imported under licence from, the patentee or the product directly derived from use of the patented process, is used, offered for sale or sold after the initial sale of such product;
2. an identical product was manufactured, an identical process was used or the necessary preparations for the manufacture of such product or use of such process were completed prior to the date of application for the patent, and the manufacturing or use only continues within the original scope;
3. the relevant patent is used by a foreign means of transportation in transit through China's territory, territorial waters or airspace for its own needs in its fittings or equipment, pursuant to the

agreement concluded between its home country and China or the international treaty to which both its home country and China have acceded, or on the basis of the principle of reciprocity; or

4. the relevant patent is used solely for the purpose of scientific research or experimentation.

Article 57 of Patent Law

Under Article 57 of the Patent Law, in the event of a dispute arising due to the working of a patent without a licence from the patentee, the parties shall resolve such dispute through consultations. If the parties are unwilling to hold consultations or if consultations are unsuccessful, the patentee or a materially interested person may institute an action in a People's Court or, alternatively, request the patent administration authority to handle the matter. If, in handling the matter, the patent administration authority determines that infringement has occurred, it may order the infringer to immediately cease the infringement. If the party concerned is dissatisfied with such order, he may institute an action in a People's Court in accordance with the Civil Procedure Law within 15 days after the date the notice concerning the handling of the case is received. If the infringer fails to institute an action and does not cease the infringement within the time limit, the patent administration authority may apply to the People's Court for enforcement. The patent administration authority that is handling the case may, at the request of a party, mediate in respect of the measure of damages for the infringement. If mediation is not successful, a party may institute an action in a People's Court in accordance with the Civil Procedure Law.

If a patent infringement dispute involves an invention patent for a process for manufacturing a new product, the unit or individual manufacturing an identical product shall provide evidence that the process for manufacturing its / his product is different from that of the patented process. If a dispute involves a utility model patent, the People's Court or the Patent Office may require the patentee to present the search report prepared by the Patent Office.

Article 58 of Patent Law

Under Article 58 of the Patent Law, if a third party's patent is passed off, the infringer shall bear civil liability in accordance with the law. Moreover, the patent administration authority shall order him to rectify the matter and shall make an announcement to that effect. Furthermore, it shall confiscate his illegal income, and may additionally impose a fine of not more than three times the illegal income. If there was no illegal income, it may impose a fine of not more than RMB50,000. If a criminal offence is constituted, the infringer's criminal liability shall be pursued in accordance with the law. If a non-patented product is passed off as a patented product or if a non-patented process is passed off as a patented process, then under Article 59 of the Patent Law, the patent administration authority shall issue an order to rectify the matter and shall make an announcement to that effect, and may impose a fine of not more than RMB50,000. For detailed provisions on the procedures and powers of the patent administration authority in administrative enforcement, see Measures for Administrative Law Enforcement in Connection with Patents.

Article 60 of Patent Law

Under Article 60 of the Patent Law, damages for infringement of patent rights shall be determined either in accordance with the loss incurred by the rights holder due to the infringement, or the benefit obtained by the infringer due to the infringement. If it is difficult to determine the injured party's loss or the benefit obtained by the infringer, the determination shall be made on the basis of a reasonable multiple of the royalty for a licence of such patent. If a patentee or a materially interested person has evidence that a third party is infringing or about to infringe his patent rights and if such infringement is not promptly halted, he will suffer irreparable damage to his legitimate rights and interests, he may, prior to instituting an action, apply to the People's Court for an injunction against the infringement and for property preservation measures under Article 61 of the Patent Law. Under Article 62 of the Patent Law, the statute of limitations for infringement of a patent right shall be two years, calculated from the date on which the patentee or materially interested person learned or ought to have learned of the infringement. The statute of limitations for an action by a patentee to demand the appropriate payment of royalties not paid for the use of an invention between the date the invention patent application was published and the granting of the patent right, shall be two years, calculated from the date on which patentee learned or ought to have learned that the third party was using his invention. However, if the patentee learned or ought to have learned of the third party's use of his invention before the date of the granting of the patent rights, the two years shall be calculated from the date on which the patent rights were granted.

Liability for damages shall not be borne for the use or sale, for production or business purposes, of a patented product manufactured or sold without a licence from the patentee or of a product directly derived from a patented process not licensed by the patentee, if the user or seller was not aware that a licence had not been obtained and is able to establish that his products came from a legitimate source.

ENTERPRISE NAMES

ENTERPRISE NAME REGISTRATION 14.36

The protection of enterprise names is principally governed by the Regulations for the Administration of the Registration of Enterprise Names (the "Enterprise Name Regulations"), which took effect on 1 September 1991, and the Implementing Measures for the Administration of the Registration of Enterprise Names (the "Enterprise Name Implementing Measures"), which took effect on 1 January 2000.

By registering an enterprise name, an enterprise is entitled to an exclusive right to use the trade name, or company business name, within its territorial scope and its registered line of business. Generally, an enterprise name lasts as long as the enterprise is in operation. Enterprise names of foreign companies are protected under the Paris Convention.

The system provides for the registration of names of domestic enterprises, foreign investment enterprises (ie equity joint ventures, cooperative joint ventures, or wholly foreign-owned enterprises) that are set up in the PRC. Only Chinese-language enterprise names can be registered. Foreign language enterprise names can be used without registration but must be literal translations of the Chinese-language enterprise names. A trade name may also be registered as a service mark in the relevant class. This will be maintained by paying a renewal fee every 10 years.

An enterprise name should consist of: (a) the administrative division where the enterprise is located; (b) the trade name which comprises at least two characters; (c) the industry in which the enterprise is in, unless its economic activities span five or more different industries, its registered capital is at least RMB100,000,000 or it is the parent company in an enterprise group and its trade name differs from other trade names registered with the AIC; and (d) the organisational form of the enterprise.

Enterprise names may be assigned or licensed.

REGISTRATION AND REGISTRABLE NAMES 14.37

Names of enterprises may not include the following elements:

1. content which is harmful to the State and public interest;
2. content which may deceive or mislead the public;
3. the names of foreign countries (or regions), and of international organisations;
4. the names of political parties, government departments, military units, and social organisations;

5. Pinyin, that is, English transliteration of Chinese words (except for foreign-language names) and numerals; and

6. other contents or words which are prohibited by laws and administrative regulations.

According to the Notice of the General Office of the State Council on Issues Concerning the Use of Words Such as 'China' at the Beginning of Company Names issued on 29 May 1995, newly established companies and other economic bodies, except those established by the State Council, may not use Chinese characters, or words, meaning 'China', 'national', 'State', or 'international'. The State Administration for Industry and Commerce shall be responsible for verifying and approving enterprise names of those types, according to the Enterprise Name Implementing Measures.

14.38 INFRINGEMENT

If a registered enterprise name is used without authorisation, the infringed party may lodge a complaint with AIC at the place where the infringer is located. The AIC has the power to order the infringer to stop its infringement, and to pay compensation to the enterprise for any loss suffered. In addition, the infringer may be liable to pay a fine of not less than RMB5,000 and not more than RMB50,000, and its income derived from such infringing use of another's name may be confiscated.

14.39 DISPUTES OVER REGISTRATION

The Enterprise Names Regulations stipulate that when two or more enterprises are involved in a dispute regarding identical or similar names, the registration authorities will handle such a dispute in accordance with the 'first-to-register' principle. Therefore, if, for example, the registration of a foreign enterprise's name pre-dates the registration of an infringing entity that is making spurious use of the name of the foreign enterprise, the foreign enterprise may apply to the AIC for enforcement action or to court.

14.40 TRADEMARK VERSUS ENTERPRISE NAME

Can one take advantage of another's trademark lawfully by registering it as an enterprise name? Can one take advantage of another's enterprise name lawfully by registering it as a trademark? Just like applying for patents for designs which are label or device trademarks owned by other parties, some Chinese entities also register other's trademarks in the hope that they will get the permit, and be able to cause confusion to the consumers.

The Notice Concerning Prohibition of the Unauthorised Use of Another's Registered Trademark as the Enterprise Name and / or on Business Signboards of Exclusive Retail Stores (Exclusive Repair Shops), issued by SAIC on 10 June 1996, prohibits the use of another's registered trademark as the enterprise name of an exclusive retail store, exclusive business store or exclusive repair shop, or to use it on a business signboard of those kinds of stores / shops, without the permission of the trademark registrant. The Notice also requires that when outlets for the sale of goods and centres which provide certain services need to indicate the goods in which the store deals or the scope of services provided, they may use such descriptive phrases as "we repair XXX products", "we sell XXX suits" etc. The typeface of the words should be uniform and may not give prominence to the word mark part.

The Opinions on Resolving Several Trademark and Enterprise Name Issues, issued by SAIC on 5 April 1999 provides that the exclusive trademark right and the right of enterprise names shall be acquired in accordance with the principle of honesty and good faith set out in the General Principles of Civil Law and PRC Anti-unfair Competition Law (to be dealt with in the next section). One must not commit unfair competition by making use of the reputation of another's trademark and enterprise name. The Opinion said that unfair competition acts, such as creating confusion (including likelihood of confusion) on the part of consumers in relation to the origin of goods or services through identicalness and similarity between a trademark and enterprise name, should be stopped. The Opinion goes on to define 'confusion' to include:

1. registering as a trademark, a word identical or similar to the trade name in another's enterprise name thereby causing the related public to mistake or confuse the enterprise name owner and the trademark registrant;
2. registering a word identical or similar to another's registered trademark as a trade name in an enterprise name thereby causing the related public to mistake or confuse the enterprise name owner and the trademark registrant.

If the trademark registrant or enterprise name owner is of the view that their rights and interests are impaired, they can file a written complaint with the provincial or State (if the case involves more than one provincial administrative region) AICs, but the complaint will have to be filed within five years from the date of trademark registration or putting on record of the enterprise name (the time limit is not applicable if the registration or putting on record is made in bad faith). The case will be handled by applying the principles of maintaining fair competition and protecting the interests of the prior lawful right holders.

There is a judicial interpretation on the issue: the Explanation of Several Issues Relating to Trial of Cases of Disputes Arising from Conflicts between Trademarks and Use of Enterprise Names, discussed and adopted by Beijing Municipal Higher People's Court on 23 December 2002. It says that in addition to regulation under the General Principles of Civil Law and PRC Anti-unfair Competition Law, should registration of a word identical or similar to another's registered trademark as a trade name in an enterprise name, and using it on identical or similar goods, create a likelihood of confusion, then it is also a kind of trademark infringement and should be regulated under the Trademark Law. An order to stop or limit the use of the enterprise name, and damages, may be granted by the court. The five-year limit applies: if the trademark registrant does not complain within five years of the putting on record of the enterprise name, no protection will be offered, unless the situation is one a well-known mark has been registered as an enterprise name in bad faith, in which case there is no limitation period. The Explanation also informs us how the court will determine whether or not there is confusion. The focus should be put on the time the infringing acts took place, and the following (but not limited to the following) should be considered: (a) the channel and manner of the sales or provision of the goods or services (b) similarity between the goods or services and the level of attention paid by the consumers when purchasing (c) evidence showing actual confusion and whether the defendant intended to take advantage or injure the trademark in question; etc. As to similarity between words in a trademark and an enterprise name, the shape, pronunciation and the meaning of the words have to be considered. If the words are basically the same in one of these three ways and will cause confusion in relation to the origin of the goods or services, the words will be considered as similar. At the same time, the distinctiveness and popularity of the mark will also have to be taken into account in considering similarity between words in a trademark and an enterprise name.

UNFAIR COMPETITION

14.41 DEFINITIONS

The PRC Anti-unfair Competition Law, effective from 1 December 1993, was formulated to stop acts of unfair competition and to protect the lawful rights and interests of business operators and consumers.

The term 'unfair competition' is defined in Article 2 of the Anti-unfair Competition Law as acts of business operators that harm the lawful rights and interests of other business operators and disrupt the social and economic order contrary to the Anti-unfair Competition Law. The term 'business operators' is defined in Article 2 to mean legal persons, other economic organisations and individuals that deal in merchandise or are engaged in the provision of services for profit.

ACTS OF UNFAIR COMPETITION   14.42
Article 5 of the Anti-unfair Competition Law
Acts of unfair competition are defined in Article 5 of the Anti-unfair Competition Law to include the following acts by business operators:

1. passing off the registered trademark of another party;
2. unauthorised use of the name, packaging or trade dress peculiar to well-known merchandise or use of a name, packaging or trade dress similar to that of well-known merchandise, thereby causing confusion with the well-known merchandise of another party and causing purchasers to mistake the merchandise for such well-known merchandise;
3. unauthorised use of the enterprise name or personal name of another party, thereby causing people to mistake the merchandise for that of another party; or
4. use on merchandise of quality marks such as certification marks, marks of fame and marks of excellence that are counterfeit or used without authorisation, falsification of the place of origin or making of misleadingly false statements as to the quality of the merchandise.

Articles 6 and 7 of the Anti-unfair Competition Law
Utility enterprises, business operators that occupy a legal monopoly, governments and their subordinate departments may not restrict other parties from purchasing the merchandise of their designated business operators in order to force out fair competition by other business operators under Article 6 of the Anti-unfair Competition Law. At the same time, as provided in Article 7 of the Anti-unfair Competition Law, governments and their subordinate departments may not abuse their administrative powers to force others to buy the goods of the operators designated by them, so as to restrict lawful business activities of operators. Also, they cannot abuse their administrative powers to restrict the entry of merchandise from elsewhere into the local market or the outflow of local merchandise to other markets.

Article 8 of the Anti-unfair Competition Law
As provided in Article 8 of the Anti-unfair Competition Law, business operators may not use bribery, by giving property or otherwise, to sell

or purchase merchandise. Those granting secret, off-the-book rebates to their opposite units or individuals shall be treated as having given bribes. Opposite units or individuals that accept secret, off-the-book rebates shall be treated as having accepted bribes. In their sale or purchase of merchandise, business operators may grant aboveboard discounts to their opposite parties and pay commissions to middlemen. When they do so, they must record the same strictly according to the facts. Business operators accepting the discounts or commissions must also record the same strictly according to the facts.

Article 9 of the Anti-unfair Competition Law

Article 9 of the Anti-unfair Competition Law provides that business operators may not make misleadingly false publicity, through advertising or otherwise, in respect of the quality, manufacturing components, functions, uses, producer, period of validity, place of origin, etc, of merchandise. Business operators in the advertising business may not act as agent for, design, make or publish advertisements that they are well aware or ought to be aware are false.

Article 10 of the Anti-unfair Competition Law

Under Article 10 of the Anti-unfair Competition Law, business operators may not infringe business secrets by any of the following methods:

1. obtaining business secrets of the party that has rights therein by theft, enticement by promises of gain, duress or other unfair methods;
2. divulging, using oneself or allowing others to use business secrets of the party that has rights therein, where such business secrets were obtained by any of the methods set forth in the preceding item; or
3. divulging, using oneself or allowing others to use business secrets in one's possession, where such is in breach of an agreement or contrary to the confidentiality requirements of the party that has rights in the business secrets.

Third parties that obtain, use or divulge business secrets of others that they are well aware or ought to be aware have been infringed by any of the methods above are deemed to have infringed business secrets. 'Business secrets' is defined under the Anti-unfair Competition Law to mean technical information and business information not known to public which can bring economic benefits to the party that has rights therein and is practical, and for which the party that has rights therein has adopted measures to maintain its confidentiality.

Article 11 of the Anti-unfair Competition Law

Under Article 11 of the Anti-unfair Competition Law, business operators are also restricted from selling merchandise below cost for the
purpose of forcing out competitors. However, under any of the following circumstances, such sales would not be regarded as an act of unfair
competition:

1. sale of fresh or live merchandise;
2. disposal of merchandise whose period of validity is due to expire
   soon or other overstocked merchandise;
3. seasonal price reductions; or
4. sale of merchandise at reduced prices in order to satisfy debts or
   due to a change in the line of production or closure of business.

Articles 12–15 of the Anti-unfair Competition Law

When selling merchandise, business operators may not link such sale to
the sale of other merchandise against the purchaser's wish or attach
other unreasonable conditions. This is provided by Article 12 of the Anti-
unfair Competition Law. Further, they cannot offer any of the following
prize sales under Article 13 of the Anti-unfair Competition Law:

1. deceitful prize sales offered by fraudulently claiming that prizes
   are offered or wilfully arranging for internally determined persons to win the prizes;
2. prize sales used to market merchandise of substandard quality
   but high price; or
3. prize sales in the form of lucky draws, where the amount of the
   highest prize exceeds RMB5,000.

Business operators may not fabricate and / or spread false facts, thereby
injuring the goodwill of competitors or the reputation of their merchandise as provided by Article 14.

Tendering parties may not collude in the submission of tenders to
force the tender price up or down, nor collude with the party that
invited the tenders to force out fair competition by competitors under
Article 15 of the Anti-unfair Competition Law.

SUPERVISION AND EXAMINATION

14.43

Supervision

Acts of unfair competition are generally supervised by AICs above the
county level, but laws or administrative regulations providing for supervision and examination by other authorities should also be
observed. All organisations and individuals are also encouraged to

supervise acts of unfair competition under Article 4 of the Anti-unfair Competition Law. People's Governments at all levels are also required to adopt measures to stop acts of unfair competition and create conditions for fair competition.

Powers

Supervision and examination authorities shall have the right to exercise the following functions and powers in their supervision and examination of acts of unfair competition under Article 17 of the Anti-unfair Competition Law:

1. to make inquiries of the business operators, interested parties and witnesses being examined, and to require them to provide evidence or other information concerning the act of unfair competition, in accordance with the prescribed procedure;
2. to inquire about and duplicate agreements, account books, bills, receipts, documents, records, business letters, business telegrams, business telexes, business facsimiles and other materials connected with the act of unfair competition; and
3. to examine property connected with acts of unfair competition as set forth in Article 5 of the Anti-unfair Competition Law and, when necessary, order the business operator being examined to give details of the source and quantity of the merchandise and to suspend sales; pending examination, such property may not be removed, concealed or destroyed.

14.44 LEGAL LIABILITY

Article 20 of the Anti-unfair Competition Law

A business operator who violates the Anti-unfair Competition Law, thereby causing other business operators to suffer loss, will be liable for damages under Article 20 of the Anti-unfair Competition Law. If the loss suffered by the injured business operator is difficult to calculate, the amount of damages shall be the profit derived from the infringement by the infringer during the infringement. (For details on calculation of the profit see the Notice of the State AIC on Calculation of Illegal Profits Derived from Unfair Competition Acts, which refers back to the method in the Notice on the Calculation of Illegal Profits in Law or Regulation Contravening Speculation and Profiteering Cases). In addition, the infringing business operator shall bear the reasonable expenses paid by the injured business operator as a result of the investigation of the infringing business operator's act of unfair competition that infringed the lawful rights and interests of the injured business operator. If the lawful rights and interests of an injured business operator are harmed by the act of unfair competition, it may institute proceedings in the People's Court.

Article 21 of the Anti-unfair Competition Law

If a business operator passes off the registered trademark of another party, makes unauthorised use of the enterprise name or personal name of another party, counterfeits or uses without authorisation quality marks such as certification marks, famous marks and marks of excellence, falsifies the place of origin or makes misleadingly false statements as to the quality of the merchandise, it shall be punished in accordance with the Trademark Law and the Product Quality Law of PRC under Article 21 of the Anti-unfair Competition Law.

Article 21 also provides that if a business operator makes unauthorised use of the name, packaging or trade dress peculiar to well-known merchandise or uses a name, packaging or trade dress similar to that of well-known merchandise, thereby causing confusion with the well-known merchandise of another party and causing purchasers to mistake the merchandise for such well-known merchandise, the supervision and examination authorities shall order it to cease the illegal act and confiscate the illegal income, and may impose a fine equivalent to more than once and not more than thrice the illegal income, depending on the circumstances; in serious cases, they may revoke its business licence. If counterfeit or substandard merchandise was sold and such sale constitutes a criminal offence, the offender shall be prosecuted according to law.

Article 22 of the Anti-unfair Competition Law

Article 22 provides that if a business operator uses bribery, by giving property or otherwise, to sell or purchase merchandise, and such bribery constitutes a criminal offence, it shall be prosecuted according to law. If such bribery does not constitute a criminal offence, the supervision and examination authorities may impose a fine of more than RMB10,000 and not more than RMB200,000, according to the circumstances. Any illegal income will also be confiscated.

Article 23 of the Anti-unfair Competition Law

Article 23 provides that if a utility enterprise or another business operator that occupies a monopoly position according to law restricts other parties to purchasing the merchandise of its designated business operator in order to force out fair competition by other business operators, the supervision and examination authorities at the provincial level or of the municipality (if such municipality has established districts) shall order it to cease the illegal act and may impose a fine of more than RMB50,000 and not more than RMB200,000, according to the circumstances. If a designated business operator takes advantage of such restriction by selling substandard merchandise at high prices or charging excessive fees, the supervision and examination authorities shall confiscate the illegal income and may impose a fine equivalent to more than twice and not more than thrice the illegal income, according to the circumstances.

Article 24 of the Anti-unfair Competition Law

Article 24 provides that if a business operator makes misleadingly false publicity in respect of merchandise, through advertising or otherwise, the supervision and examination authorities shall order it to cease the illegal act and eliminate the effects, and may impose a fine of more than RMB10,000 and not more than RMB200,000, according to the circumstances. If a business operator in the advertising business acts as agent for, designs, makes or publishes advertisements which it is well aware or ought to be aware to be false, the supervision and examination authorities shall order it to cease the illegal act, confiscate the illegal income and, in addition, impose a fine according to law.

Articles 25–28 of the Anti-unfair Competition Law

If a business secret is infringed, Article 25 provides that the supervision and examination authorities shall order the violator to cease the illegal act and may impose a fine of more than RMB10,000 and not more than RMB200,000, according to the circumstances.

If a business operator offers the kinds of prize sales which are contrary to Article 13 of the Anti-unfair Competition Law, then under Article 26 the supervision and examination authorities shall order the violator to cease the illegal act and may impose a fine of more than RMB10,000 and not more than RMB100,000, according to the circumstances.

If tendering parties collude in the submission of tenders in order to force the tender price up or down, or if a tendering party and the party that invited the tenders collude with each other in order to force out fair competition by competitors, Article 27 provides that the successful tenderer's winning of the tender shall be void. The supervision and examination authorities may impose a fine of more than RMB10,000 and not more than RMB200,000 according to the circumstances.

Article 28 provides that if a business operator violates an order to suspend sales and not to remove, conceal or destroy property connected with the act of unfair competition, the supervision and examination authorities may impose a fine equivalent to more than twice and not more than thrice the price of the property sold, removed, concealed or destroyed, according to the circumstances.

Article 30 of the Anti-unfair Competition Law

Article 30 provides that if a government or its subordinate department restricts other parties from purchasing the merchandise of its designated business operators, by restricting the fair business activities of other business operators or by restricting the normal circulation of merchandise between areas, its superior authorities shall order to it to rectify the situation; in serious cases, its directly responsible personnel shall be subject to administrative sanctions by authorities at the same or a higher level. If a designated business operator takes advantage of such restriction by selling substandard merchandise at high prices or charging excessive fees, the supervision and examination authorities shall confiscate the illegal income and may impose a fine equivalent to more than twice and not more than thrice the illegal income, according to the circumstances.

RECONSIDERATION

14.45

If a party is dissatisfied with the penalty decision made by the supervision and examination authorities, under Article 29 of the Anti-unfair Competition Law, it may apply to the competent authority at the next higher level, within 15 days after the date of receipt of the penalty decision, for reconsideration. If a party is dissatisfied with the decision made upon reconsideration, it may institute proceedings in the People's Court within 15 days after the date of receipt of the written decision made upon reconsideration. Procedures may also be instituted with the People's Court directly.

CONSUMER AND PRODUCT QUALITY LAW

OVERVIEW

14.46

In most cases, an aggrieved consumer may seek remedies under the contract (be it written, oral or by conduct) that covers the subject goods or services. Yet governments invariably enact consumer protection legislations to tip the balance in favour of the consumers. The seminal legislations in the PRC are the Product Quality Law of the PRC ("Product Quality Law"), effective from 1 September 1993 and with amendments effective from 1 September 2000, and the Law Concerning Protection of the Rights and Interests of Consumers ("Consumer Protection Law"), effective from 1 January 1994.

The Product Quality Law is the first national law of the PRC governing the manufacture and sale of goods in the PRC. The Consumer Protection Law later extended the scope of protection regarding services and incorporated and improved on those protections under the Product Quality Law. In essence, the Consumer Protection Law imposes liabilities on business operators for their malpractice or any defective quality in goods and services causing harm to a consumer's person or property. In Chapter 2 of the Consumer Protection Law, rights of a person in connection with his daily consumption of goods and services are established, examples include the following:

1. right to security of person and property – any harm or loss caused by the purchase or use of goods or services will entitle a consumer to compensation;
2. right to information – a business operator must not make false representation or conceal the relevant facts from a consumer;
3. right to freedom of choice – a consumer is entitled to choose the goods or services he prefers without undue influence from a business operator;
4. right to fair dealing – business operators must ensure their goods or services are of merchantable quality, reasonable price and correct measurements and quantity;
5. right to compensation - for injury to his person or property suffered due to the purchase or use of merchandise or the receipt of services;
6. right to association – consumers are free to organise social association to safeguard and promote their interest.

Also, according to Article 24 of the Consumer Protection Law, business operators are prohibited from imposing unreasonable requirements on consumers through the use of standard form contract, notifications, declarations or notices on their premises. Those requirements would be regarded as not valid. Business operators are also not allowed to insult or slander consumers, search the person or belongings of consumers or otherwise violate their freedom of movement, as provided by Article 25 of the Consumer Protection Law.

If a consumer cannot resolve disputes with the business operator through consultation, he may seek redress by requesting mediation through his local consumer council, filing a complaint with local AICs, initiating an arbitration proceeding (if an arbitration agreement is in place) or filing a law suit with a People's Court. These ways of resolution are listed in Article 34 of the Consumer Protection Law.

14.47 CIVIL REMEDIES

As provided by Article 40 of the Consumer Protection Law, business operators will have to bear civil responsibilities in the following cases according to the Product Quality Law:

1. if the merchandise is defective;
2. if the merchandise does not possess the properties for use that it should possess, and no clear indication of such situation is given at the time of sale;
3. if the merchandise does not conform to the merchandise standards applied, as specified on the merchandise or its packaging;
4. if the quality of the merchandise does not conform to the quality made known by means of descriptions or physical samples, etc, of the merchandise;
5. if the merchandise produced has been formally decreed obsolete by the state or if the merchandise sold has expired or deteriorated;
6. if the quantity of merchandise sold is insufficient;
7. if the substance of or fee for the service violates the agreement;
8. if the response to a consumer's demand for repair, redoing, replacement, return, making up the quantity of merchandise, refund of the payment for the merchandise or the service fee, or compensation for losses is wilfully delayed or if such demand is unreasonably refused; or
9. other circumstances where the rights and interests of consumers are harmed, as specified in laws and regulations.

The Consumer Protection Law imposes primary obligation on sellers of goods to compensate consumers for harm done to the consumers' lawful rights and interests when consumers purchase or use the merchandise. Article 35 of the Consumer Protection Law provides that if, when consumers purchase or use merchandise, their lawful rights and interests are harmed, they may claim compensation from the seller. If it turns out that the responsibility for the harm lies with the producer or with another seller that provided the merchandise to the seller, the seller will, after having compensated the consumer, have the right of recovery from the producer or the other seller. If, when consumers receive a service, their lawful rights and interests are harmed, they may claim compensation from the provider of the service. Article 42 of the Product Quality Law provides that if a product is defective due to the fault of the seller and such defect causes personal injury or damage to property other than the product itself, the seller shall be liable for damages. If the seller is unable to identify the producer of a defective product and is also unable to identify the supplier thereof, the seller shall be liable for damages. 'Defect in Product Quality Law means "an unreasonable danger in a product, which danger threatens personal safety or property other than the product itself". It also means, where a product is governed by State or industry standards for the safeguarding of health, personal safety or the safety of property, the non-compliance of the product with such standards.

Article 35 of the Consumer Protection Law also provides that if a defect in the merchandise causes harm to the person or to property, the consumer or other victim may claim compensation from the seller, and may also claim compensation from the producer. If the responsibility for the harm lies with the producer, the seller shall, after having compensated the consumer, have the right of recovery from the producer. If the responsibility for the harm lies with the seller, the producer shall, after having compensated the consumer, have the right of recovery from the seller. Article 43 of the Product Quality Law is a substantially identical provision.

As to the liability of the producer, Article 41 of the Product Quality Law says that if a defect in a product causes personal injury or damage to property other than the defective product, the producer shall be liable for damages. But defences are available. The producer shall not be liable for damages if it can prove that:

1. it has not put the product into circulation;
2. the defect causing the harm did not yet exist when the product was put into circulation; or
3. the level of science and technology at the time when the product was put into circulation was not sufficient to detect the existence of the defect.

Further, it has to be pointed out that consumers are entitled to aggravated compensation (an additional 100 per cent of the price of the goods or services involved) when the business operators acted fraudulently, as provided by Article 49 of the Consumer Protection Law. At the same time, where a consumer suffered loss on reliance of a fraudulent advertisement but cannot locate the business operator placing the advertisement, he can instead sue the advertisement publisher for compensation, if the latter cannot provide the true name and address of the business operator, as provided by Article 39 of the Consumer Protection Law.

As to limitation period, Article 45 of the Product Quality Law designates that actions must be filed within two years from the date the plaintiff knew, or should have known, about his rights being prejudiced. But where the claim is for personal injury, a shorter period of one year under Article 136 of the Civil Code applies.

The above is about the liability of the sellers and manufacturers. Due to the existence of licences and franchises, there may be situations where the owner of the trademark of the product in question is not the manufacturer and seller of the product. Is there any liability of the owner of the trademark if there is a problem with the products? The Official Reply of the Supreme People's Court on Whether or Not the

Injured Party in a Product Tort Case Can Institute a Civil Action Naming the Product's Trademark Owner as a Defendant (coming into effect on 28 July 2002) provides the answer.

The Official Reply was made upon the request of Beijing Municipal Higher People's Court for instructions in the action for damages brought by Jing Qilian and Zhang Xinrong et al against the General Motors Corporation of the US and the General Motors Overseas Corporation of the US. The General Motors Corporation of the US is the owner of the trademark on the vehicle involved in the accident that killed the sons of the Plaintiffs. It claimed that the vehicle was not produced by it but by General Motors do Brasil Ltd, so it should not be a defendant in the action. The Supreme People's Court said that any enterprise or individual that puts its or his name, trademark or other distinguishing mark on a product indicating that it or he is the manufacturer of the product is a 'manufacturer of the product' as the term is used in Article 122 of the General Principles of Civil Law of the People's Republic of China and a 'producer' as the term is used in the Product Quality Law. The Court further said that based on the action brought by the Plaintiffs and the actual circumstances of the case, there is absolutely nothing wrong with making the trademark owner a Defendant. The hearing of the case was resumed on 3 September 2003, and the actual decisions on the substantive issues are to be seen.

PENALTIES   14.48

Breaching the provisions of the Product Quality Law or the Consumer Protection Law may lead to administrative or criminal sanctions.

Article 49 of the Product Quality Law provides that anyone producing or selling products that do not comply with the state or industry standards for the safeguarding of health, personal safety or the safety of property, shall be ordered to cease such production or sale. The products shall be confiscated and a fine equivalent to not less than the value of the products (including the products which have been sold and those which have not), and not more than three times such value shall be imposed. The illegal income, if any, shall be confiscated. If the case is serious, the producer's or seller's business licence shall be revoked. If a criminal offence is constituted, the offender shall be prosecuted according to law.

Products that are adulterated or mixed with improper elements, passing off spurious products as genuine products or substandard products as quality products are also prohibited by Article 50 of the Product Quality Law. Producer or seller shall be ordered to cease the production or sale thereof, the illegally produced or sold products shall be confiscated and a fine of not less than 50 per cent of the value of the products produced or sold and not more than three times such value shall be imposed. Again, the illegal income will be confiscated. Also, if the case is serious, the producer's or seller's business licence shall be revoked. If a criminal offence is constituted, the offender shall be prosecuted according to law.

There are also provisions in relation to penalties for producing products pronounced obsolete by the state, selling products which have expired or whose quality has deteriorated, illegal product labelling, and making or facilitating arrangements (eg of transportation, custody or storage, etc) for the production or sale of products which one knows or ought to know to be products whose production and /or sale is prohibited, and provision of technology for the production of spurious products passed off as genuine products etc.

The Consumer Protection Law also lists punishable activities in Article 50. These are:

1. a business operator producing or selling merchandise that does not conform to the requirement of ensuring the safety of the person and of property;
2. a business operator adulterating merchandise, mixing improper elements with merchandise, or passing off spurious merchandise as genuine, merchandise of poor quality as quality merchandise, or substandard merchandise as merchandise that is up to standard;
3. a business operator producing merchandise formally decreed obsolete by the state or selling merchandise that has expired or deteriorated;
4. a business operator fabricating the place of origin of merchandise, forging or passing off the name and / or address of another's factory, or forging or passing off marks of quality such as certification marks, marks of fame or marks of excellence;
5. a business operator selling merchandise that should have been inspected or quarantined but has not been inspected or quarantined, or fabricating the inspection or quarantine results;
6. a business operator carrying out misleadingly false advertising for a product or service;
7. where response to a consumer's demand for repair, redoing, replacement, return, making up the quantity of merchandise, refund of the payment for the merchandise or the service fee, or compensation for losses is willfully delayed or if such demand is unreasonably refused;
8. where a consumer's human dignity is injured or personal freedom infringed; or
9. other circumstances where laws and regulations provide that a fine be imposed for harming consumers' rights and interests.

If the penalising authority and penalty methods for the above are provided for in the Law of the People's Republic of China Concerning Product Quality or other relevant laws and regulations, the matter shall be handled in accordance with those. If this is not the case, the AIC shall order rectification and, depending on the circumstances, may impose one or more of the following penalties: issuance of a warning, confiscation of the illegal income, imposition of a fine of not less than twice and not more than five times the illegal income; if there is no illegal income, a fine of not more than RMB10,000 shall be imposed; if the circumstances are serious, the business operator shall be ordered to cease business and reorganise, and its business licence shall be revoked.

ADMINISTRATIVE COMPLAINTS 14.49

In order to provide standard procedures for consumers filing complaints, the SAIC issued the Provisional Measures on Accepting Consumer Complaints by Administration Authorities for Industry and Commerce ("Provisional Consumer Complaints Measures") and the Measures for Punishing Fraudulent Acts on Consumers on 15 March 1996 ("Consumers Fraud Measures"). Implementing Measures for Handling Complaints of Consumers by Stations of Administration for Industry and Commerce were issued one year later. There is an amendment made to Provisional Consumer Complaints Measures effective from 3 December 1998.

Under the Consumer Fraud Measures, 'fraudulent acts' are broadly defined and include (a) providing goods or services of inferior standards; (b) using false description, standard or sample and falsely representing the price to be a 'special' price, 'lowest' price, etc. The Consumer Measures also shift the burden onto business operators to prove their innocence if they are found selling goods which infringe upon others' trademark rights, or goods which pirates others' packaging or name, etc. It should be noted that an administrative complaint, upon proof, would only result in a fine on the business operator. Consumers seeking compensation have recourse to civil litigation. Article 6 of the Measures is confusing and seems to suggest that AIC may order compensation. SAIC issued a reply (Reply of the SAIC on the Issue of Whether AICs Can Make a Decision on Compensation in Complaints by Consumers) on 16 July 1997 to clear the doubt, clarifying that AICs do not have the power to order compensation. Complainants have to go to People's Courts for compensation.

The limitation period for filing administrative complaints is one year from the date the consumer knew, or should have known, about his rights being prejudiced. Administrative complaints will not be accepted once civil actions or arbitration has commenced, as provided by Article 17 of Provisional Consumer Complaints Measures.

14.50 THREE GUARANTEES

Article 45 of the Consumer Protection Law requires business operators to provide guarantees on the repair, replace and return of goods (*sanbao* or 'three guarantees') designated by the State. The State Administration of Quality Supervision (now the General Administration of Quality Supervision, Inspection and Quarantine) promulgated the Regulations on Responsibilities for the Repair, Replacement and Return of Certain Goods on 25 August 1995 to implement the 'three guarantees' policy.

The said Regulations established the Catalogue of Goods Implementing the Three Guarantees and consumers are entitled to have the relevant defective goods repaired, replaced or returned for original price within respective guarantee periods. There are 18 items in the first batch of goods under the Catalogue and include household appliances, watches and motorcycles. Sellers are responsible for providing the three guarantees, which cannot be contracted out. Article 4 of the Regulations on Responsibilities for the Repair, Replacement and Return of Certain Goods also said that the Regulations would not exempt the 'three guarantees' responsibility in relation to goods not listed under the Catalogue and those responsibilities undertaken by the producer or seller were in addition to 'three guarantees' responsibility.

Since 1997, scope of 'three guarantees' for motorcycles, mobile phones, landline telephones, household audio-visual equipment and computer equipment has been provided for under separate regulations.

14.51 LATEST DEVELOPMENTS

The Regulations on the Protection of Rights and Interests and Consumers of the Shanghai Municipality ("Shanghai Regulations") came into effect on 1 January 2003 and represent the latest trend of consumer protection in the PRC.

The first innovation under the Shanghai Regulations is the protection on consumers personal data, which is broadly defined to include "name, gender, occupation, academic credential, contact details, marital status, information on income and wealth, fingerprints, blood type, medical history and other information which are closely connected to the consumer or his family". Not only must business operators not ask for personal data that is not related to the consumption of goods or services, they are also prohibited from disclosing to third parties, without the consent of the consumer, any personal data collected.

Second, a system for recall of defective goods is put into place. When a business operator becomes aware of any serious inherent defects in its goods where damage may be caused to consumers' safety or property even if the goods are used properly, it is mandated to publicly announce a recall of the defective goods. Administration authorities may initiate the recovery if the relevant business operator fails to do so. Further, the municipal consumer association may recommend recovery, upon discovery of serious inherent defects in goods.

On the national front, it has been reported that the much-anticipated Regulations on Administration of Recall of Defective Automobiles will soon become law since the General Administration of Quality Supervision, Inspection and Quarantine published the draft in October 2002. The draft previously circulated for comments defines 'defects' as "the same type of defects which are commonly found in cars of the same batch, model or type due to problems in the processes of design, manufacturing, etc". It also stipulates a 'recall period' of 10 years from the date of the first delivery of the car in question to end-users. The 'recall period' may be the period in which the use of the automobile would be safe, as specified by the manufacturer, if such period is longer than 10 years. Within the "recall period", automobile manufacturers (including those importing cars into the PRC) are responsible for initiating the recall process upon occurrence of the following triggering events:

1. the examination institution concludes that the safety standards of an automobile do not meet national or industrial standards;
2. the defects have caused damage to the person or property of end-users; or
3. it is proved by examination, experiments and demonstration that the defects may cause damage to a person or property under certain conditions.

If a manufacturer fails to initiate the recall on its own, the General Administration of Quality Supervision, Inspection and Quarantine may mandate it to do so.

PRODUCTS QUALITY (COMPULSORY CERTIFICATION)   14.52

The launching of the China Compulsory Certification ("CCC") system is part of the PRC's commitments upon accession to the WTO. The CCC system unified and replaced two separate systems previously in place in relation to product quality – the CCIB certification on imported products administered by the then State Administration of Inspection and Quarantine for Imports and Exports, and the 'Great Wall' (*Changcheng*) certification on domestic products administered by the then State Administration on Quality and Technology Supervision. The old and new systems were allowed to coexist during the one-year transition period commencing from 1 May 2002. Later, mandatory implementation of the CCC system was postponed to 1 August 2003.

The relevant legal provisions of CCC can be found in Regulations for the Administration of Mandatory Product Certification. In essence, the CCC system requires all products subject to it to complete relevant certification with designated institutions before the same are put into circulation. The Catalogue of the First Batch of Products Subject to Compulsory Certification promulgated on 3 December 2001 includes 132 products under 19 categories. In general, the certification process is comprised of the following steps:

1. application and admission for certification;
2. sample testing;
3. form testing;
4. onsite examination of the manufacturing facility where final assembly and affixing of relevant 'CCC' marks will take place;
5. evaluation and approval of certification results;
6. post-certification supervision.

Currently the Certification and Accreditation Administration of the PRC has designated nine certification institutions each responsible for certifying different products.

ADVERTISING LAW

14.53 INTRODUCTION

Some of the provisions in various advertising laws and regulations in PRC govern the use of trademarks in different forms of advertising. These have to be looked at when thinking of including a trademark in an advertisement. At the same time, using other's trademarks in comparative advertising might lead to some unfavourable consequences. Though the relevant trademark owner might rely on the trademark laws and regulations, the laws and regulations in relation to advertising might also provide the legal basis for its complaint.

14.54 MARKS IN TELEVISION ADVERTISEMENTS AND PROGRAMMES

There is a short provision in the Provisional Measures for Administration of the Broadcast of Radio and Television Commercials, promulgated on 15 September 2003 and effective on 1 January 2004, governing the use of marks (not necessarily but likely including trademarks) of enterprises or products. Its Article 22 provides that when showing a television advertisement, the television station shall not hide the mark of the station or channel. Also, during the showing of programmes the title of which has incorporated the name of an enterprise or a product, only one mark of the enterprise or product can be displayed. The mark has to be displayed at the bottom right hand corner, and it must be smaller than the mark of the station or channel, and shall not cover the usual subtitles of the programme itself.

USE OF REGISTERED TRADEMARKS IN ADVERTISEMENT 14.55

The Standards for Censorship of Advertisements (for Trial Implementation) ("the Standards") are the basic standard for censorship of advertisement before it is released (see Article 3).

Article 14(5) of the Standards requires that if a mark in an advertisement is specified as a registered trademark, the relevant registration certificates have to be submitted for censorship.

COMPARATIVE ADVERTISING 14.56
The Trademark Law

Comparative advertising does not necessarily involve the use of trademarks belonging to others. Nonetheless, as trademarks are created to be references to goods and services, trademarks are somewhat inevitable in comparative advertising. Trademark infringement includes using a trademark that is identical with or similar to a registered trademark in respect of the identical or similar goods without authorisation from the trademark registrant, as provided in Article 52 of the Trademark Law. As stipulated by Article 3 of Implementing Regulations for PRC Trademark Law, 'use of a trademark' in Trademark Law and those Regulations includes the use on goods, on packaging or containers for goods, on trade documents for goods, or in advertising, publicity, exhibitions or other business activities. The provisions literally embrace the use of another's trademark in comparative advertising as a kind of trademark infringement. (See also Cao Xinming, *Examining the Legal Questions of Comparative Advertising*, available at http://library.jgsu. edu.cn/sfxz/jingji/LWJ/LWJ%201333.htm). Article 8 of the Standards makes it clear that other people's rights should be respected when advertising. It says that approval of the owner must be obtained if its exclusive mark or registered trademark, etc, is involved in the advertisement.

The Advertising Law and Regulations

The story does not end, however, when approval of the owner is obtained. The general principle is that, as provided in Article 4 of PRC Advertising Law ("Advertising Law"), advertisements may not contain false information and may not deceive or mislead consumers. Article 9 stipulates that indications as to the performance, place of production, use, quality, price or producer of merchandise, etc, in the advertisement shall be clear and explicit. Article 3 of Regulations Concerning Control of Advertising ("Advertising Regulations") also provides that the content of an advertisement shall be factually correct, sound, clear and easily understood and shall not mislead or deceive users and consumers in any way. Article 8 also stipulates that advertising which employs trickery shall not be permitted to be published, broadcast, displayed or posted. Article 4 of The Standards provides that the content of an advertisement should be true, legal, healthy, easily understood and shall not mislead or cheat the general public. Article 36 of The Standards also says that comparative advertisements must not mislead consumers by way of allusion. Comparative advertising could turn out to be a misrepresentation (unintentional though it may be) as to the origin of the goods and services. The common law case *Mc-Donald's Hamburgers v Burger King* [1986] FSR 45 is an example. Burger King's slogan 'It's not just Big Mac' was understood by members of the public to mean that Burger King was offering Big Mac hamburgers. This was held to be a passing off. Such a situation would probably fall under the 'misleading or deceiving consumers' provisions quoted above. One must be careful in using another's trademarks in comparative advertising.

Enforcement and liabilities

False publicity for merchandise or services under the Advertising Law will be dealt with by State and local AICs. Under Article 37, they shall order the advertiser to cease publication of those advertisements and, within a corresponding scope, use an amount equal to the advertising expenses to publicly correct the falsehoods and eliminate their effects. The AIC will also impose on the advertiser a fine equivalent to not less than twice and not more than five times the advertising expenses or fee. At the same time, the AIC will confiscate the advertising fees of the responsible advertising business operator and advertisement publisher. AIC will also impose a fine equivalent to not less than twice and not more than five times the advertising expenses or fees. Serious cases will lead to the cessation of their advertising business. If the violation constitutes a criminal offence, the criminal liability of the offenders will be pursued according to law. Indications as to the performance, place of production, use, quality, price or producer of merchandise, etc, if unclear or not easily understood, may also be targeted by AICs. Under Article 40 of the Advertising Law, they will order the responsible advertiser, advertising business operator and advertisement publisher to cease the publication of the advertisement in question, and to make a public correction. AICs will also confiscate the advertising fee. A fine equivalent to not less than twice and not more than five times the advertising expenses or fees may be imposed. In addition to the above, Article 18 of the Advertising Regulations also gives AICs the power to suspend the operation until the matter is rectified or even revoke the business licence or advertising permit, depending on the seriousness of the case.

Advertisers will also have to bear civil liability, if they, by publishing false advertisements and deceiving or misleading consumers, harm the lawful rights and interests of consumers that purchase the merchandise or accept the services. This is provided in Article 38 of the Advertising Law. The provision also covers advertising business operators and advertisement publishers that design, produce or publish the advertisement in question. If they are fully aware or should be aware of the fact that the advertisement is false, they will bear joint and several liability. If they fail to provide the real names and addresses of the advertisers they shall bear full civil liability. Social or other organisations that recommend merchandise or services to consumers in false advertisements, thereby harming the lawful rights and interests of consumers, also bear joint and several liability.

Another important principle is that advertising must not belittle goods and services of other producers or business operators. This is included as one of the infringing acts that trigger liability under Article 47 of the Advertising Law. Advertisements that belittle similar products shall not be permitted to be published, broadcast, displayed or posted, as provided by Article 8 of Advertising Regulations. Chapter 4 of The Standards is devoted to comparative advertising. It says that comparative advertising shall follow the principle of fair and proper competition. The comparison shall not involve specific products or services, or direct comparison of any other type. At the same time, while an indirect and general comparison of goods or service of the same kind is allowed, scientific basis and evidence are required. Use of data and investigation results must be supported with their source and basis, and certification of a specialised examining authority of PRC should be provided. The comparison should be of goods that are identical or comparable; only the aspects that can be compared, should be compared. The description in language and words in a comparative advertisement should be precise, and should be easily understood by consumers. Injurious falsehood in a direct way or by way of an indirect inference is not allowed. As mentioned above, comparative advertisements must not mislead consumers by way of allusion. A comparative advertisement should not create the feeling that not using a particular product (other than a product of safety or protection of labour) will lead to serious loss or bad consequences. Comparative advertising not fulfilling the requirements above might not pass the censorship.

At the same time advertisers, advertising business operators and advertisement publishers have to bear the civil liability if the advertisement depreciates the merchandise or services of another producer or business operator, as provided by Article 47 of Advertising Law. Again under Article 40 of Advertising Law, AIC will also order the responsible advertiser, advertising business operator and advertisement publisher to cease the publication of the advertisement and to make a public correction. AICs will also confiscate the advertising fee. A fine equivalent to not less than twice and not more than five times the advertising expenses or fees may be imposed. The additional power of AIC in Advertising Regulations mentioned above may also come into play.

CUSTOMS RECORDAL OF INTELLECTUAL PROPERTY RIGHTS

14.57 DETAINMENT OF TRADEMARK-INFRINGING GOODS

Trademark owners now have a mechanism to take action against parties involved in the shipment into and out of China of goods that infringe their trademark rights. The Regulations of the People's Republic of China for Customs Protection of Intellectual Property Rights and its Implementing Measures, both effective from 1 October 1995, allow right-owners to request China's customs authorities to detain infringing goods at the border.

The measures, which are applicable to all types of intellectual property rights ("IPR") including trademarks, copyrights and patents, set out a system whereby the owners of IPR can apply to have such IPR recorded at the General Customs Administration in Beijing. Recordal will enable local customs posts to act promptly in the detention of infringing goods, and to establish a channel for the swift confirmation of infringements. Where a trademark owner requests local customs posts to take enforcement measures for a trademark not yet recorded with the General Customs Administration, an application for the recordal of such a trademark must be filed simultaneously with the request for protection. Failure to record a trademark with the General Customs Administration in advance may therefore cause delay in enforcement and ultimately prevent punishment of infringers.

14.58 HOW THE SCHEME WORKS

There are two aspects to trademark protection by customs: recordal and enforcement.

Recordal

Recordal of the IPR with the General Customs Administration in Beijing is a prerequisite. Applications for the customs recordal of trademarks and accompanying documentation must be submitted in Chinese. Once the IPR is recorded, a Customs IPR Protection Recordal Certificate ("Recordal Certificate") is issued by the General Customs Administration in Beijing. The Recordal Certificate constitutes preliminary evidence of the IPR owner's rights and must accompany all applications for enforcement. The Recordal Certificate is valid for seven years, and can be renewed for a further seven years.

Enforcement

When infringing goods are suspected to be passing into or out of China, an application for enforcement can be made to the relevant local customs posts. The application must provide relevant details about the trademark for which protection is sought, the infringing goods, the suspected infringer, the time and place of entry or exit and the nature of the suspected infringement. The application should be accompanied by the Recordal Certificate. Before the local customs post will detain goods, a guaranty equivalent to the cost, insurance and freight value (for imports) or free on board value (for exports) of the goods must be paid by the applicant to cover costs in case of wrongful application. Where the local customs post decides to detain goods on suspicion of an infringement, it must issue a notice of detention to the consignee / consignor and the applicant. The consignee / consignor has seven days to submit a written objection to the detention. If no objection is received, the goods will be treated as infringing. If an objection is received the applicant will be notified and must submit the dispute to the competent authorities for resolution within 15 days from the notification of detention. Upon determination that the goods are infringing, they will be confiscated. Depending on the nature of the infringement, the goods may be destroyed or otherwise disposed of, and the consignor / consignee fined.

CHAPTER 15

CONCLUSION

OVERVIEW 15.1

It is undeniable that China's intellectual property laws are amongst the most comprehensive and developed in Asia. China's legislators have taken active and continuous steps to develop a comprehensive intellectual property framework governing trademarks, copyright, and patents, and China has acceded to most international intellectual property-related conventions. Although serious problems remain, most notably in the area of enforcement, China's efforts to exact compliance with its existing body of laws and regulations have attracted a great amount of international approbation. China has made great efforts to develop a more transparent legal system. Although it may take some time to reverse China's reputation as a major violator of intellectual property rights, a strong signal is being sent to Chinese companies and individuals that large-scale counterfeiting and infringement will no longer be permitted.

LOCALISATION OF FOREIGN TRADEMARKS 15.2

As the Chinese market continues to grow, more and more foreign trademark holders are keen to protect their rights in China. In the process of localisation of a foreign trademark in China, the most important consideration for the holder, separate from the legal aspects of registering a trade mark in China, is the practical aspect of choosing a trade mark for use in China. Given the unique characteristics of Chinese culture and language, along with the inherent obstacles in translating a foreign-word mark, there are a number of key factors which must be taken into account to maximise the success of a trade mark in China.

WELL-KNOWN TRADEMARKS: THE DEBATE CONTINUES 15.3

A common concern of trademark holders is whether their marks, household names in their home and other jurisdictions and representing a large share of the right-holders' assets, will be recognised as well known and protected as such in China. This concern arises out of the oft-mentioned problem that China faces with enforcement, and from the concern that China's cultural heritage, mentioned earlier in this book, does not recognise private ownership of intellectual property rights. Mindful of its obligations under the WTO, the Chinese government has drafted legislation pertaining to well-known trademarks. Article 14 of the PRC Trademark Law, as well as the Implementing Regulations and the Well-Known Marks Regulations provide the scope of protection. This scope has been drafted with the TRIPS Agreement in mind, which extended in two aspects the protection given to well-known trademarks by the Paris Convention. First, well-known trademark protection is offered to trademarks used in respect of services also. Second, well-known trademark protection could be sought if the infringing trademark is used on goods or services not similar to those of the registered well-known trademark, provided that the use of the infringing mark would indicate a connection between those goods or services and the owner of the registered well-known trademark, and provided that the interests of that trademark owner are likely to be damaged by such use. The Chinese government has taken pains to draft its laws in like fashion. Admittedly, the interpretation of these laws is not always perfect; the Chinese judiciary and administrative authorities are learning as they go, and while foreign trademark holders are often chagrined at the scant respect their "NIKE" or "MTV" receives, the situation is steadily changing.

15.4 ADMINISTRATIVE AND ENFORCEMENT NETWORKS

The administrative and enforcement frameworks for handling trademark matters rival any of China's WTO colleagues. The Chinese government has established a sophisticated network of administrative agencies and authorities to manage the myriad aspects of its current trademark regime. From the State Council, as the apex of government in China, which is charged with responsibility over the many intellectual property-related administrative agencies, to the State Administration for Industry and Commerce ("SAIC"), which is the supervisory body for all matters concerning trademarks in China, the Trademark Office ("TMO"), which is responsible for the administration of trademarks and service marks in the PRC, the Trademark Review and Adjudication Board, which is responsible for reviewing disputes or specific petitions relating to the registration and ownership of trademark rights, to the local AICs, which are responsible for the enforcement of China's trademark laws in the market, the PRC has an established constellation of agencies that are charged with awarding and guarding trademark rights. This, in itself, is one of the biggest problems facing trademark owners when they try to enforce their rights.

FUTURE CHALLENGES   15.5

As mentioned above, it is undeniable that China has enacted laws that are in conformity with the requirements of WTO, and that it has an admirable administrative and enforcement framework. But there are some severe problems that China will need to tackle, and tackle effectively, if it wishes to cease being regarded as a flagrant violator by the intellectual property community. The biggest problem intellectual property holders face in China today is the exponential growth of trademark counterfeiting. China's post-WTO laws, regulations and standards attempt to fill gaps in the existing legal regime related to criminal prosecution of counterfeiters under China's Criminal Code. However, they still leave several critical issues unresolved. These unresolved issues may pose a barrier to prosecution in the majority of cases where criminal penalties would be appropriate, thereby frustrating the government's key objective of creating real deterrence against counterfeiting. The Chinese police are also not as trained or well-equipped as they need to be in dealing with this sensitive area, though that is probably a function of the relative novelty of China's enforcement efforts and should improve. The fact also remains that even though China is modernising and improving rapidly, most genuine goods remain far out of reach of the average consumer.

All that notwithstanding, it is equally undeniable that China has made great strides in the very short period that it has had an intellectual property protection system in place. It is a recognised fact that as intellectual property laws worldwide become more uniform, and the world economy more intertwined, China will recognise that its economic development is a natural corollary of its willingness to protect intellectual property rights, the engine of modern economies. Brand owners should not shy away from the challenges of trademark protection but fully embrace the new legal environment and the obvious business opportunities in the Middle Kingdom.

APPENDIX 1

TRADEMARK LAW OF THE PEOPLE'S REPUBLIC OF CHINA

(Adopted at the 24th Session of the Standing Committee of the Fifth National People's Congress on 23 August 1982, revised for the first time according to the Decision on the Amendment of the Trademark Law of the People's Republic of China adopted at the 30th Session of the Standing Committee of the Seventh National People's Congress, on 22 February 1993, and revised for the second time according to the Decision on the Amendment of the Trademark Law of the People's Republic of China adopted at the 24th Session of the Standing Committee of the Ninth National People's Congress on 27 October 2001.)

CHAPTER I GENERAL PROVISIONS

Article 1 This Law is enacted for the purposes of improving the administration of trademarks, protecting the exclusive right to use trademarks, and of encouraging producers and operators to guarantee the quality of their goods and services and maintaining the reputation of their trademarks, with a view to protecting the interests of consumers, producers and operators and to promoting the development of the socialist market economy.

Article 2 The Trademark Office of the administrative authority for industry and commerce under the State Council shall be responsible for the registration and administration of trademarks throughout the country.

The Trademark Review and Adjudication Board, established under the administrative authority for industry and commerce under the State Council, shall be responsible for handling matters of trademark disputes.

Article 3 Registered trademarks mean trademarks that have been approved and registered by the Trademark Office, including trademarks, service marks, collective marks and certification marks; the trademark registrants shall enjoy the exclusive right to use the trademarks, and be protected by law.

Said collective marks mean signs that are registered in the name of bodies, associations or other organisations to be used by the members thereof in their commercial activities to indicate their membership of the organisations.

Said certification marks mean signs which are controlled by organisations capable of supervising some goods or services and used by entities or individual persons outside the organisation for their goods or services to certify the origin, material, mode of manufacture, quality or other characteristics of the goods or services.

Regulations for the particular matters of registration and administration of collective and certification marks shall be established by the administrative authority for industry and commerce under the State Council.

Article 4 Any natural person, legal entity or other organisation intending to acquire the exclusive right to use a trademark for the goods produced, manufactured, processed, selected or marketed by it or him, shall file an application for the registration of the trademark with the Trademark Office. Any natural person, legal entity or other organisation intending to acquire the exclusive right to use a service mark for the service provided by it or him, shall file an application for the registration of the service mark with the Trademark Office.

The provisions set forth in this Law concerning trademarks shall apply to service marks.

Article 5 Two or more natural persons, legal entities or other organisations may jointly file an application for the registration for the same trademark with the Trademark Office, and jointly enjoy and exercise the exclusive right to use the trademark.

Article 6 As for any of such goods, as prescribed by the State, that must bear a registered trademark, a trademark registration must be applied for. Where no trademark registration has been granted, such goods cannot be marketed.

Article 7 Any user of a trademark shall be responsible for the quality of the goods in respect of which the trademark is used. The administrative authorities for industry and commerce at different levels shall, through the administration of trademarks, stop any practice that deceives consumers.

Article 8 An application may be filed for registration in respect of any visual sign capable of distinguishing the goods or service of one natural person, legal entity or any other organisation from that of others, including any word, design, letters of an alphabet, numerals, three-dimensional symbol, combinations of colours, and their combination.

Article 9 Any trademark in respect of which an application for registration is filed shall be so distinctive as to be distinguishable, and shall not conflict with any prior right acquired by another person.

A trademark registrant has the right to use the words 'registered trademark' or a symbol to indicate that his trademark is registered.

Article 10 The following signs shall not be used as trademarks:

1. those identical with or similar to the State name, national flag, national emblem, military flag, or decorations, of the People's Republic of China, with names of the places where the Central and State organs are located, or with the names and designs of landmark buildings;
2. those identical with or similar to the State names, national flags, national emblems or military flags of foreign countries, except that the foreign state government agrees otherwise on the use;
3. those identical with or similar to the names, flags or emblems or names, of international intergovernmental organisations, except where the organisations agree otherwise on the use or that it is not easy for the use to mislead the public;
4. those identical with or similar to official signs and hallmarks, showing official control or warranty by them, except that the use thereof is otherwise authorised;
5. those identical with or similar to the symbols, or names, of the Red Cross or the Red Crescent;
6. those having the nature of discrimination against any nationality;
7. those having the nature of exaggeration and fraud in advertising goods; and
8. those detrimental to socialist morals or customs, or having other unhealthy influences.

The geographical names of the administrative divisions at or above the county level and the foreign geographical names well known to the public shall not be used as trademarks, but such geographical terms as have other meanings or are a part of collective marks or certification marks shall be excluded. Where a trademark using any of the above-mentioned geographical names has been approved and registered, it shall continue to be valid.

Article 11 The following signs shall not be registered as trademarks:

1. those only comprising generic names, designs or models of the goods in respect of which the trademarks are used;
2. those having direct reference to the quality, main raw materials, function, use, weight, quantity or other features of the goods in respect of which the trademarks are used; and
3. those lacking distinctive features.

The signs under the preceding paragraphs may be registered as trademarks where they have acquired the distinctive features through use and become readily identifiable.

Article 12 Where an application is filed for registration of a three-dimensional sign as a trademark, any shape derived from the goods itself, required for obtaining the technical effect, or giving the goods substantive value, shall not be registered.

Article 13 Where a trademark, in respect of which the application for registration is filed for use for identical or similar goods, is a reproduction, imitation or translation of another person's trademark not registered in China and likely to cause confusion, it shall be rejected for registration and prohibited from use.

Where a trademark, in respect of which the application for registration is filed for use for non-identical or dissimilar goods, is a reproduction, imitation or translation of the well-known mark of another person that has been registered in China, misleads the public and is likely to create prejudice to the interests of the well-known mark registrant, it shall be rejected for registration and prohibited from use.

Article 14 Account shall be taken of the following factors in establishment of a well-known mark:

1. reputation of the mark to the relevant public;
2. time for continued use of the mark;
3. consecutive time, extent and geographical area of advertisement of the mark;
4. records of protection of the mark as a well-known mark; and
5. any other factors relevant to the reputation of the mark.

Article 15 Where any agent or representative registers, in their own name, the trademark of a person for whom it or he acts as the agent or representative without authorisation thereof, and the latter raises opposition, the trademark shall be rejected for registration and prohibited from use.

Article 16 Where a trademark contains a geographic indication of the goods in respect of which the trademark is used, and the goods are not from the region indicated therein and it misleads the public, it shall be rejected for registration and prohibited from use; however, any trademark that has been registered in good faith shall remain valid.

The geographic indications mentioned in the preceding paragraph refer to the signs that signify the place of origin of the goods in respect of which the signs are used, their specific quality, reputation or other features as mainly decided by the natural or cultural factors of the regions.

Article 17 Any foreign person or foreign enterprise intending to apply for the registration of a trademark in China shall file an application in accordance with any agreement concluded between the People's Republic of China and the country to which the applicant belongs, or according to the international treaty to which both countries are parties, or on the basis of the principles of reciprocity.

Article 18 Any foreign persons or foreign enterprises intending to apply for the registration of a trademark or for any other matters concerning a trademark in China shall appoint any of such organisations as designated by the State to act as their agent.

CHAPTER II APPLICATION FOR TRADEMARK REGISTRATION

Article 19 An applicant for the registration of a trademark shall, in a form, indicate, in accordance with the prescribed classification of goods, the class of the goods and the designation of the goods in respect of which the trademark is to be used.

Article 20 Where any applicant for registration of a trademark intends to use the same trademark for goods in different classes, an application for registration shall be filed in respect of each class of the prescribed classification of goods.

Article 21 Where a registered trademark is to be used in respect of other goods of the same class, a new application for registration shall be filed.
Article 22 Where the sign of a registered trademark is to be altered, a new registration shall be applied for.

Article 23 Where, after the registration of a trademark, the name, address or other registered matters concerning the registrant change, an application regarding the change shall be filed.

Article 24 Any applicant for the registration of a trademark who files an application for registration of the same trademark for identical goods in China within six months from the date of filing the first application for the trademark registration overseas may enjoy the right of priority in accordance with any agreement concluded between the People's Republic of China and the country to which the applicant belongs, or according to the international treaty to which both countries are parties, or on the basis of the principle whereby each acknowledges the right of priority of the other.

Anyone claiming the right of priority according to the preceding paragraph shall make a statement in writing when filing the application for the trademark registration, and submit, within three months, a copy of the application documents that was first filed for the registration of the trademark; where the applicant fails to make the claim in writing or submit the copy of the application documents within the time limit, the claim shall be deemed not to have been made for the right of priority.

Article 25 Where a trademark is first used for goods in an international exhibition sponsored or recognised by the Chinese Government, the applicant for the registration of the trademark may enjoy the right of priority within six months from the date of exhibition of the goods. Anyone claiming the right of priority according to the preceding paragraph shall make a claim in writing when filing the application for the registration of the trademark, and submit, within three months, documents showing the title of the exhibition in which the goods were displayed, proof that the trademark was used for the goods exhibited, and the date of exhibition; where the claim is not made in writing, or the proof documents not submitted within the time limit, the claim shall be deemed not to have been made for the right of priority.

Article 26 The matters reported and materials submitted in the application for trademark registration shall be true, accurate and complete.

CHAPTER III EXAMINATION FOR AND APPROVAL OF TRADEMARK REGISTRATION

Article 27 Where a trademark for which registration has been applied, is in conformity with the relevant provisions of this Law, the Trademark Office shall, after examination, preliminarily approve the trademark and publish it.

Article 28 Where a trademark for which registration has been applied, is not in conformity with the relevant provisions of this Law, or it is identical with or similar to the trademark of another person that has, in respect of the same or similar goods, been registered or, after examination, preliminarily approved, the Trademark Office shall refuse the application and shall not publish the said trademark.

Article 29 Where two or more applicants apply for the registration of identical or similar trademarks for the same or similar goods, the preliminary approval, after examination, and the publication shall be made for the trademark that was first filed. Where applications are filed on the same day, the preliminary approval, after examination, and the publication shall be made for the trademark that was used earliest, and the applications of the others shall be refused and their trademarks shall not be published.

Article 30 Any person may, within three months from the date of the publication, file an opposition against the trademark that has, after examination, been preliminarily approved. If no opposition has been filed after the expiration of the time limit from the publication, the registration shall be approved, a certificate of trademark registration shall be issued and the trademark shall be published.

Article 31 An application for the registration of a trademark shall not create any prejudice to the prior right of another person, nor unfair means be used to pre-emptively register the trademark of some reputation another person has used.

Article 32 Where the application for registration of a trademark is refused and no publication of the trademark is made, the Trademark Office shall notify the applicant of the same in writing. Where the applicant is dissatisfied, he may, within 15 days from receipt of the notice, file an application with the Trademark Review and Adjudication Board for a review. The Trademark Review and Adjudication Board shall make a decision and notify the applicant in writing.

Any interested party who is not satisfied with the decision made by the Trademark Review and Adjudication Board may, within 30 days from receipt of the notice, institute legal proceedings in the People's Court.

Article 33 Where an opposition is filed against the trademark that has, after examination, been preliminarily approved and published, the Trademark Office shall hear both the opponent and applicant state facts and grounds, and shall, after investigation and verification, make a decision. Where any party is dissatisfied, it may within fifteen days from receipt of the notification, apply for a re-examination, and the Trademark Review and Adjudication Board shall make a decision and notify both the opponent and applicant in writing.

Any interested party who is not satisfied with the decision made by the Trademark Review and Adjudication Board may, within 30 days from the date of receipt of the notice, institute legal proceedings in the People's Court. The People's Court shall notify the other party to the trademark re-examination proceeding to be a third party to the litigation.

Article 34 Where the interested party does not, within the statutory time limit, apply for the re-examination of the adjudication by the Trademark Office or does not institute legal proceedings in respect of the adjudication by the Trademark Review and Adjudication Board, the adjudication takes effect.

Where the opposition cannot be established upon adjudication, the registration shall be approved, a certificate of trademark registration shall be issued and the trademark shall be published; where the opposition is established upon adjudication, the registration shall not be approved.

Where the opposition cannot be established upon adjudication, but the registration is approved, the time of the exclusive right the trademark registration applicant has obtained to use the trademark is counted from the date on which the three months expires from the publication of the preliminary examination.

Article 35 Any application for trademark registration and trademark re-examination shall be examined in due course.

Article 36 Where any trademark registration applicant or registrant finds any obvious errors in the trademark registration documents or application documents, it or he may apply for correction thereof. The Trademark Office shall ex officio make the correction according to law and notify the interested party of the correction.

The error correction mentioned in the preceding paragraph shall not relate to the substance of the trademark registration documents or application documents.

CHAPTER IV RENEWAL, ASSIGNMENT AND LICENSING OF REGISTERED TRADEMARKS

Article 37 The period of validity of a registered trademark shall be 10 years, counted from the date of approval of the registration.

Article 38 Where the registrant intends to continue to use the registered trademark beyond the expiration of the period of validity, an application for renewal of the registration shall be made within six months before the said expiration. Where no application therefore has been filed within the said period, a grace period of six months may be allowed. If no application has been filed at the expiration of the grace period, the registered trademark shall be cancelled.

The period of validity of each renewal of registration shall be 10 years.

Any renewal of registration shall be published after it as been approved.

Article 39 Where a registered trademark is assigned, the assignor and assignee shall conclude a contract for the assignment, and jointly file an application with the trademark Office. The assignee shall guarantee the quality of the goods in respect of which the registered trademark is used.

The assignment of a registered trademark shall be published after it has been approved, and the assignee enjoys the exclusive right to use the trademark from the date of publication.

Article 40 Any trademark registrant may, by signing a trademark license contract, authorise other persons to use his registered trademark. The licensor shall supervise the quality of the goods in respect of which the licensee uses his registered trademark, and the licensee shall guarantee the quality of the goods in respect of which the registered trademark is used.

Where any party is authorised to use a registered trademark of another person, the name of the licensee and the origin of the goods must be indicated on the goods that bear the registered trademark.

The trademark license contract shall be submitted to the Trademark Office for record.

CHAPTER V ADJUDICATION OF DISPUTES CONCERNING REGISTERED TRADEMARKS

Article 41 Where a registered trademark stands in violation of the provisions of Articles 10, 11 and 12 of this Law, or the registration of a trademark was acquired by fraud or any other unfair means, the Trademark Office shall cancel the registered trademark in question; and any other organisation or individual may request the Trademark Review and Adjudication Board to make an adjudication to cancel such a registered trademark.

Where a registered trademark stands in violation of the provisions of Articles 13, 15, 16 and 31 of this Law, any other trademark owner concerned or interested party may, within five years from the date of the registration of the trademark, file a request with the Trademark Review and Adjudication Board for adjudication to cancel the registered trademark. Where a well-known mark is registered in bad faith, the genuine owner thereof shall not be restricted by the five-year limitation.

In addition to those cases as provided for in the preceding two paragraphs, any person disputing a registered trademark may, within five years from the date of approval of the trademark registration, apply to the Trademark Review and Adjudication Board for adjudication.

The Trademark Review and Adjudication Board shall, after receipt of the application for adjudication, notify the interested parties and request them to respond with arguments within a specified period.

Article 42 Where a trademark, before its being approved for registration, has been the object of opposition and decision, no application for adjudication may be filed based on the same facts and grounds.

Article 43 After the Trademark Review and Adjudication Board has made an adjudication either to maintain or to cancel a registered trademark, it shall notify the interested parties of the same in writing.

Any interested party who is dissatisfied with the adjudication made by the Trademark Review and Adjudication Board may, within 30 days from the date of receipt of the notice, institute legal proceedings in the People's Court. The People's Court shall notify the other party of the trademark adjudication proceeding to be a third party to the legal proceedings.

CHAPTER VI ADMINISTRATION OF THE USE OF TRADEMARKS

Article 44 Where any person who uses a registered trademark has committed any of the following, the Trademark Office shall order him to rectify the situation within a specified period or even cancel the registered trademark:

1. where a registered trademark is altered unilaterally (that is, without the required registration);
2. where the name, address or other registered matters concerning the registrant of a registered trademark are changed unilaterally (that is, without the required application),
3. where the registered trademark is assigned unilaterally (that is, without the required approval); or

4. where the use of the registered trademark has ceased for three consecutive years.

Article 45 Where a registered trademark is used in respect of the goods that have been roughly or poorly manufactured, or whose superior quality has been replaced by inferior quality, so that consumers are deceived, the administrative authorities for industry and commerce at different levels shall, according to the circumstances, order rectification of the situation within a specified period, and may, in addition, circulate a notice of criticism or impose a fine, and the Trademark Office may even cancel the registered trademark.

Article 46 Where a registered trademark has been cancelled or has not been renewed at the expiration, the Trademark Office shall, during one year from the date of the cancellation or removal thereof, approve no application for the registration of a trademark that is identical with or similar to the said trademark.

Article 47 Where any person violates the provisions of Article 6 of this Law, the local administrative authority for industry and commerce shall order him to file an application for the registration within a specified period, and may, in addition, impose a fine.

Article 48 Where any person who uses an unregistered trademark has committed any of the following, the local administrative authority for industry and commerce shall stop the use of the trademark, order him to rectify the situation within a specified period, and may, in addition, circulate a notice of criticism or impose a fine:

1. where the trademark is falsely represented as registered;
2. where any provision of Article 10 of this Law is violated; or
3. where the manufacture is of rough or poor quality, or where superior quality is replaced by inferior quality, so that 'consumers are deceived.

Article 49 Any party dissatisfied with the decision of the Trademark Office to cancel a registered trademark may, within 15 days from receipt of the corresponding notice, apply for a review. The Trademark Review and Adjudication Board shall make a decision and notify the applicant in writing.

Any interested party dissatisfied with the decision by the Trademark Review and Adjudication Board may, within 30 days from the date of receipt of the notice, institute legal proceedings in the People's Court.

Article 50 Any party dissatisfied with the decision of the administrative authority for industry and commerce to impose a fine under the provisions of Article 45, Article 47 or Article 48 may, within 15 days from receipt of the corresponding notice, institute legal proceedings with the People's Court. If there have been instituted no legal proceedings and no performance of the decision made at the expiration of the said period, the administrative authority for industry and commerce may request the People's Court for compulsory execution thereof.

CHAPTER VII PROTECTION OF THE EXCLUSIVE RIGHTS TO USE REGISTERED TRADEMARKS

Article 51 The exclusive right to use a registered trademark is limited to the trademark that has been approved for registration and to the goods in respect of which the use of the trademark has been approved.

Article 52 Any of the following acts shall be an infringement of the exclusive right to use a registered trademark:

1. to use a trademark that is identical with or similar to a registered trademark in respect of the identical or similar goods without the authorisation from the trademark registrant;
2. to sell goods that one knows bear a counterfeited registered trademark;
3. to counterfeit, or to make, without authorisation, representations of a registered trademark of another person, or to sell such representations of a registered trademark as were counterfeited, or made without authorisation;
4. to replace, without the consent of the trademark registrant, the registered trademark and market again the goods bearing the replaced trademark; or
5. to cause, in other respects, prejudice to the exclusive right of another person to use a registered trademark.

Article 53 Where any party has committed any such acts to infringe the exclusive right to use a registered trademark as provided for in Article 52 of this Law and has caused a dispute, the interested parties shall resolve the dispute through consultation; where they are reluctant to resolve the matter through consultation or the consultation fails, the trademark registrant or interested party may institute legal proceedings in the People's Court or request action from the administrative authority for industry and commerce.

Where it is established that an act constitutes an infringement, the administrative authority for industry and commerce handling the matter shall order the infringer to immediately stop the infringing act, confiscate and destroy the infringing goods and tools specially used for the manufacture of the infringing goods and for counterfeiting the representations of the registered trademark, and impose a fine.

Where any interested party is dissatisfied with the decision in the matter, they may, within 15 days from the date of receipt of the notice, institute legal proceedings in the People's Court, according to the Administrative Procedure Law of the People's Republic of China.

If there have been instituted no legal proceedings and performance of the decision is not made at the expiration of the said period, the administrative authority for industry and commerce shall request from the People's Court, compulsory execution thereof.

The administrative authority for industry and commerce handling the matter may, upon the request of the interested party, mediate on the amount of compensation for the infringement of the exclusive right to use the trademark; where the mediation fails, the interested party may institute legal proceedings in the People's Court according to the Civil Procedure Law of the People's Republic of China.

Article 54 The administrative authority for industry and commerce has the power to investigate and handle any act of infringement of the exclusive right to use a registered trademark according to law; where the case is so serious as to constitute a crime, it shall be transferred to the judicial authority for handling.

Article 55 When investigating and handling a suspected act of infringement of a registered trademark, the administrative authority for industry and commerce at or above the county level may, according to the obtained evidence of the suspected violation of law or informed offence, exercise the following functions and authorities:

1. to inquire of the interested parties involved, and to investigate the relevant events of the infringement of the exclusive right to use the trademark;
2. to read and make copies of the contract, receipts, account books and other relevant materials of the interested parties relating to the infringement;
3. to inspect the site where the interested party committed the alleged infringement of the exclusive right to use the trademark; and
4. to inspect any articles relevant to the infringement; any articles that prove to have been used for the infringement of another person's exclusive right to use the trademark may be sealed up or seized.

When the administrative authority for industry and commerce exercises the preceding functions and authorities, the interested party shall cooperate and help, and shall not refuse to do so or stand in the way.

Article 56 The amount of damages shall be the profit that the infringer has earned because of the infringement in the period of the infringement or the injury that the infringee has suffered from the infringement in the period of the infringement, including the appropriate expenses of the infringee for stopping the infringement.

Where it is difficult to determine the profit that the infringer has earned because of the infringement in the period of the infringement or the injury that the infringee has suffered from the infringement in the period of the infringement, the People's Court shall impose an amount of damages of no more than RMB500,000 according to the circumstances of the infringement.

Anyone who sells goods without knowing that they infringed the exclusive right to use a registered trademark, and is able to prove that the goods were obtained legitimately, and indicates the supplier thereof, shall not bear the liability for damages.

Article 57 Where a trademark registrant or interested party who has evidence to show that another person is committing or will commit an infringement of the right to use its registered trademark, and that failure to promptly stop the infringement will cause irreparable damages to its legitimate rights and interests, the registrant may file an application with the People's Court to order cessation of the relevant act and to take measures for property preservation before instituting legal proceedings in the People's Court.

The People's Court handling the application under the preceding paragraph shall apply the provisions of Articles 93 to 96 and Article 99 of the Civil Procedure Law of the People's Republic of China.

Article 58 In order to stop an infringing act, any trademark registrant or interested party may file an application with the People's Court for preservation of the evidence before instituting legal proceedings in the People's Court, where the evidence will possibly be destroyed or lost or difficult to obtain again in the future. The People's Court must make adjudication within 48 hours after receipt of the application; where it is decided to take the preservative measures, the measures shall be executed immediately. The People's Court may order the applicant to place guaranty; where the applicant fails to place the guaranty, the application shall be rejected.

Where the applicant institutes no legal proceedings within 15 days after the People's Court takes the preservative measures, the People's Court shall release the measures taken for the preservation.

Article 59 Where any party uses, without the authorisation from the trademark registrant, a trademark identical with a registered trademark, and the case is so serious as to constitute a crime, he shall be prosecuted, according to law, for his criminal liabilities in addition to his compensation for the damages suffered by the infringee.

Where any party counterfeits, or makes, without authorisation, representations of a registered trademark of another person, or sells such representations of a registered trademark that are counterfeited, or made without authorisation, and the case is so serious as to constitute a crime, he shall be prosecuted, according to law, for his criminal liabilities in addition to his compensation for the damages suffered by the infringee.

Where any party sells goods that he knows bear a counterfeited registered trademark, and the case is so serious as to constitute a crime, he shall be prosecuted, according to law, for his criminal liabilities in addition to his compensation for the damages suffered by the infringee.

Article 60 The State functionaries for the registration, administration and re-examination of trademarks must handle cases according to law, be incorruptible and disciplined, be devoted to their duties and courteous and honest in their provision of service.

The State functionaries of the Trademark Office and the Trademark Review and Adjudication Board and those working for the registration, administration and re-examination of trademarks shall not practice as trademark agent and engage in any activity to manufacture and market goods.

Article 61 The administrative authority for industry and commerce shall establish and amplify its internal supervision system to supervise and inspect the State functionaries for the registration, administration and re-examination of trademarks in their implementation of the laws and administrative regulations and in their observation of the discipline.

Article 62 Where any State functionary for the registration, administration and re-examination of trademarks neglects his duty, abuses his power, engages in malpractice for personal gain, handles the registration, administration and re-examination of trademarks in violation of law, accepts money or material wealth from any interested party or seeks illicit interest, which constitutes a crime, he or she shall be prosecuted for his or her criminal liability. If the case is not serious enough to constitute a crime, he or she shall be given disciplinary sanction according to law.

CHAPTER VIII SUPPLEMENTARY PROVISIONS

Article 63 Any application for a trademark registration and for other matters concerning a trademark shall be subject to payment of the fees as prescribed. The schedule of fees shall be prescribed separately.

Article 64 This Law shall enter into force on 1 March 1983. The Regulations Governing Trademarks promulgated by the State Council on 10 April l963 shall be abrogated on the same date, and any other provisions concerning trademarks contrary to this Law shall cease to be effective at the same time.

Trademarks registered before this Law enters into force shall continue to be valid.

IMPLEMENTING REGULATIONS FOR THE TRADEMARK LAW OF THE PEOPLE'S REPUBLIC OF CHINA

(Issued by the State Council on 3 August 2002. Effective from 15 September 2002. The regulations supersede the Detailed Implementing Rules for the Trademark Law of the People's Republic of China published by the State Council on 10 March 1983, amended for the first time with the approval of the State Council on 3 January 1988 and amended for the second time with the approval of the State Council on 15 July 1993, and the Official Reply of the State Council Concerning the Issue of the Submission of Supporting Documents
When Carrying Out Trademark Registration Procedures dated 23 April 1995.)

CHAPTER 1 GENERAL PROVISIONS

Article 1 These Regulations are formulated in accordance with the Trademark Law of the People's Republic of China (the "Trademark Law").

Article 2 The provisions of these Regulations relating to trademarks for goods shall be applicable to trademarks for services.

Article 3 For the purposes of the Trademark Law and these Regulations, the use of a trademark includes the use on goods, on the packaging or containers for goods, on trade documents for goods, or in advertising, publicity, exhibitions or other business activities.

Article 4 For the purposes of Article 6 of the Trademark Law, the phrase "goods which the state stipulates must use registered trademarks" means goods that laws or administration regulations stipulate must use registered trademarks.

Article 5 Pursuant to the Trademark Law and these Regulations, if a dispute arises in the course of trademark registration or trademark review and adjudication and a relevant party considers his trademark to constitute a well-known trademark, such party may submit an application to the Trademark Office or the Trademark Review and Adjudication Board, as the case may be, for recognition of the trademark as a well-known trademark and rejection of the trademark registration application which violates Article 13 of the Trademark Law or cancellation of the trademark registration which violates Article 13 of the Trademark Law. When submitting his application, the relevant party shall provide evidence that his trademark constitutes a well-known trademark.

Based on the application of the party and ascertainment of the facts, the Trademark Office or the Trademark Review and Adjudication Board shall, pursuant to Article 14 of the Trademark Law, determine whether or not his trademark constitutes a well-known trademark.

Article 6 A geographical indication as provided for in Article 16 of the Trademark Law may be the subject of an application for registration as a certification mark or a collective mark pursuant to the Trademark Law and these Regulations.

Where a geographical indication has been registered as a certification mark, a natural person or a legal person or other organisation whose goods satisfy the conditions for use of the geographical indication may request to use such certification mark, and the organisation that controls the mark shall permit such use. Where a geographical indication has been registered as a collective mark, a natural person or a legal person or other organisation whose goods satisfy the conditions for use of the geographical indication may request to join the group, association or other organisation that registered such geographical indication as a collective mark, and such group, association or other organisation shall accept him or it as a member pursuant to its charter; if he or it does not request to join the group, association or other organisation that registered such geographical indication as a collective mark, he or it may nonetheless make legitimate use of the geographical indication, and the said group, association or other organisation shall have no right to prohibit the same.

Article 7 An applicant entrusting a trademark agency to apply for trademark registration or to handle other trademark matters shall file a power of attorney. The power of attorney shall clearly state the matters entrusted and the limits of authority. The power of attorney of a foreigner or foreign enterprise shall also state the nationality of the principal.

The notarisation and authentication procedures for the power of attorney and the relevant supporting documents of a foreigner or foreign enterprise shall be carried out in accordance with the principle of reciprocity.

For the purposes of Article 18 of the Trademark Law, the phrase "foreigners and foreign enterprises" means foreigners and foreign enterprises that have no habitual residence or place of business in China.

Article 8 The Chinese language shall be used for applications for trademark registration or the handling of other trademark matters.

Certificates, supporting documents and evidence submitted pursuant to the Trademark Law or these Regulations that are in a foreign language shall be accompanied by a Chinese translation, failing which they shall be deemed not to have been submitted.

Article 9 A member of the working personnel of the Trademark Office or the Trademark Review and Adjudication Board shall recuse himself, and may be challenged by a party or a materially interested person, in any of the following circumstances:

1. he is a party or a close relative of a party or of an agent;
2. he is otherwise related to a party or to an agent in a way that may affect his impartiality; or
3. he is materially interested in the application for trademark registration or the handling of the other trademark matters.

Article 10 Unless otherwise provided for herein, the date on which a party files documents or materials with the Trademark Office or the Trademark Review and Adjudication Board shall be the date of delivery in the case of direct delivery and the date of the postmark affixed at the time of mailing in the case of filing by mail. If the postmark date is unclear or if there is no postmark, then the date of filing shall be the date of actual receipt by the Trademark Office or the Trademark Review and Adjudication Board, unless the party is able to provide evidence of the actual postmark date.

Article 11 Documents from the Trademark Office or the Trademark Review and Adjudication Board may be served on the parties by mail, direct delivery or otherwise. Where a party has appointed a trademark agency, documents served on the trademark agency shall be deemed to have been served on such party.

The date on which a document from the Trademark Office or the Trademark Review and Adjudication Board is served on a party shall be the date of the postmark affixed at the time of receipt by the party in the case of service by mail. If the postmark date is unclear or if there is no postmark, then the document shall be deemed to have been served on the party following the lapse of 15 days from the date of sending. In the case of direct delivery, the date of service shall be the date of delivery. If it is impossible to mail the document or to deliver it directly, it may be served on the party by public announcement, in which case it shall be deemed to have been served on the party following the lapse of 30 days from the date of issuance of the public announcement.

Article 12 International trademark registrations shall be handled pursuant to the relevant international treaties to which China has acceded. The specific measures therefore shall be formulated by the department for the administration of industry and commerce of the State Council.

CHAPTER 2 APPLICATIONS FOR TRADEMARK REGISTRATION

Article 13 When applying for registration of a trademark, application shall be made by class of goods or services according to the published classification of goods and services. For each application for registration of a trademark, an Application for Trademark Registration shall be filed with the Trademark Office, accompanied by five specimens of the trademark. For trademarks with designated colours, five coloured specimens and one black-and-white sketch shall be filed as well.

The trademark specimens must be clear and easy to paste up. They must be printed on glossy, durable paper or be replaced by photographs. Their length or width shall not exceed 10 centimetres and not be less than 5 centimetres.

If trademark registration is applied for a three-dimensional sign, the applicant shall declare the same in the application and file specimens enabling determination of the three-dimensional shape.

If trademark registration is applied for a colour combination, the applicant shall declare the same in the application and file a textual description.

When applying for registration of a collective or certification mark, the applicant shall declare the same in the application and file documents supporting his qualifications to apply as well as the rules for administration of the use of the mark.

If the trademark is in a foreign language or includes a foreign language, its meaning shall be explained.

Article 14 An applicant for trademark registration shall submit a photocopy of a valid identification document. The name of the applicant for trademark registration shall be consistent with that on the identification document submitted.

Article 15 The name of the goods or the service shall be entered in accordance with the classification of goods and services. For goods that are not named or services that are not listed in the classification of goods and services, a description of the goods or service shall be attached.

Relevant documents, such as those for application for registration of a trademark, shall be typed or printed.

Article 16 If joint application is made for registration of the same trademark, a representative shall be designated in the application. In the absence of such designation, the person ranked first in the application shall be the representative.

Article 17 If an applicant changes his name, address or agent, or narrows the scope of designated goods, he shall carry out amendment procedures with the Trademark Office.

If an applicant assigns his application for trademark registration, he shall carry out assignment procedures with the Trademark Office.

Article 18 The date of application for trademark registration shall be the date on which the application documents are received by the Trademark Office. If the application procedures have been completed and the application documents have been filled out in accordance with regulations, the Trademark Office shall accept the same and notify the applicant in writing. If the application procedures have not been completed or the application documents have not been filled out in accordance with regulations, the Trademark Office shall not accept the same and shall notify the applicant in writing, stating the grounds for the non-acceptance.

If the application procedures have been basically completed or the application documents basically conform to the regulations, but supplementation and / or correction is required, the Trademark Office shall notify the applicant to carry out supplementation and / or correction and require him to supplement and / or correct the contents indicated and return the application to the Trademark Office within 30 days from the date of receipt of the notice. If supplementation and / or correction is carried out and the application is returned to the Trademark Office within the time limit, the application date shall be reserved. If supplementation and / or correction is not carried out within the time limit, the application shall be deemed abandoned and the Trademark Office shall notify the applicant in writing.

Article 19 If two or more applicants separately apply on the same date for registration of the same or similar trademarks for use on the same or similar goods, each applicant shall, within 30 days of the date of receipt of a notice from the Trademark Office, submit evidence that he was the first to use the trademark in question prior to the application for registration. If the trademarks have been first used on the same date or none has yet been used, the applicants may hold consultations among themselves and submit their written agreement to the Trademark Office within 30 days after receipt of a notice from the Trademark Office. If the applicants do not wish to consult or consultations are unsuccessful, the Trademark Office shall notify the applicants to determine one applicant by drawing lots and shall reject the registration applications of the others. Applicants who have been notified by the Trademark Office but fail to participate in the draw shall be deemed to have abandoned their applications. Applicants who fail to participate in the draw shall be notified in writing by the Trademark Office.

Article 20 Where a right of priority is claimed pursuant to Article 24 of the Trademark Law, the copies, filed by the applicant, of the application documents he submitted when he first applied for registration of the trademark must be authenticated by the trademark authority that accepted such application, and marked with the application date and number.

Where a right of priority is claimed pursuant to Article 25 of the Trademark Law, the supporting documents filed by the applicant must be authenticated by an organisation designated by the department for the administration of industry and commerce of the State Council, unless the international exhibition at which his goods were exhibited was held in China.

CHAPTER 3 EXAMINATION OF APPLICATIONS FOR TRADEMARK REGISTRATION

Article 21 Trademark registration applications that have been accepted shall be examined by the Trademark Office in accordance with relevant provisions of the Trademark Law and these Regulations. If an application for registration conforms to the provisions or conforms to the provisions to the extent that the trademark is used on some of the designated goods only, the Trademark Office shall preliminarily approve and gazette the trademark. If an application for registration does not conform to the provisions or does not conform to the provisions vis-à-vis some of the goods for which the trademark is designated, the Trademark Office shall reject the application or reject the application with respect to some of the designated goods, and notify the applicant in writing, stating the grounds for the rejection.

If the Trademark Office preliminarily approves an application for registration which conforms to the provisions to the extent that the trademark is used on some of the designated goods only, the applicant may, prior to the expiration date of the opposition period, apply for abandonment of the application under which the trademark may be used on some of the designated goods only. If the applicant applies for abandonment of the application under which the trademark may be used on some of the designated goods only, the Trademark Office shall revoke its preliminary approval, terminate the examination procedure and gazette the matter anew.

Article 22 To oppose a trademark that has been preliminarily approved and gazetted by the Trademark Office, the opponent shall file a trademark opposition, in duplicate, with the Trademark Office. The trademark opposition shall clearly state the number of the issue of the Trademark Gazette in which the opposed trademark was gazetted as well as its preliminary approval number. The trademark opposition shall contain specific claims and be based on facts, and shall be accompanied by relevant evidence.

The Trademark Office shall serve a copy of the trademark opposition on the respondent in a timely manner and instruct him to offer a defence within 30 days from the date of receipt of the opposition. Failure on the part of the respondent to offer a defence shall not affect the Trademark Office's ruling on the opposition.

If a party needs to submit relevant supplementary evidence after he raises an opposition or offers a defence, he shall include a statement to that effect in his application or defence, and submit the evidence within three months of the date on which he filed his opposition or defence. If the supplementary evidence is not submitted within the time limit, the party shall be deemed to have abandoned his right to submit supplementary evidence.

Article 23 For the purposes of the second paragraph of Article 34 of the Trademark Law, the word 'tenable' includes tenable in respect of some of the designated goods. If an opposition is tenable in respect of some of the designated goods, the trademark registration application shall not be approved to the extent of that portion of the designated goods.

If the registration of the opposed trademark had been gazetted before the ruling on the opposition became effective, the original gazetting of the registration shall be revoked and the trademark whose registration was approved in the ruling on the opposition shall be gazetted anew.

The approval of a trademark's registration in the ruling on an opposition shall have no retroactive effect on another person's use on the same or similar goods of a sign which is the same as or similar to such trademark during the time from the expiration date of the period for opposition to the trademark until the entry into effect of the ruling on the opposition; however, damages shall be payable if the trademark registrant suffered loss as a result of bad faith on the part of the person using such sign.

The time limit for applying for review and adjudication of a trademark whose registration was approved in a ruling on an opposition shall run from the date on which the ruling is gazetted.

CHAPTER 4 AMENDMENT, ASSIGNMENT AND RENEWAL OF REGISTERED TRADEMARKS

Article 24 To change the name, address or other registered particulars of a trademark registrant, an amendment application shall be filed with the Trademark Office. Following its approval of the application, the Trademark Office shall issue a corresponding certificate to the registrant and gazette the matter. If the Trademark Office does not approve the application, it shall notify the applicant in writing, stating the grounds for the disapproval.

To change the name of a trademark registrant, a document in support of the change issued by the relevant registry shall be filed as well. If no such document has been filed, it may be supplied within 30 days after the date on which application is made. If the said document is not supplied within the time limit, the amendment application shall be deemed abandoned and the Trademark Office shall notify the applicant in writing.

When the name or address of a trademark registrant is changed, the trademark registrant shall amend the registrations of all of his trademarks simultaneously. If he fails to do so, the amendment application shall be deemed abandoned and the Trademark Office shall notify the applicant in writing.

Article 25 To apply for assignment of a registered trademark, the assignor and the assignee shall file an application for assignment of a registered trademark with the Trademark Office. The application procedures for assignment of the registered trademark shall be carried out by the assignee. After the Trademark Office has examined and approved the application, it shall issue a corresponding certificate to the assignee and gazette the assignment.

When assigning a registered trademark, the trademark registrant shall assign simultaneously the same or similar trademarks registered for the same or similar goods. If he fails to do so, the Trademark Office shall notify him that he should rectify the matter within a specified time. If he fails to rectify the matter within the time limit, the application for assignment of the registered trademark shall be deemed abandoned and the Trademark Office shall notify the applicant in writing.

If an application for assignment of a registered trademark may lead to mistaken recognition or confusion or have other negative effects, the Trademark Office shall not approve the same and shall notify the applicant in writing, stating the grounds for the disapproval.

Article 26 If the exclusive right to use a registered trademark is transferred to someone else for reasons other than assignment, the party accepting such right shall carry out the procedures for the transfer of the exclusive right to use a registered trademark with the Trademark Office on the strength of the relevant supporting documents or legal documents.

If the exclusive right to use a registered trademark is transferred to someone else, the same or similar trademarks registered for the same or similar goods by the holder of such right shall be transferred simultaneously. If he fails to cause the said trademarks to be transferred simultaneously, the Trademark Office shall notify him that he should rectify the matter within a specified time. If he fails to rectify the matter within the time limit, the application for transfer of the registered trademark to someone else shall be deemed abandoned and the Trademark Office shall notify the applicant in writing.

Article 27 If the registration of a registered trademark needs to be renewed, an application for renewal of trademark registration shall be filed with the Trademark Office. After the Trademark Office has examined and approved the application, it shall issue a corresponding certificate to the assignee and gazette the renewal.

The term of a renewed trademark registration shall run from the first day following the expiration of the preceding registration term of the trademark.

CHAPTER 5 TRADEMARK REVIEW AND ADJUDICATION

Article 28 The Trademark Review and Adjudication Board shall accept applications for trademark review and adjudication submitted pursuant to Articles 32, 33, 41 and 49 of the Trademark Law. The Trademark Review and Adjudication Board shall carry out review and adjudication on the basis of the facts and in accordance with the law.

Article 29 For the purposes of the third paragraph of Article 41 of the Trademark Law, the term 'disputed registered trademarks' refers to situations where the registrant of a trademark that was first filed for registration considers a trademark that another person subsequently filed for registration to be the same as or similar to his own trademark that he registered for the same or similar products.

Article 30 To apply for trademark review and adjudication, the applicant shall file an application with the Trademark Review and Adjudication Board, accompanied by a number of duplicates corresponding to the number of parties on the opposite side. When applying for review on the basis of a written decision or ruling of the Trademark Office, the application shall additionally be accompanied by duplicates of the written decision or ruling of the Trademark Office.

After having received the application, the Trademark Review and Adjudication Board shall accept the same if it is found to satisfy the conditions for acceptance. If the application is found not to satisfy the conditions for acceptance, the Trademark Review and Adjudication Board shall not accept it and shall notify the applicant in writing, stating the grounds for the non-acceptance. If supplementation and / or correction are required, the Trademark Review and Adjudication Board shall notify the applicant to carry out supplementation and / or correction within 30 days from the date of receipt of the notice. If the application still does not comply with the regulations after it has been supplemented and / or corrected, the Trademark Review and Adjudication Board shall not accept it and shall notify the applicant in writing, stating the grounds for the non-acceptance. If supplementation and / or correction are not carried out within the time limit, the application shall be deemed withdrawn and the Trademark Review and Adjudication Board shall notify the applicant in writing.

If the Trademark Review and Adjudication Board discovers an application for trademark review and adjudication does not satisfy the conditions for acceptance after it has accepted the same, it shall reject the application and notify the applicant in writing, stating the grounds for the rejection.

Article 31 After the Trademark Review and Adjudication Board has accepted an application for trademark review and adjudication, it shall deliver the duplicate of the trademark opposition to the respondent in a timely manner and instruct him to offer a defence within 30 days from the date of receipt of the application. Failure to offer a defence shall not affect the review and adjudication by the Trademark Review and Adjudication Board.

Article 32 If a party needs to submit relevant supplementary evidence after he applies for review and adjudication or offers a defence, he shall include a statement to that effect in his application or defence and submit the evidence within three months of the date on which he filed his application or defence. If the supplementary evidence is not submitted within the time limit, the party shall be deemed to have abandoned his right to submit supplementary evidence.

Article 33 Based on a party's request or actual need, the Trademark Review and Adjudication Board may decide to conduct an open hearing concerning an application for review and adjudication.

If the Trademark Review and Adjudication Board decides to conduct an open hearing concerning an application for review and adjudication, it shall notify the parties in writing 15 days prior to the hearing, informing them of the date and place of the hearing and of the adjudicators. The parties shall reply within the time limit specified in the notice.

If the applicant neither replies nor attends the hearing, his application for review and adjudication shall be deemed withdrawn and he shall be notified in writing by the Trademark Review and Adjudication Board. If the respondent neither replies nor attends the hearing, the Trademark Review and Adjudication Board may conduct review and adjudication by default.

Article 34 If an applicant requests to withdraw his application before the Trademark Review and Adjudication Board has made a decision or ruling, he may do so after he has given the Trademark Review and Adjudication Board a written explanation of his grounds. If the application is withdrawn, the review and adjudication process shall terminate.

Article 35 An applicant who has withdrawn his application for trademark review and adjudication may not submit another review and adjudication application based on the same facts and grounds. If the Trademark Review and Adjudication Board has already made a ruling or decision in respect of an application for trademark review and adjudication, no party may submit another review and adjudication application based on the same facts and grounds.

Article 36 Where a registered trademark is cancelled pursuant to Article 41 of the Trademark Law, the exclusive right to use the same shall be deemed not to have existed *ab initio*. A decision or ruling on the cancellation of a registered trademark shall have no retroactive effect on a judgement or ruling in a trademark infringement case that was made by a People's Court and enforced prior to the cancellation, or on a decision on the handling of an infringement made in a trademark infringement case that was made by a department for the administration of industry and commerce and enforced prior to the cancellation or on a trademark assignment or licence contract that was performed prior to the cancellation; however, damages shall be payable if bad faith on the part of the trademark registrant caused another person to suffer loss.

CHAPTER 6 CONTROL OF THE USE OF TRADEMARKS

Article 37 When a registered trademark is used, it may be marked with the phrase '注册商标'[1] or a registration symbol on the goods, the packaging for the goods, the instruction leaflet or manual, or other attachments.

The registration symbols include Ⓩ[2] and ®. When a registration symbol is used, it shall be placed at the top or bottom right corner of the trademark.

Article 38 If a Trademark Registration Certificate has been lost or damaged, application must be made to the Trademark Office for re-issuance. If the Trademark Registration Certificate has been lost, a declaration of loss shall be published in the Trademark Gazette. Damaged Trademark Registration Certificates shall be returned to the Trademark Office when the application for re-issuance is filed.

If a Trademark Registration Certificate is forged or altered, criminal liability shall be pursued according to law in accordance with the provisions of the Criminal Code on the crime of forging or altering certificates issued by state authorities or other crimes.

Article 39 If a trademark registrant commits any of the acts specified in items 1, 2 and 3 of Article 44 of the Trademark Law, the administration of industry and commerce will order him to rectify the situation within a specified time. If he refuses to do so, the administration of industry and commerce will report the matter to the Trademark Office with the request that it cancel his registered trademark.

In the event of the act mentioned in item 4 of Article 44 of the Trademark Law, anyone may apply, stating the relevant details, to the

---

1   Translator's note: These characters mean 'registered trademark'.
2   Translator's note: The character inside the circle means 'registered'.

Trademark Office for cancellation of the registered trademark. The Trademark Office shall notify the trademark registrant, requiring him to provide evidence of his use of the trademark prior to the filing of the application for cancellation, or to state legitimate reasons for non-use, within two months of the date of receipt of the notice. If the registrant fails to provide evidence or provides invalid evidence, and if he has no legitimate reasons for non-use, the Trademark Office shall cancel his registered trademark.

For the purposes of the preceding paragraph, the term 'evidence' includes evidence of the trademark registrant's use of the registered trademark and evidence of the trademark registrant's licensing of the trademark to another person.

Article 40 Registered trademarks that have been cancelled pursuant to Article 44 or 45 of the Trademark Law shall be gazetted by the Trademark Office. The exclusive right to use such a registered trademark shall be extinguished from the date on which the Trademark Office makes its decision to cancel the mark.

Article 41 If the grounds for cancellation of a registered trademark, which has been cancelled by the Trademark Office or the Trademark Review and Adjudication Board, apply to some of the designated goods only, the trademark registration shall be cancelled to the extent of that portion of the designated goods.

Article 42 The amount of a fine imposed pursuant to Article 45 or 48 of the Trademark Law shall not be more than 20 per cent of the illegal turnover or not more than twice the illegal profit.

The amount of a fine imposed pursuant to Article 47 of the Trademark Law shall not be more than 10 per cent of the illegal turnover.

Article 43 When a licensor licenses his registered trademark to another person, he shall deliver a duplicate of the trademark licence contract to the Trademark Office for the record within three months after the date of execution.

Article 44 If anyone violates the second paragraph of Article 40 of the Trademark Law, the administration of industry and commerce shall order him to rectify the situation within a specified time. If he fails to rectify the situation within the time limit, the department for the administration of industry and commerce will confiscate his trademark representations. If it is difficult to separate the trademark representations from the goods, they will be confiscated and destroyed together.

Article 45 If the use of a trademark violates Article 13 of the Trademark Law, a relevant party may request the administration of industry and commerce to prohibit such use. When submitting his application, the party shall provide evidence that his trademark constitutes a well-known trademark. If the trademark is recognised by the Trademark Office as a well-known trademark pursuant to Article 14 of the Trademark Law, the administration of industry and commerce will order the infringer to cease using the well-known trademark in violation of Article 13 of the Trademark Law and will confiscate and destroy his trademark representations. If it is difficult to separate the trademark representations from the goods, they will be confiscated and destroyed together.

Article 46 To apply for the deregistration of a registered trademark, or for deregistration of a trademark for some of the designated goods only, a trademark registrant shall file an application for the deregistration of a trademark with, and return the original Trademark Registration Certificate to, the Trademark Office.

If a trademark registrant applies for the deregistration of his registered trademark or for the deregistration of his registered trademark for some of the designated goods only, the exclusive right to use the registered trademark or the exclusive right to use the registered trademark for those of the designated goods shall be extinguished from the date of receipt by the Trademark Office of the application for its deregistration.

Article 47 If a trademark registrant dies or is closed and no procedures for the transfer of the trademark to another person are carried out within one year after the date of his death or its closure, anyone may apply to the Trademark Office for the deregistration of the trademark after the lapse of such one-year period. If deregistration is applied for, evidence shall be submitted of the death or termination of the trademark registrant.

If a registered trademark is deregistered by reason of the death or termination of its registrant, the exclusive right to use the registered trademark shall be extinguished from the date of the death or termination of its registrant.

Article 48 If a registered trademark is cancelled, or deregistered pursuant to Article 46 or 47 above, the original Trademark Registration Certificate will become void. If the registration of the trademark is cancelled as to some of the designated goods only, or if the trademark registrant applies for the deregistration of his trademark for some of the designated goods only, the Trademark Office shall annotate and return the original Trademark Registration Certificate or issue a new one, and gazette the matter.

CHAPTER 7 PROTECTION OF THE EXCLUSIVE RIGHT TO USE A TRADEMARK

Article 49 The holder of the exclusive right to use a registered trademark has no right to prohibit others from making legitimate use of the generic name, device or model number of the goods in question, or direct expressions of the quality, principal raw materials, functions, uses, weight, quantity or other characteristics of the goods, or place names, which are included in the registered trademark.

Article 50 Any of the following acts constitutes an infringement of an exclusive right to use a registered trademark as referred to in item (5) of Article 52 of the Trademark Law:

1. use as the name or trade dress of goods, of a sign which is the same as or similar to another person's registered trademark for the same or similar goods, thereby misleading the public; or
2. intentional provision of conditions facilitating the infringement of another person's exclusive right to use a trademark such as storage, transportation, mailing or concealment.

Article 51 Anyone may lodge a complaint against an infringement of the exclusive right to use a trademark with, or report such infringement to, the authority for the administration of industry and commerce.

Article 52 The amount of a fine imposed for infringement of the exclusive right to use a registered trademark shall not be more than three times the illegal turnover or, if it is impossible to calculate the illegal turnover, not more than RMB100,000.

Article 53 If a trademark owner is of the opinion that his well-known trademark has been registered by another person as such person's enterprise name and that such registration may cause the public to be deceived or give rise to misunderstanding among the public, he may apply to the authority in charge of enterprise name registration for cancellation of the enterprise name registration. The authority in charge of enterprise name registration shall handle the matter in accordance with the Regulations for the Administration of the Registration of Enterprise Names.

CHAPTER 8 SUPPLEMENTARY PROVISIONS

Article 54 Trademarks for services that have been used continuously up to 1 July 1993 and that are the same as or similar to trademarks for services registered by others for the same or similar services may continue to be used; however, those whose use has been suspended for three years or more after 1 July 1993 may not continue to be used.

Article 55 Specific measures for the administration of trademark agents will be formulated separately by the State Council.

Article 56 The classification of goods and services for the purpose of the registration of trademarks shall be formulated and published by the department for the administration of industry and commerce of the State Council.

The formats of documents for applications for trademark registration or the handling of other trademark matters shall be designed and published by the department for the administration of industry and commerce of the State Council.

The review and adjudication rules of the Trademark Review and Adjudication Board shall be formulated and published by the department for the administration of industry and commerce of the State Council.

Article 57 The Trademark Office shall establish a Trademark Register, in which it shall record registered trademarks and related registration matters.

The Trademark Office shall compile, print and publish a Trademark Gazette, in which it shall publish trademark registrations and other, related matters.

Article 58 Applications for trademark registration or the handling of other trademark matters shall require the payment of fees. The fee items and rates payable shall be stipulated and published by the department for the administration of industry and commerce of the State Council in conjunction with the department in charge of prices of the State Council.

Article 59 These Regulations shall be implemented from 15 September 2002. The Detailed Implementing Rules for the Trademark Law of the People's Republic of China published by the State Council on 10 March 1983, amended for the first time with the approval of the State Council on 3 January 1988 and amended for the second time with the approval of the State Council on 15 July 1993, and the Official Reply of the State Council Concerning the Issue of the Submission of Supporting Documents When Carrying Out Trademark Registration Procedures dated 23 April 1995 shall be repealed on the same date.

NOTICE REGARDING THE PRINTING AND ISSUANCE OF THE TRADEMARK LICENSING CONTRACT RECORDAL MEASURES

To the administration for industry and commerce of each province, autonomous region, municipality directly under the central government and municipality with independent development plans:

In order to perfect the system for recordal of trademark licensing contracts and to standardise the acts of trademark licensing, our Office has formulated Trademark Licensing Contract Recordal Measures. We hereby issue them to you. Please implement them in earnest.

Trademark Office of the State Administration for Industry and Commerce

1 August 1997

TRADEMARK LICENSING CONTRACT RECORDAL MEASURES

(Promulgated by the State Administration for Industry and Commerce on, and effective from, 1 August 1997)

Article 1 These Measures are formulated in accordance with the relevant provisions of the Trademark Law of the People's Republic of China and the Detailed Implementing Rules for the Trademark Law of the People's Republic of China, in order to strengthen the administration of trademark licensing contracts and to standardise the acts of trademark licensing.

Article 2 A trademark registrant shall sign a trademark licensing contract if it wishes to license its registered trademark to another.

Article 3 When concluding a trademark licensing contract, the principles of free will and good faith shall be observed.

No unit or individual may use a licensing contract to engage in illegal activities and harm the public interest or the rights and interests of the consumers.

Article 4 Within three months following the execution of a trademark licensing contract the licensor shall file a duplicate of the licensing contract with the Trademark Office for the record.

Article 5 The filing for the record of a trademark licensing contract with the Trademark Office may be entrusted to a trademark agency approved by the State Administration for Industry and Commerce or be carried out directly with the Trademark Office.

If the licensor is a foreigner or a foreign enterprise, he or it shall appoint a trademark agency designated by the State Administration for Industry and Commerce.

Article 6 A trademark licensing contract shall at least contain the following particulars:

1. the trademark licensed and the number of its registration certificate;
2. the scope of licensed goods;
3. the license term;
4. the way in which representations of the licensed trademark shall be provided;
5. provisions for supervision by the licensor of the quality of the licensee's goods for which the registered trademark is used; and
6. provisions requiring the licensee to indicate its name and the place of origin on the goods for which the registered trademark of the licensor is used.

Article 7 When applying for recordal of a trademark licensing contract, the following documents shall be provided:

1. the recordal form for the trademark licensing contract;
2. a duplicate of the trademark licensing contract; and
3. a photocopy of the registration certificate of the trademark licensed.

A valid certificate obtained by the licensee from the administrative department for public health shall also be filed in case the trademark licensing contract that is placed on record involves pharmaceuticals for human use.

A valid certificate approving production obtained by the licensee from the state department in charge of tobacco shall also be filed in cases where the trademark licensing contract that is placed on record involves cigarettes, cigars or packaged cut tobacco.

Documents in a foreign language shall be accompanied by a Chinese translation.

Article 8 In case a trademark registrant licenses its registered trademark to a third party through a licensee, then the trademark licensing contract shall contain a clause permitting the licensee to license the trademark to a third party, or the licensor shall issue a letter of authorisation to that effect.

Article 9 When applying for recordal of a trademark licensing contract, one trademark licensing contract recordal form shall be completed for every trademark licensed and be accompanied by a duplicate of the trademark licensing contract in question and a photocopy of the Trademark Registration Certificate.

In case a number of trademarks are licensed to one licensee under one contract, the licensor shall file the same number of trademark licensing contract recordal forms and Trademark Registration Certificate photocopies, but need file only one duplicate of the licensing contract.

Article 10 When applying for recordal of a trademark licensing contract, the licensor shall pay a recordal fee according to the number of trademarks licensed.

The recordal fee may be paid directly to the Trademark Office or by an appointed trademark agency. The specific fee standards shall be determined according to the regulations on charges for relevant trademark business.

Article 11 The Trademark Office shall not grant recordal under any of the following circumstances:

1. the licensor is not the registrant of the licensed trademark;
2. the licensed trademark is different from the registered trademark;
3. the registration certificate number of the licensed trademark does not agree with the provided trademark registration certificate number;
4. the license term exceeds the term of validity of the registered trademark;
5. the goods for which the registered trademark is licensed exceed the scope of goods for which use of the trademark has been approved;
6. the trademark licensing contract lacks the particulars mentioned in Article 6 hereof;
7. the application for recordal does not contain all documents required in Article 7 hereof;
8. the trademark licensing contract recordal fee has not been paid in full;
9. the foreign language documents in the application for recordal are not accompanied by a Chinese translation; or
10. other circumstances under which recordal shall not be granted.

Article 12 The Trademark Office shall grant recordal of a trademark licensing contract when all the documents to be filed have been filed and comply with the relevant provisions of the Trademark Law and the Detailed Implementing Rules for the Trademark Law.

After a trademark licensing contract has been recorded, the Trademark Office shall send a recordal notice to the recordal applicant. In addition, it shall publish all recordals in the second volume of the month of the *Trademark Gazette*.

Article 13 Applications that do not comply with the recordal requirements shall be returned by the Trademark Office together with an explanation of the reason.

Within one month upon receipt of the returned recordal materials, the licensor shall make additions and corrections according to the Trademark Office's directions and resubmit the materials for recordal purposes.

Article 14 A new application for recordal of a trademark licensing contract shall be made under any of the following circumstances:

1. the scope of goods for which the trademark is licensed has changed;
2. the license term has changed;
3. ownership of the licensed trademark has been transferred; or
4. any other circumstances requiring the making of a new application for recordal.

Article 15 The licensor and the licensee shall notify in writing the Trademark Office and the authorities for the administration of industry and commerce at county level in their respective locations under any of the following circumstances:

1. a change in the name of the licensor has occurred;
2. a change in the name of the licensee has occurred;
3. the trademark licensing contract has been terminated early; or
4. any other circumstances that need to be reported

Article 16 If recordal was obtained through fraud or other irregular means, the Trademark Office shall cancel the recordal of the trademark licensing contract and publicly announce the same.

Article 17 After a trademark licensing contract has been filed for the record, any unit or person may apply in writing for information, in which case an inquiry fee shall be paid according to the relevant regulations.

Article 18 In accordance with Article 35 of the Detailed Implementing Rules for the Trademark Law, the licensor and the licensee shall file, within three months from the date of execution of the trademark licensing contract, a duplicate of the said contract with the authorities for the administration of industry and commerce of the places where they are located to be kept for reference. As to the specific methods for keeping such duplicates for reference, reference may be made to these Measures.

Article 19 The authorities for the administration of industry and commerce at county level and above[1] shall be responsible for guidance, supervision and control of trademark licensing, in accordance with the Trademark Law and other laws, rules and regulations.

Article 20 The use of the trademark licensing contract to engage in illegal activities shall be dealt with by the authorities for the administration of industry and commerce at county level and above[2] in accordance with the Trademark Law and other laws, rules regulations. If such use constitutes a criminal offence, criminal liability shall be pursued according to law.

Article 21 For the purposes of these Measures, the term 'trademark licensor' shall mean the person in a trademark licensing contract that licenses its registered trademark to another person; and the term 'trademark licensee' shall mean a person that complies with the relevant provisions of the Trademark Law and the Detailed Implementing Rules for the Trademark Law and that has been authorised by a trademark registrant to use its trademark.

The provisions of these Measures that relate to trademarks for goods are applicable to trademarks for services.

Article 22 The Trademark Office shall formulate and publish a model trademark licensing contract.

Article 23 These Measures shall be implemented from the date of promulgation. The Points for Attention on the Recordal of Trademark Licensing Contracts promulgated by the Trademark Office on 25 February 1985 shall cease to be effective on the same date.

---

1 Translator's note: The phrase translated here as 'at county level and above' could also be interpreted as 'above county level'.
2 Same as note 3 above.

OPINIONS ON SEVERAL ISSUES CONCERNING THE ADMINISTRATIVE ENFORCEMENT OF TRADEMARK LAWS

(Issued by the State Administration for Industry and Commerce of the People's Republic of China as document Gong Shang Biao Zi [1999] No 331 on 29 December 1999.)

To the administrations for industry and commerce of each province, autonomous region, municipality directly under the central government and municipality with independent development plans, we hereby set forth the following opinions on several issues concerning the administrative enforcement of trademark laws in order to improve the administrative enforcement of trademark laws, strengthen trademark administration, improve the handling of trademark cases, and better implement the Trademark Law and related laws, rules and regulations:

1. The main trademark law violations investigated and handled by the trademark administration departments of administration authorities for industry and commerce include:
   (1) cases of the infringement or counterfeiting of trademarks;
   (2) cases of the illegal use of trademarks;
   (3) cases of the illegal printing or sale and purchase of trademark representations;
   (4) cases of illegal trademark licensing; and
   (5) cases of other violations of trademark laws, rules and regulations.
2. For the purposes of trademark infringement cases, the term 'place of infringement' means the territory involved during the course of commission of a trademark infringement, including the place where the infringing article is produced, the place to where it is transported, the place where it is sold, the place where it is

stored, etc. If two or more local administration authorities for industry and commerce have jurisdiction over the same trademark infringement case, jurisdiction shall fall to the administration authority for industry and commerce which first placed the case on file.

3. The three trademark infringement acts set forth below constitute acts of counterfeiting a registered trademark as stipulated in the Trademark Law and the Law Against Unfair Competition:
   (1) use of a trademark that is the same as a registered trademark on the same goods without the permission of the owner of the registered trademark;
   (2) sale of goods that one is fully aware to be goods bearing counterfeits of a registered trademark; and
   (3) forgery or unauthorised manufacture of representations of another's registered trademark, or sale of representations of a registered trademark that were forged or manufactured without authorisation.

4. The Criminal Law of the People's Republic of China as implemented from 1 October 1997 specifies three illegal acts constituting trademark crimes. According to the Regulations of the Supreme People's Court Concerning the Determination of Charges in Implementing the Criminal Law of the People's Republic of China, the charges for trademark crimes and / or violations of trademark laws are as follows: the crime of counterfeiting a registered trademark, the crime of selling merchandise bearing a counterfeit registered trademark and the crime of illegally manufacturing, or selling illegally manufactured, representations of a registered trademark.

   The crime of counterfeiting a registered trademark is only one of the types of trademark crime.

   If the administration authority for industry and commerce suspects that a trademark infringement it is investigating and handling is a trademark crime, it shall transfer the case to the public security authority for placement on file and investigation, according to law. In the interval before the public security authority formulates the relevant standard for placing trademark crime cases on file, such crimes shall be handled with reference to the Regulations of the Supreme People's Procuratorate Concerning the Standards for Placing Crimes of Counterfeiting Registered Trademarks on File (ref. *Gao Jian Fa Yan Zi* [1993] No 12).

5. The phrase 'a trademark that is the same' means that compared with another trademark, the text or device or the combination of text and device of the trademark is the same as that of the other trademark or that visually there is no difference between the two.

The phrase 'a trademark that is similar' means that compared with another trademark, the shape, pronunciation and meaning of the text, or the composition and colour(s) of the device, or the overall structure of the text and device of the trademark is similar to those / that of the other trademark and likely to cause confusion among consumers as to the origin of the goods or services.

6. Determination of the sameness or similarity of trademarks:
   (1) the trademark whose registration was approved shall be taken as the standard, not the trademark actually used by the trademark registrant;
   (2) a comprehensive judgement shall be arrived at by using the average consumer's general power of observation as a subjective judging standard and adopting the method of combining comparisons of the trademarks as a whole with comparisons of their distinctive parts.

7. The term 'similar goods' means goods that are related or specifically connected to each other in terms of function, purpose, targeted consumer, sales channel, etc.

   The term 'similar services' means services that are related or specifically connected to each other in terms of service goal, method, target, etc.

   If the use of the same or similar trademarks on goods or for services is likely to cause confusion among consumers as to the origin of the goods or services, such goods or services shall be determined to be similar.

8. Determination of the similarity of goods or services:
   (1) a comprehensive judgement shall be arrived at by considering the average consumer's objective knowledge of the goods or services;
   (2) the *International Classification of Goods and Services for the Purposes of the Registration of Marks* and the *List for Differentiating Similar Goods and Services* may be consulted to determine the similarity of goods or services, but shall not be used as the sole basis for such determination.

9. The following use of text or a device that is the same as, or similar to, that of a registered trademark is not trademark infringement:
   (1) using one's own name or address in good faith;
   (2) describing the characteristics or properties of a product or service in good faith, particularly when describing the quality, purpose, geographical origin, type, value or supply date of goods or services.

10. The acts of trademark infringement specified in Article 41 of the Detailed Implementing Rules for the Trademark Law are acts as

referred to in item (4) of Article 38 of the Trademark Law. Other acts which prejudice the exclusive right to use a registered trademark are also acts of trademark infringement as mentioned in item (4) of Article 38 of the Trademark Law.

11. Acts of using a trademark that is the same as or similar to a relatively well-known and relatively distinctive trademark on dissimilar goods or services, thereby resulting in unfair use of, or damage to, the distinctiveness or reputation of the trademark, may be handled by applying the provisions of item (4) of Article 38 of the Trademark Law, provided that matters are handled in accordance with the Regulations for Supervision and Control of the Investigation and Handling by Administration Authorities for Industry and Commerce of Violations of Trademark Laws.

12. If during the grace period for extension of a registered trademark the trademark registrant submits an application for extension and such extension is approved, the exclusive right to use the trademark shall continue to exist, and the use by a third party of a trademark that is the same as, or similar to, such trademark during this period shall constitute an act of trademark infringement. If the trademark registrant does not submit an application for extension, or submits an application for extension but such extension is not approved, the exclusive right to use the trademark shall cease to be afforded the protection of the law upon the expiration of the term thereof.

If a petition is made for the protection of a trademark during the grace period for extension, the complainant shall submit proof of the application for extension, otherwise the administration authority for industry of commerce shall refuse to place the case on file, and if the case has been placed on file, it shall stay proceedings and wait until the extension approval situation is clarified before recommencing proceedings.

13. If the representations of a trademark printed on behalf of the commissioning party infringe the exclusive right of a third party to use the trademark, the commissioning party shall also be liable for infringement.

14. The use by a trademark licensee of the licensor's registered trademark shall be deemed to be use of the registered trademark by the registrant.

15. If during the processing of goods that are to bear a designated brand, the processor is to produce and sell products bearing the registered trademark of the commissioning party, the parties shall enter into a trademark license contract.

16. Trademark license contracts shall be submitted to the Trademark Office for the record. If the parties to such a contract fail to submit the same for the record, they shall bear corresponding

administrative legal liability, but the validity of such contract shall not be affected. If a license contract expressly stipulates recordal as a condition precedent for entry into effect thereof, the contract shall not become effective if not submitted for the record.

17. The assignment of a registered trademark shall not affect the validity of trademark license contracts that became effective before the assignment, unless otherwise provided in such license contracts.

18. The term 'exclusive trademark license' means a trademark license whereby the trademark registrant, within the scope of his exclusive right to use the trademark, licenses the trademark to one licensee only and also relinquishes his own right to use the trademark. During the term of the license contract, the exclusive licensee may, as the holder of the trademark rights, file complaints with the administration authority for industry and commerce in his own name.

19. If a trademark licensee breaches the provisions of the license contract by exceeding the scope of the goods and / or services covered under the license, the term of the license or the quantity of goods and such breach constitutes trademark infringement, the administration authority for industry and commerce may, at the request of the licensor, examine and handle the matter in accordance with the law.

    If there is a dispute between the licensor and the licensee concerning the particulars of a trademark license contract and such dispute may affect the handling of the case, the administration authority for industry and commerce may stay its handling of the case and wait until the dispute is resolved before recommencing proceedings.

20. The administration authority for industry and commerce shall halt, and impose a time limit for rectification of the trademark law violation of selling goods which one is fully aware, or ought to be aware, to be bearing counterfeits of a registered trademark or which violate the relevant provisions of Article 8 of the Trademark Law.

21. When investigating and handling trademark infringement cases, the administration authority for industry and commerce may order the sealing of articles related to the infringement activities. The sealed articles may be kept in the custody of the suspected infringer himself; alternatively, the administration authority for industry and commerce may keep them in its own custody or entrust them to the custody of a third party. If the suspected infringer is to keep the articles in his own custody, he shall issue a written undertaking.

22. Where the administration authority for industry and commerce registers and preserves evidence in advance, or seals evidence in advance, at the request of a complainant, it may require the complainant to provide appropriate security in accordance with relevant laws, depending on actual circumstances.

23. When the administration authority for industry and commerce is conducting an investigation and gathering evidence, it may, in accordance with circumstances, impose a fine of not more than three times the illegal income, up to a maximum of RMB30,000, for refusal to carry out an order to suspend sales, or an order to wait for investigation, or an order to not to transfer, conceal or destroy relevant property, etc, pursuant to Article 43 of the Provisional Regulations for the Administration of Industry and Commerce; if there is no illegal income, it may impose a fine of not more than RMB10,000.

24. If the complainant applies to withdraw his complaint in a trademark infringement case which the administration authority for industry and commerce has placed on file but in which it has not yet rendered an administrative decision on the handling thereof, the administration authority for industry and commerce shall not render a decision ordering compensation, but it may, depending on actual circumstances, pursue the administrative legal liability of the infringing party in accordance with the law.

25. When imposing a fine for trademark infringement, the administration authority for industry and commerce shall base its punishment on the relevant provisions of the Trademark Law and the Detailed Implementing Rules issued thereunder. The fine for counterfeiting of a registered trademark may not be less than 30 per cent of the illegal turnover or three times the profit earned from the infringement. The fine for other serious acts of trademark infringement may not be less than 20 per cent of the illegal turnover or twice the profit earned from the infringement.

26. When investigating and handling a trademark infringement case *ex officio*, the administration authority for industry and commerce may, at the request of the owner of the trademark rights, decide to order compensation before it has rendered its administrative decision on the handling of the case.

27. In accordance with Article 39 of the Trademark Law, when the infringed party petitions the administration authority for industry and commerce for an order for compensation, he may elect to have the damages calculated on the basis of the infringer's profits from the infringement derived during the period of infringement or on the basis of the infringed party's losses due to the infringement incurred during the period of infringement.

The term 'the infringer's profits from the infringement derived during the period of infringement' generally means sales revenue less costs and payable taxes. The calculation of sales revenue shall only involve the infringer's actual revenue, ie the revenue from the goods that have already been sold, and shall not include the goods in stock.

The term 'the infringed party's losses due to the infringement incurred during the period of infringement' means actual losses, including direct losses and indirect losses. Direct losses are the decrease in profits suffered by the infringed party during the period of infringement or the product of multiplying the infringer's sales proceeds by the infringed party's average profit rate on the sale of his normal goods. Indirect losses are such reasonable expenses as the agency fees, investigation fees, etc, incurred by the infringed party in investigating the infringing acts of the infringer.

APPENDIX 6

CIVIL PROCEDURE LAW OF THE PEOPLE'S REPUBLIC OF CHINA

(Adopted at the Fourth Session of the Seventh National People's Congress on 9 April 1991, promulgated by Order No 44 of the President of the People's Republic of China on 9 April 1991, and effective as of the date of promulgation)

CONTENTS

PART ONE GENERAL PROVISIONS

CHAPTER I THE AIM, SCOPE OF APPLICATION AND BASIC PRINCIPLES

Article 1 The Civil Procedure Law of the People's Republic of China is formulated on the basis of the Constitution and in the light of the experience and actual conditions of our country in the trial of civil cases.

Article 2 The Civil Procedure Law of the People's Republic of China aims to protect the exercise of the litigation rights of the parties and ensure the ascertaining of facts by the people's courts, distinguish right from wrong, apply the law correctly, try civil cases promptly, affirm civil rights and obligations, impose sanctions for civil wrongs, protect the lawful rights and interests of the parties, educate citizens to voluntarily abide by the law, maintain the social and economic order, and guarantee the smooth progress of the socialist construction.

Article 3 In dealing with civil litigation arising from disputes on property and personal relations between citizens, legal persons or other organisations and between the three of them, the people's courts shall apply the provisions of this Law.

Article 4 Whoever engages in civil litigation within the territory of the People's Republic of China must abide by this Law.

Article 5 Aliens, stateless persons, foreign enterprises and organisations that bring suits or enter appearance in the people's courts shall have the same litigation rights and obligations as citizens, legal persons and other organisations of the People's Republic of China. If the courts of a foreign country impose restrictions on the civil litigation rights of the citizens, legal persons and other organisations of the People's Republic of China, the people's courts of the People's Republic of China shall follow the principle of reciprocity regarding the civil litigation rights of the citizens, enterprises and organisations of that foreign country.

Article 6 The people's courts shall exercise judicial powers with respect to civil cases. The people's courts shall try civil cases independently in accordance with the law, and shall be subject to no interference by any administrative organ, public organisation or individual.

Article 7 In trying civil cases, the people's courts must base themselves on facts and take the law as the criterion.

Article 8 The parties in civil litigation shall have equal litigation rights. The people's courts shall, in conducting the trials, safeguard their rights, facilitate their exercising the rights, and apply the law equally to them.

Article 9 In trying civil cases, the people's courts shall conduct conciliation for the parties on a voluntary and lawful basis; if conciliation fails, judgements shall be rendered without delay.

Article 10 In trying civil cases, the people's courts shall, according to the provisions of the law, follow the systems of panel hearing, withdrawal, public trial and the court of second instance being that of last instance.

Article 11 Citizens of all nationalities shall have the right to use their native spoken and written languages in civil proceedings. Where minority nationalities live in aggregation in a community or where several nationalities live together in one area, the people's courts shall conduct hearings and issue legal documents in the spoken and written languages commonly used by the local nationalities. The people's courts shall provide translations for any participant in the proceedings who is not familiar with the spoken or written languages commonly used by the local nationalities.

Article 12 Parties to civil actions are entitled in the trials by the people's courts to argue for themselves.

Article 13 The parties are free to deal with their own civil rights and litigation rights the way they prefer within the scope provided by the law.

Article 14 The people's procuratorates shall have the right to exercise legal supervision over civil proceedings.

Article 15 Where an act has infringed upon the civil rights and interests of the State, a collective organisation or an individual, any State organ, public organisation, enterprise or institution may support the injured unit or individual to bring an action in a people's court.

Article 16 The people's conciliation committees shall be mass organisations to conduct conciliation of civil disputes under the guidance of the grass-roots level people's governments and the basic level people's courts. The people's conciliation committee shall conduct conciliation for the parties according to the Law and on a voluntary basis. The parties concerned shall carry out the settlement agreement reached through conciliation; those who decline conciliation or those for whom conciliation has failed or those who have backed out of the settlement agreement may institute legal proceedings in a people's court. If a people's conciliation committee, in conducting conciliation of civil disputes, acts contrary to the law, rectification shall be made by the people's court.

Article 17 The people's congresses of the national autonomous regions may formulate, in accordance with the Constitution and the principles of this Law, and in conjunction with the specific circumstances of the local nationalities, adaptive and supplementary provisions. Such provisions made by an autonomous region shall be submitted to the Standing Committee of the National People's Congress for approval; those made by an autonomous prefecture or autonomous county shall be submitted to the standing committee of the people's congress of the relevant province or autonomous region for approval and to the Standing Committee of the National People's Congress for the record.

CHAPTER II JURISDICTION

Section 1 Jurisdiction by Forum Level

Article 18 The basic people's courts shall have jurisdiction as courts of first instance over civil cases, unless otherwise provided in this Law.

Article 19 The intermediate people's courts shall have jurisdiction as courts of first instance over the following civil cases:

1. major cases involving foreign elements;
2. cases that have major impact on the area under their jurisdiction; and
3. cases as determined by the Supreme People's Court to be under the jurisdiction of the intermediate people's courts.

Article 20 The high people's courts shall have jurisdiction as courts of first instance over civil cases that have major impact on the areas under their jurisdiction.

Article 21 The Supreme People's Court shall have jurisdiction as the court of first instance over the following civil cases:

1. cases that have major impact on the whole country; and
2. cases that the Supreme People's Court deems it should try.

Section 2 Territorial Jurisdiction

Article 22 A civil lawsuit brought against a citizen shall be under the jurisdiction of the people's court of the place where the defendant has his domicile; if the place of the defendant's domicile is different from that of his habitual residence, the lawsuit shall be under the jurisdiction of the people's court of the place of his habitual residence. A civil lawsuit brought against a legal person or any other organisation shall be under the jurisdiction of the people's court of the place where the defendant has his domicile. Where the domiciles or habitual residences of several defendants in the same lawsuit are in the areas under the jurisdiction of two or more people's courts, all of those people's courts shall have jurisdiction over the lawsuit.

Article 23 The civil lawsuits described below shall be under the jurisdiction of the people's court of the place where the plaintiff has his domicile; if the place of the plaintiff's domicile is different from that of his habitual residence, the lawsuit shall be under the jurisdiction of the people's court of the place of the plaintiff's habitual residence:

1. those concerning personal status brought against persons not residing within the territory of the People's Republic of China;
2. those concerning the personal status of persons whose whereabouts are unknown or who have been declared as missing;
3. those brought against persons who are undergoing rehabilitation through labour; and
4. those brought against persons who are in imprisonment.

Article 24 A lawsuit brought on a contract dispute shall be under the jurisdiction of the people's court of the place where the defendant has his domicile or where the contract is performed.

Article 25 The parties to a contract may agree to choose in their written contract the people's court of the place where the defendant has his domicile, where the contract is performed, where the contract is signed, where the plaintiff has his domicile or where the object of the action is located to exercise jurisdiction over the case, provided that the provisions of this Law regarding jurisdiction by forum level and exclusive jurisdiction are not violated.

Article 26 A lawsuit brought on an insurance contract dispute shall be under the jurisdiction of the people's court of the place where the defendant has his domicile or where the insured object is located.

Article 27 A lawsuit brought on a bill dispute shall be under the jurisdiction of the people's court of the place where the bill is to be paid or where the defendant has his domicile.

Article 28 A lawsuit arising from a dispute over a railway, road, water, or air transport contract or over a combined transport contract shall be under the jurisdiction of the people's court of the place of dispatch or the place of destination or where the defendant has his domicile.

Article 29 A lawsuit brought on a tortious act shall be under the jurisdiction of the people's court of the place where the tort is committed or where the defendant has his domicile.

Article 30 A lawsuit brought on claims for damages caused by a railway, road, water transport or air accident shall be under the jurisdiction of the people's court of the place where the accident occurred or where the vehicle or ship first arrived after the accident or where the aircraft first landed after the accident, or where the defendant has his domicile.

Article 31 A lawsuit brought on claims for damages caused by a collision at sea or by any other maritime accident shall be under the jurisdiction of the people's court of the place where the collision occurred or where the ship in collision first docked after the accident or where the ship at fault was detained, or where the defendant has his domicile.

Article 32 A lawsuit instituted for expenses of maritime salvage shall be under the jurisdiction of the people's court of the place where the salvage took place or where the salvaged ship first docked after the disaster.

Article 33 A lawsuit brought for general average shall be under the jurisdiction of the people's court of the place where the ship first docked or where the adjustment of general average was conducted or where the voyage ended.

Article 34 The following cases shall be under the exclusive jurisdiction of the people's courts herein specified:

1. a lawsuit brought on a dispute over real estate shall be under the jurisdiction of the people's court of the place where the estate is located;
2. a lawsuit brought on a dispute over harbour operations shall be under the jurisdiction of the people's court of the place where the harbour is located; and

3. a lawsuit brought on a dispute over succession shall be under the jurisdiction of the people's court of the place where the decedent had his domicile upon his death, or where the principal part of his estate is located.

Article 35 When two or more people's courts have jurisdiction over a lawsuit, the plaintiff may bring his lawsuit in one of these people's courts; if the plaintiff brings the lawsuit in two or more people's courts that have jurisdiction over the lawsuit, the people's court in which the case was first entertained shall have jurisdiction.

Section 3 Transfer and Designation of Jurisdiction

Article 36 If a people's court finds that a case it has entertained is not under its jurisdiction, it shall refer the case to the people's court that has jurisdiction over the case. The people's court to which a case has been referred shall entertain the case, and if it considers that, according to the relevant regulations, the case referred to it is not under its jurisdiction, it shall report to a superior people's court for the designation of jurisdiction and shall not independently refer the case again to another people's court.

Article 37 If a people's court that has jurisdiction over a case is unable to exercise the jurisdiction for special reasons, a superior people's court shall designate another court to exercise jurisdiction. In the event of a jurisdictional dispute between two or more people's courts, it shall be resolved by the disputing parties through consultation; if the dispute cannot be so resolved, it shall be reported to their common superior people's court for the designation of jurisdiction.

Article 38 If a party to an action objects to the jurisdiction of a people's court after the court has entertained the case, the party must raise the objection within the period prescribed for the submission of defence. The people's court shall examine the objection. If the objection is established, the people's court shall order the case to be transferred to the people's court that has jurisdiction over it; if not, the people's court shall reject it.

Article 39 The people's courts at higher levels shall have the power to try civil cases over which the people's courts at lower levels have jurisdiction as courts of first instance; they may also transfer civil cases over which they themselves have jurisdiction as courts of first instance to people's courts at lower levels for trial. If a people's court at a lower level that has jurisdiction over a civil case as court of first instance deems it necessary to have the case to be tried by a people's court at a higher level, it may submit it to and request the people's court at a higher level to try the case.

CHAPTER III TRIAL ORGANISATION

Article 40 The people's court of first instance shall try civil cases by a collegial panel composed of both judges and judicial assessors or of judges alone. The collegial panel must have an odd number of members. Civil cases in which summary procedure is followed shall be tried by a single judge alone. When performing their duties, the judicial assessors shall have equal rights and obligations as the judges.

Article 41 The people's court of second instance shall try civil cases by a collegial panel of judges. The collegial panel must have an odd number of members. For the retrial of a remanded case, the people's court of first instance shall form a new collegial panel in accordance with the procedure of first instance. If a case for retrial was originally tried at first instance, a new collegial panel shall be formed according to the procedure of first instance; if the case was originally tried at second instance or was brought by a people's court at a higher level to it for trial, a new collegial panel shall be formed according to the procedure of second instance.

Article 42 The president of the court or the chief judge of a division of the court shall designate a judge to serve as the presiding judge of the collegial panel; if the president or the chief judge participates in the trial, he himself shall serve as the presiding judge.

Article 43 When deliberating a case, a collegial panel shall observe the rule of majority. The deliberations shall be recorded in writing, and the transcript shall be signed by the members of the collegial panel. Dissenting opinions in the deliberations must be truthfully entered in the transcript.

Article 44 The judicial officers shall deal with all cases impartially and in accordance with the law. The judicial officers shall not accept any treat or gift from the parties or their agents *ad litem*. Any judicial officer who commits embezzlement, accepts bribes, engages in malpractice for personal benefits or who perverts the law in passing judgement shall be investigated for legal responsibility; if the act constitutes a crime, the offender shall be investigated for criminal responsibility according to the law.

319

CHAPTER IV WITHDRAWAL

Article 45 A judicial officer shall of himself withdraw from the case, and the parties thereto shall be entitled to apply orally or in writing for his withdrawal in any of the following circumstances:

1. he being a party to the case or a near relative of a party or an agent *ad litem* in the case;
2. he being an interested party in the case; or
3. he having some other kind of relationship with a party to the case, which might affect the impartiality of the trial.

The above provisions shall also apply to clerks, interpreters, expert witnesses and inspection personnel.

Article 46 In applying for the withdrawal, the party shall state the reason and submit the application at the beginning of the proceedings; the application may also be submitted before the closing of arguments in court if the reason for the withdrawal is known to him only after the proceedings begin. Pending a decision by the people's court regarding the withdrawal applied for, the judicial officer concerned shall temporarily suspend his participation in the proceedings, with the exception, however, of cases that require the taking of emergency measures.

Article 47 The withdrawal of the presiding judge who is president of the court shall be decided by the judicial committee; the withdrawal of judicial officers shall be decided by the court president; and the withdrawal of other personnel by the presiding judge.

Article 48 The decision of a people's court on an application made by any party for withdrawal shall be made orally or in writing within three days after the application is made. If the applicant is not satisfied with the decision, he may apply for reconsideration, which can be granted only once. During the period of reconsideration, the person whose withdrawal has been applied for shall not suspend his participation in the proceedings. The decision of a people's court on the reconsideration shall be made within three days after receiving the application and the applicant shall be notified of it accordingly.

CHAPTER V PARTICIPANTS IN PROCEEDINGS

Section 1 Parties

Article 49 Any citizen, legal person and any other organisation may become a party to a civil action. Legal persons shall be represented by their legal representatives in the litigation. Other organisations shall be represented by their principal heads in the proceedings.

Article 50 Parties to an action shall have the right to appoint agents, apply for withdrawals, collect and provide evidence, proffer arguments, request conciliation, file an appeal and apply for execution. Parties to an action may have access to materials pertaining to the case and make copies thereof and other legal documents pertaining to the case. The scope of and rules for consulting and making copies of these materials shall be specified by the Supreme People's Court. Parties to an action must exercise their litigation rights in accordance with the law, observe the procedures and carry out legally effective written judgements or orders and conciliation statements.

Article 51 The two parties may reach a compromise of their own accord.

Article 52 The plaintiff may relinquish or modify his claims. The defendant may admit or rebut the claims and shall have the right to file counterclaims.

Article 53 When one party or both parties consist of two or more than two persons, their object of action being the same or of the same category and the people's court considers that, with the consent of the parties, the action can be tried combined, it is a joint action. If a party of two or more persons to a joint action have common rights and obligations with respect to the object of action and the act of any one of them is recognised by the others of the party, such an act shall be valid for all the rest of the party; if a party of two or more persons have no common rights and obligations with respect to the object of action, the act of any one of them shall not be valid for the rest.

Article 54 If the persons comprising a party to a joint action are large in number, the party may elect representatives from among themselves to act for them in the litigation. The acts of such representatives in the litigation shall be valid for the party they represent. However, modification or waiver of claims or admission of the claims of the other party or pursuing a compromise with the other party by the representatives shall be subject to the consent of the party they represent.

Article 55 Where the object of action is of the same category and the persons comprising one of the parties are large but uncertain in number at the commencement of the action, the people's court may issue a public notice, stating the particulars and claims of the case and informing those entitled to participate in the action to register their rights with the people's court within a fixed period of time. Those who have registered their rights with the people's court may elect representatives from among themselves to proceed with the litigation; if the election fails its purpose, such representatives may be determined by the people's court through consultation with those who have registered their rights with the court. The acts of such a representative in the litigation shall be valid for the party they represent; however, modification or waiver of claims or admission of the claims of the other party or pursuing a compromise with the other party by the representatives shall be subject to the consent of the party they represent. The judgements or written orders rendered by the people's court shall be valid for all those who have registered their rights with the court. Such judgements or written orders shall apply to those who have not registered their rights but have instituted legal proceedings during period of limitation of the action.

Article 56 If a third party considers that he has an independent claim to the object of action of both parties, he shall have the right to bring an action. Where the outcome of the case will affect a third party's legal interest, such party, though having no independent claim to the object of action of both parties, may file a request to participate in the proceedings or the people's court shall notify the third party to participate. A third party that is to bear civil liability in accordance with the judgement of the people's court shall be entitled to the rights and obligations of a party in litigation.

Section 2 Agents ad litem

Article 57 Any person with no legal capacity to engage in litigation shall have his guardian or guardians as statutory agents to act for him in a lawsuit. If the statutory agents try to shift responsibility as agents *ad litem* upon one another, the people's court shall appoint one of them to represent the person in litigation.

Article 58 A party to an action, or statutory agent may appoint one or two persons to act as his agents *ad litem*. A lawyer, a near relative of the party, a person recommended by a relevant social organisation or a unit to which the party belongs or any other citizen approved by the people's court may be appointed as the party's agent *ad litem*.

Article 59 When a person appoints another to act on his behalf in litigation, he must submit to the people's court a power of attorney bearing his signature or seal. The power of attorney must specify the matters entrusted and the powers conferred. An agent *ad litem* must obtain special powers from his principal to admit, waive or modify claims, or to compromise or to file a counterclaim or an appeal. A power of attorney mailed or delivered through others by a citizen of the People's Republic of China residing abroad must be certified by the Chinese embassy or consulate accredited to that country. If there is no Chinese embassy or consulate in that country, the power of attorney must be certified by an embassy or a consulate of a third country accredited to that country that has diplomatic relations with the People's Republic of China, and then transmitted for authentication to the embassy or consulate of the People's Republic of China accredited to that third country, or it must be certified by a local patriotic overseas Chinese organisation.

Article 60 A party to an action shall inform the people's court in writing if he changes or revokes the powers of an agent *ad litem*, and the court shall notify the other party of the change or revocation.

Article 61 A lawyer who serves as an agent *ad litem* and other agents *ad litem* shall have the right to investigate and collect evidence, and may have access to materials pertaining to the case. The scope of and rules for consulting materials pertaining to the case shall be specified by the Supreme People's Court.

Article 62 In a divorce case in which the parties to the action have been represented by their agents *ad litem*, the parties themselves shall still appear in court in person, unless they are incapable of expressing their own will. A party who is truly unable to appear in court due to a special reason shall submit his views in writing to the people's court.

CHAPTER VI EVIDENCE

Article 63 Evidence shall be classified as follows:

1. documentary evidence;
2. material evidence;
3. audio-visual material;
4. testimony of witnesses;

5. statements of the parties;
6. expert conclusions; and
7. records of inspection.

The above-mentioned evidence must be verified before it can be taken as a basis for ascertaining a fact.

Article 64 It is the duty of a party to an action to provide evidence in support of his allegations. If, for objective reasons, a party and his agent *ad litem* are unable to collect the evidence by themselves or if the people's court considers the evidence necessary for the trial of the case, the people's court shall investigate and collect it. The people's court shall, in accordance with the procedure prescribed by the law, examine and verify evidence comprehensively and objectively.

Article 65 The people's court shall have the right to make investigation and collect evidence from the relevant units or individuals; such units or individuals may not refuse to provide information and evidence. The people's court shall verify the authenticity, examine and determine the validity of the certifying documents provided by the relevant units or individuals.

Article 66 Evidence shall be presented in court and cross-examined by the parties concerned. But evidence that involves State secrets, trade secrets and personal privacy shall be kept confidential. If it needs to be presented in court, such evidence shall not be presented in an open court session.

Article 67 The people's court shall take the acts, facts and documents legalised by notarisation according to legal procedures as the basis for ascertaining facts, unless there is evidence to the contrary sufficient to invalidate the notarisation.

Article 68 Any document submitted as evidence must be the original. Material evidence must also be original. If it is truly difficult to present the original document or thing, then reproductions, photographs, duplicates or extracts of the original may be submitted. If a document in a foreign language is submitted as evidence, a Chinese translation must be appended.

Article 69 The people's court shall verify audio-visual materials and determine after their examination in the light of other evidence in the case whether they can be taken as a basis for ascertaining the facts.

Article 70 All units and individuals who have knowledge of a case shall be under the obligation of giving testimony in court. Responsible heads of the relevant units shall support the witnesses to give testimony. When it is truly difficult for a witness to appear in court, he may, with the consent of the people's court, submit a written testimony. Any person who is incapable of expressing his will properly shall not give testimony.

Article 71 The people's court shall examine the statements of the parties concerned in the light of other evidence in the case to determine whether the statements can be taken as a basis for ascertaining the facts. The refusal of a party to make statements shall not prevent the people's court from ascertaining the facts of a case on the basis of other evidence.

Article 72 When the people's court deems it necessary to make an expert evaluation of a problem of a technical nature, it shall refer the problem to a department authorised by the law for the evaluation. In the absence of such a department, the people's court shall appoint one to make the expert evaluation. The authorised department and the experts designated by the department shall have the right to consult the case materials necessary for the evaluation and question the parties and witnesses when circumstances so require. The authorised department and the experts it designated shall present a written conclusion of the evaluation duly sealed or signed by both. If the evaluation is made by an expert alone, the unit to which the expert belongs shall certify his status by affixing its seal to the expert's conclusion.

Article 73 When inspecting material evidence or a site, the inspector must produce his credentials issued by a people's court. He shall request the local grass-roots organisation or the unit to which the party to the action belongs to send persons to participate in the inspection. The party concerned or an adult member of his family shall be present; their refusal to appear on the scene, however, shall not hinder the inspection. Upon notification by the people's court, the relevant units and individuals shall be under the obligation of preserving the site and assisting the inspection. The inspector shall make a written record of the circumstances and results of the inspection, which shall be duly signed or sealed by the inspector, the party concerned and the participants requested to be present.

Article 74 Under circumstances where there is a likelihood that evidence may be destroyed or lost, or difficult to obtain later, the participants in the proceedings may apply to the people's court for preservation of the evidence. The people's court may also on its own initiative take measures to preserve such evidence.

CHAPTER VII TIME PERIODS AND SERVICE

Section 1 Time Periods

Article 75 Time periods shall include those prescribed by the law and those designated by a people's court. Time periods shall be calculated by the hour, the day, the month and the year. The hour and day from which a time period begins shall not be counted as within the time period. If the expiration date of a time period falls on a holiday, then the day immediately following the holiday shall be regarded as the expiration date. A time period shall not include travelling time. A litigation document that is mailed before the deadline shall not be regarded as overdue.

Article 76 In case of failure on the part of a party to an action to meet a deadline due to force majeure or for other justified reasons, the party concerned may apply for an extension of the time limit within 10 days after the obstacle is removed. The extension applied for shall be subject to approval by a people's court.

Section 2 Service

Article 77 A receipt shall be required for every litigation document that is served and it shall bear the date of receipt noted by the signature or seal of the person on whom the document was served. The date noted on the receipt by the person on whom the document was served shall be regarded as the date of service of the document.

Article 78 Litigation documents shall be sent or delivered directly to the person on whom they are to be served. If that person is a citizen, the documents shall, in case of his absence, be receipted by an adult member of his family living with him. If the person on whom they are to be served is a legal person or any other organisation, the documents shall be receipted by the legal representatives of the legal person or the principal heads of the other organisation or anyone of the legal person or the other organisation responsible for receiving such documents; if the person on whom they are to be served has an agent *ad litem*, the documents may be receipted by the agent *ad litem*; if the person on whom they are to be served has designated a person to receive litigation documents on his behalf and has informed the people's court of it, the documents may be receipted by the person designated. The date put down in the receipt and signed by the adult family member living with the person or whom the litigation documents are to be served, or by the person responsible for receiving documents of a legal person or any other organisation, or by the agent ad litem, or the person designated to receive documents shall be deemed the date of service of the documents.

Article 79 If the person on whom the litigation documents are to be served or the adult family member living with him refuses to receive the documents, the person serving the documents shall ask representatives from the relevant grass-roots organisation or the unit to which the person on whom the documents are to be served belongs, to appear on the scene, explain the situation to them, and record on the receipt the reasons of the refusal and the date of it. After the person serving the documents and the witnesses have affixed their signatures or seals to the receipt, the documents shall be left at the place where the person on whom they are to be served lives and the service shall be deemed completed.

Article 80 If direct service proves to be difficult, service of litigation documents may be entrusted to another people's court, or done by mail. If the documents are served by mail, the date stated on the receipt for postal delivery shall be deemed the date of service of the documents.

Article 81 If the person on whom the litigation documents are to be served is a military-man, the documents shall be forwarded to him through the political organ of the unit at or above the regimental level in the force to which he belongs.

Article 82 If the person on whom the litigation documents are to be served is in imprisonment, the documents shall be forwarded to him through the prison authorities or the unit of reform through labour where the person is serving his term. If the person on whom the litigation documents are to be served is undergoing rehabilitation through labour, the documents shall be forwarded to him through the unit of his rehabilitation through labour.

Article 83 The organisation or unit that receives the litigation documents to be forwarded must immediately deliver them to and have them receipted by the person on whom they are to be served. The date stated on the receipt shall be deemed the date of service of the documents.

Article 84 If the whereabouts of the person on whom the litigation documents are to be served is unknown, or if the documents cannot be served by the other methods specified in this Section, the documents shall be served by public announcement. The documents shall be deemed to have been served 60 days after the public announcement is made. The reasons for service by public announcement and the process gone through shall be recorded in the case files.

CHAPTER VIII CONCILIATION

Article 85 In the trial of civil cases, the people's court shall distinguish between right and wrong on the basis of the facts being clear and conduct conciliation between the parties on a voluntary basis.

Article 86 When a people's court conducts conciliation, a single judge or a collegial panel may preside over it. Conciliation shall be conducted on the spot as much as possible. When a people's court conducts conciliation, it may employ simplified methods to notify the parties concerned and the witnesses to appear in court.

Article 87 When a people's court conducts conciliation, it may invite the units or individuals concerned to come to its assistance. The units or individuals invited shall assist the people's court in conciliation.

Article 88 A settlement agreement reached between the two parties through conciliation must be of their own free will and without compulsion. The content of the settlement agreement shall not contravene the law.

Article 89 When a settlement agreement through conciliation is reached, the people's court shall draw up a conciliation statement. The conciliation statement shall clearly set forth the claims, the facts of the case, and the result of the conciliation. The conciliation statement shall be signed by the judge and the court clerk, sealed by the people's court, and served on both parties. Once it is received by the two parties concerned, the conciliation statement shall become legally effective.

Article 90 The people's court need not draw up a conciliation statement for the following cases when a settlement agreement is reached through conciliation: (1) divorce cases in which both parties have become reconciled after conciliation; (2) cases in which adoptive relationship has been maintained through conciliation; (3) cases in which the claims can be immediately satisfied; and (4) other cases that do not require a conciliation statement. Any settlement agreement that needs no conciliation statement shall be entered into the written record and shall become legally effective after being signed or sealed by both parties concerned, by the judge and by the court clerk.

Article 91 If no agreement is reached through conciliation or if either party backs out of the settlement agreement before the conciliation statement is served, the people's court shall render a judgement without delay.

CHAPTER IX PROPERTY PRESERVATION AND ADVANCE EXECUTION

Article 92 In the cases where the execution of a judgement may become impossible or difficult because of the acts of either party or for other reasons, the people's court may, at the application of the other party, order the adoption of measures for property preservation. In the absence of such application, the people's court may of itself, when necessary, order the adoption of measures for property preservation. In adopting property preservation measures, the people's court may enjoin the applicant to provide security; if the applicant fails to do so, his application shall be rejected. After receiving an application, the people's court must, if the case is urgent, make an order within 48 hours; if the order for the adoption of property preservation measures is made, the execution thereof shall begin immediately.

Article 93 Any interested party whose lawful rights and interests would, due to urgent circumstances, suffer irretrievable damage without immediately applying for property preservation, may, before filing a lawsuit, apply to the people's court for the adoption of property preservation measures. The applicant must provide security; if he fails to do so, his application shall be rejected. After receiving an application, the people's court must make an order within 48 hours; if the court orders the adoption of property preservation measures, the execution thereof shall begin immediately. If the applicant fails to bring an action within 15 days after the people's court has adopted the preservation measures, the people's court shall cancel the property preservation.

Article 94 Property preservation shall be limited to the scope of the claims or to the property relevant to the case. Property preservation shall be effected by sealing up, distraining, freezing or other methods as prescribed by the law. After the people's court has frozen the property, it shall promptly notify the person whose property has been frozen. The property that has already been sealed up or frozen shall not be sealed up or frozen for a second time.

Article 95 If the person against whom the application for property reservation is made provides security, the people's court shall cancel the property reservation.

Article 96 If an application for property preservation is wrongfully made, the applicant shall compensate the person against whom the application is made for any loss incurred from property preservation.

Article 97 The people's court may, upon application of the party concerned, order advance execution in respect of the following cases:

1. those involving claims for alimony, support for children or elders, pension for the disabled or the family of a decedent, or expenses for medical care;
2. those involving claims for remuneration for labour; and
3. those involving urgent circumstances that require advance execution.

Article 98 Cases in which advance execution is ordered by the people's court shall meet the following conditions:

1. the relationship of rights and obligations between the parties concerned is clear and definite, and denial of advance execution would seriously affect the livelihood or production operations of the applicant; and
2. the person against whom the application for advance execution is made is capable of fulfilling his obligations. The people's court may enjoin the applicant to provide security; if the applicant fails to do so, his application shall be rejected. If the applicant loses the lawsuit, he shall compensate the person against whom the application is made for any loss of property incurred from the advance execution.

Article 99 If the party concerned is not satisfied with the order made on property preservation or execution, he may apply for reconsideration, which can be granted only once. Execution of the order shall not be suspended during the time of reconsideration.

CHAPTER X COMPULSORY MEASURES AGAINST OBSTRUCTION OF CIVIL PROCEEDINGS

Article 100 If a defendant is required to appear in court, but having been served twice with summons, still refuses to do so without a justified reason, the people's court may constrain him to appear in court by a peremptory writ.

Article 101 Participants and other persons in the court proceedings shall abide by the court rules. If a person violates the court rules, the people's court may reprimand him, or order him to leave the courtroom, or impose a fine on or detain him. A person who seriously disrupts court order by making an uproar in the court or rushing at it, or insulting, slandering, threatening, or assaulting the judicial officers, shall be investigated for criminal responsibility by the people's court according to the law; if the offence is a minor one, the offender may be detained or a fine imposed on him.

Article 102 If a participant or any other person in the proceedings commits any one of the following acts, the people's court shall, according to the seriousness of the act, impose a fine on him or detain him; if the act constitutes a crime, the offender shall be investigated for criminal responsibility according to law:

1. forging or destroying important evidence, which would obstruct the trial of a case by the people's court;
2. using violence, threats or subordination to prevent a witness from giving testimony, or instigating, suborning, or coercing others to commit perjury;
3. concealing, transferring, selling or destroying property that has been sealed up or distrained, or property of which an inventory has been made and which has been put under his care according to court instruction, or transferring the property that has been frozen;
4. insulting, slandering, incriminating with false charges, assaulting or maliciously retaliating against judicial officers or personnel, participants in the proceedings, witnesses, interpreters, evaluation experts, inspectors, or personnel assisting in execution;
5. using violence, threats or other means to hinder judicial officers or personnel from performing their duties; or
6. refusing to carry out legally effective judgements or orders of the people's court.

With respect to a unit that commits any one of the acts specified above, the people's court may impose a fine on or detain its principal heads or the persons who are held actually responsible for the act; if the act constitutes a crime, investigations for criminal responsibility shall be made according to the law.

Article 103 Where a unit which is under an obligation to assist in investigation and execution commits any one of the following acts, the people's court may, apart from enjoining it to perform its obligation, also impose a fine:

1. refusing or obstructing the investigation and collection of evidence by the people's court;
2. refusing by banks, credit cooperatives or other units dealing with savings deposit, after receiving a notice for assistance in execution from the people's court, to assist in inquiring into, freezing or transferring the relevant deposit;
3. refusing by the unit concerned, after receiving a notice for assistance in execution from the people's court, to assist in withholding the income of the party subject to execution, in going through the formalities of transferring the relevant certificates of property rights or in transferring the relevant negotiable instruments, certificates, or other property; or
4. refusing to provide other obligatory assistance in the execution.

With respect to a unit that commits any one of the acts specified above, the people's court may impose a fine on its principal heads or the persons who are held actually responsible for the act. The people's court may also put forward a judicial proposal to the supervisory organ or any relevant organ for the imposition of disciplinary sanctions.

Article 104 A fine on an individual shall not exceed RMB1,000. A fine on a unit shall not be less than RMB1,000 and shall not exceed RMB30,000. The period of detention shall not be longer than 15 days. The people's court shall deliver detained persons to a public security organ for custody. The people's court may decide to advance the time of release, if the detainee admits and mends his wrongdoings.

Article 105 Constrained appearance in court, imposition of a fine or detention shall be subject to the approval of the president of the people's court. A peremptory writ shall be issued for constraining appearance in court. A decision in writing shall be made for the imposition of a fine or detention. The offender, if dissatisfied with the decision, may apply to a people's court at a higher level for reconsideration, which can be granted only once. The execution of the decision shall not be suspended during the time of reconsideration.

Article 106 Decision on the adoption of compulsory measures against obstruction of proceedings shall be made only by the people's court. Any unit or individual that extorts repayment of a debt by illegal detention of a person or illegal distrainment of property shall be investigated for criminal responsibility according to the law, or shall be punished with detention or a fine.

CHAPTER XI LITIGATION COSTS

Article 107 Any party filing a civil lawsuit shall pay court costs according to the rules. For property cases, the party shall pay other fees in addition to the court costs. Any party that has genuine difficulty in paying litigation costs may, according to the relevant rules, apply to the people's court for deferment or reduction of the payment or for its exemption. Particulars for payment of litigation costs shall be laid down separately.

PART TWO TRIAL PROCEDURE

CHAPTER XII ORDINARY PROCEDURE OF FIRST INSTANCE

Section 1 Bringing a Lawsuit and Entertaining a Case

Article 108 The following conditions must be met when a lawsuit is brought:

1. the plaintiff must be a citizen, legal person or any other organisation that has a direct interest in the case;
2. there must be a definite defendant;
3. there must be specific claim or claims, facts, and cause or causes for the suit; and
4. the suit must be within the scope of acceptance for civil actions by the people's court and under the jurisdiction of the people's court where the suit is entertained.

Article 109 When a lawsuit is brought, a statement of complaint shall be submitted to the people's court, and copies of the statement shall be provided according to the number of defendants. If the plaintiff has genuine difficulty in presenting the statement of complaint in writing, he may state his complaint orally; the people's court shall transcribe the complaint and inform the other party of it accordingly.

Article 110 A statement of complaint shall clearly set forth the following:

1. the name, sex, age, ethnic status, occupation, work unit and home address of the parties to the case. If the parties are legal persons or any other organisations, their names, addresses and the names and posts of the legal representatives or the principal heads;
2. the claim or claims of the suit, the facts and grounds on which the suit is based; and
3. the evidence and its source, as well as the names and home addresses of the witnesses.

Article 111 The people's court must entertain the lawsuits filed in conformity with the provisions of Article 108 of this Law. With respect to lawsuits described below, the people's court shall deal with them in the light of their specific circumstances:

1. for a lawsuit within the scope of administrative actions in accordance with the provisions of the Administrative Procedure Law, the people's court shall advise the plaintiff to institute administrative proceedings;
2. if, according to the law, both parties have on a voluntary basis reached a written agreement to submit their contract dispute to an arbitral organ for arbitration, they may not institute legal proceedings in a people's court. The people's court shall advise the plaintiff to apply to the arbitral organ for arbitration;
3. in case of disputes which, according to the law, shall be dealt with by other organs, the people's court shall advise the plaintiff to apply to the relevant organ for settlement;
4. with respect to cases that are not under its jurisdiction, the people's court shall advise the plaintiff to bring a lawsuit in the competent people's court;
5. with respect to cases in which a judgement or order has already taken legal effect, but either party brings a suit again, the people's court shall advise that party to file an appeal instead, except when the order of the people's court is one that permits the withdrawal of a suit;
6. with respect to an action that may not be filed within a specified period according to the law, it shall not be entertained, if it is filed during that period;
7. in a divorce case in which a judgement has been made disallowing the divorce, or in which both parties have become reconciled after conciliation, or in a case concerning adoptive relationship in which a judgement has been made or conciliation has been

successfully conducted to maintain the adoptive relation-ship, if the plaintiff files a suit again within six months in the absence of any new developments or new reasons, it shall not be entertained.

Article 112 When a people's court receives a statement of complaint or an oral complaint and finds after examination that it meets the requirements for acceptance, the court shall place the case on the docket within seven days and notify the parties concerned; if it does not meet the requirements for acceptance the court shall make an order within seven days to reject it. The plaintiff, if not satisfied with the order, may file an appeal.

Section 2 Preparations for Trial

Article 113 The people's court shall send a copy of the statement of complaint to the defendant within five days after docketing the case, and the defendant shall file a defence within 15 days from receipt of the copy of the statement of complaint. When the defendant files a defence, the people's court shall send a copy of it to the plaintiff within five days from its receipt. Failure by the defendant to file a defence shall not prevent the case from being tried by the people's court.

Article 114 The people's court shall, with respect to cases whose acceptance has been decided, inform the parties in the notification of acceptance and in the notification calling for responses to the action of their relevant litigation rights and obligations of which the parties may likewise be informed orally.

Article 115 The parties shall be notified within three days after the members of the collegial panel are determined.

Article 116 The judicial officers must carefully examine and verify the case materials and carry out investigations and collection of necessary evidence.

Article 117 The personnel sent by a people's court to conduct investigations shall produce their credentials before the person to be investigated. The written record of an investigation shall be checked by the person investigated and then signed or sealed by both the investigator and the investigated.

Article 118 A people's court may, when necessary, entrust a people's court in another locality with the investigations. The entrusting people's court shall clearly set out the matters for and requirements of the entrusted investigations. The entrusted people's court may on its own initiative conduct supplementary investigations. The entrusted people's court shall complete the investigations within 30 days after receiving the commission in writing. If for some reason it cannot complete the investigations, the said people's court shall notify the entrusting people's court in writing within the above-mentioned time limit.

Article 119 If a party who must participate in a joint action fails to participate in the proceedings, the people's court shall notify him to participate.

Section 3 Trial in Court

Article 120 Civil cases shall be tried in public, except for those that involve State secrets or personal privacy or are to be tried otherwise as provided by the law. A divorce case or a case involving trade secrets may not be heard in public if a party so requests.

Article 121 For civil cases, the people's court shall, whenever necessary, go on circuit to hold trials on the spot.

Article 122 For civil cases, the people's court shall notify the parties and other participants in the proceedings three days before the opening of a court session. If a case is to be tried in public, the names of the parties, the cause of action and the time and location of the court session shall be announced publicly.

Article 123 Before a court session is called to order, the court clerk shall ascertain whether or not the parties and other participants in the proceedings are present and announce the rules of order of the court. At the beginning of a court session, the presiding judge shall check the parties present, announce the cause of action and the names of the judicial officers and court clerks, inform the parties of their relevant litigation rights and obligations and ask the parties whether or not they wish to apply for the withdrawal of any court personnel.

Article 124 Court investigation shall be conducted in the following order:

1. statements by the parties;
2. informing the witnesses of their rights and obligations, giving testimony by the witnesses and reading of the written statements of absentee witnesses;
3. presentation of documentary evidence, material evidence and audio-visual material;

4. reading of expert conclusions; and
5. reading of records of inspection.

Article 125 The parties may present new evidence during a court session. With the permission of the court, the parties may put questions to witnesses, expert witnesses and inspectors. Any request by the parties concerned for a new investigation, expert evaluation or inspection shall be subject to the approval of the people's court.

Article 126 Additional claims by the plaintiff, counterclaims by the defendant and third-party claims related to the case may be tried in combination.

Article 127 Court debate shall be conducted in the following order:

1. oral statements by the plaintiff and his agents *ad litem*;
2. defence by the defendant and his agents *ad litem*;
3. oral statement or defence by the third party and his agents *ad litem*;
4. debate between the two sides.

At the end of the court debate, the presiding judge shall ask each side, first the plaintiff, then the defendant, and then the third party, for their final opinion respectively.

Article 128 At the end of the court debate, a judgement shall be made according to the law. Where conciliation is possible prior to the rendering of a judgement, conciliation efforts may be made; if conciliation proves to be unsuccessful, a judgement shall be made without delay.

Article 129 If a plaintiff, having been served with a summons, refuses to appear in court without justified reasons, or if he withdraws during a court session without the permission of the court, the case may be considered as withdrawn by him; if the defendant files a counterclaim in the mean time, the court may make a judgement by default.

Article 130 If a defendant, having been served with a summons, refuses to appear in court without justified reasons, or if he withdraws during a court session without the permission of the court, the court may make a judgement by default.

Article 131 If a plaintiff applies for withdrawal of the case before the judgement is pronounced, the people's court shall decide whether to approve or disapprove it. If withdrawal of the case is not allowed by an order of the people's court, and the plaintiff, having been served with a summons, refuses to appear in court without justified reasons, the people's court may make a judgement by default.

Article 132 Under any of the following circumstances, the trial may be adjourned:

1. the parties concerned and other participants in the proceedings required to appear in court fail to do so for justified reasons;
2. any party concerned makes an extempore application for the withdrawal of a judicial officer;
3. it is necessary to summon new witnesses to court, collect new evidence, make a new expert evaluation, new inspection, or to make a supplementary investigation; or
4. other circumstances that warrant the adjournment.

Article 133 The court clerk shall make a written record of the entire court proceedings, which shall be signed by him and the judicial officers. The court record shall be read out in court, or else the parties and other participants in the proceedings may be notified to read the record while in court or within five days. If they consider that there are omissions or errors in the record of their own statements, the parties or other participants in the proceedings shall have the right to apply for rectifications. If such rectifications are not made, the application shall be placed on record in the case file. The court record shall be signed or sealed by the parties and other participants in the proceedings. Refusal to do so shall be put on record in the case file.

Article 134 The people's court shall publicly pronounce its judgement in all cases, whether publicly tried or not. If a judgement is pronounced in court, the written judgement shall be issued and delivered within ten days; if a judgement is pronounced later on a fixed date, the written judgement shall be issued and given immediately after the pronouncement. Upon pronouncement of a judgement, the parties concerned must be informed of their right to file an appeal, the time limit for appeal and the court to which they may appeal. Upon pronouncement of a divorce judgement, the parties concerned must be informed not to remarry before the judgement takes legal effect.

Article 135 A people's court trying a case in which the ordinary procedure is followed, shall conclude the case within six months after docketing the case. Where an extension of the period is necessary under special circumstances, a six-month extension may be allowed subject to the approval of the president of the court. Further extension, if needed, shall be reported to the people's court at a higher level for approval.

Section 4 Suspension and Termination of Legal Proceedings

Article 136 Legal proceedings shall be suspended in any of the following circumstances:

1. one of the parties dies and it is necessary to wait for the heir or heiress to make clear whether to participate or not in the proceedings;
2. one of the parties has lost the capacity to engage in litigation and his agent ad item has not been designated yet;
3. the legal person or any other organisation as one of the parties has dissolved, and the successor to its rights and obligations has not been determined yet;
4. one of the parties is unable to participate in the proceedings for reasons of force majeure;
5. the adjudication of the case pending is dependent on the results of the trial of another case that has not yet been concluded; or
6. other circumstances that warrant the suspension of the litigation. The proceedings shall resume after the causes of the suspension have been eliminated.

Article 137 Legal proceedings shall be terminated in any of the following circumstances:

1. the plaintiff dies without a successor, or the successor waives the right to litigate;
2. the decedent leaves no estate, nor anyone to succeed to his obligations;
3. one of the parties in a divorce case dies; or
4. one of the parties dies who is a claimant to alimony, support for elders or children or to the termination of adoptive relationship.

Section 5 Judgement and Order

Article 138 A judgement shall clearly set forth the following:

1. cause of action, the claims, facts and cause or causes of the dispute;
2. the facts and causes as found in the judgement and the basis of application of the law;

3. the outcome of adjudication and the costs to be borne; and
4. the time limit for filing an appeal and the appellate court with which the appeal may be filed.

The judgement shall be signed by the judicial officers and the court clerk, with the seal of the people's court affixed to it.

Article 139 If some of the facts in a case being tried by the people's court are already evident, the court may pass judgement on that part of the case first.

Article 140 An order in writing is to be made in any of the following conditions:

1. refusal to entertain a case;
2. objection to the jurisdiction of a court;
3. rejection of a complaint;
4. property preservation and advance execution;
5. approval or disapproval of withdrawal of a suit;
6. suspension or termination of legal proceedings;
7. correction of errata in the judgement;
8. suspension or termination of execution;
9. refusal to enforce an arbitration award;
10. refusal to enforce a document of a notary office evidencing the rights of a creditor and entitling him to its compulsory execution;
11. other matters to be decided in the form of an order in writing. An appeal may be lodged against an order in writing in Items 1, 2 and 3 mentioned above.

An order in writing shall be signed by the judicial officers and the court clerk, with the seal of the people's court affixed to it. If it is issued orally, the order shall be entered in the record.

Article 141 All judgements and written orders of the Supreme People's Court, as well as judgements and written orders that may not be appealed against according to the law or that have not been appealed against within the prescribed time limit, shall be legally effective.

CHAPTER XIII SUMMARY PROCEDURE

Article 142 When trying simple civil cases in which the facts are evident, the rights and obligations clear and the disputes trivial in character, the basic people's courts and the tribunals dispatched by them shall apply the provisions of this Chapter.

Article 143 In simple civil cases, the plaintiff may lodge his complaint orally. The two parties concerned may at the same time come before a basic people's court or a tribunal dispatched by it for a solution of their dispute. The basic people's court or the tribunal it dispatched may try the case immediately or set a date for the trial.

Article 144 In trying a simple civil case, the basic people's court or the tribunal dispatched by it may use simplified methods to summon at any time the parties and witnesses.

Article 145 Simple civil cases shall be tried by a single judge alone and the trial of such cases shall not be bound by the provisions of Articles 122, 124, and 127 of this Law.

Article 146 The people's court trying a case in which summary procedure is followed shall conclude the case within three months after placing the case on the docket.

CHAPTER XIV PROCEDURE OF SECOND INSTANCE

Article 147 If a party refuses to accept a judgement of first instance of a local people's court, he shall have the right to file an appeal with the people's court at the next higher level within 15 days after the date on which the written judgement was served. If a party refuses to accept a written order of first instance of a local people's court, he shall have the right to file an appeal with a people's court at the next higher level within 10 days after the date on which the written order was served.

Article 148 For filing an appeal, a petition for the purpose shall be submitted. The content of the appeal petition shall include the names of the parties, the names of the legal persons and their legal representatives or names of other organisations and their principal heads; the name of the people's court where the case was originally tried; file number of the case and the cause of action; and the claims of the appeal and the reasons.

Article 149 The appeal petition shall be submitted through the people's court that originally tried the case, and copies of it shall be provided according to the number of persons in the other party or of the representatives thereof. If a party appeals directly to a people's court of second instance, the said court shall within five days transmit the appeal petition to the people's court that originally tried the case.

Article 150 The people's court that originally tried the case shall, within five days after receiving the appeal petition, serve a copy of it on the other party, who shall submit his defence within 15 days from the receipt of such copy. The people's court shall, within five days after receiving the defence, serve a copy of it on the appellant. Failure by the other party to submit a defence shall not prevent the case from being tried by the people's court. After receiving the appeal petition and the defence, the people's court which originally tried the case shall, within five days, deliver them together with the entire case file and evidence to the people's court of second instance.

Article 151 With respect to an appealed case, the people's court of second instance shall review the relevant facts and the application of the law.

Article 152 With respect to a case on appeal, the people's court of second instance shall form a collegial panel to conduct the trial. After verification of the facts of the case through consulting the files, making investigations and questioning the parties, if the collegial panel considers that it is not necessary to conduct a trial, it may make a judgement or a written order directly. The people's court of second instance may try a case on appeal at its own site or in the place where the case originated or where the people's court that originally tried the case is located.

Article 153 After trying a case on appeal, the people's court of second instance shall, in the light of the following situations, dispose of it accordingly:

1. if the facts were clearly ascertained and the law was correctly applied in the original judgement, the appeal shall be rejected in the form of a judgement and the original judgement shall be affirmed;
2. if the application of the law was incorrect in the original judgement, the said judgement shall be amended according to the law;
3. if in the original judgement the facts were incorrectly or not clearly ascertained and the evidence was insufficient, the people's court of second instance shall make a written order to set aside the judgement and remand the case to the original people's court for retrial, or the people's court of second instance may amend the judgement after investigating and clarifying the facts; or
4. if there was violation of legal procedure in making the original judgement, which may have affected correct adjudication, the

judgement shall be set aside by a written order and the case remanded to the original people's court for retrial. The parties concerned may appeal against the judgement or written order rendered in a retrial of their case.

Article 154 The people's court of second instance shall decide in the form of orders in writing all cases of appeal against the written orders made by the people's court of first instance.

Article 155 In dealing with a case on appeal, a people's court of second instance may conduct conciliation. If an agreement is reached through conciliation, a conciliation statement shall be made and signed by the judicial officers and the court clerk, with the seal of the people's court affixed to it. After the conciliation statement has been served, the original judgement of the lower court shall be deemed as set aside.

Article 156 If an appellant applies for withdrawal of his appeal before a people's court of second instance pronounces its judgement, the court shall decide whether to approve the application or not.

Article 157 In the trial of a case on appeal, the people's court of second instance shall, apart from observing the provisions of this Chapter, follow the ordinary procedure for trials of first instance.

Article 158 The judgement and the written order of a people's court of second instance shall be final.

Article 159 The people's court trying a case on appeal shall conclude the case within three months after docketing the case. Any extension of the period necessitated by special circumstances shall be subject to the approval of the president of the court. The people's court trying a case on appeal against a written order shall, within 30 days after docketing the case for second instance trial, make a written order which is final.

CHAPTER XV SPECIAL PROCEDURE

Section 1 General Provisions

Article 160 When the people's courts try cases concerning the qualification of voters, the declaration of a person as missing or dead, the adjudgement of legal incapacity or restricted legal capacity of a citizen and the adjudgement of a property as ownerless, the provisions of this

Chapter shall apply. For matters not covered in this Chapter, the relevant provisions of this Law and other laws shall apply.

Article 161 In cases tried in accordance with the procedure provided in this Chapter, the judgement of first instance shall be final. A collegial panel of judges shall be formed for the trial of any case in involving the qualification of voters or of any major, difficult or complicated case; other cases shall be tried by a single judge alone.

Article 162 If a people's court, while trying a case in accordance with the procedure provided in this Chapter, finds that the case involves a civil dispute over rights and interests, it shall make a written order to terminate the special procedure and inform the interested parties to otherwise institute an action.

Article 163 A people's court trying a case in which special procedure is followed shall conclude the case within 30 days after placing the case on the docket or within 30 days after expiration of the period stated in the public notice. Any extension of the time limit necessitated by special circumstances shall be subject to the approval of the president of the court, excepting, however, a case concerning the qualification of voters.

Section 2 Cases Concerning the Qualification of Voters

Article 164 If a citizen refuses to accept an election committee's decision on an appeal concerning his voting qualification, he may, five days before the election day, bring a suit in the basic people's court located in the electoral district.

Article 165 After entertaining a case concerning voting qualification, a people's court must conclude the trial before the election day. The party who brings the suit, the representative of the election committee and other citizens concerned must participate in the proceedings. The written judgement of the people's court shall be served on the election committee and the party who brings the suit before the election day; other citizens concerned shall be notified of the judgement.

Section 3 Cases Concerning the Declaration of a Person as Missing or Dead

Article 166 With respect to a citizen whose whereabouts are unknown for two years in full, if the interested party applies for declaring the person as missing, the application shall be filed with the basic people's court in the locality where the missing person has his domicile. The application shall clearly state the facts and time of the disappearance of the person missing as well as the motion; documentary evidence from a public security organ or other relevant organs concerning the disappearance of the citizen shall be appended to the application.

Article 167 With respect to a citizen whose whereabouts are unknown for four years in full or whose whereabouts are unknown for two years in full after an accident in which he was involved, or with respect to a citizen whose whereabouts are unknown after such an accident, and, upon proof furnished by the relevant authorities that it is impossible for him to survive, if the interested party applies for declaring such person as dead, the application shall be filed with the basic people's court in the locality where the missing person has his domicile. The application shall clearly state the facts and time of the disappearance as well as the motion; documentary evidence from a public security organ or other relevant organs concerning the disappearance of the citizen shall be appended to the application.

Article 168 After entertaining a case concerning the declaration of a person as missing or dead, the people's court shall issue a public notice in search of the person missing. The period of the public notice for declaring a person as missing shall be three months, and that for declaring a person as dead shall be one year. Where a citizen's whereabouts are unknown after an accident in which he was involved and, upon proof furnished by the relevant authorities that it is impossible for him to survive, the period of the public notice for proclaiming such person as dead shall be three months. On the expiration of the period of the public notice, the people's court shall, depending on whether the fact of the missing or death of the person has been confirmed, make a judgement declaring the person missing or dead or make a judgement rejecting the application.

Article 169 If a person who has been declared missing or dead by a people's court reappears, the people's court shall, upon the application of that person or of an interested party, make a new judgement and annul the previous one.

Section 4 Cases Concerning the Adjudgement of Legal Incapacity or Restricted Legal Capacity of Citizens

Article 170 An application for adjudgement of legal incapacity or restricted legal capacity of a citizen shall be filed by the citizen's near relatives or any other interested party with the basic people's court in the locality where the citizen has his domicile. The application shall clearly state the fact and grounds of the citizen's legal incapacity or restricted legal capacity.

Article 171 After accepting such an application, the people's court shall, when necessary, have an expert evaluation of the citizen of whom the determination of legal incapacity or restricted legal capacity or upon the application of his guardian, the people's court confirms that the causes of that person's legal incapacity or restricted legal capacity have been eliminated, a new judgement shall be made annulling the previous one.

Section 5 Cases Concerning the Determination of a Property as Ownerless

Article 174 An application for determining a property as ownerless shall be filed by a citizen, legal person or any other organisation with the basic people's court in the place where the property is located. The application shall clearly state the type and quantity of the property and the grounds on which the application for determining the property as ownerless is filed.

Article 175 The people's court shall, after accepting such an application and upon examination and verification of it, issue a public notice calling on the owner to claim the property. If no one claims the property one year after the issue of the public notice, the people's court shall make a judgement determining the property as ownerless and turn it over to the State or the collective concerned.

Article 176 If, after a property has been determined by a judgement as ownerless, the owner of the property or his successor appears, such a person may file a claim for the property within the period of limitation specified in the General Principles of the Civil Law. The people's court shall, after examination and verification of the claim, make a new judgement, annulling the previous one.

CHAPTER XVI PROCEDURE FOR TRIAL SUPERVISION

Article 177 If the president of a people's court at any level finds definite error in a legally effective judgement or written order of his court and deems it necessary to have the case retried, he shall refer it to the judicial committee for discussion and decision. If the Supreme People's Court finds definite error in a legally effective judgement or written order of a local people's court at any level, or if a people's court at a higher level finds some definite error in a legally effective judgement or written order of a people's court at a lower level, it shall respectively have the power to bring the case up for trial by itself or direct the people's court at a lower level to conduct a retrial.

Article 178 If a party to an action considers that there is error in a legally effective judgement or written order, he may apply to the people's court that originally tried the case or to a people's court at the next higher level for a retrial; however, execution of the judgement or order shall not be suspended.

Article 179 If an application made by a party meets any of the following conditions, the people's court shall retry the case:

1. there is sufficient new evidence to set aside the original judgement or written order;
2. the main evidence on which the facts were ascertained in the original judgement or written order was insufficient;
3. there was definite error in the application of the law in the original judgement or written order;
4. there was violation by the people's court of the legal procedure which may have affected the correctness of the judgement or written order in the case; or
5. the judicial officers have committed embezzlement, accepted bribes, done malpractices for personal benefits and perverted the law in the adjudication of the case. The people's court shall reject the application that meets none of the conditions specified above.

Article 180 With respect to a legally effective conciliation statement, if evidence furnished by a party proves that the conciliation violates the principle of voluntariness or that the content of the conciliation agreement violates the law, the party may apply for a retrial. If the foregoing proves true after its examination, the people's court shall retry the case.

Article 181 With respect to a legally effective judgement on dissolution of marriage, neither of the two parties shall apply for a retrial.

Article 182 Application for a retrial made by a party must be submitted within two years after the judgement or written order becomes legally effective.

Article 183 When a decision is made to retry a case in accordance with the procedure for trial supervision, the execution of the original judgement shall be suspended by a written order, which shall be signed by the president of the court with the seal of the people's court affixed to it.

Article 184 With respect to a case pending retrial by a people's court in accordance with the procedure for trial supervision, if the legally effective judgement or written order was made by a court of first instance, the case shall be tried in accordance with the procedure of first instance, and the parties concerned may appeal against the new judgement or order; if the legally effective judgement or written order was made by a court of second instance, the case shall be tried in accordance with the procedure of second instance, and the new judgement or written order shall be legally effective; if it is a case which was brought up for trial by a people's court at a higher level, it shall be tried in accordance with the procedure of second instance, and the new judgement or written order shall be legally effective. The people's court shall form a new collegial panel for the purpose of the retrial.

Article 185 If the Supreme People's Procuratorate finds that a legally effective judgement or written order made by a people's court at any level involves any of the following circumstances, or if a people's procuratorate at a higher level finds that a legally effective judgement or written order made by a people's court at a lower level involves any of the following circumstances, the Supreme People's Procuratorate or the people's procuratorate at a higher level shall respectively lodge a protest in accordance with the procedure for trial supervision:

1. the main evidence for ascertaining the facts in the previous judgement or written order was insufficient;
2. there was a definite error in the application of the law in the previous judgement or written order;
3. there was violation by the people's court of the legal procedure which may have affected the correctness of the judgement or written order; or
4. the judicial officers have committed embezzlement, accepted bribes, done malpractice for personal benefits and perverted the law in the trial of the case.

If a local people's procuratorate at any level finds that a legally effective judgement or written order made by a people's court at the corresponding level involves any of the circumstances specified above, it shall refer the matter to the people's procuratorate at a higher level with the request that a protest be lodged by the latter in accordance with the procedure for trial supervision.

Article 186 Cases in which protest was made by the people's procuratorate shall be retried by the people's court.

Article 187 When a people's procuratorate decides to lodge a protest against a judgement or written order made by a people's court, it shall make the protest in writing.

Article 188 The people's court shall, in retrying a case in which protest was lodged by a people's procuratorate, notify the procuratorate to send representatives to attend the court session.

CHAPTER XVII PROCEDURE FOR HASTENING DEBT RECOVERY

Article 189 When a creditor requests payment of a pecuniary debt or recovery of negotiable instruments from a debtor, he may, if the following requirements are met, apply to the basic people's court that has jurisdiction for an order of payment:

1. no other debt disputes exist between the creditor and the debtor; and
2. the order of payment can be served on the debtor. The application shall clearly state the requested amount of money or of the negotiable instruments and the facts and evidence on the basis of which the application is made.

Article 190 After the creditor has submitted his application, the people's court shall within five days inform the creditor whether it accepts the application or not.

Article 191 After accepting the application and upon examination of the facts and evidence provided by the creditor, the people's court shall, if the rights and obligations relationship between the creditor and the debtor is clear and legitimate, issue within 15 days after accepting the application an order of payment to the debtor; if the application is unfounded, the people's court shall make an order to reject it. The debtor shall, within 15 days after receipt of the order of payment, clear off his debts or submit to the people's court his dissent in writing. If the debtor has neither dissented from nor complied with the order of payment within the period specified in the preceding paragraph, the creditor may apply to the people's court for execution.

Article 192 The people's court shall, on receiving the dissent in writing submitted by the debtor, make an order to terminate the procedure for hastening debt recovery and the order of payment shall of itself be invalidated. The creditor may bring an action in the people's court.

CHAPTER XVIII PROCEDURE FOR PUBLICISING PUBLIC NOTICE FOR ASSERTION OF CLAIMS

Article 193 Any holder of a bill transferable by endorsement according to the law may, if the bill is stolen, lost, or destroyed, apply to the basic people's court of the place where the bill is to be paid for publication of public notice for assertion of claims. The provisions of this Chapter shall apply to other matters for which, according to the law, an application for publication of a public notice for assertion of claims may be made. The applicant shall submit to the people's court an application that clearly states the main contents of the bill such as the face amount, the drawer, the holder, the endorser, and the facts and reasons in respect of the application.

Article 194 The people's court shall, upon deciding to accept the application, notify the payor concerned in the meantime to suspend the payment, and shall, within three days, issue a public notice for the interested parties to assert their rights. The period of the public notice shall be decided at the discretion of the people's court; however, it shall not be less than 60 days.

Article 195 The payor shall, upon receiving the notification by the people's court to suspend the payment, do so accordingly till the conclusion of the procedure for publicising a public notice for assertion of claims. Within the period of the public notice, assignment of rights on the bill shall be void.

Article 196 Interested party or parties as claimants shall report their claims to the people's court within the period of the public notice. After receiving the report on the claims by interested party or parties, the people's court shall make a written order to terminate the procedure for publicising public notice for assertion of claims, and notify the applicant and the payor. The applicant or the claimants may bring an action in the people's court.

Article 197 If no claim is asserted, the people's court shall make a judgement on the basis of the application to declare the bill in question null and void. The judgement shall be published and the payor notified accordingly. As of the date of publication of the judgement, the applicant shall be entitled to payment by the payor.

Article 198 If an interested party for justified reasons was unable to submit his claim to the people's court before the judgement is made, he may, within one year after the day he knows or should know the publication of the judgement, bring an action in the people's court which has made the judgement.

CHAPTER XIX PROCEDURE FOR BANKRUPTCY AND DEBT REPAYMENT OF LEGAL PERSON ENTERPRISES

Article 199 If a legal person enterprise has suffered serious losses and is unable to repay the debts at maturity, the creditors may apply to a people's court for declaring the debtor bankrupt for debts to be repaid; the debtor may likewise apply to a people's court for declaring bankruptcy for debts to be repaid.

Article 200 After making an order to declare the initiation of the bankruptcy and debt repayment proceedings, the people's court shall notify the debtor and the known creditors within ten days and also make a public announcement. Creditors who have been notified shall, within 30 days after receiving the notice, and those who have not been notified shall, within three months after the date of the announcement, lodge their claims with the people's court. Creditors who fail to lodge their claims during the respective periods shall be deemed to have abandoned their rights. Creditors may organise a creditors' meeting to discuss and approve of a formula for the disposition and distribution of bankrupt property, or for a composition agreement.

Article 201 The people's court may appoint a liquidation commission formed by relevant state organs and persons concerned. The liquidation commission shall take charge of the custody of the bankrupt property, its liquidation, assessment, disposition and distribution. The liquidation commission may also engage in necessary activities of a civil nature according to the law. The liquidation commission shall be responsible and report its work to the people's court.

Article 202 If the legal person enterprise and the creditors reach a composition agreement, the people's court shall, after approving the agreement, make a public announcement of it and terminate the bankruptcy and debt repayment proceedings. The composition agreement shall be legally effective as of the date of the public announcement.

Article 203 With respect to the property mortgaged or otherwise used as security for bank loans or other obligations, the bank and other creditors shall have priority in the repayment of debts as regards the property mortgaged or used as security for other kinds of obligations. If the money value of the property mortgaged or used as security for other kinds of obligations exceeds the amount of loans secured, the surplus shall go to the bankrupt property for debt repayment.

Article 204 After deduction of bankruptcy proceedings expenses from the bankrupt property, first repayment shall be made in the following order of priority:

1. wages and salaries of staff and workers and labour insurance expenses that are owned by the bankrupt enterprise;
2. taxes owed by the bankrupt enterprise; and
3. claims by creditors in the bankruptcy proceedings. Where the bankrupt property is insufficient to meet the repayment claims of the same order of priority, it shall be distributed on a pro-rata basis.

Article 205 The debt repayment of a bankrupt legal person enterprise shall be under the jurisdiction of the people's court of the place where the legal person enterprise is located.

Article 206 The provisions of the Law of the People's Republic of China on Enterprise Bankruptcy shall apply to bankruptcy and debt repayment of enterprises owned by the whole people. The provisions of this Chapter shall not apply to non-legal person enterprises, individual businesses, lease-holding farm households and partnerships by private individuals.

PART THREE PROCEDURE OF EXECUTION

CHAPTER XX GENERAL PROVISIONS

Article 207 Legally effective judgements or written orders in civil cases, as well as the parts of judgements or written orders that relate to property in criminal cases, shall be executed by the people's court of first instance. Other legal documents, which are to be executed by a people's court as prescribed by the law, shall be executed by the people's court of the place where the person subjected to execution has his domicile or where the property subject to execution is located.

Article 208 If, in the course of execution, an outsider raises an objection with respect to the object subjected to execution, the execution officer shall examine the objection in accordance with the procedure prescribed by the law. If the reasons for the objection are untenable, the objection shall be rejected; if otherwise, execution shall be suspended with the approval of the president of the court. If definite error is found in the judgement or the written order, it shall be dealt with in accordance with the procedure for trial supervision.

Article 209 Execution work shall be carried out by the execution officer. When carrying out a compulsory execution measure, the execution officer shall produce his credentials. After the execution is completed, the execution officer shall make a record of the particulars of the execution, and have it signed or sealed by the persons concerned on the scene. The basic people's court and the intermediate people's court may, when necessary, establish execution organs, whose functions shall be defined by the Supreme People's Court.

Article 210 If a person or property subjected to execution is in another locality, the people's court in that locality may be entrusted with the carrying out of the execution. The entrusted people's court shall begin the execution within 15 days after receiving a letter of entrustment and shall not refuse to do so. After the execution has been completed, the entrusted people's court shall promptly inform the entrusting people's court, by letter, of the result of the execution. If the execution has not been completed within 30 days, the entrusted people's court shall also inform the entrusting people's court, by letter, of the particulars of the execution. If the entrusted people's court does not carry out the execution within 15 days after receiving the letter of entrustment, the entrusting people's court may request the people's court at a higher level over the entrusted people's court to instruct the entrusted people's court to carry out the execution.

Article 211 If in the course of execution the two parties become reconciled and reach a settlement agreement on their own initiative, the execution officer shall make a record of the contents of the agreement, and both parties shall affix their signatures or seals to the record. If either party fails to fulfil the settlement agreement, the people's court may, at the request of the other party, resume the execution of the legal document which was originally effective.

Article 212 In the course of execution, if the person subjected to execution provides a guaranty, the people's court may, with the consent of the person who has applied for execution, decide on the suspension of the execution and the time limit for such suspension. If the person subjected to execution still fails to perform his obligations after the time limit, the people's court shall have the power to execute the property he provided as security or the property of the guarantor.

Article 213 If the citizen subjected to execution dies, his debts shall be paid off from the deceased estate; if a legal person or any other organisation subjected to execution dissolves, the party that succeeds to its rights and obligations shall fulfil the obligations.

Article 214 After the completion of execution, if definite error is found in the executed judgement, written order or other legal documents resulting in the annulment of such judgement, order or legal documents by the people's court, the said court shall, with respect to the property which has been executed, make a written order that persons who have obtained the property shall return it. In the event of refusal to return such property, compulsory execution shall be carried out.

Article 215 The provisions of this Part shall be applicable to the execution of the conciliation statement as drawn up by the people's court.

CHAPTER XXI APPLICATION FOR EXECUTION AND REFERRAL

Article 216 The parties concerned must comply with legally effective judgements or written orders in civil cases. If a party refuses to do so, the other party may apply to the people's court for execution, or the judge may refer the matter to the execution officer for enforcement. The parties concerned must comply with the conciliation statement and other legal documents that are to be executed by the people's court. If a party refuses to do so, the other party may apply to the people's court for enforcement.

Article 217 If a party fails to comply with an award of an arbitral organ established according to the law, the other party may apply for execution to the people's court which has jurisdiction over the case. The people's court applied to shall enforce the award. If the party against whom the application is made furnishes proof that the arbitral award involves any of the following circumstances, the people's court shall, after examination and verification by a collegial panel, make a written order not to allow the enforcement:

1. the parties have had no arbitration clause in their contract, nor have subsequently reached a written agreement on arbitration;
2. the matters dealt with by the award fall outside the scope of the arbitration agreement or are matters which the arbitral organ has no power to arbitrate;
3. the composition of the arbitration tribunal or the procedure for arbitration contradicts the procedure prescribed by the law;
4. the main evidence for ascertaining the facts is insufficient;
5. there is definite error in the application of the law; or
6. the arbitrators have committed embezzlement, accepted bribes or done malpractice for personal benefits or perverted the law in the arbitration of the case.

If the people's court determines that the execution of the arbitral award is against the social and public interest, it shall make an order not to allow the execution. The above-mentioned written order shall be served on both parties and the arbitral organ. If the execution of an arbitral award is disallowed by a written order of the people's court, the parties may, in accordance with a written agreement on arbitration reached between them, apply for arbitration again; they may also bring an action in a people's court.

Article 218 If a party fails to comply with a document evidencing the creditor's rights made enforceable according to the law by a notary office, the other party may apply to the people's court which has jurisdiction over the case for execution. The people's court applied to shall enforce such document. If the people's court finds definite error in the document of creditor's rights, it shall make an order not to allow the execution and serve the order on both parties concerned as well as the notary office.

Article 219 The time limit for the submission of an application for execution shall be one year, if both or one of the parties are citizens; it shall be six months if both parties are legal persons or other organisations. The above-mentioned time limit shall be calculated from the last day of the period of performance specified by the legal document. If the legal document specifies performance in stages, the time limit shall be calculated from the last day of the period specified for each stage of performance.

Article 220 The execution officer shall, after receiving the application for execution or the writ of referral directing execution, send an execution notice to the person subjected to execution, instructing him to comply within the specified time. If the person fails to comply accordingly, compulsory execution shall be carried out.

CHAPTER XXII EXECUTION MEASURES

Article 221 If the person subjected to execution fails to fulfil according to the execution notice the obligations specified in the legal document, the people's court shall be empowered to make inquiries with banks, credit cooperatives or other units that deal with savings deposit into the deposit accounts of the person subjected to execution, and shall be empowered to freeze or transfer his deposits; however, the inquiries, freezing or transfer of the deposits shall not exceed the scope of the obligations to be fulfilled by the person subjected to execution. The people's court shall, in deciding to freeze or transfer a deposit, make a written order and issue a notice for assistance in execution. Banks, credit cooperatives or other units that deal with savings deposit must comply with it.

Article 222 If the person subjected to execution fails to fulfil according to the execution notice the obligations specified in the legal document, the people's court shall be empowered to withhold or withdraw part of the income of the person subjected to execution, for the fulfilment of his obligations. However, it shall leave out the necessary living expenses for the person subjected to execution and his dependant family members. The people's court shall, when withholding or withdrawing the income, make a written order and issue a notice for assistance in execution. The unit in which the person subjected to execution works, banks, credit cooperatives or other units that deal with savings deposit must comply with the notice.

Article 223 If the person subjected to execution fails to fulfil according to the execution notice the obligations specified in the legal document, the people's court shall be empowered to seal up, distrain, freeze, sell by public auction, or sell off part of the property of the person subjected to execution for the fulfilment of his obligations. However, it shall leave out the necessaries of life for the person subjected to execution and his dependant family members. The people's court shall make an order for the adoption of the measures specified in the preceding paragraph.

Article 224 When the people's court seals up or distrains a property, it shall, if the person subjected to execution is a citizen, notify him or an adult member of his family to appear on the scene; if the party subjected to execution is a legal person or any other organisation, it shall notify its legal representatives or its principal heads to be present. Their refusal to appear on the scene shall not hinder the execution. If the person subjected to execution is a citizen, his unit or the grass-roots organisation of the place where his property is located shall send a representative to attend the execution. An inventory of the sealed-up or distrained property must be made by the execution officer and, after the inventory has been signed or sealed by the persons on the scene, a copy of it shall be given to the person subjected to execution. If the person subjected to execution is a citizen, another copy may be given to an adult member of his family.

Article 225 The execution officer may commit the sealed-up property to the person subjected to execution for safekeeping, and the person shall be held responsible for any losses incurred due to his fault.

Article 226 After a property has been sealed up or distrained, the execution officer shall instruct the person subjected to execution to fulfil, within the prescribed period, the obligations specified in the legal document. If the person has not fulfilled his obligations upon expiration of the period, the people's court may, in accordance with the relevant legal provisions, entrust the relevant units with selling by public auction or selling off the sealed-up or distrained property. Articles that are prohibited from free trading by the State shall be delivered to and purchased by the relevant units at the price fixed by the State.

Article 227 If the person subjected to execution fails to fulfil his obligations specified in the legal document and conceals his property, the people's court shall be empowered to issue a search warrant and search him and his domicile or the place where the property was concealed. In adopting the measure mentioned in the preceding paragraph, the president of the people's court shall sign and issue the search warrant.

Article 228 With respect to the property or negotiable instruments specified for delivery in the legal document, the execution officer shall summon both parties concerned and deliver them in their presence or the execution officer may forward them to the recipient, who shall sign and give a receipt. Any unit concerned that has in possession the property or negotiable instruments shall turn them over to the recipient in accordance with the notice of the people's court for assistance in execution, and the recipient shall sign and give a receipt. If any citizen concerned has in possession the property or negotiable instruments, the people's court shall notify him to hand them over. If he refuses to do so, compulsory execution shall be carried out.

Article 229 Compulsory eviction from a building or a plot of land shall require a public notice signed and issued by the president of a people's court, instructing the person subjected to execution to comply within a specified period of time. If the person subjected to execution fails to do so upon the expiration of the period, compulsory execution shall be carried out by the execution officer. When compulsory execution is being carried out, if the person subjected to execution is a citizen, the person or an adult member of his family shall be notified to be present; if the party subjected to execution is a legal person or any other organisation, its legal representatives or principal heads shall be notified to be present; their refusal to be present shall not hinder the execution. If the person subjected to execution is a citizen, his work unit or the grass-roots organisation in the locality of the building or the plot of land shall send a representative for attendance. The execution officer shall make a record of the particulars of the compulsory execution, with the signatures or seals of the persons on the scene affixed to it. The people's court shall assign personnel to transport the property removed in a compulsory eviction from a building to a designated location and turn it over to the person subjected to execution or, if the person is a citizen, to an adult member of his family; if any loss is incurred due to such person's refusal to accept the property, the loss shall be borne by the person subjected to execution.

Article 230 In the course of execution, if certain formalities for the transfer of certificates of property right need to be gone through, the people's court may issue a notice for assistance in execution to the relevant units, and they must comply with it.

Article 231 If the person subjected to execution fails to perform acts specified in a judgement or written order or any other legal document according to the execution notice, the people's court may carry out compulsory execution or entrust the task to a relevant unit or other persons, and the person subjected to execution shall bear the expenses thus incurred.

Article 232 If the person subjected to execution fails to fulfil his obligations with respect to pecuniary payment within the period specified by a judgement or written order or any other legal document, he shall pay double interest on the debt for the belated payment. If the person subjected to execution fails to fulfil his other obligations within the period specified in the judgement or written order or any other legal document, he shall pay a charge for the dilatory fulfilment.

Article 233 After the adoption of the execution measures stipulated in Articles 221, 222 and 223 of this Law, if the person subjected to execution is still unable to repay the debts, he shall continue to fulfil his obligations. If the creditor finds that the person subjected to execution has any other property, he may at any time apply to the people's court for execution.

CHAPTER XXIII SUSPENSION AND TERMINATION OF EXECUTION

Article 234 The people's court shall make a written order to suspend execution under any of the following circumstances:

1. the applicant indicates that the execution may be postponed;
2. an outsider raises an obviously reasonable objection to the object of the execution;
3. a citizen as one of the parties dies and it is necessary to wait for the successor to inherit the rights of the deceased or to succeed to his obligations;
4. a legal person or any other organisation as one of the parties dissolves, and the party succeeding to its rights and obligations has not been determined; or
5. other circumstances occur under which the people's court deems the suspension of execution necessary.

Execution shall be resumed when the circumstances warranting the suspension of execution have disappeared.

Article 235 The people's court shall make a written order to terminate execution under any of the following circumstances:

1. the applicant has withdrawn his application;
2. the legal document on which the execution is based has been revoked;
3. the citizen subjected to execution dies and there is no estate that may be subjected to execution, nor anyone to succeed to his obligations;
4. the person entitled to claim alimony or support for elders or children dies;
5. the citizen subjected to execution is too badly off to repay his debts, has no source of income and has lost his ability to work as well; or

6. other circumstances occur under which the people's court deems the termination of execution necessary.

Article 236 A written order to suspend or terminate execution shall become effective immediately after being served on the parties concerned.

PART FOUR SPECIAL PROVISIONS FOR CIVIL PROCEDURE OF CASES INVOLVING FOREIGN ELEMENTS

CHAPTER XXIV GENERAL PRINCIPLES

Article 237 The provisions of this Part shall be applicable to civil proceedings within the territory of the People's Republic of China in regard to cases involving foreign element. Where it is not covered by the provisions of this Part, other relevant provisions of this Law shall apply.

Article 238 If an international treaty concluded or acceded to by the People's Republic of China contains provisions that differ from provisions of this Law, the provisions of the international treaty shall apply, except those on which China has made reservations.

Article 239 Civil actions brought against a foreign national, a foreign organisation or an international organisation that enjoys diplomatic privileges and immunities shall be dealt with in accordance with the relevant law of the People's Republic of China and the provisions of the international treaties concluded or acceded to by the People's Republic of China.

Article 240 The people's court shall conduct trials of civil cases involving foreign elements in the spoken and written language commonly used in the People's Republic of China. Translation may be provided at the request of the parties concerned, and the expenses shall be borne by them.

Article 241 When foreign nationals, stateless persons or foreign enterprises and organisations need lawyers as agents *ad litem* to bring an action or enter appearance on their behalf in the people's court, they must appoint lawyers of the People's Republic of China.

Article 242 Any power of attorney mailed or forwarded by other means from outside the territory of the People's Republic of China by a foreign national, stateless person or a foreign enterprise and organisation that has no domicile in the People's Republic of China for the appointment of a lawyer or any other person of the People's Republic of China as an agent *ad litem* must be notarised by a notarial office in the country of domicile and authenticated by the Chinese embassy or consulate accredited to that country or, for the purpose of verification, must go through the formalities stipulated in the relevant bilateral treaties between China and that country before it becomes effective.

CHAPTER XXV JURISDICTION

Article 243 In the case of an action concerning a contract dispute or other disputes over property rights and interests, brought against a defendant who has no domicile within the territory of the People's Republic of China, if the contract is signed or performed within the territory of the People's Republic of China, or if the object of the action is located within the territory of the People's Republic of China, or if the defendant has distrainable property within the territory of the People's Republic of China, or if the defendant has its representative office within the territory of the People's Republic of China, the people's court of the place where the contract is signed or performed, or where the object of the action is, or where the defendant's distrainable property is located, or where the torts are done, or where the defendant's representative office is located, shall have jurisdiction.

Article 244 Parties to a dispute over a contract concluded with foreign elements or over property rights and interests involving foreign elements may, through written agreement, choose the court of the place which has practical connections with the dispute to exercise jurisdiction. If a people's court of the People's Republic of China is chosen to exercise jurisdiction, the provisions of this Law on jurisdiction by forum level and on exclusive jurisdiction shall not be violated.

Article 245 If in a civil action in respect of a case involving foreign element, the defendant raises no objection to the jurisdiction of a people's court and responds to the action by making his defence, he shall be deemed to have accepted that this people's court has jurisdiction over the case.

Article 246 Actions brought on disputes arising from the performance of contracts for Chinese-foreign equity joint ventures, or Chinese-foreign contractual joint ventures, or Chinese-foreign cooperative exploration and development of the natural resources in the People's Republic of China shall fall under the jurisdiction of the people's courts of the People's Republic of China.

CHAPTER XXVI SERVICE AND TIME PERIODS

Article 247 A people's court may serve litigation documents on a party who has no domicile within the territory of the People's Republic of China in the following ways:

1. in the way specified in the international treaties concluded or acceded to by both the People's Republic of China and the country where the person on whom service is to be made resides;
2. by making the service through diplomatic channels;
3. with respect to the person on whom the service is to be made and who is of the nationality of the People's Republic of China, service may be entrusted to the embassy or consulate of the People's Republic of China accredited to the country where the person resides;
4. by making the service on the agent ad litem who is authorised to receive the documents served;
5. by serving the documents on the representative office established in the People's Republic of China by the person on whom the service is to be made or on his branch office or business agents there who have the right to receive the documents;
6. by making service by mail if the law of the country where the person on whom the service is to be made resides so permits; in the event that the receipt of delivery is not returned six months after the date on which the documents were mailed, and that circumstances justify the assumption that service has been made, the service shall be deemed completed upon the expiration of the said time period; and
7. by making service by public notice, if none of the above-mentioned methods can be employed. The service shall be deemed completed six months after the date on which the public notice was issued.

Article 248 If a defendant has no domicile within the territory of the People's Republic of China, the people's court shall serve a copy of the statement of complaint on the defendant and notify him to submit his defence within 30 days after he receives the copy of the statement of complaint. Extension of the period requested by the defendant shall be at the discretion of the people's court.

Article 249 If a party who has no domicile within the territory of the People's Republic of China is not satisfied with a judgement or written order made by a people's court of first instance, he shall have the right to file an appeal within 30 days from the date the written judgement or order is served. The appellate shall submit his defence within 30 days after receipt of a copy of the appeal petition. If a party who is unable to file an appeal or submit a defence within the period prescribed by the law requests an extension of the period, the people's court shall decide whether to grant it.

Article 250 The period for the trials of civil cases involving foreign element by the people's court shall not be restricted by the provisions of Articles 135 and 159 of this Law.

CHAPTER XXVII PROPERTY PRESERVATION

Article 251 The parties to an action may, in accordance with the provisions of Article 92 of this Law, apply to the people's court for property preservation. Interested parties may, in accordance with the provisions of Article 93 of this Law, apply to the people's court for property preservation before an action is brought.

Article 252 After a people's court makes an order granting property preservation before litigation, the applicant shall bring an action within 30 days. If he fails to bring the action within the period, the people's court shall cancel the property preservation.

Article 253 After the people's court makes an order granting property preservation, if the party against whom the application is made provides a guaranty, the people's court shall cancel the property preservation.

Article 254 If the application is wrongfully made, the applicant shall compensate the party against whom the application is made for losses incurred from the property preservation.

Article 255 If the property to be preserved by a people's court needs supervision, the court shall notify the unit concerned to be responsible for the supervision, and the party against whom the application is made shall bear the expenses.

Article 256 The order to cancel the preservation issued by a people's court shall be carried out by an execution officer.

CHAPTER XXVIII ARBITRATION

Article 257 In the case of a dispute arising from the foreign economic, trade, transport or maritime activities of China, if the parties have had an arbitration clause in the contract concerned or have subsequently reached a written arbitration agreement stipulating the submission of the dispute for arbitration to an arbitral organ in the People's Republic of China handling cases involving foreign elements, or to any other arbitral body, they may not bring an action in a people's court. If the parties have not had an arbitration clause in the contract concerned or have not subsequently reached a written arbitration agreement, they may bring an action in a people's court.

Article 258 If a party has applied for property preservation measures, the arbitral organ of the People's Republic of China handling cases involving foreign elements shall refer the party's application for a decision to the intermediate people's court of the place where the party against whom the application is made has his domicile or where his property is located.

Article 259 In a case in which an award has been made by an arbitral organ of the People's Republic of China handling cases involving foreign elements, the parties may not bring an action in a people's court. If one party fails to comply with the arbitral award, the other party may apply for its enforcement to the intermediate people's court of the place where the party against whom the application for enforcement is made has his domicile or where his property is located.

Article 260 A people's court shall, after examination and verification by a collegial panel of the court, make a written order not to allow the enforcement of the award rendered by an arbitral organ of the People's Republic of China handling cases involving foreign element, if the party against whom the application for enforcement is made furnishes proof that:

1. the parties have not had an arbitration clause in the contract or have not subsequently reached a written arbitration agreement;
2. the party against whom the application for enforcement is made was not given notice for the appointment of an arbitrator or for the inception of the arbitration proceedings or was unable to present his case due to causes for which he is not responsible;
3. the composition of the arbitration tribunal or the procedure for arbitration was not in conformity with the rules of arbitration; or
4. the matters dealt with by the award fall outside the scope of the arbitration agreement or which the arbitral organ was not empowered to arbitrate.

If the people's court determines that the enforcement of the award goes against the social and public interest of the country, the people's court shall make a written order not to allow the enforcement of the arbitral award.

Article 261 If the enforcement of an arbitral award is disallowed by a written order of a people's court, the parties may, in accordance with a written arbitration agreement reached between them, apply for arbitration again; they may also bring an action in a people's court.

CHAPTER XXIX JUDICIAL ASSISTANCE

Article 262 In accordance with the international treaties concluded or acceded to by the People's Republic of China or with the principle of reciprocity, the people's courts of China and foreign courts may make mutual requests for assistance in the service of legal documents, in investigation and collection of evidence or in other litigation actions. The people's court shall not render the assistance requested by a foreign court, if it impairs the sovereignty, security or social and public interest of the People's Republic of China.

Article 263 The request for the providing of judicial assistance shall be effected through channels provided in the international treaties concluded or acceded to by the People's Republic of China; in the absence of such treaties, they shall be effected through diplomatic channels. A foreign embassy or consulate accredited to the People's Republic of China may serve documents on its citizens and make investigations and collect evidence among them, provided that the laws of the People's Republic of China are not violated and no compulsory measures are taken. Except for the conditions provided in the preceding paragraph, no foreign organisation or individual may, without the consent of the competent authorities of the People's Republic of China, serve documents or make investigations and collect evidence within the territory of the People's Republic of China.

Article 264 The letter of request for judicial assistance and its annexes sent by a foreign court to a people's court shall be appended with a Chinese translation or a text in any other language or languages specified in the relevant international treaties. The letter of request and its annexes sent to a foreign court by a people's court for judicial assistance shall be appended with a translation in the language of that country or a text in any other language or languages specified in the relevant international treaties.

Article 265 The judicial assistance provided by the people's courts shall be rendered in accordance with the procedure prescribed by the laws of the People's Republic of China. If a special form of judicial assistance is requested by a foreign court, it may also be rendered, provided that the special form requested does not contradict the laws of the People's Republic of China.

Article 266 If a party applies for enforcement of a legally effective judgement or written order made by a people's court, and the opposite party or his property is not within the territory of the People's Republic of China, the applicant may directly apply for recognition and enforcement to the foreign court that has jurisdiction. The people's court may also, in accordance with the relevant provisions of the international treaties concluded or acceded to by China, or with the principle of reciprocity, request recognition and enforcement by the foreign court. If a party applies for enforcement of a legally effective arbitral award made by an arbitral organ in the People's Republic of China handling cases involving foreign elements and the opposite party or his property is not within the territory of the People's Republic of China, he may directly apply for recognition and enforcement of the award to the foreign court which has jurisdiction.

Article 267 If a legally effective judgement or written order made by a foreign court requires recognition and enforcement by a people's court of the People's Republic of China, the party concerned may directly apply for recognition and enforcement to the intermediate people's court of the People's Republic of China which has jurisdiction. The foreign court may also, in accordance with the provisions of the international treaties concluded or acceded to by that foreign country and the People's Republic of China or with the principle of reciprocity, request recognition and enforcement by a people's court.

Article 268 In the case of an application or request for recognition and enforcement of a legally effective judgement or written order of a foreign court, the people's court shall, after examining it in accordance with the international treaties concluded or acceded to by the People's Republic of China or with the principle of reciprocity and arriving at the conclusion that it does not contradict the basic principles of the law of the People's Republic of China nor violates State sovereignty, security and social and public interest of the country, recognise the validity of the judgement or written order, and, if required, issue a writ of execution to enforce it in accordance with the relevant provisions of this Law; if the application or request contradicts the basic principles of the law of the People's Republic of China or violates State sovereignty, security and social and public interest of the country, the people's court shall not recognise and enforce it.

Article 269 If an award made by a foreign arbitral organ requires the recognition and enforcement by a people's court of the People's Republic of China, the party concerned shall directly apply to the intermediate people's court of the place where the party subjected to enforcement has his domicile or where his property is located. The people's court shall deal with the matter in accordance with the international treaties concluded or acceded to by the People's Republic of China or with the principle of reciprocity.

Article 270 This Law shall come into force as of the date of promulgation, and the Civil Procedure Law of the People's Republic of China (for Trial Implementation) shall be abrogated simultaneously.

AMENDMENTS TO CIVIL PROCEDURE LAW OF THE PEOPLE'S REPUBLIC OF CHINA

(Adopted at the Fourth Session of the Seventh National People's Congress on 9 April 1991, promulgated by Order No 44 of the President of the People's Republic of China on 9 April 1991, and effective as of the date of promulgation)

Article 217 If a party fails to perform an award of an arbitration organ established according to law, the other party may apply for an enforcement to the competent People's Court. The Peoples' Court to which an application is made shall enforce the award.

If the party against whom the application is made presents evidence that proves that the arbitral award involves any of the following circumstances, the Peoples' Court shall, after examination and verification by a collegiate bench formed by the People's Court, rule to deny enforcement:

1. the parties have neither included an arbitration clause in their contract nor subsequently reached a written arbitration agreement;
2. matters decided in the award exceed the scope of the arbitration agreement or are beyond the arbitral authority of the arbitration organ;
3. the composition of the arbitral tribunal or the arbitration procedure was not in conformity with statutory procedure;
4. the main evidence for ascertaining the facts was insufficient;
5. the law was truly applied incorrectly; or
6. one or several arbitrators committed embezzlement, accepted bribes, practiced favouritism or made an award that perverted the law.

If the People's Court determines that enforcement of the award would be against the public interest, it shall rule to deny enforcement.

The written ruling shall be served on both parties and on the arbitration organ.

If a People's Court rules to deny enforcement of an arbitral award, a party may, in accordance with the written arbitration agreement between the two parties, reapply to the arbitration organ for arbitration or institute an action in a People's Court.

PART 4 SPECIAL PROVISIONS FOR CIVIL PROCEDURES INVOLVING FOREIGN PARTIES

CHAPTER 24 GENERAL PROVISIONS

Article 237 This Part shall apply to civil actions within the territory of the People's Republic of China involving foreign parties. For matters not covered by this Part, the other relevant provisions of this law shall apply.

Article 238 If an international treaty to which the People's Republic of China has concluded or acceded contains provisions that are inconsistent with this Law, the provisions of the international treaty shall prevail, except for those provisions to which the People's Republic of China has declared reservations.

Article 239 Civil actions instituted against foreigners, foreign organisations or international organisations that enjoy diplomatic privileges and immunities shall be handled in accordance with the relevant laws of the People's Republic of China and the relevant international treaties concluded or acceded to by the People's Republic of China.

Article 240 In trying civil cases involving foreign parties, a People's Court shall use the written and spoken language commonly used in the People's Republic of China. At the request of a party, translation may be provided at the expense of such party.

Article 241 If a foreigner, stateless person, foreign enterprise or foreign organisation who or which sues or is sued in a People's Court is required to appoint a lawyer as his or its agent *ad litem*, he or it must entrust a lawyer of the People's Republic of China.

Article 242 When a foreigner, stateless person, foreign enterprise or foreign organisation without a domicile within the territory of the People's Republic of China appoints a lawyer or another person of the People's Republic of China as his or its agent *ad litem*, the power of attorney sent or forwarded from outside the territory of the People's Republic of China shall become effective only after it has been notarised by a notary public of his or its state and (i) been authenticated by the embassy or a consulate of the People's Republic of China in that state; or (ii) certification procedures provided for in the relevant treaty between the People's Republic of China and that state have been carried out.

CHAPTER 25 JURISDICTION

Article 243 With respect to an action instituted against a defendant without a domicile within the territory of the People's Republic of China which involves a dispute over a contract or over rights and interests in property, if the contract was executed or performed within the territory of the People's Republic of China, or the subject matter of the action is located within the territory of the People's Republic of China, or the defendant has distrainable property within the territory of the jurisdiction of the People's Republic of China, or the defendant maintains a representative in the People's Republic of China, the action may come under the jurisdiction of the People's Court of the place where the contract was executed, the place where the contract was performed, the place where the object of the action is located, the place where the distrainable property is located, the place where the tort was committed or the place where the representative office is domiciled.

Article 244 The parties to a dispute involving a foreign party over a contract or over rights and interests in property may, by written agreement, select the jurisdiction of the court in the place of actual connection with the dispute. If they select to come under the jurisdiction of the People's Court of the People's Republic of China, such selection may not violate the provisions of this Law concerning jurisdiction by level and exclusive jurisdiction.

Article 245 If a defendant in a civil action involving a foreign party does not object to the jurisdiction of a People's Court and responds to the suit by filing a bill of defence, he shall be deemed to have recognised the jurisdiction of such People's Court.

Article 246 An action instituted for a dispute arising from the performance in the People's Republic of China of a Chinese-foreign equity joint venture contract, a Chinese-foreign cooperative joint venture contract or a contract for Chinese-foreign cooperative exploration and development of natural resources shall come under the jurisdiction of the People's Republic of China.

CHAPTER 26 SERVICE AND TIME PERIODS

Article 247 A People's Court may serve procedural documents on a party without a domicile within the territory of the People's Republic of China in the following ways:

1. service in the way specified in the international treaty concluded between or acceded to by the state of the person to be served and the People's Republic of China;
2. service through diplomatic channels;
3. if the person to be served has the nationality of the People's Republic of China, entrustment of the embassy or a consulate of the People's Republic of China in the state where such person is located with service on its behalf;
4. service on the agent *ad litem* appointed by the person to be served and authorised to accept service on his behalf;
5. service on the representative office, or the branch or business agent authorised to accept service, established within the territory of the People's Republic of China by the person to be served;
6. service by post, if permitted by the law of the state of the person to be served. If the acknowledgment of service is not returned within six months from the date of posting, but various circumstances justify the assumption that the documents have been served, the documents shall be deemed to have been served on the date of expiry of the time limit;
7. if the documents cannot be served by any of the above methods, service by public announcement. The documents shall be deemed to have been served when six months have elapsed since the date of the public announcement.

Article 248 If a defendant does not have a domicile within the territory of the People's Republic of China, the People's Court shall serve the copy of the bill of complaint on the defendant and notify the defendant to submit a bill of defence within 30 days upon receipt of the copy of the bill of defence. If the defendant applies for an extension of the time limit, the People's Court shall decide on the application.

Article 249 If a party without a domicile within the territory of the People's Republic of China disagrees with the judgement or ruling rendered by the People's Court of first instance, he shall have the right to lodge an appeal within 30 days from the date on which the judgement or ruling is served. The appellee shall file a statement of defence within 30 days after the date of receipt of the copy of the appeal petition. If a party is unable to lodge an appeal or to submit a bill of defence within the statutory time limit and applies for an extension thereof, the People's Court shall decide on the application.

Article 250 The period for the trial by the People's Court of civil cases involving foreign parties shall not be subject to the restrictions of Articles 135 and 159 hereof.

CHAPTER 27 PRESERVATION OF PROPERTY

Article 251 A party may apply to a People's Court for preservation of property prior to the institution of an action in accordance with Article 93 hereof.

An interested party may apply to a People's Court for preservation of property prior to the institution of an action in accordance with Article 93 hereof.

Article 252 After the People's Court has ruled to allow preservation of property prior to the institution of an action, the applicant shall institute an action within 30 days. If the applicant fails to institute an action within the time limit, the People's Court shall cancel the preservation of property.

Article 253 If, after the People's Court has rendered a ruling to allow preservation of property prior to the institution of an action, the person against whom an application is made provides security, the People's court shall cancel the preservation of property.

Article 254 If an application for preservation of property is made wrongfully, the applicant shall compensate the person against whom the application is made for any loss incurred as a result of the preservation of property.

Article 255 If a People's Court decides that the preserved property needs to be kept under surveillance, it shall notify the relevant unit to take charge of the surveillance. The surveillance expenses shall be borne by the person against whom the application is made.

Article 256 An order from a People's Court to cancel preservation shall be carried out by an enforcement officer.

CHAPTER 28 ARBITRATION

Artcle 257 With respect to disputes which arise from economic, trade, transport or maritime activities involving foreign parties, if the parties have included an arbitration clause in their contract or have subsequently reached a written arbitration agreement which provides that such disputes shall be submitted for arbitration to an arbitration organ of the People's Republic of China for foreign-related disputes or to another arbitration organ, no party may institute an action in a People's Court.

If the parties have neither included an arbitration clause in their contract nor subsequently reached a written arbitration agreement, an action may be instituted in a People's Court.

Article 258 If a party applies for preservation of property, the arbitration organ of the People's Republic of China for foreign-related disputes shall submit the application to the Intermediate People's Court of the place where the domicile of the person against whom the application is made is located or where the property is located.

Article 259 After an award has been made by an arbitration organ of the People's Republic of China for foreign-related disputes, no party may institute an action in a People's Court. If a party fails to perform the arbitral award, the other party may apply for enforcement to the Intermediate People's Court of the place where the domicile of the person against whom the application is made is located or where the property is located.

Article 260 If the person against whom the application is made presents evidence which proves that the arbitral award made by an arbitration organ of the People's Republic of China for foreign-related disputes involves any of the following circumstances, the People's Court shall, after examination and verification by a collegiate bench formed by the People's Court, rule to deny enforcement of the award:

1. the parties have neither included an arbitration clause in their contact nor subsequently reached a written arbitration agreement;

2. the person against whom the application is made was not notified to appoint an arbitrator or to take part in the arbitration proceedings or the said person was unable to state his opinions due to reasons for which he was not responsible;
3. the composition of the arbitral tribunal or the arbitration procedure was not in conformity with the rules of arbitration; or
4. matters decided in the award exceeded the scope of the arbitration agreement or are beyond the arbitral authority of the arbitration authority.

If the People's Court determines that enforcement of the said award would be against the public interest, it shall rule to deny enforcement.

Article 261 If a People's Court rules to deny enforcement of an arbitral award, a party may, in accordance with the written arbitration agreement between two parties, reapply to the arbitration organ for arbitration, or institute an action in a People's Court.

CHAPTER 29 JUDICIAL ASSISTANCE

Article 262 Pursuant to international treaties concluded or acceded to by the People's Republic of China or in accordance with the principle of reciprocity, People's Courts and foreign courts may request mutual assistance in the service of legal documents, investigation, taking evidence, and other acts in connection with litigation, on each other's behalf.

If any matter in which a foreign court requests assistance would harm the sovereignty, security or public interest of the People's Republic of China, the People's Court shall refuse to comply with the request.

Article 263 The request for and provision of judicial assistance shall be conducted through the channels stipulated in the international treaties concluded or acceded to by the People's Republic of China. Where no treaty relations exist, the request for and provision of judicial assistance shall be conducted through diplomatic channels.

The embassy or a consulate in the People's Republic of China of a foreign state may serve documents on, investigate, and take evidence from its citizens, provided that the law of the People's Republic of China is not violated and that no coercive measures are adopted.

Except for the circumstances set forth in the preceding paragraph, no foreign agency or individual may, without the consent of the competent authorities of the People's Republic of China, serve documents, carry out an investigation or take evidence within the territory of the People's Republic of China.

Article 264 The letter of request for judicial assistance and its annexes submitted to a People's Court by a foreign court shall be accompanied by a Chinese translation or a text in another language as specified in the relevant international treaty.

The letter of request for judicial assistance and its annexes submitted to a foreign court by the People's Court shall be accompanied by a translation in the language of that state or a text in another language as specified in the relevant international treaty.

Article 265 The judicial assistance provided by a People's Court shall be carried out in accordance with the procedure prescribed by the law of the People's Republic of China. If a special method is requested by a foreign court, judicial assistance may also be provided by the method requested, provided that such special method does not contradict the law of the People's Republic of China

Article 266 If a party applies for enforcement of a legally effective judgement or ruling made by a People's Court and the party subject to enforcement or his property is not located within the territory of the People's Republic of China, it may directly apply for recognition and enforcement to the competent foreign court. Alternatively, the People's Court may, pursuant to an international treaty concluded or acceded to by the People's Republic of China or in accordance with the principle of reciprocity, request the foreign court to recognise and enforce the judgement or ruling.

If a party applies for enforcement of a legally effective arbitral award made by an arbitration organ of the People's Republic of China for foreign-related disputes, and the party subject to enforcement or its property is not located within the territory of the People's Republic of China, it shall directly apply for recognition and enforcement to the competent foreign court.

Article 267 If a legally effective judgement or ruling made by a foreign court requires recognition and enforcement by a People's Court of the People's Republic of China, the party concerned may directly apply for recognition and enforcement to the competent Intermediate People's Court of the People's Republic of China. Alternatively, the foreign court may, pursuant to the provisions of the international treaty concluded or acceded to by the foreign state and the People's Republic of China, or in accordance with the principle of reciprocity, request the People's Court to recognise and enforce the judgement or ruling.

Article 268 Having received an application or a request for recognition and enforcement of a legally effective judgement or ruling of a foreign court, a People's Court shall review such judgement or ruling pursuant to the international treaty concluded or acceded to by the People's Republic of China or in accordance with the principle of reciprocity. If, upon such review, the People's Court considers that such judgement or ruling neither contradicts the basic principles of law of the People's Republic of China nor violates state sovereignty, security and the public interest, it shall rule to recognise its effectiveness. If enforcement is necessary, it shall issue an order of enforcement, which shall be implemented in accordance with the relevant provisions of this Law. If such judgement or ruling contradicts the basic principles of the law of the People's Republic of China or violates state sovereignty, security or public interest, the People's Court shall refuse to recognise and enforce the same.

Article 269 If an award made by a foreign arbitration organ requires recognition and enforcement by a People's Court of the People's Republic of China, the party concerned shall directly apply to the Intermediate People's Court of the place where the party subject to enforcement is domiciled or where his property is located. The People's Court shall handle the matter pursuant to the international treaty concluded or acceded to by the People's Republic of China or in accordance with the principle of reciprocity.

Article 270 This law shall be implemented from the date of the promulgation. At the same time, the Civil Procedure Law of the People's Republic if China (for Trial Implementation) shall be repealed.

SOME PROVISIONS OF THE SUPREME PEOPLE'S COURT ON EVIDENCE IN CIVIL PROCEDURES

Public Announcement of the Supreme People's Court

Some Provisions of the Supreme People's Court on Evidence in Civil Procedures have been passed at the 1201st meeting of the Judicial Committee of the Supreme People's Court on 6 December 2001, and are hereby promulgated for implementation as of 1 April 2002.

December 21, 2001

Some Provisions of the Supreme People's Court on Evidence in Civil Procedures

(No. 33 of [2001])

The present Provisions have been formulated on the basis of the Civil Procedure Law of the People's Republic of China and other relevant laws by combining the civil trial experience with the actual practice for the purpose of ensuring the People's Courts' finding of facts, impartial and timely trial of civil cases, and safeguarding and facilitating the parties concerned to exercise their litigation rights according to law.

I. PRODUCING EVIDENCE BY THE PARTIES CONCERNED

Article 1 The plaintiff that files a lawsuit or the defendant that files a counterclaim at the People's Court shall produce eligible evidential materials.

Article 2 The parties concerned shall be responsible for producing evidence to prove the facts on which their own allegations are based or the facts on which the allegations of the other party are refuted.

Where any party cannot produce evidence or the evidence produced cannot support the facts on which the allegations are based, the party concerned that bears the burden of proof shall undertake unfavourable consequences.

Article 3 The People's Court shall inform the parties concerned of the requirements for producing evidence and of the corresponding legal liabilities so that the parties concerned may produce evidence actively, completely, correctly and honestly within reasonable time period.

Any party who cannot independently collect evidence due to objective reasons may request the People's Court to collect after investigations.

Article 4 The burden of proof in the tort actions shall be assumed according to the following rules:

1. in a patent infringement action resulting from the innovation-creation of ways of producing new products, the entity or individual that produces the same product shall prove that the ways used are different from those of the patent holder;
2. in an infringement action resulting from personal damage caused by highly dangerous operations, the infringing person shall be responsible for producing evidence to prove the argument that the victim caused the injury;
3. in a compensation lawsuit for damages caused by environmental pollution, the infringing party shall be responsible for producing evidence to prove the existence of exemptions of liabilities as provided in laws, or that there is no causal relationship between the act and the harmful consequences;
4. in an infringement action of damages caused by the collapse, breaking off or falling of a building or other facilities and the thing that is laid or hung on the building, the owner of administrator of the building shall be responsible for producing evidence;
5. in an infringement action of damages caused by an animal, the person who raises or manages the animal shall be responsible for producing evidence to prove that the victim is at fault or any third party is at fault;
6. in an infringement action of damages caused by a defective product, the producer of the product shall be responsible for producing evidence to prove that there exist the exemptions of liabilities as provided in laws;

7. in an infringement action of damages caused by common danger, the persons who commit the common danger shall be responsible for producing evidence to prove that there is no causal relationship between the act thereof and the harmful consequences;

8. in an infringement action of damages caused by medical acts, the medical institution shall be responsible for producing evidence to prove that there is no causal relationship between the medical act and the harmful consequences, or it is not at fault.

Where there are special provisions in relevant laws concerning the producing of evidence, such provisions shall prevail.

Article 5 In a contractual dispute, the party that claims the establishment of contractual relationship and the contract has taken effect shall be responsible for producing evidence to prove that the contract has been concluded and that it has taken effect; the party that claims that the contract has been altered, dissolved, terminated or cancelled shall be responsible for producing evidence to prove the changes of the contract.

In a dispute over whether a contract is performed, the party under the obligation of performing the contract shall be responsible for producing evidence.

In a dispute over the power of agency, the party that claims the existence of such power shall be responsible for producing evidence.

Article 6 In a dispute of labour, if the dispute is caused by the employing entity's decision of kick-out, removal from the name roll, dismissal, dissolution of contract, reducing remuneration, calculation of working years of the labourer, the employing entity shall be responsible for producing evidence.

Article 7 Where there are no explicit statutory provisions and it is not possible to define who shall be responsible for producing evidence according to the present Provisions or other judicial interpretations, the People's Court may determine the burden of proof according to the principle of fairness and the principle of honesty and credit and taking such elements as the ability to produce evidence into consideration.

Article 8 In the process of litigation, if a party explicitly acknowledges the facts alleged by the other party, the other party needs not to produce evidence, with the exception, however, of cases that involve personal identification.

If the other party neither acknowledges nor denies the facts alleged by a party and still fails to explicitly express confirmation or denial after the judge has made adequate accounts and inquiries, it shall be deemed as confirming the said facts.

If any of the parties concerned entrusts agents to participate in the litigation, the affirmation of the agent shall be that of the parties concerned, however, with the exception of the affirmation of facts made by the agent without special authorisation that leads to the affirmation of the litigation allegations of the other party. If the party concerned is present but fails to deny the affirmation made by the agent thereof, the affirmation shall be deemed as the affirmation of the party concerned.

If any of the parties concerned withdraws its affirmation and obtains the approval of the other party prior to the end of court debate, or has adequate evidence to prove that its affirmation has been made due to threat or gross misunderstanding or the affirmation is not consistent with the facts, the party concerned shall not be exempted from the burden of proof.

Article 9 The parties concerned need not present evidence to prove the facts as mentioned below:

1. The facts that are known by all people;
2. Natural laws and theorems;
3. The facts that can be induced according to legal provisions or known facts or the rule of experience of daily life;
4. The facts affirmed in the judgement of the People's Court that has taken effect;
5. The facts affirmed in the award of the arbitration organ that has taken effect;
6. The facts that have been proved in the valid notary documents.

The facts as mentioned in items 1, 3, 4, 5, 6 of the preceding paragraph shall be excluded if they can be overthrown by contrary evidence of the parties concerned.

Article 10 When producing evidence to the People's Court, the parties concerned shall submit the original document or original thing. If the party concerned needs to preserve the original document or original thing of evidence or if it is difficult to submit the original document or original thing, a photocopy or reproduction that has been deemed as the original by the People's Court after verification may be submitted.

Article 11 If the evidence submitted by the parties concerned is formed beyond the territory of the People's Republic of China, the evidence shall be subject to the certification of the notarisation organ of the country concerned and shall be authenticated by the embassy of the People's Republic of China stationed in the said country, or shall be subject to the certification formalities as provided in the relevant treaties concluded between the People's Republic of China and the said country.

If the evidence submitted by the parties concerned is formed in Hong Kong, Macao or Taiwan, relevant formalities shall also be gone through.

Article 12 The foreign-language written documents or foreign-language specification materials submitted by the parties concerned shall be accompanied by the Chinese translation thereof.

Article 13 The People's Court may order the parties concerned to produce relevant evidence in relation to facts to which both parties consent, but which concern the interests of the state or the public interests of the society or the lawful rights and interests of other people.

Article 14 The parties concerned shall categorise and number the evidential materials submitted thereby, make a brief specification of the sources of the evidential materials, the object and content of proof, put on their signatures and mark the date of submission and submit as many copies according to the number of opposite parties concerned.

The People's Court shall, upon receiving the evidential materials submitted by the parties concerned, issue receipts, noting the title copies and pages of the evidence as well as the time when the evidence is received, and shall put signatures or official seals to the receipts.

II. THE INVESTIGATION UPON AND COLLECTION OF EVIDENCE BY THE PEOPLE's COURT

Article 15 The "evidence deemed as necessary by the People's Court for hearing the case" as mentioned in Article 64 of the Civil Procedure Law of the People's Republic of China shall refer to the following:

1. the facts that may injure the interest of the state, the public interest of the society or the lawful interest of other people;
2. the procedural matters that have nothing to do with the substantial dispute, such as adding parties concerned, suspending the litigation, ending the litigation, withdrawing, etc, on the basis of authority of the courts.

Article 16 Unless provided in Article 15 of the present Provisions, the investigation upon and collection of evidence by the People's Court shall be based on the application of the parties concerned.

Article 17 The parties concerned and the agent *ad litum* thereof may plead the People's Court to investigate upon and collect evidence, in any of the following circumstances:

1. the evidence applied for investigation and collection are the archive files kept by relevant organs of the state and must be accessed by the People's Court upon authority;
2. the materials concern state secrets, commercial secrets or personal privacy;
3. other materials cannot be collected by the parties concerned or the agents *ad litum* thereof due to objective reasons.

Article 18 To plead the People's Court for investigating upon and collecting evidence, the parties concerned and the agents *ad litum* thereof shall submit a written application.

The application shall clearly specify the basic information of the evidence, such as the name of the person investigated or the title of the entity, the dwelling place, the contents of the evidence to be investigated upon and collected, the reasons why the evidence needs to be investigated upon and collected by the People's Court and the facts to be proved.

Article 19 The application of the parties concerned and the agents *ad litum* thereof to the People's Court for investigating upon and collecting evidence shall be filed at no later than seven days prior to the expiration of the term for producing evidence.

If the People's Court refuses to approve the application of the parties concerned or the agents *ad litum* thereof, it shall serve a notice to them. The parties concerned and the agents *ad litum* thereof may file a written application to the People's Court that accepts the application for reconsideration, within three days after receiving the notice. The People's Court shall give a reply within five days after receiving the application for reconsideration.

Article 20 The written evidence to be investigated upon and collected by the investigators may be the original document or the reproduction or photocopy thereof which has been verified as correct. In the case of a reproduction or a photocopy, the sources and the collection of evidence shall be specified in the investigation notes.

Article 21 The physical evidence investigated upon and collected by the investigators shall be the original things. If it is indeed difficult for the person investigated to provide the original thing, he may provide a reproduction or a photo thereof. In the case of a reproduction or a photo, the investigation notes shall specify how the evidence was obtained.

Article 22 The investigators, who investigate upon and collect computer data or audio-visual materials such as sound recordings and visual recordings, etc, shall request the person investigated to provide the original carrier of the relevant data. If it is difficult to provide the original carrier, a reproduction may be provided. If the case of a reproduction, the investigators shall specify the source of the evidence and the process of its making in the investigation notes.

Article 23 The parties concerned who apply for the preservation of evidence as pursuant to Article 74 of the Civil Procedure Law of the People's Republic of China shall make the application at no later than 7 days prior to the term for producing evidence.

Where any party concerned applies for the preservation of evidence, the People's Court may demand the party to provide relevant guarantees.

In case there are different provisions in laws or judicial interpretations concerning the prior-litigation preservation of evidence, such provisions shall prevail.

Article 24 When preserving evidence, the People's Court may, according to the specific circumstances, adopt the ways of preservation like sealing up, detaining, taking photos, make sound recordings or visual recordings, making reproductions, authenticating, taking transcripts, etc.

When preserving evidence, the People's Court may demand the parties concerned or the agents *ad litum* thereof to be present at the scene.

Article 25 The parties concerned who apply for the preservation of evidence shall make the application within the time period for producing evidence and shall be in conformity with Article 27 of the present Provisions unless the parties concerned apply for re-authentication.

If any party concerned who bears the burden of proof for the matters that need to be authenticated fails to file an application for authentication within the time limit prescribed by the People's Court or fails to pay in advance the expenses for authentication or refuses to provide relevant materials without good reason so that the facts under dispute cannot be affirmed by way of a conclusion of authentication, it shall undertake the harmful consequences of inability to produce evidence.

Article 26 After the concerned party's application for authentication is approved by the People's Court, both parties shall determine, through negotiations, the eligible authentication institution and the authenticators. In case such consent cannot be reached through negotiations, the People's Court shall designate the authentication institution and authenticators.

Article 27 In case any party concerned refuses to accept the authentication conclusions made by the authentication institution designated by the People's Court and applies for re-authentication, the People's Court shall approve the application if there is evidence that can prove the existence of any of the following circumstances:

1. the authentication institution or authenticator does not have relevant qualifications;
2. the process of authentication is seriously illegal;
3. there is obviously inadequate evidence for the authentication conclusions;
4. other circumstance that, after cross-examinations, cannot be used as evidence.

If any defective authentication conclusion can be made up by way of supplementary authentications, re-authentications or supplementary cross-examinations, it shall not be re-authenticated.

Article 28 If the authentication conclusion is made by relevant departments upon the independent entrustment of any party concerned and the other party has adequate evidence to rebut and applies for re-authentication, such application shall be approved by the People's Court.

Article 29 The judges shall examine the reports of authentication made by the authenticators so as to confirm whether the following contents are included:

1. the name or title of the client, and the content of the entrusted authentication;
2. the materials for the entrusted authentication;
3. the basis of entrustment and the scientific or technological means adopted;
4. specifications of the authentication process;
5. a definite conclusion of authentication;
6. specifications of the qualifications of the authenticators;
7. the signatures of the authenticator and the official seal of the authentication institution.

Article 30 The People's Court shall take notes for the inquisition of the physical evidence on the spot of the scene, recording the time and venue of the inquisition, the inquisitors, the people at the scene, the process and result of the inquisition, etc, and have the notes signed or sealed by the people on the spot of the scene. If any map is drawn, the time and direction of the drawing, the name and identification of the drawers shall be specified in the map.

Article 31 In case excerpts are taken from the relevant documents or materials formulated by relevant departments, the excerpts shall specify the sources and be affixed with the cachet of the entity that has formulated or that keeps the documents or materials, and the person who makes the excerpt or other investigators shall put their signatures or seals on the excerpts.

The excerpts of the documents or materials shall be relatively complete in content and may not be made unscrupulously.

III. THE TIME PERIOD FOR PRODUCING EVIDENCES AND THE EXCHANGE OF EVIDENCES

Article 32 The defendant shall submit a written reply before the expiration of the prescribed time period, specifying his opinions concerning the facts and reasons on which the allegations of the plaintiff are based.

Article 33 The People's Court shall serve a notice for accepting the case and a notice for responding to the suit to the parties concerned, and at the same time serve a notice for producing evidence to them. The notice for producing evidence shall specify the principle and requirements of distributing the burden of proof, the circumstances under which the parties concerned may plead the People's Court to investigate upon and collect evidence, the time period prescribed by the People's Court for producing evidence and the harmful consequences for failure to produce evidence during the prescribed time period.

The time period for producing evidence may be agreed upon by the parties concerned and be affirmed by the People's Court.

If the time period for producing evidence is designated by the People's Court, the designated time period shall be not less than 30 days, starting from the next day when the parties concerned receive the notice of acceptance of the case and the notice for responding to the suit.

Article 34 The parties concerned shall submit evidential materials to the People's Court within the time period for producing evidence; in case any party fails to submit evidence during this time period, they shall be deemed as giving up the right to produce evidence.

The evidential materials submitted by the parties concerned beyond the time period shall not be cross-examined during the court hearing of the People's Court, unless both parties agree to have the evidence cross-examined.

In case any party changes or makes additional allegations or lodges a counterclaim, he shall do so prior to the expiration of the time period for producing evidence.

Article 35 If, in the process of litigation, the nature of the legal relations alleged by the parties concerned or the validity of the civil acts are inconsistent with the findings of fact made by the People's Court on the basis of the facts of the case, the provisions of Article 34 of the present Provisions shall not be applicable, and the People's Court shall inform the parties concerned that the allegations litigation may be changed.

Where the parties concerned change their allegations of litigation, the People's Court shall prescribe the time period for producing evidence anew.

Article 36 If any party concerned has real difficulty in producing evidence during the prescribed time period, it shall apply to the People's Court for extending the period during the time period for producing evidence. It may delay the producing of evidence upon the approval of the People's Court. If the party concerned still has difficulty in producing evidence during the extended time period, it may apply to the People's Court for another extension of the time period for producing evidence. It is up to the People's Court to decide whether to approve the application or not.

Article 37 The People's Court may, upon the application of the parties concerned, arrange for them to exchange evidence prior to holding a session of court hearing.

As for the cases for which there are plenty of evidence or which are difficult in nature, the People's Court shall arrange for the parties concerned to exchange evidence after the expiration of the time period for reply but prior to holding a session of court hearing.

Article 38 The time for exchanging evidence may be agreed upon by the parties concerned and be subject to the approval of the People's Court, or it may be determined by the People's Court.

Where the People's Court arranges for the parties concerned to exchange evidence, the day when evidence is exchanged is the day when the time period for producing evidence expires. Where the concerned parties' application for extending the time period for producing evidence is approved by the People's Court, the date for exchanging evidence shall also be extended accordingly.

Article 39 The exchange of evidence shall be conducted under the charge of the judges.

In the process of changing evidence, the judges shall record in the case files the facts and evidence to which the parties concerned have no objection. If they have any objection to any of the evidence, such evidence shall be recorded according to the classified facts that need to be proved, and shall specify the reasons for such objection. Through the exchange of evidence, the major issues about the disputes of both parties concerned are determined.

Article 40 Where any party concerned rebuts and submits new evidence after receiving the evidence exchanged by the other party, the People's Court shall inform them to exchange the new evidence at a designated time.

As a general rule, there shall not be more than two exchanges of evidence, unless the case is very important, difficult or very complicated in nature and the People's Court believes it necessary to have another exchange of evidence.

Article 41 The new evidence as provided in paragraph 1 of Article 125 of the Civil Procedure Law shall refer to any of the following circumstances:

1. the new evidence of the first instance hearing includes: the evidence newly found by the parties concerned after the expiration of the time period for producing evidence in the first instance court hearing; the evidence which the parties concerned cannot provide during the time period for producing evidence due to objective reasons and still cannot provide during the extended time period approved by the People's Court;
2. the new evidence of the second instance hearing includes: the evidence newly found after the first instance hearing is finished; the evidence which the parties concerned applied, prior to the expiration of the time period for producing evidence in the first instance hearing, to the People's Court for investigation and collection but failed to be approved but collected by the second instance court upon the application of the parties concerned which believes it necessary to grant approval to the application thereof.

Article 42 Where any party concerned submits new evidence in the first instance hearing, such evidence shall be submitted prior to the start of the first instance hearing or prior to the holding of a session.

Where any party concerned submits new evidence in the process of the second instance hearing, such evidence shall be submitted prior to the start of the second instance or prior to the holding of a session. Where it is not necessary to hold a session, they shall be submitted during the time period designated by the People's Court.

Article 43 Where the evidence submitted by the parties concerned, after the time period for producing evidence expires, is not new evidence, it shall not be accepted by the People's Court.

Where any evidence fails to be provided by the parties concerned during the extended time period upon the approval of the People's Court due to objective reasons and the failure to hear such evidence may result in injustice, such evidence may be deemed as new evidence.

Article 44 The term 'new evidence' as mentioned in Item 1, Paragraph 1 of Article 179 of the Civil Procedure Law shall refer to the evidence newly found after the court hearing of the original instance is finished.

Where any party concerned submits new evidence in the process of retrial, it shall submit such evidence when it applies for retrial.

Article 45 Where any party concerned produces new evidence, the People's Court shall inform the other party to put forward its opinions or produce evidence during a reasonable period of time.

Article 46 Where a case is remanded for a new trial or the judgement of which is changed during the second trial or retrial as a result that any party concerned failed to produce evidence during the prescribed time limit, the original judgement shall not be considered to be a wrong judgement. Where a party pleads that the other party that produces new evidence bear the reasonable expenses incurred from the travelling, loss of working time, the witness' appearance at court, litigation, etc, and the direct losses incurred therefrom, such pleadings shall be affirmed by the People's Court.

IV. CROSS-EXAMINATION

Article 47 Evidences shall be presented at court and be cross-examined by the parties concerned. Any evidence that has not been cross-examined shall not be rendered as the basis for affirming the facts of the case.

The evidence that is affirmed and recorded down in the case files in the process of exchanging evidence may, upon the statement of judges at court hearing, be taken as the basis for affirming the facts of the case.

Article 48 The evidence that involves the state secrets, business secrets, personal privacy or other evidence that shall be kept secret according to relevant provisions of law, may not be cross-examined in public at the court hearings.

Article 49 When cross-examining written evidence, physical evidence or audio-visual materials, the parties concerned shall be entitled to demand the other party to present the original document or original thing with the exception of any of the following circumstances:

1. it is indeed difficult to present the original document or original thing and it is approved by the People's Court to present the reproduction or photocopy thereof;
2. the original document or original thing is not existing but evidence shows that the production or photocopy is identical to the original document or original thing.

Article 50 When cross-examining evidence, the parties concerned shall concentrate on the genuineness, relativity, lawfulness of the evidence, and make interrogations, accounts and debates concerning the validity and forcefulness of the evidence.

Article 51 The cross-examination shall be conducted in the following sequence:

1. the plaintiff presents evidence, and the defendant or third party cross-examine;
2. the defendant presents evidence, and the plaintiff or third party cross-examine;
3. the third party presents evidence, and the defendant and the plaintiff cross-examine.

The evidence collected by the People's Court upon the application of the parties concerned shall be deemed as the evidence provided by the party that has made the application.

The People's Court shall present the evidence collected according to its functions, listen to the opinions of the parties concerned and make account of the investigation upon and collection of the evidence.

Article 52 Where there are more than two independent allegations, the parties concerned may present items of evidence one by one for cross-examination.

Article 53 Anyone who cannot express her or his mind may not be a witness.

Persons with no capacity for civil conduct or persons with limited capacity for civil conduct who are suitable for the facts to be affirmed in terms of age, intelligibility or mental health may be witnesses.

Article 54 The application of the parties concerned for having witnesses appear at court shall be filed 10 days before the time period for producing evidence expires and shall be subject to the approval of the People's Court.

In case the People's Court approves the application of the party concerned, it shall inform the witnesses involved, prior to the opening of the court hearing, that they shall testify on the basis of facts as well as the legal consequences of giving false testimony.

The reasonable expenses incurred from the witness' appearance at court for testimony shall be paid in advance by the party that provides the witnesses and be borne by the party that loses the suit.

Article 55 Witnesses shall appear in court to testify and shall accept the cross-examination of the parties concerned.

Where the witness appears at the exchange of evidence organised by the People's Court and makes statements as testimony, it may be deemed as having appeared in court as a witness.

Article 56 The phrase "the witness cannot appear in court due to real difficulties" as mentioned in Article 70 of the Civil Procedure Law shall refer to any of the following circumstances:

1. being unable to appear in court due to old age, debility or unable to travel;
2. being unable to leave due to the special post thereof;
3. being unable to appear in court due to long distance and inconvenient communications;
4. being unable to appear in court due to force majeure such as natural disaster, etc;
5. other special circumstances of being unable to appear in court.

In any of the circumstances as mentioned in the preceding paragraph, the witness may, upon the approval of the People's Court, bear witness by way of submitting a written testimony or audiovisual materials or by means of two-way audiovisual transmission technology.

Article 57 The witness that appears in court to bear witness shall objectively state the facts that he has felt in person. If the witness is deaf or mute, he may bear witness by other means.

When bearing witness, the witnesses may not use language of conjecture, induction or comments.

Article 58 The judges and the parties concerned may interrogate the witnesses. No witness may audit the court hearing. When interrogating a witness, no other witness may be present. When it thinks necessary, the People's Court may allow the witnesses to cross-examine each other.

Article 59 The authenticators shall appear in court to accept the interrogations of the parties concerned.

Where any authenticator is unable to appear in court due to special reasons, he may, upon the approval of the People's Court, answer the interrogations of the parties concerned in writing.

Article 60 The parties concerned may, upon the approval of the court, interrogate the witnesses, authenticators and investigators.

When interrogating the witnesses, authenticators or investigators, no menacing, insulting or misleading language or means may be used.

Article 61 The parties concerned may apply to the People's Court to have one or two persons with professional knowledge appear in court to make accounts of the specialised questions relating to the case. If the People's Court approves such applications, the relevant expenses shall be borne by the party that makes the application.

The judges and parties concerned may interrogate the persons with professional knowledge that appear in court.

The persons with professional knowledge may interrogate the authenticators.

Article 62 The court shall write down the interrogations of the parties into the case files, which shall be signed or sealed by the parties concerned after verfication.

V. THE VERIFICATION AND AFFIRMATION OF EVIDENCES

Article 63 The People's Court shall take the facts that can be proved by evidence as the basis of judgement according to law.

Article 64 The judges shall verify the evidence according to the legal procedures all-roundly and objectively, shall observe the provisions of law, follow the professional ethics of judges, use logical reasoning and daily life experience to make independent judgements concerning the validity and forcefulness of the evidence, and publicise the reasons and result of judgement.

Article 65 The judges may examine and verify a single piece of evidence from the following aspects:

1. whether the evidence is the original document or thing; whether the photocopy or reproduction is identical to the original document or original thing;
2. whether the evidence is relevant to the facts of the present case;
3. whether the forms and sources of the evidence is consistent with the legal provisions;
4. whether the evidence is real;
5. whether the witness or evidence provider has an interest in any party concerned.

Article 66 The judges shall make a comprehensive examination and judgement of all evidence from the degree of connection of each item of evidence with the fact of the case, and the relation between pieces of evidence.

Article 67 In the process of litigation, the evidence that has been affirmed through compromise, for the sake of reaching a mediation or agreement or reconciliation, may not be used by the parties concerned in later litigations as evidence unfavourable to the other party.

Article 68 The evidence obtained by infringing upon the lawful rights and interests of other people or by those means prohibited by law may not be taken as the basis for affirming the facts of the case.

Article 69 The following evidence may not be used independently as the basis for affirming the facts of a case:

1. the testimony of a minor, which is not suitable to his age or intelligence;
2. the testimony of a witness that has an interest in a party or the agent thereof;
3. doubtful audiovisual materials;
4. photocopies or reproductions that cannot be verified against the original document or original thing;
5. the testimony of a witness that fails to appear in court to bear witness.

Article 70 If any of the following evidence submitted by any party concerned is objected to by the other party, who does not have opposite evidence forceful enough to rebut them, the People's Court shall affirm the forcefulness thereof:

1. the original document of written evidence or the photocopy, photo, duplicate, or excerpt that is verified as identical with the original document of the written evidence;
2. the original thing of physical evidence or the reproduction, photo, or visual recordings that are verified as identical with the original thing of the physical evidence;
3. the audiovisual materials that are obtained by lawful means, without any doubt and are supported by other evidence or the reproductions of the audiovisual materials that have been verified as correct;
4. on-the-spot inquisition records about the physical evidence or the scene made according to legal procedures by the People's Court upon the application of a party concerned.

Article 71 The validity of the authentication conclusions made by the authentication institutions upon the entrustment of the People's Court shall be affirmed if the parties concerned do not have opposite evidence or reasons forceful enough to rebut them.

Article 72 If the evidence produced by one of the parties is affirmed by the other party or cannot be rebutted by the opposite evidence produced by the other party, the forcefulness thereof shall be affirmed by the People's Court.

If the evidence produced by one of the parties is objected to by the other party or is rebutted by the opposite evidence of the other party, and if the opposite evidence of the other party is affirmed, the forcefulness of the opposite evidence shall be affirmed.

Article 73 Where both parties concerned produce contradicting evidence to prove the same fact but neither has enough evidence to rebut the evidence of the other party, the People's Court shall determine which evidence is obviously more forceful than the other by taking the case into consideration, and shall affirm the evidence that is more forceful.

If the facts of a case are not identifiable due to the inability to determine the forcefulness of the evidence, the People's Court shall make a judgement according to the rules for distributing the burden of proof.

Article 74 In the process of litigation, the facts that are affirmed as unfavourable to a party itself and the evidence that has been affirmed by the parties concerned in the bill of complaint, bill of defence, statements of the parties concerned or the statement of the procurator shall be affirmed by the People's Court, unless the party concerned goes back on its own words and has adequate evidence to overthrow the said evidence.

Article 75 Where there is evidence to prove that a party possesses the evidence but refuses to provide it without good reasons and if the other party claims that the evidence is unfavourable to the possessor of the evidence, it may be deduced that the claim stands.

Article 76 Where a party makes statements for its allegations but fails to provide other relevant evidence, the allegations thereof shall not be affirmed, unless the other party so affirms.

Article 77 The forcefulness of more than one piece of evidence concerning the same fact may be determined by the People's Court according to the following principles:

1. the documents formulated by state organs or social bodies according to their respective functions are, as a general rule, more forceful than other written evidence;
2. the physical evidence, archive files, authentication conclusions, on-the-spot inquisition recordings and the written evidence that has been notarised or registered are, as a general rule, more forceful than other written evidence, audiovisual materials and testimonies;
3. the original evidence is, as a general rule, more forceful than the derivative evidence;
4. direct evidence is, as a general rule, more forceful than indirect evidence;
5. the testimony of a witness that is favourable to the party concerned who is a relation thereof or with whom the party concerned is in other close relations are, as a general rule, less forceful than the testimony of other witnesses.

Article 78 When affirming the testimony of a witness, the People's Court may decide on the basis of comprehensive analysis of the intelligence, moral character, knowledge, experience, legal consciousness, professional abilities, etc, of the witnesses.

Article 79 The People's Court shall specify in the judgements the reasons why evidence is adopted.

The reasons why evidence, to which the parties concerned have no objection, is adopted need not be specified in the judgements.

VI. OTHER PROVISIONS

Article 80 The lawful rights and interests of the witnesses, authenticators and inquisitors shall be protected.

In case any party concerned or other participant of litigation counterfeits or destroys evidence, or produces false evidence, or prevents any witness from bearing witness, or instigates or bribes or threatens other people to give false testimonies, or takes revenge against any witness, authenticator or inquisitor, it shall be dealt with as pursuant to Article 102 of the Civil Procedure Law.

Article 81 The cases heard by the People's Court on the basis of simplified procedures shall not be confined to the provisions of Article 32, Paragraph 3 of Article 33 and Article 79 of the present Provisions.

Article 82 Where any of the judicial interpretations made by this court in the past contradicts the present Provisions, the present Provisions shall prevail.

Article 83 The present Provisions shall be implemented as of 1 April 2002. The present Provisions shall not be applicable to the cases of first instance, second instance or retrial that have not been ended by 1 April 2002.

As for the civil cases that have been heard prior to the implementation of the present Provisions, if any party requests for retrial on the ground that the hearing of the case was against the present Provisions, such request shall not be supported by the People's Court.

The civil cases accepted for retrial after the implementation of the present Provisions and the People's Court hears the cases on the basis of the provisions of Article 184 of the Civil Procedure Law, the present Provisions shall apply.

PROVISIONAL ADMINISTRATIVE RULES FOR REGISTRATION OF DOMAIN NAMES ON CHINA'S INTERNET

Note: This English version is only for reference. Any official interpretation should be based on the original Chinese version.

CHAPTER 1 GENERAL PROVISIONS

Article 1 These Administrative Rules are formulated in order to ensure and promote the development of China's internet and to strengthen the administration of China's internet domain name system. All of the domain name registrations within China shall be carried out in accordance with these Administrative Rules.

Article 2 The Office of the State Council's Steering Committee on Informatisation ("State Council's Informatisation Office") is the official Chinese agency responsible for China's internet domain name system. These responsibilities include the following:

1. formulate policies and procedures to establish, allocate and administer China's internet domain names;
2. select, authorise and cancel top-level and second-level domain names; and
3. supervise and monitor the registration of domain names at each level.

Article 3 The Steering Committee of the China Internet Network Information Center ("CNNIC") shall assist the State Council's Informatisation Office with the administration of China's internet domain name system.

Article 4 With authorisation from, and under the leadership of, the State Council's Informatisation Office, the CNNIC shall be the day-to-day administrative organisation of the CNNIC Steering Committee. The CNNIC shall formulate the Detailed Implementation Rules for the Registration of Domain Names on China's internet and be responsible for administration and registration of China's top-level domain name CN.

Article 5 The administrators of domain names at and below the third level shall be determined by means of authorisation granted from the next highest adjacent level. The administrators of domain names at each level shall be responsible for registration of domain names one level below their level. Second-level domain name administrators must regularly submit registration statements of their third-level domain names to CNNIC.

Article 6 Applicants for domain name registration must be organisations that have been registered according to law and can independently assume civil liability.

CHAPTER 2 STRUCTURE OF THE DOMAIN NAME SYSTEM OF CHINA's INTERNET

Article 7 The top-level domain name officially registered by China with InterNIC and being operated by China is CN. The domain names at each level below the top level CN shall be established according to a tree/hierarchy structure.

Article 8 Second-level domain names of China's internet are divided into category domain names and administrative division domain names.

There are six category domain names, namely: AC for scientific research institutions; COM for enterprises in the fields of industry, commerce, finance, etc; EDU for educational institutions; GOV for government agencies; NET for information centres (NICs) and operation centers (NOCs) of interconnecting and accessing networks; and ORG for all kinds of non-profit organisations.

There are 34 administrative division domain names assigned for China's provinces, autonomous regions and municipalities directly under the central government, namely: BJ (Beijing Municipality); SH (Shanghai Municipality); TJ (Tianjin Municipality); CQ (Chongqing Municipality); HE (Hebei Province); SX (Shanxi Province); NM (Inner Mongolia Autonomous Region); LN (Liaoning Province); JL (Jilin Province); HL (Heilongjiang Province); JS (Jiangsu Province);

ZJ (Zhejiang Province); AH (Anhui Province); FJ (Fujian Province); JX (Jiangxi Province); SD (Shandong Province); HA (Henan Province); HB (Hubei Province); HN (Hunan Province); GD (Guangdong Province); GX (Guangxi Zhuang Autonomous Region); HI (Hainan Province); SC (Sichuan Province); GZ (Guizhou Province); YN (Yunnan Province); XZ (Tibet Autonomous Region); SN (Shaanxi Province); GS (Gansu Province); QH (Qinghai Province); NX (Ningxia Hui Autonomous Region); XJ (Xinjiang Uygur Autonomous Region); TW (Taiwan); HK (Hong Kong); MO (Macao).

Article 9 The proposal for addition, cancellation or modification of second-level domain names shall be filed by the CNNIC Steering Committee and promulgated after approval by the State Council's Informatisation Office.

Article 10 Naming principles for third-level domains:

1. third-level domain names shall be composed of letters (A–Z, a–z, not case-sensitive), digits (0–9) and the hyphen (-). Each level of the domain name shall be separated by a dot (.). Any third-level domain name may not be longer than 20 characters;
2. it is recommended that the applicant's English names (or abbreviations thereof) or Chinese names romanised according to the pinyin system (or abbreviations thereof) be used as third-level domain names, so as to preserve their clarity and simplicity.

Article 11 Restrictions for the naming of domains at and below the third level:

1. without official approval from the relevant state authorities, domain names including words such as CHINA, CHINESE, CN, NATIONAL, etc, may not be used;
2. well-known names of other countries or regions, foreign location names and names of international organisations may not be used;
3. without approval from the local government at relevant levels, full or abbreviated names of administrative divisions at and above county level may not be used;
4. classifications of industries or generic names of goods may not be used;
5. enterprise names or trademark names already registered in China by others may not be used;
6. names that are harmful to the interests of the state, society or the public may not be used.

CHAPTER 3 APPLICATION FOR DOMAIN NAME REGISTRATION

Article 12 Applicants shall have the right to select the name for the domain one level higher. Organisations that apply for a domain name from the category domain names shall apply under the second-level domain name corresponding to the nature of their organisations.

Article 13 Applications for domain name registration must submit to the domain name administrator one level higher.

Article 14 To apply for domain name registration, the following conditions must be met:

1. the domain name application for registration conforms to all the provisions hereof;
2. the applicant's primary domain name server is operated within China and provides continuous service for the domain name; and
3. the applicant designates an administrative contact and a technical contact respectively responsible for the administration and the operation of the domain name server at the requested level.

Article 15 When applying for domain name registration, the following documents and certificates shall be submitted:

1. an application form for domain name registration;
2. a formal letter of request from the organisation applying for domain name registration;
3. a photo identification card of the individual filing the application; and
4. a photocopy of the document stating that the organisation has been registered according to law.

Article 16 The application form for domain name registration shall contain at least the following particulars: the name of the organisation (including its Chinese name and its full and abbreviated English name and Chinese name romanised according to the pinyin system), the location of the organisation, the individual responsible for the organisation, the administrative contact and technical contact responsible for the domain name, the applicant's information, the correspondence address, the telephone number, the electronic mail address, the names and locations of the primary and secondary domain name servers, the network address, the models and operating systems of the servers, the domain name proposed to be registered, the reason and purpose, and other particulars.

Article 17 The name of the applicant shall be consistent with the name on the seal and relevant certificates.

Article 18 Applications for registration may be delivered by electronic mail, facsimile, post, etc. All the other documents specified in Article 15 shall be submitted by any means within 30 days thereafter. The date of an application shall be the date on which the first application for registration is received. If all the documents specified in Article 15 are not received within 30 days, the application shall automatically be null and void.

Article 19 Responsibilities of the applicant:

1. the applicant must observe China's laws and regulations of the internet;
2. the applicant shall be responsible for the domain name selected by him / her;
3. the applicant shall warrant that the contents of his / her application documents are true and accurate and, to the best of his / her knowledge, that registration of the domain name selected will not harm the interests of any third party; the applicant shall warrant that registration of the domain name is not for any illegal purpose; and
4. upon approval of the application, the applicant will become the administrator of the domain name registered and must administer and operate the domain name in accordance with these Administrative Rules.

CHAPTER 4 EXAMINATION AND APPROVAL OF DOMAIN NAME REGISTRATION

Article 20 Domain name registration shall be conducted on a first-come first-served basis. Domain name reservations shall not be accepted.

Article 21 The domain name administrator shall complete the approval of registration, make the name operational and issue a domain name registration certificate within 10 working days after receiving the documents specified in Article 15, if the domain name requested and the documents submitted conform to the provisions of these Administrative Rules.

Article 22 The domain name administrator shall notify the applicant within 10 working days after receiving the documents specified in Article 15, if the domain name requested or the documents submitted do not conform to the provisions of these Administrative Rules. The applicant will have 30 days to revise and resubmit the application. The application shall automatically be null and void, if the applicant does not reply within 30 days or if the documents resubmitted do not comply with the provisions hereof.

Article 23 The administrators of domain names at each level shall not be responsible for checking inquiries with the State Administration Agency for industry and commerce, and the agencies for trademark administration as to whether or not a user's domain name is in conflict with a registered trademark, enterprise name, or is harmful to the interests of any third party. The applicant shall be responsible for handling any dispute arising from such a conflict and bearing the legal liability. Where a third-level domain name is identical to a trademark or enterprise name registered in China but the registered domain name is not owned by the holder of the registered trademark or enterprise name, the holder of the domain name may continue using its domain name if the holder of the registered trademark or enterprise name has not filed an opposition. If the holder of the registered trademark or enterprise name files an opposition, the administrators of domain names at each level shall retain the domain name service for the holder of the domain name for 30 days from the date on which it is confirmed that the opponent owns the registered trademark rights or enterprise name rights, and the domain name service shall automatically cease after 30 days. Domain name administrators are not responsible for any legal liability or economic disputes.

CHAPTER 5 CHANGE AND CANCELLATION OF REGISTERED DOMAIN NAMES

Article 24 Registered domain names may be changed or cancelled, but are not permitted to be transferred, sold or purchased.

Article 25 To apply for change of a registered domain name or other registration particulars, the applicant shall submit a domain name registration form and the documents specified in Article 15 as well as the original domain name registration certificate.

Following verification and approval by the domain name administrator, the original domain name registration certificate shall be annotated and returned, and the domain name shall be made accessible within 10 working days.

Article 26 To apply for the cancellation of a registered domain name, the applicant shall submit a domain name registration form, the documents specified in Article 15, and return the original domain name registration certificate. Following verification and approval by the domain name registrar, operation of the domain name shall cease and the domain name registration certificate shall be revoked.

Article 27 An annual inspection shall be implemented for registered domain names. The domain name administrators at each level shall be responsible for the implementation of the inspection.

CHAPTER 6 SUPPLEMENTARY PROVISIONS

Article 28 Servers located in China and connected to China's internet, whose registered top-level domain names are not CN, must report and file a record with the CNNIC.

Article 29 An administrative fee shall be paid when registering domain names and handling other matters concerning domain names. The detailed fee structure shall be determined separately.

Article 30 The State Council's Informatisation Office shall be responsible for the interpretation of these Administrative Rules.

Article 31 These Administrative Rules shall be implemented from the date of ratification.

DETAILED IMPLEMENTATION RULES FOR REGISTRATION OF DOMAIN NAMES ON CHINA'S INTERNET

Note: This English version is only for reference. Any official interpretation should be based on the original Chinese version.

CHAPTER 1 GENERAL PROVISIONS

Article 1 These Implementation Rules are formulated in accordance with the Provisional Administrative Rules of Registration of Domain Names on China's internet (the Administrative Rules), in order to implement the registration and the operation of third-level domain names of China's internet.

Article 2 Applicants for domain name registration must be organisations that have been registered according to law and can independently assume civil liability. Individuals may not apply for domain name registration.

Article 3 The WWW server installed at the China Internet Network Information Centre ("CNNIC") (www.cnnic.net.cn) shall be used to announce information on domain name registrations and other relevant matters.

CHAPTER 2 APPLICATION FOR EXAMINATION AND APPROVAL OF DOMAIN NAME REGISTRATION

Article 4 Applicants for registration of third-level domain names ("Applicants") shall satisfy the conditions set forth in Article 14 of the Administrative Rules.

Article 5 When registering third-level domain names, Applicants shall submit all the documents specified in Article 15 of the Administrative Rules. Enterprises applying for domain name registration under COM must submit a photocopy of their business license registered in China. Government authorities applying for domain name registration under GOV must submit a photocopy of the approval document of the corresponding department in charge. Organisations applying for domain name registration under ORG must submit a photocopy of the approval document of the corresponding department in charge. Applicants may obtain Application Forms for Domain Name Registration (see Annex 1) via the WWW, by electronic mail, by facsimile, by post, in person, etc.

Article 6 Applicants may submit their applications for registration via the WWW, by electronic mail, by facsimile, by post, in person, etc. All the documents required for domain name registration shall be delivered within 30 days thereafter. The date of an application shall be the date on which the first application for registration is received. If any of the documents required for domain name registration are not received by the CNNIC within 30 days, the application shall automatically be null and void.

Article 7 The Applicant shall be responsible for the domain name selected. When completing and submitting the application form for domain name registration, the Applicant shall warrant that the contents thereof are true and that registration of the domain name selected will not harm the interests of any third party. The Applicant must warrant that registration of her or his domain name is not for any illegal purpose. The name of the Applicant shall be consistent with the name on the seal and relevant certificates.

Article 8 A power of attorney shall be issued if the Applicant appoints an agent to apply for and handle domain name registration or handle other domain name matters. The power of attorney shall specify the substance and authority of agency. When the agent handles domain name registration, he shall submit the power of attorney, the domain name registration documents of his principal, a letter of introduction from the unit of the agent and a photocopy of the identity card of the person handling the application.

Article 9 Whether the Applicant applies for domain name registration herself or himself or through an appointed agent, the domain name administrative contact must be a full member of the organisation applying for the domain name.

Article 10 The CNNIC shall examine accepted applications in accordance with the Administrative Rules. It shall approve any application conforming to the relevant provisions of the Administrative Rules. The CNNIC shall, within 10 working days, complete registration, issue a Domain Name Registration Certificate to the Applicant and make an announcement through the WWW. If the CNNIC considers that the contents of an application for domain name registration require revision, it shall issue an Opinion Upon Examination and make an announcement through the WWW. The Applicant shall make the revisions within 30 days from the date of its first application for registration. If it does not make revisions, or if it makes revisions after expiration of the time limit, or if the revised contents still do not conform to the relevant provisions of the Administrative Rules, the application shall be rejected and the Applicant shall be issued a Notice of Rejection. An announcement of the rejection shall be made through the WWW.

In order to avoid disputes that might arise from non-receipt by the Applicant of the Opinion Upon Examination or the Notice of Rejection, the Applicant shall use the internet to check the status of its domain name registration 10 working days after submitting the documents.

CHAPTER 3 CHANGE AND CANCELLATION OF REGISTERED DOMAIN NAMES AND RULINGS ON DISPUTES

Article 11 To apply for the change of registration of a registered domain name or other registered particulars, the Applicant shall submit the documents specified in Article 15 of the Administrative Rules and return the original Domain Name Registration Certificate. Following the verification and approval by the CNNIC, the original Domain Name Registration Certificate shall be annotated and returned, and the domain name shall be made operational.

Article 12 To apply for the cancellation of a registered domain name, the Applicant shall submit the documents specified in Article 15 of the Administrative Rules and return the original Domain Name Registration Certificate. Following the verification and approval by the CNNIC, operation of the domain name shall cease and the Domain Name Registration Certificate shall be revoked.

Article 13 In the event of a dispute between a domain name registrant and a third party arising from the registration or use of the domain name, the CNNIC shall not act as a mediator and the domain name registrant itself shall be responsible for handling the dispute and bearing the legal liability. Where a third-level domain name is identical to a trademark or enterprise name registered in China, but the registered domain name is not owned by the holder of the registered trademark or enterprise name, the domain name registrant may continue using its domain name if the holder of the registered trademark or enterprise name has not filed an opposition. If the holder of the registered trademark or enterprise name files an opposition, the CNNIC shall retain domain name service for the holder of the domain name for 30 days from the date on which it is confirmed that the opponent owns the registered trademark rights or enterprise name rights, and the domain name service shall automatically cease after 30 days. The CNNIC shall not be responsible for any legal liability or economic dispute.

CHAPTER 4 ADMINISTRATION OF, AND STANDARDS FOR, REGISTERED DOMAIN NAMES

Article 14 The CNNIC shall implement an annual inspection of registered domain names ("Annual Inspection"), in order to ensure correct, standardised and effective operation of the domain name system. For provisions concerning the date of Annual Inspection, see Article 19.

Article 15 At the time of Annual Inspection, the domain name registrant shall complete and submit to the CNNIC the Annual Inspection form online through the WWW. In event of problems, it may contact the CNNIC by electronic mail.

Article 16 At the time of Annual Inspection, if a domain name or particulars of a domain name registration that were registered prior to the ratification of the Administrative Rules does not conform to current regulations, the CNNIC shall suggest that the domain name registrant make corrections or supplement the necessary approval documents.

Article 17 If anyone violates Article 24 of the Administrative Rules by transferring, selling or purchasing a registered domain name, the CNNIC shall cancel the domain name and suspend the operation of all her or his registered domain names for six months.

Article 18 In accordance with Article 8 of the Administrative Rules, the original second-level domain names CO.CN, GO.CN, OR.CN, EB.CN, EN.CN, HA.CN and CANET.CN ("Old Domain Names") shall be changed to COM.CN, GOV.CN, ORG.CN, HE.CN, HA.CN and HI.CN ("New Domain Names"), respectively, within 180 days after the date of the ratification of the Administrative Rules. Third-level domain names shall no longer be registered under the Old Domain Names from the date of the ratification of Administrative Rules. Where third-level domain names have already been registered under CO.CN, GO.CN, OR.CN, EB.CN, EN.CN or HA.CN, the CNNIC will register identical third-level domain names under the corresponding New Domain Names. Where third-level domain names have already been registered under CANET.CN, the users may select a second-level domain name from among those set forth in Article 8 of the Administrative Rules and register the same with the CNNIC. During the said 180-day transition period, the CNNIC will permit concurrent use of New and Old Domain Names. After the 180-day period, the operation of Old Domain Names will cease.

CHAPTER 5 DOMAIN NAME ADMINISTRATIVE FEES

Article 19 In accordance with Article 29 of the Administrative Rules and the principle of being non-profit-seeking and providing remunerated services, the CNNIC shall charge annual administrative fees for registered domain names (covering registration, change and cancellation of domain names; annual administrative fees are not refundable upon cancellation). The annual fee is RMB300 per registered third-level domain name.

1. with respect to domain names registered on or after 1 July 1997, the fee for the first year shall be paid at the time of registration, and each anniversary of such date shall be the date for Annual Inspection and date for fee payment;
2. with respect to domain names registered on or before 30 June 1997, the fee for the first year shall be paid on 1 July 1997, and 1 July of each subsequent year shall be the date for Annual Inspection and date for fee payment;
3. domain names for which Annual Inspection and fee payment are completed within 30 days from the date for Annual Inspection and date for fee payment shall be regarded as valid. The operation of domain names for which Annual Inspection and fee payment are not completed within 30 days from the date for Annual Inspection and date for fee payment shall be suspended. Domain

names for which Annual Inspection and fee payment are not completed within 60 days from the date for Annual Inspection and date for fee payment shall be cancelled.

CHAPTER 6 CONTACT METHODS

Article 20 Applicants who wish to register a third-level domain name under the second level domain name EDU shall contact the China Education and Research Network Information Centre. The contact methods are:

Email: hostmaster@nic.edu.cn
Homepage: www.nic.edu.cn/rs/templates
Telephone: (+86 10) 6278 4049
Facsimile: (+86 10) 6278 5933
Postal address: Room 224, Main Central Building, Qinghua University, Beijing 100084

Applicants who wish to register a third-level domain name under a second level domain name other than EDU shall contact CNNIC. The contact methods are:

Email: hostmaster@cnnic.net.cn
Homepage: www.cnnic.net.cn
Telephone: (+86 10) 6253 3515, (+86 10) 6261 9750
Facsimile: (+86 10) 6255 9892
Postal address: Mailbox 349, Beijing 100080, Attn.: CNNIC
Visiting address: 4 South Fourth Street, Zhongguancun, Beijing (Computer Network Information Center of the Chinese Academy of Sciences)

CHAPTER 7 SUPPLEMENTARY PROVISIONS

Article 21 Those that conform to the provisions of Article 28 of the Administrative Rules must report and file a record with the CNNIC. When filing a record, a Record Form for a Domain Name Registered Abroad (see Annex 2) may be obtained from CNNIC's WWW server. The said form shall be truthfully completed and be returned to the CNNIC after the official seal has been affixed thereto.

Article 22 In the absence of an express statement of the Applicant to the contrary, all information entered in the Applicant's Application

Form for Domain Name Registration will be recorded by the CNNIC into a publicly accessible database as one of the directory services provided by the CNNIC to internet users.

Article 23 Foreign enterprises or institutions applying for registration of a domain name under the second-level domain name of the CN must have a branch or an office in China. Their primary domain name server must be located in China.

EXPLANATION OF THE SUPREME PEOPLE'S COURT ON SEVERAL ISSUES CONCERNING THE APPLICATION OF THE LAW TO THE TRIAL OF CIVIL DISPUTE CASES INVOLVING COMPUTER NETWORK DOMAIN NAMES

(Adopted at the 1182nd Meeting of the Adjudication Commission of the Supreme People's Court on 26 June 2001. Issued by the Supreme People's Court with document reference Fa Shi [2001] No 24 on 17 July 2001. Effective from 24 July 2001.)

In accordance with laws such as the General Provisions of the Civil Code of the People's Republic of China (the "General Provisions of the Civil Code"), the Law of the People's Republic of China against Unfair Competition (the "Law against Unfair Competition") and the Civil Procedure Code of the People's Republic of China (the "Civil Procedure Code"), we hereby give the following explanation in order to cause civil dispute cases concerning the registration and / or use, etc, of computer network domain names ("Domain Name Dispute Cases") to be tried correctly.

Article 1 Where a party to a civil dispute concerning the registration and / or use, etc, of a domain name files a suit with a People's Court, the People's Court should accept the case if, after examination, it finds the same to accord with Article 108 of the Civil Procedure Code.

Article 2 Intermediate People's Courts of the place of the infringement or the place of the defendant's domicile shall have jurisdiction over infringement disputes involving domain names. Where the place of the infringement and the place of the defendant's domicile are difficult to determine, the location of the equipment, such as a computer terminal, through which the plaintiff discovered the domain name may be regarded as the place of the infringement.

Foreign-related Domain Name Disputes Cases include cases in which one or both of the parties are foreigners, stateless persons, foreign enterprises or organisations or international organisations, or in which the domain name in question is registered abroad. For foreign-related Domain Name Disputes Cases occurring within the territory of the People's Republic of China, jurisdiction shall be determined according to the provisions of Section 4 of the Civil Procedure Code.

Article 3 The cause of action for Domain Name Disputes Cases shall be determined in accordance with the character of the legal relationship of the dispute between the parties. The cause of action shall commence with the phrase "computer network domain name". If the character of the legal relationship of the dispute is difficult to determine, it may be generally referred to as a "computer network domain name dispute".

Article 4 When trying a Domain Name Disputes Case, the People's Court should determine that the defendant's registration and / or use, etc, of a domain name constitutes infringement or unfair competition if each of the following criteria is satisfied:

1. the civil rights or interests for which the plaintiff seeks protection are legitimate and effective;
2. the defendant's domain name or its main part constitutes a copy, imitation, translation or transliteration of a well-known trademark of the plaintiff; or it is identical with or similar to a registered trademark, domain name, etc, of the plaintiff to a degree sufficient to cause mistaken identification among the relevant public;
3. the defendant does not enjoy rights or interests to the domain name or its main part, and has no justification to register and / or use the domain name; and
4. the defendant's registration and / or use of the domain name is in bad faith.

Article 5 The People's Court should determine that the defendant acted in bad faith if his conduct is shown to constitute any one of the following:

1. for commercial purposes, registering another's well-known trademark as a domain name;

2. for commercial purposes, registering and / or using a domain name that is the same as or similar to the plaintiff's registered trademark, domain name, etc, and deliberately causing confusion with the products and/or services provided by the plaintiff or with the plaintiff's website in order to mislead network users into accessing one's own website or another online site;
3. having offered to sell, lease or otherwise transfer the domain name at a high price and obtained unfair benefits;
4. the defendant neither uses nor intends to use the domain name after registration, but intentionally prevents the registration of the domain name by the person holding rights therein;
5. other situations involving bad faith.

If the defendant produces evidence that the domain name he owns has gained a certain degree of notoriety before the dispute occurred, and is distinct from the plaintiff's registered trademarks, domain names, etc, or if there are other circumstances sufficient to show that he has not acted in bad faith, the People's Court is not required to determine that the defendant acted in bad faith.

Article 6 When trying a Domain Name Disputes Case, the People's Court may determine according to law whether a registered trademark involved is well-known or not based on a party's request and the actual circumstances of the case.

Article 7 When trying a Domain Name Disputes Case that satisfies the criteria set forth in Article 4 hereof and, according to the relevant laws, constitutes infringement, the People's Court should apply the stipulations of the corresponding laws. If the case constitutes unfair competition, the People's Court may apply Article 4 of the General Provisions of the Civil Code and the first paragraph of Article 2 of the Law against Unfair Competition.

Foreign-related domain name dispute cases should be handled according to the relevant provisions of Chapter 8 of the Civil Procedure Code.

Article 8 Once the People's Court determines that conduct such as the registration and / or use of a domain name constitutes infringement or unfair competition, it may order the defendant to cease the infringement and / or deregister the domain name, or, at the request of the plaintiff, order that the domain name be registered and used by the plaintiff. If the said conduct has caused actual damage to the holder of the rights, the People's Court may order the defendant to pay damages.

CIETAC SUPPLEMENTAL RULES TO CNNIC DOMAIN NAME DISPUTE RESOLUTION POLICY ("THE SUPPLEMENTAL RULES")

(in effect as of 30 September 2002)

Article 1 – Definitions

1. "The Rules" refer to the Rules for China Internet Network Information Centre Domain Name Dispute Resolution Policy as approved and implemented by CNNIC on 30 September 2002.
2. "The Policy" refers to China Internet Network Information Centre Domain Name Dispute Resolution Policy as approved and implemented by CNNIC on 30 September 2002.
3. "The Supplemental Rules" mean these Rules which are Supplemental to the Policy and are adopted by China International Economic and Trade Arbitration Commission ("CIETAC") to assess complaints regarding domain name dispute and administer proceedings in conformity with "the Rules" and where required supplement them.
4. "The Centre" refers to The Domain Name Dispute Resolution Centre of China International Economic and Trade Arbitration Commission (CIETAC).
5. Any terms defined in the Rules shall have the same meaning in these Supplemental Rules.

Article 2 – Scope

1. The Supplemental Rules are to be read and used in connection with the Policy and the Rules.
2. Any Complaint submitted to the Centre shall abide by the Policy, the Rules and the Supplemental Rules.

Article 3 Communications between Parties and the Centre

1. Unless otherwise agreed beforehand with the Centre, any submission that may or is required to be made to the Centre pursuant to the Rules, the Policy and the Supplemental Rules may be made:
   (a) by telecopy or facsimile, with a confirmation of transmission; or
   (b) by postal or courier service, with postage pre-paid and documentary verification of service and, for the purposes of this sub-rule, double registered post shall constitute good service; or
   (c) electronically via the internet, provided that a record of its transmission is available. For any electronic communications to the Centre, the email address domain@cietac.org shall be used.
2. All documentation submitted in hard copy form to the Centre by the Parties shall be submitted in two (in case of one-member Panel) or four sets (in case of three-member Panel) together with the original copy marked 'Original'.
3. The Centre shall maintain an archive of all communications received or required to be made under the Rules and the Supplemental Rules for a period of one year from the date of filing the initial Complaint from the Complainant. Subsequently, all communications and documentation received shall be destroyed.

Article 4 Communications Between Parties and the Panel

1. Where a Party intends to send any communications that are required to be made to the Panel members, it shall be addressed through the case administrator designated by the Centre. No party may have any unilateral communications with any member of the Panel.
2. Where a Party sends any communications to the Centre, it shall at the same time send a copy to the other Party with verification of service lodged with the Centre.
3. The Parties may communicate with the Centre by phone, fax, email, or the ordinary postal or courier service. Any communication by post shall be deemed to be received in four days after posting in the case of local mail or in seven days in respect of overseas mail. While any instantaneous means of communications shall be deemed to be received on the same day as transmitted.

Article 5 – The Complaint

1. The Complaint filed by the Complainant to the Centre shall be submitted in hard copy and (except to the extent not available for annexes) in electronic form, and the uniform standard format set out by the Centre shall be adopted.
2. The Complainant shall be required to send its Complaint to the Centre in accordance with the Complainant Filing Guidelines, using Form C under the cover of the Complaint Transmittal Coversheet ("CTC") which are set out and posted on the Centre's Web site http://dndrc.cietac.org.
3. In accordance with Article 4 and Article 12(12) of the Rules, the Complainant shall provide a copy of the Complaint to the Respondent and the concerned Registrars at the same time as it submits its Complaint to the Centre.
4. In accordance with Article 14 of the Rules, the Centre shall forward the Complaint to the Respondent(s) within three calendar days following receipt of the fixed initial fee by the Complainant.
5. The case proceedings shall be deemed to have commenced on the date that the Centre forwards the Complaint to the Respondent(s).

Article 6 – The Response

1. Within 20 days of the date of commencement of the case proceedings, the Respondent shall submit a Response to the Centre.
2. The Response submitted by the Respondent to the Centre shall be submitted in hard copy and (except to the extent not available for annexes) in electronic form, and the uniform standard format set out by the Centre shall be adopted.
3. The Respondent shall be required to send its Response to the Centre in accordance with the Response Filing Guidelines, using Form R which is set out and posted on the Centre's Web site http://dndrc.cietac.org.
4. In accordance with Article 4 and Article 18(7) of the Rules, the Respondent shall provide a copy of the Response to the concerned Complainant(s).

Article 7 – The Centre's Compliance Review

1. The Centre shall, within three calendar days of acknowledging the Complaint, examine the Complaint for compliance with the Policy, the Rules and the Supplemental Rules.

2. If in compliance, the Centre shall forward the copy of the Complaint to the Respondent, in the manner prescribed by the Rules, within three calendar days following receipt of the fees to be paid by the Complainant in accordance with the Rules.
3. If the Centre finds the Complaint to be administratively deficient, it shall promptly notify the Complainant of the nature of the deficiencies identified. The Complainant shall remedy any deficiencies identified by the Centre within five calendar days. Failing this, the case proceedings shall be deemed withdrawn in accordance with Article 14 of the Rules.

Article 8 – Appointment of Panelist(s)

The Centre shall maintain and publish a list of Panelist(s) and their qualifications. Any Party may refer to the Centre's Web site at http://dndrc.cietac.org for details. For the panelist(s) appointment to a specific case, the Centre shall appoint suitable person(s) from the list, having regard to:

(a) the nature of the dispute;
(b) the availability of the Panelist(s);
(c) the identity of the Parties;
(d) the independence and impartiality of the Panelist(s);
(e) any stipulation in the relevant Registration Agreement.

Article 9 – Impartiality and Independence

1. The Panelist(s) shall be and remain at all times wholly independent and impartial, and shall not act as advocate for any Party during the proceedings.
2. Prior to the appointment, any proposed Panelist(s) shall declare in writing to the Parties and the Centre any circumstances that are likely to create an impression of bias or prevent a prompt resolution of the dispute between the Parties. Except by consent of the Parties, no person shall serve as a Panelist(s) in any dispute in which that person has any interest, which, if a Party knew of it, might lead him/her to think that the Panelist(s) might be biased.
3. After a Panelist(s) has been appointed but before rendering a decision, a Panelist(s) dies, is unable to act, or refuses to act, the Centre will, upon request by either Party, appoint a replacement Panelist(s).

Article 10 – Panel Decision

1. A Panel shall make its decision in electronic form and in hard copy and state the reasons upon which the decision is based. The

decision shall be dated and signed by the Panellist(s) according to the requirements set forth in Article 40 of the Rules.

2. The Panel shall forward its decision to the Centre within 14 days of its appointment. In exceptional circumstances, the Centre may extend the time limit as required for the Panel to forward its Decision.

Article 11 – Publication of Panel Decision

The Centre shall within three calendar days of its receipt of a decision from the Panelist(s) submit the decision to the Parties, the concerned Registrar(s) and CNNIC. Unless the Panel determines otherwise, the Centre shall publish the full decision on the Centre's Web site, listing:

(a) the case number;
(b) the Domain Name that is in dispute and is the subject of a Complaint;
(c) the names of the Complainant and the Respondent;
(d) the decision rendered by the Panelist(s);
(e) the publishing date of the Decision.

Article 12 – Correction of Panel Decision

1. Within seven days of receiving the decision, a Party may, by written notice to the Centre and the other Party, request the Panel to correct in the decision any errors in computation, any clerical or typographical errors or any errors of a similar nature. Any such corrections shall be given in electronic form and in hard copy to the Parties and shall become a part of the decision.
2. The Panel may correct any errors on its own initiative of the type referred to in Article 12(1) within seven days of the date of the decision being rendered.

Article 13 – Limits on Description of Written Statements

1. In accordance with Article 12(9)(3) and Article 18(1) of the Rules, the (maximum) word limit in the 'Facts and Legal Grounds' part of the Complaint and Response shall be 3,000 words respectively. Parties are required to observe this as the Panel in its own discretion shall have liberty to ignore those words exceeding the maximum stated limit.
2. In accordance with Article 39 and 40 of the Rules, the Panel in its own discretion shall have liberty to determine the length of its Decision. There shall be no set word limit of the Panel's Decision.

Article 14 – Appointment of Case Administrator

1. Upon acceptance of the Complaint, the Centre shall appoint a member of its staff who shall be the Case Administrator and shall be responsible for the procedural matters relating to the dispute. The Case Administrator shall provide administrative assistance to the Panel, but shall have no authority to decide matters of a substantive nature concerning the domain name dispute.
2. Communication between the Panelist(s) and the Parties shall be coordinated through the Case Administrator.

Article 15 – Fees (RMB)

1. The applicable fees for documents-only administrative procedure are specified as follows:

Panel	Domain Name Number	Total Fees	Administration Fee	Fee for Panelists
Single Panellist	1	3,000	1,500	1,500
	2 to 5	5,000	2,000	3,000
	6 to 10	7,000	3,500	3,500
	10 or more	8,000	4,000	4,000
Three Panellists	1	6,000	3,000	Presiding Panellist: 1,500 Each Co-Panellist: 750
	2 to 5	9,000	3,000	Presiding Panellist: 3,000 Each Co-Panellist: 1,500
	6 to 10	11,000	4,000	Presiding Panellist: 3,500 Each Co-Panellist: 1,750
	10 or more	13,000	5,000	Presiding Panellist: 4,000 Each Co-Panellist: 2,000

2. Within three days after submitting the Complaint to the Centre, the Complainant shall, based on the number of the Panelists designated and the number of the disputed domain names, pay the initial fixed fees to the Centre in accordance with the above Fee Schedule. If the Complainant fails to make the payment within eight days after the submission of the Complaint, the Complaint shall be deemed withdrawn and the proceedings terminated thereupon.
3. Fees to be paid to the Centre in accordance with the Supplemental Rules may be paid by cash, check, telegraphic transfer or draft made payable to 'China International Economic and Trade

Arbitration Commission'. Generally, all fees to be paid are in Chinese currency (RMB). If the US Dollar is used, the exchange rate calculation shall be based on the current prevailing rate of exchange.

4. The Complainant shall be responsible for paying the total fees provided that the Respondent has to share the fees when the Respondent chooses to have the Complaint decided by three Panelists while the Complainant has chosen one Panellist.

5. The said fees do not include any payments that might have to be made to a lawyer representing a Party.

6. All bank charges, transfer fees or other amounts that may be levied in connection with a payment made to the Centre shall be the responsibility of the Party making the payment.

Article 16 – Exclusion of Liability

1. Without prejudice to any existing rule of law, no Panelist shall be liable to any Party, a concerned Registrar or CNNIC for any act or omission in connection with the administrative proceedings conducted under the Rules, the Policy and the Supplemental Rules, save in the case of fraud or dishonesty or deliberate wrongdoing.

2. Without prejudice to any existing rule of law, the Centre, its officers and its staff, shall not be liable to any Party, a concerned Registrar or CNNIC, for any act or omission in connection with any administrative proceedings conducted under the Rules, the Policy and the Supplemental Rules, save in the case of fraud or dishonesty or deliberate wrongdoing.

Article 17 – Amendments

Subject to the Rules and the Policy, the Centre may amend the Supplemental Rules from time to time at its sole discretion. The amended Supplemental Rules shall come into force after with the express approval of CNNIC.

Article 18 – Interpretation

This Supplemental Rules are subject to the interpretation of CIETAC.

RULES FOR CNNIC DOMAIN NAME DISPUTE RESOLUTION POLICY

CHAPTER I GENERAL PROVISIONS AND DEFINITIONS

Article 1 In order to ensure the fairness, convenience and promptness of a domain name dispute resolution procedure, these Rules are formulated in accordance with CNNIC Domain Name Dispute Resolution Policy.

Article 2 The proceedings for the resolution of disputes under CNNIC Domain Name Dispute Resolution Policy adopted by CNNIC shall be governed by these Rules and the Supplemental Rules of the Domain Name Dispute Resolution Provider.

Article 3 The following terms in the Rules for CNNIC Domain Name Dispute Resolution Policy (hereinafter referred to as "these Rules" or "CNDRP Rules") have the following definitions:

(a) **CNDRP** means CNNIC Domain Name Dispute Resolution Policy adopted by CNNIC, which is incorporated by reference and made a part of the Registration Agreement, and binding to the holders of the domain names.
(b) **Registration Agreement** means the domain name registration agreement between a Registrar and a domain name holder.
(c) **Party** means a Complainant or a Respondent.
(d) **Complainant** means the party initiating a complaint concerning a domain name registration with Domain Name Dispute Resolution Provider in accordance with CNDRP and the CNDRP Rules.
(e) **Respondent** means the holder of the domain name against which a complaint is initiated.
(f) **Registry** refers to China Internet Network Information Center (CNNIC).

(g) **Registrar** refers to the entity authorised by CNNIC and responsible for acceptance of the domain name registration applications and completion of domain name registrations.

(h) **Agency** refers to the entity that accepts the applications for registrations of the domain names on behalf of the Registrar.

(i) **Provider** refers to a dispute resolution service provider approved by CNNIC to resolve the domain name disputes.

(j) **Panel** means a panel composed of one or three Panelists who are appointed by the Provider to be responsible for the resolution of a domain name dispute.

(k) **Panelist** means the individual who are listed among the Name List of Panelists approved by the Provider and published at the Provider's website, and qualified to be members of the Panel for the resolution of the domain name disputes.

(l) **Supplemental Rules** means the rules adopted by the Provider to supplement CNDRP in accordance with CNDRP and these Rules.

CHAPTER II COMMUNICATIONS

Article 4 Any communication under these Rules shall abide by the following principles:

(a) any communication provided by a Party shall be copied and served to the other Party, the Panel and the Provider, as the case may be;

(b) any communication by the Provider to any Party shall be copied and served to the other Party;

(c) any communication by the Panel to any Party shall be copied and served to the other Party and the Provider;

(d) it shall be the responsibility of the sender to retain records of the fact and circumstances of sending, which shall be available for inspection by affected parties and for reporting purposes;

(e) in the event a Party sending a communication receives notification of non-delivery of the communication, or thinks by himself that he has not delivered the communication successfully, the Party shall promptly notify the Provider of the circumstances of the notification. Further proceedings concerning the communication and any response shall be as directed by the Provider;

(f) either Party may update its contact details by notifying the Provider.

Article 5 When forwarding a complaint to the Respondent, it shall be the Provider's responsibility to employ reasonably available means calculated to achieve actual notice to Respondent. Achieving actual notice, or employing the following measures to do so, shall discharge this responsibility:

(a) sending the complaint to all postal-mail and facsimile addresses shown in the Registry's and the Registrar's WHOIS database for the registered domain name holder, administrative contact, the technical contact, the undertaker and the bill contact;

(b) sending the complaint in electronic form (including annexes to the extent available in that form) by e-mail to the e-mail addresses shown in the Registry's and the Registrar's WHOIS database for the registered domain name holder, administrative contact, the technical contact, the undertaker and the bill contact, or if the domain name resolves to an active web page, sending the complaint in electronic form (including annexes to the extent available in that form) by e-mail to the e-mail addresses shown on that web page; and

(c) sending the complaint to any address the Respondent has notified the Provider it prefers and, to the extent practicable, to all other addresses provided to the Provider by the Complainant.

Article 6 Except as provided in the preceding Article, any written communication to Complainant or Respondent provided for under these Rules shall be made by the preferred means stated by the Complainant or Respondent respectively, or in the absence of such specification,

(a) by facsimile transmission, with a confirmation of transmission;

(b) by postal or courier service, postage pre-paid and return receipt requested; or

(c) electronically via the internet, provided a record of its transmission is available.

Article 7 Any communication by the Complaint or the Respondent to the Provider or the Panel shall be made by the means and in the manner (including number of copies) stated in the Provider's Supplemental Rules.

Article 8 Unless otherwise agreed by the Parties or determined in exceptional cases by the Panel, the language of the domain name dispute resolution proceedings shall be Chinese. The Panel may order that any documents submitted in languages other than Chinese be wholly or partially translated into Chinese.

Article 9 Except as otherwise provided in these Rules, or decided by a Panel, all communications provided for under these Rules shall be deemed to have been made:

- (a) if by facsimile transmission, on the date shown on the confirmation of transmission;
- (b) if by postal or courier service, on the date marked on the receipt; or
- (c) if via the internet, on the date that the communication was transmitted, provided that the date of transmission is verifiable.

Article 10 Except as otherwise provided in these Rules, the date calculated under these Rules when a communication begin to be made shall be the earliest date that the communication is deemed to have been made in accordance with the preceding Article.

CHAPTER III THE COMPLAINT

Article 11 Any person or entity may initiate a domain name dispute resolution proceedings by submitting a complaint in accordance with CNDRP and these Rules to any Provider approved by CNNIC.

Article 12 The complaint shall be submitted in hard copy and (except to the extent not available for annexes) in electronic form, and shall:

- (a) request that the complaint be submitted for decision in accordance with CNDRP and these Rules;
- (b) provide the name, postal and e-mail addresses, and the telephone and telefax numbers of the complaint and of any representative authorised to act for the Complainant in the proceedings;
- (c) specify a preferred method for communications directed to the Complainant in domain name dispute resolution proceedings, including person to be contacted, medium to be adopted and address information, for each of electronic-only material and material including hard copy;
- (d) designate whether Complainant elects to have the dispute decided by a single-member Panel or a three-member Panel and, in the event Complainant elects a three-member Panel, provide the names of three candidates from the Provider's list of panelists to serve as one of the Panelists in the order of its own preference. The Complainant may also entrust the Provider to appoint the panelist on his behalf;

(e) provide the name of the Respondent (domain name holder) and all information (including any postal and e-mail addresses and telephone and telefax numbers) known to Complainant regarding how to contact Respondent or any representative of Respondent, in sufficient detail to allow the Provider to send the complaint as described in Article 5 of these Rules;

(f) specify clearly the domain name (s) that is / are the subject of the complaint;

(g) identify the Registrar and/or the Agency with whom the domain name (s) is / are registered at the time the complaint is filed;

(h) specify the rights or legitimate interests on which the complaint is based with regard to the disputed domain name, annexing all materials evidencing the rights or interests;

(i) describe, in accordance with CNDRP, the grounds on which the complaint is made including, in particular:

(A) the disputed domain name is identical with or confusingly similar to the complainant's name or mark in which the Complainant has civil rights or interests;

(B) the disputed domain name holder has no right or legitimate interest in respect of the domain name or major part of the domain name;

(C) the disputed domain name holder has registered or is using the domain name in bad faith.

(The description should, for item C, discuss any aspects of Article 9 of CNDRP. The description shall comply with any word or page limit set forth in the Provider's Supplemental Rules.)

(j) specify, in accordance with Article 13 of CNDRP, the remedies sought;

(k) identify any other legal or arbitral proceedings which have been commenced or terminated in connection with or related to any of the domain name(s) that are the subject of the complaint. All materials concerning the above proceedings that can be obtained by Complainant shall be submitted;

(l) state that a copy of the complaint has been sent or transmitted to the Respondent (domain name holder) as well as the concerned Registrar and / or the Agency respectively;

(m) Conclude with the following statement followed by the signature or stamp of the Complainant or its legal representative or its authorised representative:

"Complainant certifies that the complaint was filed in accordance with CNNIC Domain Name Dispute Resolution Policy and Rules for Domain Name Dispute Resolution Policy as well as the relevant laws; that the information contained in this Complaint is to the best of Complainant's knowledge complete and accurate; that the corresponding claims and remedies shall be solely against the domain name holder and waives all such claims and remedies against the dispute resolution Provider and Panelists, the Registry and the Registrar, the registry administrator as well as the Agency";

(n) Annex, as attachments, any documentary or other evidence upon which the complaint relies.

Article 13 The Complaint may relate to more than one domain name, provided that the domain names are registered by the same domain name holder.

Article 14 After receipt of the complaint, the Provider shall review the complaint for administrative compliance with CNDRP and these Rules and, if in compliance, shall forward the copy of the complaint to the Respondent, in the manner prescribed by Article 5 of these Rules, within three calendar days following receipt of the fees to be paid by the Complainant in accordance with Chapter VIII of these Rules.

If the Provider finds the complaint to be administratively deficient, it shall promptly notify the Complainant of the nature of the deficiencies identified. The Complainant shall have five calendar days within which to correct any such deficiencies of the complaint. If the Complainant does not correct the deficiencies identified or the corrected complaint cannot satisfy the requirements under CNDRP and these Rules, the complaint will be deemed withdrawn without prejudice to submission of a different complaint by Complainant.

Article 15 The date of commencement of the domain name dispute resolution proceedings shall be the date on which the Provider completes its responsibilities under Article 5 of these Rules in connection with forwarding the Complaint to the Respondent.

Article 16 The Provider shall immediately notify the parties, the concerned Registrar and CNNIC of the date of commencement of the domain name dispute resolution proceedings.

CHAPTER IV THE RESPONSE

Article 17 Within 20 calendar days of the date of commencement of the proceedings the Respondent shall submit a response to the Provider.

Article 18 The response shall be submitted in hard copy and (except to the extent not available for annexes) in electronic form, and shall:

(a) respond specifically to the statements and allegations contained in the complaint and include any and all bases for the Respondent (domain name holder) to retain registration and use of the disputed domain name. (This portion of the response shall comply with any word or page limit set forth in the Provider's Supplemental Rules);

(b) provide the name and contact details of the Respondent and of any representative authorised to act for the Respondent in the proceedings (postal and e-mail addresses, and the telephone and telefax numbers);

(c) specify a preferred method for communications directed to the Respondent in the domain name dispute resolution proceedings, including person to be contacted, medium to be adopted and address information, for each of electronic-only material and material including hard copy;

(d) if Complainant has elected a single member Panel in the Complaint, state whether Respondent elects instead to have the dispute decided by a three-member panel;

(e) if either Complainant or Respondent elects a three-member Panel, provide the names of three candidates from the Provider's list of panelists to serve as one of the Panelists in the order of its own preference. The Respondent may also entrust the Provider to appoint the panelist on his behalf;

(f) identify and state any other legal or arbitral proceedings which have been commenced or terminated in connection with or relating to any of the domain name(s) that is / are the subject of the complaint and provide all information available concerning such proceedings;

(g) state that a copy of the response has been sent or transmitted to the Complainant in accordance with these Rules;

(h) conclude with the following statement followed by the signature or stamp of the Respondent or its legal representative or its authorised representative:

"Respondent certifies that the response was filed in accordance with CNNIC Domain Name Dispute Resolution Policy and Rules for CNNIC Domain Name Dispute Resolution Policy as well as the relevant law; that the information contained in this Response is to the best of Respondent's knowledge complete and accurate; that the corresponding defences and assertions shall be solely against the Complainant and waives all such defences and assertions against the Provider and Panelists, the Registry and the Registrar, the registry administrator as well as the Agency."

(i) Annex, as attachments, any documentary or other evidence upon which the response relies.

Article 19 If Complainant has elected to have the dispute decided by a single member Panel and Respondent elects a three-member Panel, Respondent shall be required to pay one-half of the applicable fees for a three-member Panel as set forth in the Provider's Supplemental Rules. This payment shall be made together with the submission of the response to the Provider. In the event that the required payment is not made, the dispute shall be decided by a single member Panel.

Article 20 At the request of the Respondent, the Provider may, under some special circumstances, extend appropriately the period of time for the filing of the response. The period may also be extended by the agreement between the parties, provided that the agreement is approved by the Provider.

CHAPTER V APPOINTMENT OF THE PANEL

Article 21 The Provider shall maintain and publish a publicly available name list of panelists. The Panel in charge of the domain name dispute resolution shall be composed by either one single Panelist or three Panelists.

Article 22 If neither the Complainant nor the Respondent has elected a three-member Panel, the Provider shall appoint, within five calendar days following receipt of the response by the Provider, or the lapse of the time period for the submission thereof, a single Panelist from its list of panelists. The fees for a single member Panel shall be paid entirely by the Complainant.

Article 23 If either the Complainant or the Respondent elects to have the dispute decided by a three-member Panel, the Provider shall appoint three Panelists in accordance with the procedures identified in Article 25 and 26 of these Rules. The fees for a three-member Panel shall be paid in their entirety by the Complainant, except where the election for a three-member Panel was made by the Respondent, in which case the applicable fees shall be shared equally between the Parties.

Article 24 Unless it has already elected a three-member Panel and provided the names of the three candidates, the Complainant shall submit to the Provider, within three calendar days of communication of a response in which the Respondent elects a three-member Panel, the names of three candidates to serve as one of the Panelists.

Article 25 In the event that either the Complainant or the Respondent elects a three-member Panel, the Provider shall endeavour to appoint one Panelist from the list of candidates provided by each of the Complainant and the Respondent. In the event the Provider is unable within five calendar days to secure the appointment of a Panelist on its customary terms from either Party's list of candidates, the Provider shall make that appointment from its list of panelists. The third Panelist shall be appointed by the Provider from its list of panelists. The third Panelist shall be the Presiding Panelist.

Article 26 Where the Respondent fails to submit the response or, has submitted the response but fails to indicate how to designate the Panel; the Provider shall proceed to appoint the Panel as follows:

    (a) if the Complainant has designated a single member Panel, the Provider shall appoint the Panelist from its list of panelists;

    (b) if the Complainant has designated a three-member Panel, the Provider shall, subject to availability, appoint one Panelist from the list of candidates provided by the Complainant and shall appoint the second Panelist and the Presiding Panelist from its list of panelists.

Article 27 The Panelists shall have the right to decide by themselves whether to accept the appointment. To ensure the promptness and smoothness of the domain name dispute resolution proceedings, if any of the Panelists designated cannot accept the appointment, the Provider shall appoint another Panelist from its list of panelists at its own discretion.

Article 28 Once the entire Panel is appointed, the Provider shall promptly forward the case file to all members of the Panel and shall notify immediately the parties of the Panelists appointed and the date by which the Panel shall forward its decision on the complaint to the Provider.

Article 29 A Panelist shall be impartial and independent and shall have, before accepting appointment, disclosed to the Provider any circumstances giving rise to justifiable doubt as to the Panelist's impartiality or independence. If, at any stage during the proceedings, new circumstances arise which could give rise to justifiable doubt as to the impartiality or independence of the Panelist, that Panelist shall promptly disclose such circumstances to the Provider. In such event, the Provider shall have the discretion to appoint a substitute Panelist.

Prior to the acceptance of appointment as a Panelist, a candidate shall be required to submit to the Provider a Declaration of Independence and Impartiality in writing.

Where either party thinks that any Panelist has material interests with the opposing party and that such circumstance may affect the fair ruling of the case, that party may request to the Provider for removing the Panelist before the Panel has rendered its decision. Removal of the Panelist shall be in the Provider's discretion.

Article 30 No Party or anyone acting on its behalf may have any unilateral communication with the Panel. All communications between a Party and the Panel or the Provider shall be made to a case administrator appointed by the Provider in the manner prescribed in the Provider's Supplemental Rules.

CHAPTER VI HEARING AND RULING

Article 31 The Panel shall conduct the proceedings in such manner as it considers appropriate according to these Rules, and decide a complaint on the basis of the statements and documents submitted and in accordance with CNDRP, as well as any rules and principles of law which it deems applicable. If a Respondent does not submit a response, the Panel shall, in absence of exceptional circumstances, decide the dispute based upon the complaint.

In all cases, the Panel shall ensure that the parties are treated with equality and that each party is given a fair opportunity to present its case, give out its reasons and provide the evidence.

The Panel shall ensure that the proceedings take place with due expedition. It may, at the request of a party, extend, under some special circumstances, a period of time fixed by these Rules.

The Panel shall determine the admissibility, relevance, materiality and weight of the evidence.

Article 32 In addition to the complaint and the response, the Panel may request, in its sole discretion, further statements or documents from either of the parties.

Article 33 Under the normal circumstances, there shall be no in-person hearings (including hearings by teleconference, video conference, and web conference), unless the Panel determines that such a hearing is necessary for deciding the complaint. Either of the parties may request the Panel to hold an in-person hearing at his own expenses.

Article 34 In the event that a party, in the absence of exceptional circumstances, does not comply with any of the provisions established by these Rules or any of the time periods fixed by the Panel, the Panel shall proceed to a decision on the complaint.

Article 35 If a party, in the absence of exceptional circumstances, does not comply with any provisions of these Rules or any request from the Panel, the Panel shall draw such inferences therefrom as it considers appropriate.

Article 36 In the event of multiple disputes between the parties, either party may petition to consolidate the disputes before a single Panel. This petition shall be made to the first Panel appointed to hear a pending dispute between the parties. This Panel may consolidate before it any or all such disputes in its sole discretion, provided that the disputes being consolidated are governed by CNDRP adopted by CNNIC.

Article 37 In the absence of exceptional circumstances, the Panel shall render its decision on the complaint and forward the decision to the Provider within 14 calendar days of its appointment.

Article 38 The Panelists shall submit the draft decision to the Provider before signing the decision. The Provider may review the form of the award on condition that the Panelists' independence of decision is not affected.

Article 39 In the case of a three-member Panel, the Panel's decision shall be made by a majority. Each Panelist possesses an equal vote. Where the majority cannot be reached, the decision shall be decided by the Presiding Panelist. Any dissenting opinion shall accompany the majority decision.

Article 40 The Panel's decision shall be made in electronic form and in hard copy, provide the final decision and the reasons on which it is based, indicate the date on which it was rendered and identify the name(s) of the Panelists.

If the Panel concludes that the dispute is not within the scope of the CNDRP, it shall so state. If after considering the submissions the Panel finds that the complaint was brought in bad faith, the Panel may declare in its decision that the complaint constitutes an abuse of the domain name dispute resolution procedure.

Article 41 In the event of any legal or arbitral proceedings initiated prior to or during the domain name dispute resolution proceedings in respect of a domain name which is the subject of the complaint, the Provider or the Panel shall have the discretion to decide whether to suspend or terminate the proceedings, or to proceed to a decision.

Where a party initiates any legal or arbitral proceedings while the domain name dispute resolution proceedings are still pending, in respect of a domain name which is the subject of the complaint, it shall promptly notify the Panel and the Provider.

Article 42 Before the Panel's decision, the domain name dispute resolution proceedings may be terminated, if

(a) the parties agree on a settlement; or
(b) the Panel thinks that it becomes unnecessary or impossible to continue the proceedings for other reasons, unless a party raises justifiable grounds for objection within a period of time to be determined by the Panel.

CHAPTER VII COMMUNICATION AND PUBLICATION OF THE DECISION

Article 43 Within three calendar days after receiving the decision from the Panel, the Provider shall communicate the full text of the decision to each party, the Registrar and CNNIC.

Article 44 Unless the Panel, at request of one party or considering the specific situation of the Case, determines otherwise, the Provider shall publish the full decision on a publicly accessible web site within the time limit stipulated in Article 43.

CHAPTER VIII FEES

Article 45 The Complainant shall pay to the Provider an initial fixed fee, in accordance with the Provider's Supplemental Rules, within the time and in the amount required. A Respondent electing to have the dispute decided by a three-member Panel, rather than the single member Panel elected by the Complainant, shall pay the Provider one-half the fixed fee for a three-member Panel. In all other cases, the Complainant shall bear all of the Provider's fees.

Article 46 No action shall be taken by the Provider on a complaint until it has received from Complainant the initial fee in accordance with the Provider's Supplemental Rules.

Article 47 If the Provider has not received the fees within eight calendar days of receiving the complaint, the complaint shall be deemed withdrawn and the proceedings terminated.

Article 48 In exceptional circumstances, in the event the Panel, at the request of a party, determines that an in-person hearing is to be held, the Provider shall request the parties for the payment of additional fees, which shall be established in agreement with the Parties and the Panel.

CHAPTER IX SUPPLEMENTARY PROVISIONS

Article 49 Except in the case of deliberate wrongdoing, neither the Provider nor a Panelist shall be liable to a party for any act or omission in connection with any proceedings under these Rules.

Article 50 These Rules are subject to the interpretation of CNNIC.

Article 51 These Rules are effective as from 30 September 2002.

CHAPTER IX SUPPLEMENTARY PROVISIONS

CNNIC DOMAIN NAME DISPUTE RESOLUTION POLICY

Article 1 This Policy is formulated in accordance with relevant Chinese laws, administrative regulations and policies, as well as the provisions of the China Internet Domain Names Regulations, in order to resolve the domain name disputes on the internet.

Article 2 This Policy is applied to resolve the disputes stemming from registration or use of the .CN domain names and Chinese domain names, which are subject to the management of the China Internet Network Information Centre ("CNNIC").

Article 3 The Domain name disputes shall be resolved with the Dispute Resolution Service Providers recognised by CNNIC.

The Dispute Resolution Service Providers shall, in accordance with this Policy and the Rules for CNNIC Domain Name Dispute Resolution Policy, formulate the supplemental rules of dispute resolution procedure and Panellist appointment.

Article 4 The Dispute Resolution Service Providers shall implement a system whereby Panels of experts are responsible for the resolution of disputes. The Panels are composed of one or three Panelists, who have expertise on computer networks and laws, possess a high sense of professional ethics and are capable of rendering independent and unbiased decisions in domain name disputes. The Dispute Resolution Service Providers shall publish the List of the Panelists on-line, and the Complainants and the Respondents may select the Panelists there from.

Article 5 Any institution or person who considers that a registered domain name conflicts with the legitimate rights or interests of that institution or person may file a Complaint with any of the Dispute Resolution Service Providers.

Upon the acceptance of the Complaint, Dispute Resolution Service Providers shall form a Panel in accordance with the procedural rules.

The Panel shall, in accordance with this Policy, the relevant procedural rules, and the principle of independence, impartiality and convenience, render a decision to the dispute within 14 days from the date of the appointment of the Panel.

Article 6 The language of the domain name dispute resolution proceeding shall be Chinese, unless otherwise agreed by the parties or determined by the Panel.

Article 7 The Complainant and the Respondent shall bear the burden of proof for their own claims.

Article 8 Support of a Complaint against a registered domain name is subject to the following conditions:

1. the disputed domain name is identical with or confusingly similar to the Complainant's name or mark in which the Complaint has civil rights or interests;
2. the disputed domain name holder has no right or legitimate interest in respect of the domain name or major part of the domain name;
3. the disputed domain name holder has registered or is being used the domain name in bad faith.

Article 9 Any of the following circumstances may be the evidence of the registration or use of a domain name in bad faith:

1. the disputed domain name holder has registered or acquired the domain name for the purpose of selling, renting or otherwise transferring the domain name to obtain unjustified benefits;
2. the disputed domain name holder registered the domain name in order to prevent the owners of the name or mark from reflecting the name or the mark in a corresponding domain name, provided that the domain name holder has been engaged in a pattern of such conduct;
3. the disputed domain name holder has registered or acquired the domain name for the purpose of damaging the Complainant's reputation, disrupting the Complainant's normal business or creating confusion with the Complainant's name or mark so as to mislead the public;
4. other circumstances which may prove the bad faith.

Article 10 If a Complainant files Complaints against multiple domain names owned by the same domain name holder, the Complainant or the Respondent may request that the Dispute Resolution Service Providers consolidate the disputes before a single Panel. The Panel may determine whether to make the consolidation.

Article 11 Before the Panel makes the Decision to a dispute, either party who believes that any of the Panelists has a material interest in the opposite party and the material interest could influence the impartiality of the Decision may request the Dispute Resolution Service Provider to ask the Panellist to withdraw from the Panel. In the request, the facts and reasons shall be stated and the supporting evidence be provided. Dispute Resolution Service Provider shall have the discretion to determine whether the Panellist shall withdraw.

Article 12 CNNIC and the registrars shall not participate in the domain name resolution proceedings in any capacity or manner other than providing the information relevant to the registration and use of the domain name upon the request of the Dispute Resolution Service Providers.

Article 13 The Panel shall make the Decisions on the basis of the facts related to the dispute and the evidence submitted by the Complainant and the Respondent.

Where the Panel supports the Complaint, the registered domain name shall be cancelled or transferred to the Complainant; otherwise, the Complaint shall be rejected.

Article 14 Before a Complaint is filed pursuant to this Policy, or during the dispute resolution proceedings, or after the expert Panel has rendered its Decision, either party may institute an action concerning the same dispute with the Chinese court at the place where CNNIC 's principal office is located or subject to the agreement between the parties, submit the dispute to a Chinese arbitration institution for arbitration.

Article 15 If the Dispute Resolution Service Provider rules in its Decision to cancel the registered domain name or to transfer it to the Complainant, the domain name Registrar, before enforcing the Decision, shall wait 10 calendar days calculating from the date on which the Decision is published. If during such waiting period the Respondent submits valid proof attesting that a competent judicial authority or arbitration institution has accepted the relevant dispute, the registrar shall not enforce the Decision of the Dispute Resolution Service Provider.

After the Decision of the Dispute Resolution Service Provider is suspended, the Registrar shall take the further action as follows:

1. if any proof attests that the parties have reached a settlement by themselves, the Registrar shall enforce such settlement.
2. if any proof attests that the party that instituted the judicial action or applied for arbitration has withdrawn the Complaint or the relevant action or Complaint has been rejected, the Registrar shall enforce the Dispute Resolution Service Provider's Decision;
3. if the judicial authority or arbitration institution has rendered a judgement or an award that has become legally effective, the Registrar shall enforce such judgement or award;

Article 16 During the dispute resolution proceedings and 10 calendar days after the Decision is published, the domain name holder shall not apply for the transfer or cancellation of the disputed domain name, unless the transferee agrees in writing to accept the Decision of the Dispute Resolution Service Provider.

Article 17 A Dispute Resolution Service Provider shall establish a dedicated website, receive Complaints concerning domain name disputes on line and make relevant materials concerning the domain name dispute cases publicly available. However, the Dispute Resolution Service Provider, upon the request of the Complainant or the Respondent, may keep confidential materials and information that may cause damage to the interests of the party if made publicly available.

Article 18 CNNIC has the right to amend this Policy in accordance with the development of the internet and the domain name system and revision of the relevant Chinese laws, administrative regulations and policies, etc. The amended Policy will be published on the website and be implemented 30 calendar days after the date of publication. The amended Policy shall not apply to domain name disputes that had been submitted to a Dispute Resolution Service Provider prior to the amendment of this Policy.

The amended Policy will automatically become a part of existing domain name registration agreements between the domain name holder and the Registrar. If a domain name holder does not agree to be bound by the Policy or its amended version thereof, he shall notify the Registrar in a timely manner. The Registrar will continue the domain name services for the domain name holder for 30 calendar days after the receipt of such notification and cancel the relevant domain name registration after the passage of the 30 calendar days.

Article 19 This Policy is subject to the interpretation of CNNIC.

Article 20 This Policy shall be implemented as of Sep. 30, 2002. Chinese Character Domain Name Dispute Resolution Policy (Trial Implementation) ceases effect simultaneously.

SEVERAL GUIDING OPINIONS CONCERNING THE HEARING OF INTELLECTUAL PROPERTY CIVIL DISPUTES ARISING FROM THE REGISTRATION OR USE OF DOMAIN NAMES

(Formulated by the General Office of the Beijing Municipal Higher People's Court. Dated 15 August 2000.)

Domain names are the network names and addresses of internet users. They have both a technical function and a labelling function, the technical function being that they serve as the network address of the domain name registrant and the identifying function being that they serve as the indication by which the domain name registrant represents itself on the internet. Given the complex characteristics of domain names, the registration and use of domain names has led to a constant stream of intellectual property civil disputes ("Domain Name Disputes"). Theorists and judicial practitioners in the field of intellectual property law have different views on how to apply the law in hearing these kinds of cases. The said difference in views is affecting the correct and timely trial of these kinds of disputes by the People's Courts. Following investigation and research of the issues, we therefore put forward the following opinions for reference by the Beijing courts at all levels in the course of hearing cases of this kind.

1. Acceptance of Domain Name Disputes
Civil disputes in which a party institutes proceedings with a People's Court because the registration or use of a domain name has given rise to a conflict with a registered trademark or an enterprise's or other organisation's registered name, etc, shall be accepted by the People's

Court if they are found to satisfy the conditions of Article 108 of the Civil Procedure Law.

2. Jurisdiction Over Domain Name Disputes

Intermediate People's Courts shall be the courts of first instance for Domain Name Disputes. The Higher People's Court shall be the court of first instance if the amount of the suit's subject matter exceeds RMB3,000,000.

The People's Courts with jurisdiction over a Domain Name Dispute shall be that of the defendant's place of domicile and that of the place of infringement. If the place of registration of the domain name is also the place of infringement, the People's Court of the place of registration may take jurisdiction.

3. Causes of Action in Domain Name Disputes

The cause of action in a Domain Name Dispute shall be determined according to the nature of the legal relationship involved in the dispute between the parties. If the plaintiff instituted proceedings on the grounds of infringement of his trademark rights by a domain name, the case shall be determined to be a trademark rights infringement dispute. If the proceedings are instituted on the grounds of unfair competition, the cause of action shall be determined according to the nature of the act of unfair competition.

4. Application of the Law to Bad Faith Registration or Pirating of Another's Well-Known Trademark as a Domain Name

The bad faith registration or pirating of another's well-known trademark as a domain name violates the principle of good faith and is contrary to generally accepted business ethics. Accordingly, it constitutes unfair competition and, as such, is regulated by the General Provisions of the Civil Code and the Law Against Unfair Competition.

5. Determination of Bad Faith Registration of a Domain Name

To determine whether an act of domain name registration constitutes bad faith registration of a domain name, it shall be examined whether the act satisfies all of the following three essential conditions:

1. the domain name registered is identical or confusingly similar to the right-holder's mark;
2. the holder of the domain name does not own any other prior rights in the domain name's mark; and
3. the domain name was registered or is used in bad faith, which specifically means the following:

the holder of the domain name proposes to sell, lease, or otherwise assign for consideration, the domain name to the rights-holder; or the holder of the domain name entices network users to access his web page or other online services by wilfully mixing up the domain name and the rights-holder's trademark or trade name for profit-seeking purposes; or the sole purpose of the domain name registration is to prevent others from registering a trademark or trade name as a domain name; or the domain was registered to harm another's goodwill; etc.

6. Assumption of Legal Liability

Where the registration of a domain name constitutes unfair competition, the People's Court may render a judgement ordering the holder or user of the domain name to cease using the domain name and, in the case of the holder, to apply for cancellation or change of the name. If the rights-owner suffers harm as a result of the act of unfair competition, the judgement shall additionally order the holder or user of the domain name to compensate for the loss.

MEASURES FOR THE ADMINISTRATION OF THE REGISTRATION OF CHINESE-LANGUAGE DOMAIN NAMES (FOR TRIAL IMPLEMENTATION)

Article 1 These Measures have been formulated in order to ensure and promote the healthy development of Chinese-language domain names and regulate the registration and administration of Chinese-language domain names.

Article 2 These Measures shall apply to the application for, and registration of, Chinese-language domain names in the People's Republic of China.

Article 3 The China Internet Network Information Center ("CNNIC") is an impartial, non-profit domain name registration and administration institution authorised by, and under the leadership of, the Ministry of Information Industry. It is responsible for operating and administering the top level Chinese-language domain name system, researching and developing related technologies and standards, formulating measures related to the administration of Chinese-language domain names and certifying the services of, and granting technology permits to, Chinese-language domain name registrars.

Article 4 Chinese-language domain name registrars ("Registrars") shall accept applications to register Chinese-language second level domain names in accordance with the principle of fairness and the 'first-file' principle and complete the registration of domain names in accordance with these Measures and relevant policies.

Article 5 An applicant for the registration of a Chinese-language domain name must be a legally registered organisation that can independently assume civil liability.

Article 6 There shall be two types of top-level Chinese-language domain names, namely CN names and pure Chinese names. Applications for second level domain names may be made directly under the top level Chinese-language domain name.

Article 7 Chinese-language domain names shall contain Chinese characters and may contain roman letters (A–Z, a–z, not case sensitive), numerals (0–9) or hyphens (-). The Chinese-language domain names at the various levels shall be separated by a dot (.) and no Chinese-language domain name at any level may exceed 20 characters and symbols in length.

Article 8 No name that is detrimental to the interests of the state, society or the public may be used as a Chinese-language domain name at any level.

Article 9 The responsibilities of an applicant include:

1. complying with relevant state laws and regulations on the internet and related rules;
2. assuming all liability for the Chinese-language domain name for which it is applying and all legal issues connected with the name;
3. ensuring the truthfulness, accuracy and completeness of its submission; and
4. ensuring that the Chinese-language domain name is not registered or used in bad faith or with any unlawful intent.

Article 10 After the registration of a Chinese-language domain name is complete, the applicant shall be the owner and administrator of such domain name and must comply with these Measures and related laws, regulations and policies.

Article 11 If anyone files a complaint with a CNNIC-authorised Chinese-language domain name dispute resolution institution against a Chinese-language domain name that has been registered and is being used and such complaint complies with the conditions stipulated in the Measures for Resolving Chinese-Language Domain Names Disputes (for Trial Implementation), the domain name owner shall submit to the jurisdiction of the dispute resolution institution and participate in the dispute handling process.

Article 12 When an applicant applies to register a Chinese-language domain name, it may submit its application form to a Registrar by such means as online registration, e-mail, etc. The date on which the Registrar receives the first valid application for registration shall be the application date.

Article 13 The following particulars shall be specified in the application form for the registration of a Chinese-language domain name:

1. the second-level domain name applied for and the top-level domain name under which it falls;
2. the IP addresses of the main and secondary domain name servers for the second-level domain name;
3. the corresponding domain names of the aforementioned domain name servers;
4. the name and address of the owner of the second-level domain name; and
5. the names, correspondence addresses, e-mail addresses, telephone numbers and facsimile numbers of the technical contact person, the administration contact person and fee payment contact person for the second level domain name.

Article 14 Unless expressly stated otherwise by the applicant, the various pieces of information entered on the application form for the registration of a Chinese-language domain name may be input by the Chinese-language domain name registration and administration institution or the Registrar into a publicly accessible database or other publication as content of the directory services provided to internet subscribers by the domain name registration and administration institution or the Registrar.

Article 15 The Chinese-language domain name registration and administration institution and the Registrars shall not be responsible for determining whether the second-level domain names that they register infringe upon the rights and interests of third parties. Any domain name disputes arising from such conflicts shall be resolved, and the legal liability thereof shall be borne by the disputing parties themselves. The Chinese-language domain name registration and administration institution and the Registrars shall unconditionally enforce judgments and awards involving the status of a domain name rendered by competent courts, arbitration institutions and domain name dispute resolution institutions.

Article 16 If a change occurs in the particulars registered in connection with a registered domain name, the domain name owner shall timely apply to the original Registrar to amend its registration. When applying to amend its registered particulars, the applicant shall file the submission for the change in domain name by the method for confirming changes selected at the time it applied to register the domain name. After the original Registrar has given its approval, it shall make the changes to the domain name and cause the changed name to become operational.

Article 17 When applying to deregister a registered domain name, the applicant shall submit to the Registrar an application form for the deregistration of a domain name bearing the official seal of the applying unit. After the Registrar verifies the application, it shall deregister the domain name.

Article 18 When applying to assign a registered domain name, the assignor shall submit to the original Registrar an application form for the assignment of a domain name bearing the official seal of the applying unit. After the original Registrar has given its approval, it shall make the changes to the domain name and cause the assigned name to become operational.

Article 19 The Registrar that originally registered a Chinese-language domain name has the power to deregister it:

1. if the domain name owner or the authorised agent thereof submits an application to deregister the domain name;
2. if the information provided in the submission for the registration of the domain name is untruthful, incomplete or inaccurate;
3. if the domain name owner fails to pay the pertinent fees in accordance with regulations;
4. if the Registrar is required to cancel the relevant domain name pursuant to a judgment or award rendered by a competent court, arbitration institution or domain name dispute resolution institution; or
5. for another reason as stipulated herein or in relevant laws, regulations or policies.

Article 20 When registering a Chinese-language domain name or carrying out procedures for other domain name related matters, pertinent fees shall be paid to the Registrar. If the fees have not been paid in full within 40 days from the fee payment date, the Registrar shall suspend the operation of the relevant domain name. If such fees are not paid in full within 60 days, the Registrar shall de-register the relevant domain name.

Article 21 CCNIC has the right to amend these Measures in line with the development of the internet and the Chinese-language domain name system, changes in relevant Chinese laws, administrative regulations and policies, etc.

Article 22 CCNIC shall be in charge of interpreting these Regulations.

Article 23 These Measures shall be implemented from the date of publication.

INDEX